RESPONSE
ABILITY

Response Ability

THE LANGUAGE, STRUCTURE, AND CULTURE OF THE AGILE ENTERPRISE

RICK DOVE

JOHN WILEY & SONS, INC.

New York • Chichester • Weinheim • Brisbane • Singapore • Toronto

Published by John Wiley & Sons, Inc.
Published simultaneously in Canada.

Library of Congress Cataloging-in-Publication Data:

Dove, Rick, 1943–
   Response ability: the language, structure, and culture of the agile enterprise / by Rick Dove.
       p.   cm.
   Includes bibliographical references and index.
   ISBN 0-471-35018-4 (cloth : alk. paper)
       1. Organizational change.   2. Strategic planning.   I. Title: Responsibility.
   II. Title.
   HD58.8.D68   2001
   658.4′06—dc21

                                                        00-064918

Printed in the United States of America.

10   9   8   7   6   5   4   3   2   1

To my wife and daughter I dedicate my life.
This book I dedicate to those who have inspired it,
those who have helped develop it,
and those who have encouraged its completion.

They are:
Steve Benson, Joan Bigham, Bob Dove, Steve Goldman,
Ted Goranson, Gene Guglielmo, Cy Hannon,
Sue Hartman, Paul Kidd, Chuck Kimzy, Charon Lohara,
Mel Pirtle, Ken Preise, Jack Ring, Larry Rhodes,
Orapong Thein-Ngern, and Gary Vasilash.

Each in some way helped cause this book.

Preface

This book addresses the practical and physical aspects of *how* to become agile. We do not deal with *why* or what to do with the *response ability* once you have it. There are already books dealing with these topics. People seldom perceive a problem in any tangible, actionable form until they appreciate that a solution exists—and then they begin to define and understand the problem in terms of the solution. Here, we will show the solution.

In 1991 I co-led an industry/government project at Lehigh University to identify the competitive frontier in 2005. This project gave birth to the concept of the *agile enterprise*. Our predictions were based on observations that the business environment was becoming less stable, that the driving forces toward more uncertainty were and would continue to accelerate, and that current organizations were not equipped to operate under these conditions. Our intention was to illuminate an inevitable future and motivate business organizations to begin preparing for it immediately and seriously.

This was an idea whose time had come: Others were thinking about the same inevitability, the consequences, and the strategies both for coping with increasing change and for turning this situation into advantage. Mass customization and organizational learning were two of the front-runners then—one a prescription for marketing and manufacturing strategy, the other a prescription for cultural strategy. At about the same time, tactical programs for change management and reengineering were sweeping through the business community, and lean manufacturing started removing the inertial fat.

As the 1990s progressed, more books were published with new ideas on how to cope with, and take advantage of, increasing uncertainty and accelerating market cycles. By and large, these books focused on strategies for specific aspects of business such as business strategy, marketing strategy, manufacturing strategy, information technology, and knowledge management. Two books *Agile Competitors and Virtual Organizations* and *Cooperate to Compete,* written by Steve Goldman, Ken Preiss, and Roger Nagel, colleagues from the original agility project, took a broader enterprise view, creating a call to arms, illuminating a cross section of agile microstrategies being tested in various industries, and suggesting new priorities.

But still something was missing. New and valuable ideas and strategies must be implemented, changing some or all aspects of the organization. The real underlying message was that these changes, however advantageous they might be when made, would have to be changed all too soon thereafter.

How do you design an organization and all of its parts so that it is naturally agile—able to transform itself with competence into whatever the new situation requires? My research has focused on just that question. This research employed collaborative industry teams analyzing hundreds of highly adaptable business structures over an eight-year period, looking for common underlying fundamentals. We found them.

Being *able to respond* to proactive strategic direction, and being *able to respond* to reactive necessity, is what this book is about.

This book illustrates what it is that makes a business and any of its systems easy to change, and then demonstrates how to apply these principles to any system in a company, at any level. It shows you how to analyze opportunities and problems for their operational dynamics, and describes ways to use these tools to establish a solution strategy. It also demonstrates how to measure change proficiency, and how to use this tool for profiling a company and establishing improvement strategies. It then focuses on the role played by culture, and how to establish and insert these new values and competencies compatibly into an established corporate culture.

This is a book for those who want to know how things work under the hood: for leaders, for strategists, for change agents, for operational managers, and for business planners who seek knowledge as well as the tools for a persuasive edge. In the hands of such people, this book is also a supporting reference and tutorial for all others who will be part of the transformation.

■ TIMELINESS AND APPLICABILITY

When our 1991 investigation proclaimed accelerated and constant change as the coming business environment, it was an intellectual concept that had not yet materialized. There was no emotional understanding in the business community. Since then, the scramble toward e-Commerce brought near panic to most established companies in many industries, as well as to the new fireflies whose five minutes of flame is extinguished as each new generation is born. E-Commerce is not the driving force behind this uncertainty and upheaval, it is only the first major wave coming from a deeper reality: the explosion and rapid application of new knowledge coupled with increasing connectivity and communication. True business complexity has arrived, and there is no going back.

E-Commerce provides a good current backdrop. Everyone understands the need for an e-Commerce strategy, but a company doesn't get an effective one without reengineering the organization considerably, and that's the hard part. An online order entry port is not what this is all about. E-Commerce is so new its broader possibilities are not yet explored. If getting a first e-Commerce strategy was a late wake-up call and cause for panic, getting another and another that is competitive will continue to cause panic for some time. Start-ups keep discovering new ways to redefine how e-Commerce can change the rules. Welcome to the twenty-first century.

To shift the focus away from e-Commerce, look at the satellite communications network business. Many of us watched Iridium's multibillion dollar 1999 bust, and turned our attention to Teledesic. But right in the middle of the Teledesic start-up comes a pronouncement[1] that manned aircraft on overlapping rotating schedules can provide sky-beamed communications services at considerably less cost than satellites. Whether that turns out to be pie in the sky or not, six months after that announcement comes one about a combination helicopter rocket,[2] which promises dramatic drops in satellite launch cost. New technology (knowledge) is threatening slightly-less-new technology with obsolescence even before it comes to market.

I will not talk much about e-Commerce or communications networks; but I will deal with how an organization can be made *response able* when e-Commerce requires a different organization, a different distribution logistics, a different production capability, a different innovation capability, a different set of resources, a different product design, a different service strategy, or a different approach to anything.

This book addresses the nuts and bolts and analytical side of organizational change proficiency. It clears the haze surrounding the concepts of business agility and the agile enterprise by showing the fundamental principles that underlie an organization's ability to respond, and by explaining how to apply these principles in real situations. It is the physics of the agile enterprise that is exposed here.

As a by-product, this fundamental viewpoint provides a strategic context for lean operating practices, puts knowledge management and the learning organization in perspective, and offers a framework for incorporating today's best advice on new business practices and strategic focus.

■ THE USER'S MANUAL

This book breaks many traditional rules. First, it attempts to speak both to enterprise leadership and to operational management—two audiences with different interests and different perspectives. Next, it speaks across the organization to various functional managers, each with a different viewpoint and strategic focus. The reward is that leaders understand the concepts and know that there is an implementation plan, that implementers respect the strategic context that justifies and guides implementation, and that managers understand that they all have something very much in common. The style of the book, also unconventional, attempts to make it fruitful for all.

The material in this book is both broad and deep. In some respects, it is written to the mythical business engineer and architect: that person who would know something about all aspects of the enterprise and take responsibility for enabling both leadership and viability under dynamic conditions. There may be times when this book doesn't speak to your experience base, when it gets too low in the organization or too high, when it gets too strategic or too tactical, or when it gets too social or too technical. If you plow through the unfamiliar terrain, you will find a common theme throughout and a common language and perspective that binds them all.

Reading this book may get your hands dirty. Many of the case examples are taken from the production floor, from product designs, and from information technology; and from the automotive, electronics, semiconductor, and aerospace industries. But there are also many examples that deal with other industries and service sectors, and illustrate organization design, supply chains, teaming, customer relationships, training tools, knowledge management strategies, knowledge worker relationships, and practically every other aspect of business.

As a learner, I need answers to my questions as they come to mind. You have in your hands a bound collection of paper that doesn't have a point-and-click interface as yet—so it is linear by nature. But like all such books, it does have a big advantage over today's on-screen text, hyperlinked or not—you can quickly flip through it and, in the process, have some sense of what you are bypassing. This book has been crafted with that style in mind, and the understanding that we all learn differently.

If you are a visual learner, you can get a pretty good overview from a cursory scan of the graphics in this book, and a reasonable amount of detail by reading the captions. Some of you may get a sufficiently complete story from only the pictures and tables and never investigate the chapter text. Others will want to see the many different data points that create the final patterns.

Reading erratically is expected and encouraged. In the text, we generally discuss the nature of a problem before exploring our approach to a solution, often with anecdotes and metaphors, sometimes directly. If you already understand the problems, skip ahead. But if you do skip, and the solution doesn't make sense, step back and review the perspective on the problem. After an overview scan, the book will be comprehensible when taken in random bites.

This book employs examples from many companies, but leans heavily on specific examples from four different companies. You will see a pattern emerge that makes the material independent of any specific case. There are enough familiar examples here that the more obscure will bare their souls as the patterns emerge.

■ NOTES

1. C. Platt (1999), "Ethernet at 60,000 Feet," *Wired,* June, pp. 150–155, 208–209. "Already Proteus has made more than a dozen test flights in preparation for its ultimate mission: to cruise at 60,000 feet . . . where it can do the kind of tasks routinely done by satellites. . . . It could bring broadband wireless voice, interactive video, and data service to American consumers three or four years ahead of low Earth orbit satellite constellations such as Teledesic. . . . A city can be served by a fleet of three Proteus airplanes, each carrying a 15-foot communications dish beneath its curved belly. One plane will circle for 8 hours, providing telecommunications for an area 50 to 75 miles in diameter. As it runs out of fuel, it hands off to the next plane, and so on, enabling uninterrupted 24-hour coverage." All of Teledesic's $9 billion system needs to be up and running before services can be provided, but Proteus can dominate a major market as soon as it puts three planes in the air—at a cost of $30 million; using revenues to finance additional major market coverage and leaving the sparse areas for Teledesic when it finally arrives.

2. O. Port (ed.) (1999), "It's a Rocket! It's a Chopper? It's Both," *Business Week,* March 22, 1999, p. 65. "It looks like a huge traffic cone that has sprouted a palm tree. But the 63-foot-tall Roton is a hybrid rocket-helicopter that Rotary Rocket Co. hopes will slash the cost of putting

satellites into orbit—by as much as 90 percent . . . To make it happen, he [founder Gary Hudson] has created a lightweight vehicle that will use whirling rockets to climb into orbit, then descend for a soft touchdown by unfolding helicopter blades. Roton's 72 rockets whirl like a fireworks wheel to create centrifugal force. That pushes fuel into the rockets and eliminates the need for the heavy and expensive turbo-pumps otherwise required."

RICK DOVE

Acknowledgments

I conducted some of the research for this book while I was associated with the Agility Forum. The nature of that association was collaborative by design, and so in addition to the Forum and its DARPA and NSF sponsors, all of the people and organizations who participated in the Forum's various discovery workshops have played important contributing roles.

In 1997 and 1998, I conducted a series of discovery workshops that focused on proofing and refining the 10 principles presented as the core material in this book. The participants in this series, along with their organizations, are due a special acknowledgment for their collaborative interest and serious thoughtful work, and in many cases, for the real-life examples provided in this book. They include:

- *Companies:* Agility Forum, Boeing Rocketdyne, Concurrent Technologies Corporation, Dupont, Eastman Kodak, General Motors, The Hartman Group, Innovation Management, LSI Logic, Lyceum Group, Miles Burke Technologies, Motorola, Pratt & Whitney, Procter & Gamble, Rockwell Avionics & Communications, and SAP America.

- *Participants:* Jack Adams, Leon Agnew, Mike Bell, Steve Benson, Lisa Bogusz, John Bricklemeyer, Al Beam, Rick Carrabello, Jim Cook, Mark Correll, Nicole DeBlieck, Bob Dove, Bill Drake, Dave Ervin, Al Hall, Sue Hartmen, Dan Henke, Pete Holmes, Jerry Hudson, Jim Hughes, Stephen Jacques, Mary Jane Kleinosky, Patrick Kraus, Howard Kuhn, Keith Kutner, Kent Longenecker, Joe Leone, Leland Leong, Joe Lichwalla,

Bob Meyer, Mike Paytas, Jim Pazehoski, Dan Praschan, Jack Ring, Joe Rutledge, Emil Sarady, Mary Jo Scheldrup, Dave Schmidt, Bill Shanklin, Tom Shaw, Bob Swanson, Gary Toyama, Guy Volponi, and Julie Youngblut Smith.

Two people helped considerably during the writing of this book with their chapter-by-chapter critique, encouragement, and direction: Jack Ring was invaluable in his willingness to understand and correct some of my tortured attempts at definition and systematic presentation and provided collaborative support for the hard-side system issues. Bob Dove, brother and coincidental fellow-traveler, provided collaborative support on the soft-side knowledge-management and learning issues, and helped improve readability and comprehension. Both have my respect as colleagues who share knowledge, interest, and curiosity.

I must also acknowledge the important role played by Silterra and its president, Cy Hannon. My conscious association with Cy and his company began when this book was half finished, whereupon I discovered that the LSI Logic examples I had already included in the book were creations of his when he was vice president at LSI. Cy understands the messages in this book viscerally. He set out to build a company that would thrive in a fast-changing environment, understanding that success would be found in the depths of infrastructure. The last half of this book was written while implementing its concepts at Silterra. The realities of business often lead good ideas astray in the heat of battle. Cy Hannon is unswerving in his belief that strategic advantage is realized with high adaptability, uncompromising in his expectations, and convinced that anything less today is a sure path to fast irrelevance. The implementation continues as this book ends.

Much of the research behind this book was first published in the various publications of the Agility Forum, at that time a member corporation of the Iacocca Institute at Lehigh University in Bethlehem, Pennsylvania. Subsequently, the Forum was officially separated from Lehigh, and eventually ceased to exist.

From 1994 to 1999, I wrote 60 essays that were published by Gary Vasilash of Gardner Publications in *Production, Automotive Production,* and *Automotive Manufacturing & Production* magazines. These essays chronicled the ongoing research behind this book as it was in process, and portions of them are scattered throughout this book.

Remmele Engineering is due special thanks for letting us include their mission and strategic guiding principles in Tables 2.2, 2.3, 2.4,

2.5, and 2.6 and for helping us understand the value of corporate ideology in an agile enterprise. Bert Casper, Tom Moore, and Red Heitkamp were especially supportive and appreciative of the study we did at Remmele.

Portions of Chapter 1 and Chapter 10 first appeared in "Knowledge Management, Response Ability, and the Agile Enterprise" in 1999 in the *Journal of Knowledge Management* (Vol. 3, No. 1), MCB University Press.

Thanks are also due to Bill Schneider and Bill Bliss.

Pierre Dillenbourg and Daniel Schneider have graciously permitted me to include my adaptation and interpretation of their eight collaborative learning mechanisms in Chapter 10.

R.D.

Contents

Part One   Agility, Response Ability, and Culture   1

Chapter 1:   Putting Agility in Its Place   3

Basic Concepts   3
Agility Does Not Come in a Can   6
Key Concepts and Terms   9
Getting a Handle on the Issues   13
Knowledge Is What Fuels Change   14
Organizing for Change and Complexity   16
The Handles of Understanding and Action   20
You Are What You Eat   26
Moving On   27
Notes   28

Chapter 2:   Change-Enabling Structure and Culture   30

Adaptable Structure   30
Adaptable Products   31
Adaptable Processes   35
Adaptable Practices   40
RRS Structure   43
Adaptable Culture   45
Remmele Engineering—Engineered for Response Ability   48
Structure and Culture in Perspective   59
Notes   62

Part Two   Change Proficiency: The Language of
Agile Enterprise   65

Chapter 3:   Frameworks for Change Proficiency   67

Change Proficiency in Perspective   67
Measuring Change Proficiency   70

	Quality of Change	79
	Categorizing Change in a Framework	87
	Proactive Dynamics	92
	Reactive Dynamics	100
	The Language of Change Proficiency	107
	Notes	108
Chapter 4:	**Response Situation Analysis**	**109**
	The Problem with Problems	109
	Establishing Response-Able Design Requirements—Four Diverse Examples	112
	Methodology—Defining Problems and Opportunities with Response Situation Analysis	120
	Final Notes on the Analysis Process	128
	Conclusion	129
Part Three	**Adaptable Structure: The Enabler of Agile Enterprise**	**131**
Chapter 5:	**Enabling Response Ability**	**133**
	Control in Response-Able Systems	133
	Response-Able Structure	135
	General Principles of Response-Able Systems	138
	Conclusion	160
	Notes	160
Chapter 6:	**Response-Able Enterprise Systems**	**161**
	Who's in Charge?	161
	Examples of Response-Able Enterprise Systems	163
	Case Stories as Models	180
	Conclusion	186
	Notes	187
Chapter 7:	**Systematic Design of Response-Able Systems**	**188**
	Systematic Design	188
	A Preliminary Framework/Component Architecture	192
	Conclusion	213
	Notes	213
Chapter 8:	**Intuitive Design of Response-Able Systems**	**214**
	Intuitive Design	214
	Defining the Problem	218
	Encapsulated Implementation	225

	Unique IT Approach Provides Unique	
	Competitive Advantage	228
	Systems Integrity Management	232
	Conclusion	233
	Notes	235
Part Four	Knowledge and Culture: The Way of the Agile Enterprise	237
Chapter 9:	Waking Up the Enterprise	239
	Change Proficiency Maturity Profiles	239
	An Introduction to the Reference Model	242
	Twenty-Four Critical Business Practices—The Reference Model Armature	244
	The Maturity Model	245
	Examples	254
	How and Why to Use Maturity Profiling	267
	Deliverables	269
	Objectives and Teams	270
	Methodology and Technique	272
	A Sheep in Wolf's Clothing—Putting a Hard Edge on Soft Science	274
	Notes	275
Chapter 10:	Becoming and Managing the Response-Able Enterprise	276
	A Perspective on Knowledge Management	277
	Learning	280
	Organizational Learning	289
	On the Power and Nature of Insight	292
	Local Metaphors—Knowledge Packaged for Diffusion	298
	Realsearch—One Method for Building the Response-Able Enterprise	304
	Knowledge Portfolio Management—One Method for Managing the Response-Able Enterprise	317
	Conclusion	323
	Notes	325
References		327
Index		335

Part One

Agility, Response Ability, and Culture

Part One of this book lays a foundation of concepts and leverage. Definitions attempt to clear up the slipperiness that the word agility acquires when applied to business and enterprise. The roles of culture and knowledge management are discussed. A common set of structural patterns is shown as the enabler for highly adaptable enterprise systems.

Chapter 1

Putting Agility in Its Place

Agility is a word that has immediate and personal definition for almost everyone. It can capture cycle-time reduction, with everything happening faster. It can encompass mass customization, with customer responsive product variation. It can embrace virtual enterprise, with streamlined supplier networks and opportunistic partnerships. It can echo reengineering, with a process and transformation focus. It can demand a learning organization, with systemic training and education. It can build on lean production, with high resource productivity. As a descriptive word, agility can embrace almost any competitiveness interest with considerable intuitive appeal.

In this opening chapter, we establish some firm guidelines and definitions for examining agility and its enabling components.

■ BASIC CONCEPTS

Agility is not a brand-new concept. Ever since the first humans banded together for a purpose, organizations have existed in a changing environment that required adaptation. Like profitability, organizational adaptability is a core viability requirement (see Figure 1.1). To continue as a viable entity, an organization must meet two conditions: (1) It must generate at least as much fuel as it consumes (profitability) and (2) It must continuously adapt as necessary to changing environmental conditions. If either of these conditions is not met, the organization is threatened with extinction. In this sense, an organization is

3

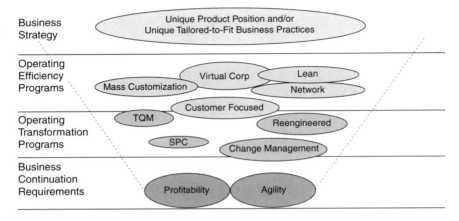

Agility Is an Objective, Not a Competitor, of Operating Programs

When agility first emerged as a competitive concern, it was confused by many as a repackaging of popular operating programs such as lean, TQM, mass customization, and virtual corporations. This confusion arose because the need was recognized before the means, and early attempts at describing supporting behavior borrowed operating modes and examples from existing programs. As a business continuation requirement, agility is not a new concept. The widespread difficulty is keeping up with a changing business environment. Though agility may also be wielded as a business strategy, that is an *option*.

Figure 1.1 Sorting Programs by Purpose

like an organism. Both lead a transitory life in a hostile environment that requires the consumption of energy and constant vigilance, followed by either adaptation or extinction.

In the life metaphor, we talk about evolution and mutation as ways to accommodate a changing environment, and we look for the enabling mechanisms in the genome of life. However, although the life metaphor has organizational lessons, we do not base the agile enterprise on it: Evolutionary life works within a much longer time frame than business. Life does not possess willful consciousness and the ability for leadership-directed mutation; and life on the grand scale knows no sense of pain or loss from its failed experiments. The proponents of biological and ecological metaphors[1] often go too far in their infatuation with mindless evolution and adaptation.

Efficiency programs[2] (e.g., lean production) and transformation programs (e.g., process reengineering) are all facilitated by an underlying proficiency for change. If the organization is proficient at change, it can and will adapt to and take advantage of unpredictable opportunity and will counter the unpredictable threat.

Being agile means being proficient at change. Agility allows an organization to do anything it wants to do whenever it wants to—or has to—do it. Thus, an agile organization can employ business process reengineering as a core competency when transformation is called for. It can hasten its conversion to lean production when greater efficiencies are useful. And, importantly, it can continue to succeed when constant innovation becomes the dominant competitive strategy. Agility can be wielded overtly as a business strategy as well as inherently as a sustainable-existence competency.

Agility is a core fundamental requirement of all organizations. It was not a conscious interest when environmental change was relatively slow and predictable. Now there is virtually no choice; organizations must develop a conscious competency. Practically all enterprises now need some method to assess their agility and determine whether it is sufficient or needs improvement. In this book I introduce techniques for characterizing, measuring, and comparing agility in all aspects of business and among different businesses. I offer methodologies for sensitizing a corporate culture to the values and modes of agile

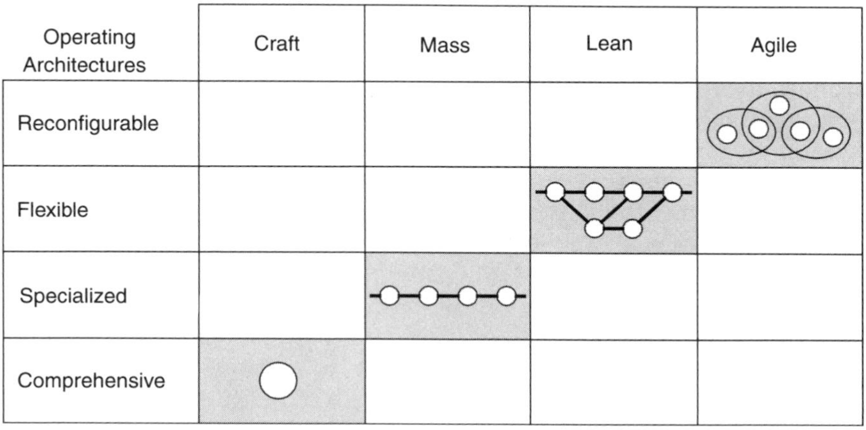

Operating Architectures	Craft	Mass	Lean	Agile
Reconfigurable				⬤⬤⬤⬤
Flexible			⬤⬤⬤⬤	
Specialized		⬤⬤⬤⬤		
Comprehensive	⬤			

Agility initially carried with it a manufacturing focus—a result of its birth in response to the Japanese success with new manufacturing approaches in the 1980s—in answer to early questions of how agility in manufacturing differed from flexibility and lean concepts agility was placed in the evolutionary continuum of manufacturing paradigms. This succeeded in helping many differentiate agility from older and more familiar ideas and in helping focus thought on the structural aspects of response-*able* systems. But it also lodged agility too firmly in the manufacturing environment and made it more difficult for some to visualize this concept in any and all aspects of enterprise organization. Worse yet, for some it cast agility as just one more operational paradigm—ignoring both the strategic and the fundamental places it timelessly occupies in the concept of enterprise.

Figure 1.2   A Manufacturing Metaphor for Agile Resource Relationships

activity and practice, and I suggest fundamental methods for increasing the agility of any business practice.

In the early 1990s, businesspeople wanted to know how agility differed from flexibility, or from the body of knowledge gathered under the *lean* rubric. These were (principally) manufacturing concepts, and agility initially, had a manufacturing focus—a result of its birth in response to Japan's success with new manufacturing approaches. In one of my own contributions to the confusion, I responded to these questions head-on, and placed agility in the evolutionary continuum of manufacturing paradigms: craft, mass, lean, agile (Figure 1.2). This characterization was a two-edged sword. It succeeded in helping (1) to differentiate new agile concepts from older and more familiar ideas, and (2) to focus thought on the structural aspects of "response-able" systems. But it also lodged agility too firmly in the manufacturing environment and made it more difficult to visualize this concept in any and all aspects of enterprise organization. Worse yet, it cast agility as just one more transient operational paradigm, ignoring both the strategic and the fundamental places that agility timelessly occupies in the concept of enterprise.

■ AGILITY DOES NOT COME IN A CAN

We may ascribe to the belief that self-organization and personal autonomy are required to navigate the turbulence of today's chaotic business environment, or that an organization cannot be successful if it lacks strong leadership and strong management. Do collaboration and team consensus offer the only way to success for an organization, or are competence and excellence compromised with consensus?

What people believe or know to be true is a product of their experience and environment and quite likely is proven true daily if their experience and current environment are in alignment. Autonomous operating concepts from complex adaptive systems (chaos) theory cannot be forced onto a polar-opposite organization that lives and breathes a command-and-control culture; and a culture that values unmitigated competency above all else cannot be persuaded that a committee consensus is the best way to make critical decisions. Conversely, a new manager who brings unquestionable procedural rules to a highly successful but independent and unpredictable creative team will either lose the team or be ignored; and an experienced team leader who is hired away from a company for his or her technical expertise may fail miserably in another company when he or she refuses to compromise ideals for the sake of team agreement.

Bill Schneider, a clinical psychologist focused on organizations, suggests that corporate cultures fall into one of four core categories: control, competence, collaborative, and cultivative.[3] Figure 1.3 shows one of his characterization maps. He argues that reengineering works when the underlying principles of new management practices are translated into concepts compatible with the underlying culture—and doesn't work otherwise.

In the early days of my proselytizing the agile enterprise concepts, one of my most poignant learning moments occurred when I addressed a group of a hundred or so manufacturing managers and executives at DuPont. The Q&A session opened with: "It's nice to know that you have all that theory about agility, but I need to know *what* to do. Tell me the five things to do!" I didn't know how many people he was speaking for, but this sentiment struck a dissonant chord deep inside me. I was sharing my most insightful thoughts about what managers had to consider when they chose a strategy, but I was talking to a person—or maybe many persons—who did not want to make that decision. This man did not even want to know what was behind a decision that someone else might make and hand to him. He wanted marching orders, and he wanted them quickly and simply. Production was what he lived for, and he kept it humming—at least while he was at work and not off listening to some academic gobbledegook. Welcome to the real world!

Schneider notes that in a corporation, a *core* culture of one type may coexist with other, even polar opposite, cultures in localized areas. My experience has been that manufacturing is a functional area that tends to favor the command-and-control operational culture, regardless of the core culture of the greater organization. Thus, what works within one part of the company may not work well in another, unless some cultural translation of the underlying principles is communicated.

When this agile *characteristic* was identified in the 1990s as a new and necessary competitive focus, there was immediate and impatient pressure within the manufacturing community to identify exactly how one became agile. An organization may exhibit this characteristic in many ways. *Agility* is not a brand name for management practice, business strategy, or manufacturing theory, though you may have *an* agile strategy, *an* agile practice, or *an* agile manufacturing capability. One company's effort to maintain this capability is likely to be very different from that of a similar competitor.

A football team exhibits agility. The quarterback tells the other 10 players on the field what the next play will be, and each player knows exactly how that play is supposed to unfold. Independent

Actuality

Impersonal

COLLABORATION (Personal / Actuality)

Leadership Focus:
Team builder–Coach
First among equals–Participative
Representative–Integrator
Trust builder–Commitment builder
Realistic–Ensure utilization of diversity
Bring in the right mix of talent

COLLABORATION

Management Style:
Participative–Collegial
Democratic–Relational
Supportive–People driven
Personal–Emotional
Adaptive–Informal
Trusting

CONTROL (Impersonal / Actuality)

Authoritative/directive
Maintain power
Conservative/cautious
Commanding–Firm/assertive
Definitive–Tough-minded
Shot caller–Realistic

CONTROL

Methodical–Systematic
Careful–Conservative
Policy and procedure oriented
Task driven–Impersonal
Prescriptive
Objective

Personal

CULTIVATION (Personal / Possibility)

Leadership Style:
Catalyst–Cultivator/harvester
Empower/enable–Inspire/enliven
Commitment builder–Potentializer
Appeal to common vision–Steward
Promoter/motivator–Maker of meaning
Foster self expression

CULTIVATION

Management Style:
People driven–Personal
Relaxed–Emotional
Attentive–Promotive
Nurturant–Humanistic
Enabling/empowering
Purposive–Committed

COMPETENCE (Impersonal / Possibility)

Standard setter–Challenge subordinates
Set exacting expectations–Visionary
Stretch people/push limits–Taskmaster
Recruit the most competent–Incentivizer
Emphasize what's possible–Architect of systems
Assertive convincing persuader

COMPETENCE

Task driven–Objective
Rational/analytical–Intense
Challenging–Efficient/crisp
Impersonal–Hard to satisfy
MBO/MBR in nature
Formal–Emotionless

Possibility

Figure 1.3   Core Cultures and the Leadership/Management Focus

Source: William E. Schneider, *The Reengineering Alternative: A Plan for Making Your Current Culture Work*. This is one of five tables characterizing the four core organizational cultures mapped by Schneider, a clinical psychologist, who consults on organizational development and change. He argues that reengineering works when the underlying principles of new management practices are extracted and then translated into concepts compatible with the underlying culture. The vertical axis reflects what a culture pays attention to—the content—and ranges from *what is* to *what might be*. The horizontal axis reflects how a culture makes decisions and forms judgments—the process—and ranges from *impersonal analysis* to *personal/interpersonal involvement.*

ideas and play modifications are not tolerated. Once the ball is snapped, however, independent interpretation of what to do from one second to the next is expected. Fortunately, team members have a shared goal in mind and they all know where it is. Every player knows what competence and excellence mean in the role he is expected to play. Teams that do not simultaneously exhibit high group discipline and opportunistic individual innovation are not among the best. Teams that are not agile enough to fluidly seize unexpected moments, recover from unanticipated setbacks, or modify their game plan to fit an uncooperative competitor are not winners. How a football team manifests agility, however, may not work at all in a fundamentally different environment.

Agility does not come in a can. One size does not fit all. There are no five common steps to achievement. And there is not a simple set of four variations to match the Schneider cultural map. Cultural models map an infinite continuum and mixture of style into a few black-and-white categories. Cultural maps are highly useful to help us understand and develop variation of approach; but they are just sketchy reflections, not reality.

This book introduces fundamental principles and frameworks for examining your own need for agility and for establishing the requirements of appropriate solutions. It offers methodologies for involving as much of the organization as is appropriate in the development of these understandings and plans. It emphasizes that an understanding of the situation is necessary before solutions can be considered, evaluated, and selected, and provides methods for doing this. And it stresses the need and value of thinking and learning rather than blindly following a recipe.

■ KEY CONCEPTS AND TERMS

Figure 1.4 defines key terms as I use them in this book. This is done to eliminate ambiguity in the discussions. I do not pretend to have some authoritative claim over their absolute meanings. I have arrived at these meanings after many years of testing them in various ways—using them in working groups to describe concepts and build understanding—and have been guilty of using some of them interchangeably at different times as their evolution developed.

We look at *agility* as deriving from both the physical ability to act (*response ability*) and the intellectual ability to find appropriate things to act on (*knowledge management*). Agility is expressed as the ability to manage and apply knowledge effectively, so that an organization has

KM + RA ⇒ A   **Knowledge management + Response ability ⇒ Agility**
This expresses agility as derived from the ability to manage and apply knowledge effectively—providing the potential for an organization to thrive in a continuously changing, unpredictable business environment.

CP + RRS ⇒ RA   **Change proficiency + Reusable/reconfigurable/scalable structural relationships ⇒ Response ability**
This expresses the dynamics and statics of agility; recognizing change proficiency (CP) as a dynamic characteristic manifested during a change activity, and RRS as a design discipline evident in the architectural structure of relationships among the things/people/resources involved in a change.

KPM + CLF ⇒ KM   **Knowledge portfolio management + Collaborative learning facilitation ⇒ Knowledge management**
This expresses KM as having both a directed strategic component and a fostered grass roots component.

CP: **Change proficiency is a dynamic competency that facilitates change.**
Proficiency is a multidimensional assessment of competency measured on a five-stage maturity scale characterized by the specific metric focus, nature of the working knowledge, and competency developed in four progressively difficult types of proactive and reactive change. (Part Two)

RRS: **Reusable/reconfigurable/scalable structural relationships are static principles that enable change.**
Analysis of business organizations, procedures, and systems shows a structure of reusable elements reconfigurable in a scalable framework as an effective way to enable high adaptability. (Part Three)

KPM: **Knowledge portfolio management.**
This includes the directed identification, acquisition, diffusion, and renewal of knowledge that the organization requires strategically. (Part Four)

CLF: **Collaborative learning facilitation.**
This includes the cultural and infrastructural support for creating and maintaining collaborative learning networks and collaborative learning events and activities. (Part Four)

For two of these terms I neither claim that they represent what others mean by them, nor carry some quality of superior correctness—both *agility* and *knowledge management* are terms carrying strong subjective meaning for many and are also being applied to products and concepts with special interest champions. It should also be understood that agility is not viewed here as an all-encompassing paradigm of organizational or business theory—only as one very necessary characteristic. For instance, the definitional span does not include the complimentary concept of leadership—yet it is obvious that wielding the characteristic of agility to superior competitive effect requires someone (or some process) to make superior decisions.

Figure 1.4   Key Concept Relationships

the potential to thrive in a continuously changing and unpredictable business environment. This book focuses on providing this potential. How you exercise this potential strategically does not concern us here, for that, as Michael Porter points out,[4] is where unique positioning is developed to differentiate one competitor from another. But first, the potential must exist.

Going a level deeper, we look at *response ability,* the ability to act, as deriving from two sources: an organizational structure that enables change and an organizational culture that facilitates change. This term is used throughout this book because its two components indicate the book's principal contribution. We look at some important aspects of knowledge management as well.

The organizational structure that enables change is based on *reusable* elements that are *reconfigurable* in a *scalable* framework (RRS). I use the phrases *organizational structure* and *system structure* interchangeably when referring to a collection of distinct resources (or elements) that are related as a group interacting together for some common purpose. A human resources director may not feel comfortable applying the term *system structure* to the structural relationship evident among a team of people. Similarly, a production manager may not find "organizational structure" is the phrase that captures the structural relationships in a production process.

The organizational culture I discuss focuses on *change proficiency* (CP) and is a subculture of beliefs and values that coexists compatibly with the corporate culture. Figure 1.5 depicts the principal tools I apply when analyzing, comparing, and developing *response-able* business practices.

Knowledge management, response ability's companion in the agile enterprise, carries at least as many different popular, proprietary, and expert interpretations as *agility.* There is widespread interest in this concept despite its relative newness as a focused enterprise factor. As an element in the agility equation, knowledge management contains both a top-down and directed component I call *knowledge portfolio management* (KPM) and a bottom-up grass-roots support component I call *collaborative learning facilitation* (CLF). There are elements of knowledge management that don't involve collaboration in any form, but in the context of the agile enterprise this is our focus.

Someone at General Motors once asked me what relationship existed between size and agility, suspecting the two were inversely related. My answer was that the larger the corporation, the more knowledge it had access to, and the more leverage it could gain from effective mobilization. Agility has two components, and whereas a smaller company may be able to act more quickly, a larger company may know what to act on sooner and more thoroughly.

Supplier Relationships

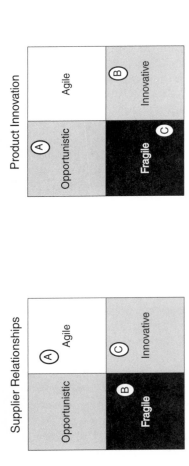

Product Innovation

Knowledge Acquisition

Assessment and Competitive Evaluation

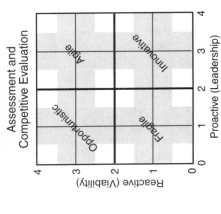

Change Proficiency Maturity Model

Maturity Stage	Metric Focus	Working Knowledge	Competency Development	
			Reactive	Proactive
0 Accidental	Pass/fail	Examples	None	None
1 Repeatable	Time	Concepts	Creation	Correction
2 Defined	Cost	Metrics	Improvement	Variation
3 Managed	Quality	Rules	Migration	Expansion
4 Mastered	Scope	Principles	Modification	Reconfiguration

Figure 1.5 Comparing Change Proficiency among Companies A-B-C

The five-stage maturity framework is used to assess existing corporate competency at change proficiency, as well as to prioritize and guide improvement strategies. Maturity progresses through five states of working knowledge and metric focus, with separate competency tracks for both proactive and reactive proficiencies. A *Change Proficiency Maturity Profile* for an organization can be built from this framework across any selected critical set of business practices.

Part One of this book provides a conceptual base. Part Two provides a language for sensitizing the organization and offers an analysis methodology. Part Three looks closely at structural issues and 10 enabling principles of reconfigurable organizations and systems, and offers a design methodology. Part Four looks at culture, knowledge, and learning issues, and offers a corporate assessment methodology as well as a cultural transformation methodology.

■ GETTING A HANDLE ON THE ISSUES

I blame the increased uncertainty in our business environment on the increasing generation of new knowledge. To get a handle on the problem, we must understand the root cause. Addressing the problem instead of the symptoms requires both some conscious management of knowledge and some competency to apply knowledge effectively—and these two capabilities should be reasonably balanced (see Figure 1.6) to avoid wasted effort.

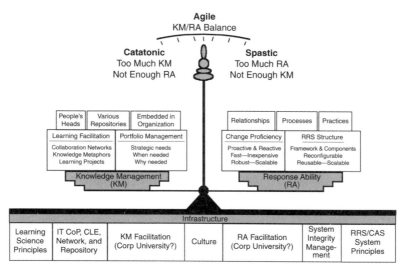

Agility—The Ability to *Manage and Apply* Knowledge Effectively

Abbreviations: CAS: Complex Adaptive Systems; CLE: Collaborative Learning Environment; CoP: Community of Practice; IT: Information Technology; KM: Knowledge Management; RA: Response Ability; RRS: Reusable, Reconfigurable, Scalable.

Figure 1.6 Balancing Knowledge Management Response Ability

The explosion of knowledge causes change and disruption in the business environment through instant and ubiquitous modern communications: television, Internet, intranet, satellite, cable, fiber optics, and e-mail connecting humans who make countless decisions each day about what to believe in, desire, wait for, and buy, and about what to turn against, shun, and throw away—both as personal consumers and as business employees. The world's people, the employees in the business, customers, suppliers, and the machines on the factory floor suddenly are connected in interactive communities—trading and using information.

This complexity is not going away, but dealing with it can actually be simple if we respond with a compatible approach.

■ KNOWLEDGE IS WHAT FUELS CHANGE

Business managers, consultants, and academics are all exploring agile enterprise, knowledge management, organizational learning, and collaboration concepts. Their general motivation is that organizations are finding it more difficult to stay in synch with the pace of change in their operational and competitive environments. Though many of these explorations have a myopic focus on a single issue, more and more are recognizing a convergence.

The capacity to generate and apply knowledge distinguishes humans from other life forms. Our increasing population is steadily enlarging the body of past knowledge, which accelerates new knowledge generation and speeds the decay of old knowledge value. This makes the general business environment unstable and dynamic because it is based in knowledge.

New knowledge demands to be applied. When one business applies new knowledge valuably, others have no choice but to follow, if they can. Knowledge does not generate a value until an enterprise applies it to introduce a change into the environment. Change that comes from the application of new knowledge is called *innovation* when the value is positive. Knowledge that cannot be applied has no value. Knowing about a new assembly technology that cannot be implemented is as useless to an automotive assembly plant as knowing about the canals on Mars.

Knowledge management is one of two key enablers for agility. The other key enabler is *response ability*—the ability of an organization to apply knowledge effectively, whether it is knowledge of a market opportunity, a production process, a business practice, a product technology, a person's skills, or a competitor's threat. My preferred working definition for agility is *the ability to manage and apply knowledge effectively,* as it illuminates the current leverage points.

We often use the word agile to describe cats. When we say a cat is agile, we observe that it is both physically and mentally adept at choosing movements appropriate for the situation. Agile carries with it the elements of timeliness, grace, purpose, and benefit as well as nimbleness. A cat that simply moves quickly, but inappropriately and to no gain, might be called reactive, spastic, or confused, but never agile. It is a cat on a hot tin roof. Conversely, a cat that knows what it should do but finds itself unable to move might be called afraid, catatonic, or paralyzed, but never agile. It is a cat up a tree.

Prior to the 1991 study that kicked off the interest in agility, I had pursued a career involving start-up and turnaround management, where speed and urgency are important. Firsthand experience helped me appreciate the difference between developing a strategy and implementing it successfully. Because knowledge about what to do was too often mismatched with the ability to do it, I started using my engineering background to look for obstacles and solutions in the design aspect of organizational systems. Rather than go back to the entrepreneurial world, I began a series of collaborative learning events with industry, seeking to understand why some business practices and processes are highly adaptable while most are extremely difficult to change.

Concurrently, the concepts of knowledge management and learning organizations were capturing increasing interest in other circles for the same underlying reasons. Our collaborative investigations have converged on the codependent relationships of change and learning. You cannot do one without the other. In terms of knowledge management, nothing happens unless and until somebody learns something.

The concepts of knowledge management and response ability are not new. Organizations throughout time have practiced both successfully or they have ceased to exist. What is new is that the quickening pace of knowledge development and knowledge obsolescence has created the need for more formal and conscious understandings of these practices, raising them to the level of a recognized competency. What used to be done unconsciously and in its own good time is no longer adequate in competitive enterprise.

Balancing these two competencies is important. A few years ago, a Canadian auto plant decided to abandon the chain drive that moved all cars synchronously through the factory from workstation to workstation. They foresaw advantages in an asynchronous movement, and placed each car-in-process on its own automated guided vehicle (AGV), capable of independent movement and not in harness to the car in front. This promised more flexibility for adding mass customized features to individual cars without dragging all cars through stations where no work was performed. More importantly, if a workstation was shut down for any reason, cars could be pool-buffered or rerouted to other stations first and then return while the rest of the factory continued to operate.

When the plant went live, the expected high throughput turned out to be considerably less than the traditional chain drive had provided. Under the old system, a failed workstation shut down the entire production line and the silence was deafening—gaining immediate and total attention. With the highly fluid AGV flow, cars simply bypassed out-of-service stations and the comforting noise of industry continued. A classic architecture for increasing response ability resulted in a major failure because it failed to recognize the knowledge management issues.

Because we do not yet have a general theory of knowledge management, this shop-floor example may not appear to illustrate the need for that expertise. Nevertheless, this situation occurred because of a disproportionate focus on response ability without a balancing knowledge base of how and why to use it.

To view a mismatched balance on the other side, revisit the classic story of Xerox and its Palo Alto Research Center. PARC brought together a group of extremely innovative thinkers and learners, organized around active collaborative learning concepts.[5] Despite some elements of progressive knowledge management techniques, few research results were transferred and applied within the Xerox family.

■ ORGANIZING FOR CHANGE AND COMPLEXITY

In 1996, Peter Drucker suggested: "Big companies have no future. . . . By and large there are no more advantages to big business. There are only disadvantages. . . . In fact, today's big business is in such turbulence and crisis that it isn't even a model for business (let alone government)." After taking top management to task for "unconscionable greed" and outright "cruelty" in the downsizing process, he commented on global differences in business restructuring: "In this country, the restructuring has caused amazingly few social problems because our labor force is so mobile, so adaptable. Our disorder is a great advantage. The Germans and the Japanese are programmed for order—and it gets in their way." On the future of organizational structures, he offers: "The model for management we have right now is the opera. . . . The soloists, the chorus, the ballet, the orchestra, all have to come together—but they have a common score. What we are increasingly talking about today are diversified groups that have to write the score while they perform. What you need now is a good jazz group."[6] And the jazz group will make good music whether the bassist shows up or not, will continue to make good music when the saxophonist has to leave, and will still make good music even when the accordionist sits in. It is adaptable by nature.

Also in 1996, the University of Michigan's Karl Weick, Professor of Organizational Behavior and Psychology, had a compatible view that arrived at a different conclusion: ". . . in a wired world of constant change, chaotic action is preferable to orderly inaction . . . there's no more middle management; and midsize organizations really don't exist anymore. More importantly, there'll be a lot of chronic ambiguity. For instance, many organizations have stopped publishing organizational charts because they become obsolete the day they get circulated. . . . If you take chaos theory seriously, it asserts that the world is both unknowable and unpredictable. All you can do is engage in transient moments of sensemaking." He then relates a story about a labor strike in outer space. "Back in 1973, the third Skylab crew had a tight schedule of experiments to run. NASA kept leaning on them to take on more experiments. The crew got more behind, more overloaded, so it turned off the microphone for 24 hours and spent some time reading and looking out the window. This says something about how companies blend control and autonomy. People are better able to get complex assignments done when given more discretion within a framework of common values."[7]

Whether it's Drucker seeing the demise of big business or Weick seeing the end of midsize business, these and other wise people believe that the future of organizational structures is based on small, interacting, self-organizing, autonomous units, sharing a common framework that facilitates reconfiguration and adaptation. And it doesn't matter if we are talking about top-level corporate structure or looking inside at functional subdivisions, the concept of loosely coupled interacting *components* reconfigurable within a framework is the central design attribute that brings adaptability.

You can employ this reconfigurable framework/component concept just as fruitfully in the design of adaptable production processes, upgradeable products, responsive supply chains, flexible distribution logistics, high-performance teams, evolving information systems, adaptable procedures, reconfigurable facilities, and any other aspect of business that must thrive in a constantly changing environment.

Though agility is a broad enterprise issue, looking at the impact on production of product realization[8] will provide a tangible illustration and some fundamental insight. Decreasing innovation cycles in all market sectors are increasing the product introduction frequency. Bringing new or improved products to market involves changes in the production process. Whether these changes are fairly small or quite sweeping, there is usually a transition period of adjustment and settling in.

During this transition period, two principal sources of turmoil are at work: (1) When the changed portion of the process is put to the test of actual use, it requires fine-tuning before it can satisfy its purpose, and (2) the interaction of the changed portion with the unchanged portion of the process (its environment) has undesirable side effects that need to be resolved. Change here refers to the total production environment and is not limited to the modification of some process or piece of production equipment. Thus, it includes both the addition of something new and the elimination of something old as these, too, are changes in the overall production environment.

Simply stated, after we design, build, and install a change, we must deal with a transition period before we have what we want, or decide to settle for what we get. Making this change incurs cost and takes time. Some of this cost and time involves pure design, development, acquisition, and installation; and some is transition turmoil from integration and shakeout. In the agile ideal, this transition period takes no time, incurs no cost, is not prematurely terminated, and is not an inhibiting factor on the latitude of change that one is willing to consider.

In addition, a new machine or production cell introduced into the production environment requires shakeout of the machine itself, integration of the machine into its interactive environment, operator training, maintenance training, and service training, to name the easy parts. Then we have the operational idiosyncrasies and failure modes that are learned the hard way through surprises and experience.

In the past, such product changes occurred infrequently and the transition costs were easy to ignore. But product introduction frequency in all markets continues to rise, and already in many markets ignorance of transition cost and time is intolerable. The toll of the transition period is reflected in true product cost, product quality, and market responsiveness.

An obvious way to reduce the toll of transition is to reduce the quantity and complexity of things in transition. If we want to do this while accommodating more new product than ever before, we have to learn how to build new product with old proven process—reusable process, reconfigurable for a new purpose. Reusability and reconfigurability are construction concepts—they have to do with the way things are built, no matter whether these things are manufacturing cells, work procedures, production teams, or information automation systems.

To bring a new or improved product to market, we want to introduce as little new process as possible. For example, instead of designing and building a completely new welding cell (a collection of machines and/or people involved in a specific subassembly or subprocess such as welding four or five individual metal stampings into an automotive door frame), we might duplicate and modify an existing well-understood cell. While this cell certainly will have some new elements to accommodate the new product, a good bit of the cell will be time tested and familiar. It may not be as technically appealing as a completely new design, but it will be up and running a lot sooner and a lot cheaper, produce less scrap and rework, reuse prior service training and require less new training, and generally function more predictably.

This does not mean an end to capital investment or a continuous cannibalism of used equipment. It means an important new focus on the structure of the production elements that must be reconfigurable. And it is physical reconfigurability we need, not programmed reconfigurability. We need the ability to make unanticipated new things from reusable pieces, not simply select some predefined subset of flexible capability or embedded options. Reconfigurable structures, whether they organize subunits in a piece of equipment, equipment relationships in a cell, cell relationships in a production area, or production areas in a plant, require some form of facilitated component reusability. For maximum benefit, these structures must be scalable as well as reusable and reconfigurable. Scalability eliminates size restrictions imposed by the structure, allowing any number of reusable components to be included or omitted as desired.

What we have discussed applies to changes in any business area: new procedures or business practices, new personnel, different personnel, introduction of teaming concepts, different suppliers or customers, a change in work instructions—all incur a transition period of integration and fine-tuning before the turmoil is settled.

Our business environment has become complex and we must address it with complexity-compatible approaches. The old ideas of integration are dangerous, though still seductive to many. Just as lean tells us to remove all waste from the system while ignoring the loss of adaptability if we are highly successful, so integration tells us to couple ourselves intimately with everything else while ignoring that single-point failures can have a broad and catastrophic reach. In a static environment, the integrated system will dance with efficient grace; but if one part breaks, the whole mass becomes a whole mess. And forget about modifying or improving an integrated system, the unanticipated side effects will return you to the equivalent of a broken system.

If General Motors and Chrysler are locked into Ryder Trucking for delivering cars to market, all it takes is a Teamsters strike against Ryder to stop the flow of product to the dealers.[9] Ford wasn't hurt noticeably by the 1995 Ryder strike; but in the same month it shut six plants down when one supplier couldn't deliver a power-steering-systems component.[10] High tech is just as vulnerable: When Apple Computer relied on sole sources for its subassemblies, all it took was a supplier problem to destroy what the 1995 Christmas buying season could have been.[11] The problem in each of these cases wasn't really single-source supply, but the inability to replace that single source when it failed. When interacting with today's complex world, you can't model your participation after a well-oiled integrated clockworks.

Lean designs and integrated designs are neither forgiving nor malleable. There are still investments to be made in business for things we cannot afford to throw out too early, but neither can we afford to keep them when they become inadequate.

■ THE HANDLES OF UNDERSTANDING AND ACTION

In Figure 1.7, the four objects of customer, producer, competitor, and knowledge, and their relationship vectors are not especially new; but the adjectives in the top three capture the inevitable behavior we see emerging today. New understandings in the relationship vectors are also worth exploring. We talk today about listening to the voice of the

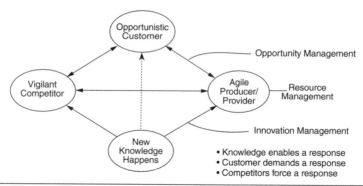

New knowledge happens independent of plans and forecasts and brings both threat and opportunity to the conditions that bind producer to customer. Listening to the voice of the customer is necessary to maintain a relationship; but it is unlikely to be the source of innovation-producing knowledge. Competitors will encroach with new knowledge that changes the rules. Response ability is both a proactive and a reactive competency.

Figure 1.7 Agile Competition Model

customer, about being customer responsive, about delighting the customer, and even exceeding the customer's expectations. It is politically incorrect to suggest otherwise, and these concepts are the fundamental platform for many corporate strategies.

In the late 1970s, the American machine tool industry made a point of asking the Detroit automakers, their biggest customers, what to do next. They listened carefully to the automakers and then watched as Detroit, the opportunistic customer, bought new innovations from Japan, the vigilant competitor.[12] In the 1980s, McDonald's asked their customers what they wanted next in fast food and the resounding answer in the United States was less fat. Customers backed up their voice by confirming their interests in a taste test. Then they turned their back on the concept when it was rolled out.[13] Listen to the voice of the customer, but do not trust it.

Customers cannot be expected to have the same command of new technology and its possibilities that a supplier's product development engineers have—users' core competencies are purposely focused elsewhere.[14] Nevertheless, they can suggest valuable improvements to products they already understand, and their ideas will probably be picked up by the competition as well. Not listening to the voice of the customer creates an easy opportunity for that competition.

The voice of the customer, whether offered or sought, is a pointed demand for reaction made by the customer to the producer. If the current relationship is managed well, the vigilant competitor cannot dislodge it, at least not under the current rules. Managing the opportunity from the competitor's point of view means introducing a new set of rules, proactively bringing an innovation to the opportunistic customer. Successful opportunity management requires an active point on both ends of the communication vector between customer and producer. You can be sure that there is a two-way vector between customer and competitor: Number two has to try harder and your customer wants to keep you honest.

At the heart of all this, the engine room of ceaseless knowledge development makes innovations and improvements possible. Fairly independent of producer, customer, and competitor, knowledge happens. New possibilities suddenly exist where *nothing* was before. What to do about this, how to foster it internally, and how to harness it effectively constitute the innovation management issue.

Being agile means being a master of change, and allows one to seize opportunity as well as initiate innovations. The agility of your company or any of its constituent elements is a function of both opportunity management and innovation management—one brings robust viability and the other brings preemptive leadership. Having one without the other is not safe; having neither is a time bomb with a short fuse. How much of each is needed at any time is a relative question and depends on the dynamics of the competitive operating environment. Though it is only necessary to be as agile as the competition, it can be strategically advantageous to be more agile.

This talk about "how agile" and "more agile" implies we can quantify the concept and compare similar elements for degrees of agility. However, there is an open question about value trade-offs between an increment of leadership and an increment of viability. Leadership may win if the leader always chooses the most optimal path to advance, but one false step allows a competitor to seize the advantage putting the previous leader in reaction mode. A competitor with excellent viability can track the leader, waiting for that sure-to-come mistake. Thereafter, poor viability may keep the fallen-from-grace ex-leader spending scarce resources on catch-up.

In the 1980s, Sun Microsystems' president, Scott McNealy, impressed me when he announced that they would be sharing much of the innovative knowledge that they had developed, the kind that others would typically hide with proprietary marks. His rationale was that potential competitors would find a new set of innovations ascending by the time they could act on this knowledge in any threatening way. In the meantime, Sun's leadership would gain support and followers. McNealy made this statement when Sun was the leader to catch. It still has validity in my book—but the company got blindsided by the rocket ascendancy and encroaching power of the personal computer, which grew to threaten the workstation market. Sun also suffered in the early 1990s when their SuperSPARC microprocessor was two years late into production and took another two years to reach its rated speed of 75 MHZ. "The lengthy delay allowed Sun's competitors to gain workstation market share at its expense."[15] Good proactively, not so good reactively—at least not in those heady days of leadership arrogance.

That Java eventually saw the light of day is a sign that Sun might be developing some reactive capability. Bill Joy, Sun's founding technologist, is credited for eventually seeing its innovative potential as an Internet play. It's hard not to look at Java as a proactive move, but it languished for years in the bowels of Sun, and though it may have sparked Joy's innovative juices, the company's backing appears to be primarily an anti-Microsoft move. Sun believed that licensing Java to Microsoft was one sure way to success. Though this was purported to be an option should Bill Gates initiate the call, "Others [Sun insiders] doubt whether McNealy could bring himself to consort with the enemy even if Gates showed up at the door. They believe that Sun's desire to beat Microsoft may be even stronger than its desire to see Java succeed."[16] In fact, McNealy's often quoted acerbicisms in the press throughout the 1990s suggest that Sun is reactively fixated on Microsoft. Sun is an example of the relentless pressures that push seemingly agile companies out of the agile zone.

How about Intel? Andy Grove's now famous statement "Only the paranoid survive" would lead you to believe that this is a company that pays attention to reactive capability. On the other hand, they haven't been put to the reactive test; they haven't really stumbled yet, and their leadership is clear in the microprocessor area. Dogging their heels, however, are two companies that appear to have mastered reactive capabilities: AMD (Advanced Micro Devices) and Cyrex. Against all odds, these two companies have quickly brought to market lower priced compatible versions of the latest Intel processors and made a business of it. They aren't simply cloning Intel designs; they have to reverse-engineer an Intel chip before they can do their own designs from scratch. As a result, while providing functional compatibility, they also can provide customer-desired improvements. AMD was quick to grab the opportunity created when Intel introduced the Pentium Pro, a multichip processor.[17] AMD's K6 was functionally equivalent but was packaged in a single chip, something that customers valued. At the same time, AMD was poised to offer a Pentium II equivalency that would plug into the same motherboards used in the previous generation, while Intel's offering would require redesigned motherboards. This is good reactive and proactive strategy, backed up by some obvious ability to act on those strategies. AMD didn't overtake Intel and isn't likely to do so as long as Intel keeps running down the Pentium path in a reasonable fashion. If it reaches too far, however, these companies will move in fast.

As to proactive capabilities, Grove has said that keeping the Intel freight train on the track is all consuming, and he is sure they will smash into a brick wall somewhere down the road. That brick wall may well be the *systems-on-a-chip* approach. This concept packages an entire computer on a single chip, not just the processor that Intel has focused on. The concept is not new; LSI Logic pioneered the concept in the early 1980s and has made a good market in this area since. To offer systems-on-a-chip requires technical capabilities, business strategies, and market relationships that Intel doesn't possess. Fast designs, custom designs, cheap production, and shorter product lives are some characteristics of this market in which Intel lacks experience. If the next intelligent-chip frontier shapes up as expected, small appliances, automotive gadgetry, light switches and plug sockets, cell phones, and other personal accoutrements will create huge demands for low-cost intelligent system chips. *Fortune* summarized the situation as 1998 began: "[Intel] . . . has no such products in development, nor does it have the [necessary] analog technology SGS, TI, and National have. But then, any world-class chipmaker with $10 billion in cash could move into this business fast—and Intel will, if systems-on-a-chip proliferate as much as their proponents expect."[18] Cash is not a substitute for proactive and reactive change capability—the best it can do is buy time while massive restructuring of business relationships, strategies, and cultures occur—and that only works if the competition is sluggish or shackled.

Intel has smart people who know how to run fast and leverage a front-runner's position. They're damn good street fighters, the best in the neighborhood they grew up in—but they haven't left the neighborhood yet. Grove's admiration for what he lauds as strength is telling: "We could still turn on a dime. Our people still put the interests of the company ahead of their own interests and, when problems arose, employees from all different divisions would still rally around and *put in incredible hours* without anyone ordering them to do so [emphasis mine]." Being agile and response-able is about not having to put in incredible hours. That is the brute-force response pattern of a good street fighter, but not of a martial artist with deep insight and automatic moves designed for the purpose. I am at a loss as to where I might place Intel in the four quadrants of the agile arena depicted in Figure 1.8.

While dealing with icons of market leadership, we will take on Microsoft as well. Here is a company that has exhibited excellent reactive response ability: The browser about-face triggered by Netscape required the redeployment of sizable resources in short order. Another reactive move, though not as onerous in resource reconfiguration, was a ". . . major about-face for Bill Gates. In August [1995] Microsoft Corp. launched a massive effort to catch up with America Online Inc. and CompuServe Inc. by offering Microsoft Network, a new proprietary online service accessible only through Windows 95 software. . . . Then Gates abruptly decided he was fighting the wrong battle. In early December, Microsoft's chairman announced that next year, MSN would be available to all of the estimated 11 million users of the Internet. . . . Gates' new vision for MSN is much more democratic. . . . *The change in strategy leaves Microsoft with far less control over its product* [my emphasis]."[19] A decision that results in less control is different for them and testament to their recognition that catching up is hindered with restrictions. I give them high points for reactive decisiveness and the ability to act well on reactive decisions,

Dynamic Environment

- Skills and competencies
- Service requirements
- Process knowledge
- Customer expectations
- Supply chain strategies
- Product technology
- Strategic issues
- Information technology
- Alternative materials
- Competition

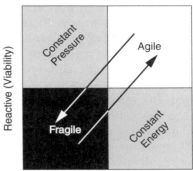

Corporate Change Proficiency

Change proficiency is a competency that allows an organization to apply knowledge effectively—knowledge of a market opportunity, a production process, a service requirement, a product technology, a person's skills, a competitor's threat, or whatever. Defensively it is wielded in reaction to events that occur independent of plan and schedule and is necessary to maintain viability. Offensively, it is wielded proactively to innovate and develop unique advantage that defines and supports leadership. Until agility becomes an installed organizational competency across whole industries, however, it will be a relative, rather than an absolute, competency. There will be companies who are the paragons for a while, who will spur the contenders into deeper understandings, who will in turn replace last year's heroes, and the cycle will spiral ever closer to the limit.

Figure 1.8 Amateurs in the Agility Arena Work Harder to Stay There as Industries Develop Professional Agile Competencies with Time

at least in the business and product strategy areas. But overall I look at Microsoft much like Intel—brute force incarnate.

Microsoft has a reputation for hiring the best and the brightest. I know some of their superstars personally having shared office space and development work with them in start-up ventures of old, and they are everything the press cracks them up to be. But I cannot figure out what benefits their combined IQs have provided for me as a customer. I've been a heavy and exclusive Microsoft user since the beginning, and I have never seen any evidence of IQ at work in delivered product—in strategy yes, but not in product. Neither response-able resource management nor product design would have that problem. Microsoft is not an agile competitor in the *absolute* sense—they simply have better strategic moves and more assets to leverage than anyone else who has stepped into the ring. "We are very fortunate that every employee of Microsoft is today ten years older than they were ten years ago" jokes Mike Murray, Microsoft's head of human resources in a 1998 *Fortune* magazine article.[20] "Hopefully this aging process will make us more empathetic to customers and suppliers, help us listen better. I think we'll learn these lessons either from the marketplace or from 'other forces,' [the implication being the Justice department]." Right from the horse's mouth: This is not an agile, response-able company.

Intel and Microsoft are far less than agile companies even though they are respected for their demonstrated abilities to thrive in fast-changing, unpredictable environments—the very core definition of agility. Most other companies would gladly trade places with Intel or Microsoft. If these two aren't agile, who needs it? They probably do, the most. They are directly responsible for creating a much more agile set of contenders than ever seen before in the market. The likes of AMD and Cyrex are developing and honing strong reactive skills as they follow Intel through the microprocessor market and develop proactive capabilities at the same time. They aren't alone, just more obvious than LSI, TI, National, SGS, and others who aren't addressing the clone market, but are poised for the next generation of intelligent chips. When these companies step out, Intel will be in unfamiliar territory.

Lacking agility on an absolute scale does not doom companies, it just shows how far they are from where they or their competitors could go, and will go without choice. Until agility becomes an installed organizational competency across whole industries, however, it will be a relative issue. There will be companies that are the paragons for a while; they will spur the contenders into deeper understandings, who will in turn replace last year's heroes; and the cycle will spiral ever closer to the limit. By the time you are reading this book, some metamorphosis may have already occurred in the companies I have taken to task. Perhaps they will have begun the pursuit of agility as a studied competency, but the lessons of history do not make that a good bet. Culture has everything to do with being response-able, as we illustrate later in a detailed company example.

■ YOU ARE WHAT YOU EAT

Agility results in appropriate response to threats and opportunities and may be present in any or all business practices and systems. Agility can be achieved in different ways. At the highest corporate level, either an effective dictatorship or a ruthless resource portfolio management strategy can be agile. Small companies and start-ups are often agile with these techniques. We are not concerned here with this type of agility, as it is not sustainable across dictators, and is not scalable into the inanimate systems of the corporation. Portfolio management techniques are easier to implement with people and business units than at the lower levels of business practices and processes. Although you may replace a business practice overnight, you cannot get your people to understand the replacement quickly. Here we focus instead on systemic agility: You must prepare people culturally for change and structure flexibility for change into the systems they use.

How innovative is your organization, relative to your competitive needs and environmental situation? How fast are the rules changing in your industry? Do you introduce a few changes of your own? If so, what fundamental capability allows you to do that? What do innovation and leadership mean in your organization? To whom? Does it have real meaning in every functional area of the organization? Do people speak of it in manufacturing, in the purchasing department, in the accounting department, and in customer support?

What does organizational viability mean in your organization? Does it mean reliable employment, reliable dividends, reliable profits, reliable demand, reliable growth, reliable markets? Does it mean reliable anything, or does it mean sustainable something, or something else completely? Is this a universal meaning throughout the company? Who subscribe to that meaning? What would be their response if it is threatened? What could threaten it? How much time will you have to deal with a serious threat to viability? Will a threat come alone or with a gang? Will weathering a serious threat be a temporary setback or a permanent position change? Can you transform your business practices and processes into something different as easily as a child changes a Lego creation?

■ MOVING ON

Somewhere in Zen Buddhist literature is the story of the Zen master so enlightened that he walks between the raindrops—or seems to. As a young man, I had difficulty with that story, not knowing if I was expected to see one real skinny, real fast Zen master, or think that he had already transcended the space-time continuum. Older now in my perspectives, I think dodging and weaving between the raindrops takes too much energy, and a misstep is inevitable somewhere. Likewise, the quantum theory of transcendence is too much to buy. So now I figure he's either controlling where the rain falls while walking where he pleases, knows where the rain will not fall next and steps accordingly, or is part of the rain system—interacting with the raindrops in concert like the bodies in a complex adaptive system. Whatever, he's not getting wet and people continue to follow him in awe at his agility.

■ NOTES

1. Biological and ecological models of self-organizing and adaptable business and economic models have been increasingly promoted as the investigations into complex adaptive systems (chaos theory) by the Santa Fe Institute gain exposure. Interesting and worthwhile books on the subject from various angles include: Kaufman's *At Home in the Universe*, Kelly's *Out of Control*, Morgan's *Images of Organization*, Postrel's *Enemies of the Future*, and Rothschild's *Bionomics*.

2. Porter (1996), "What is Strategy?" Michael Porter suggests that managers have forgotten what real strategy is in an attempt to regain lost ground to the Japanese. They are engaged in best practice benchmarking, outsourcing, developing core competencies, and other such programs to make them lean and nimble, mistaking these for strategies. He identifies them instead as operating efficiency programs, allows that they have a definite benefit to offer, but reminds the reader that strategy is positioning a company uniquely in the market.

3. See Schneider (1994), *The Reengineering Alternative*; and/or Schneider (1998), "Why Good Management Ideas Fail," for an excellent and succinct coverage of the material (www.cdg-corp.com).

4. Porter (1996), "What is Strategy?"

5. Bennis and Biederman (1997), *Organizing Genius—The Secrets of Creative Collaboration*, pp. 22, 27, 76–78, 122, 212–213.

6. In the August 1996 issue of *Wired*, Peter Drucker was interviewed by Peter Schwartz and Kevin Kelly as "The Relentless Contrarian," pp. 116–120, 182–184.

7. In *Wired*, April 1996, John Geirland interviews Karl Weick in "Complicate Yourself," p. 137.

8. The phrase *product realization* encompasses all activities from the initial conceptualization of a product through finished production and readiness to ship. It came into common use in the mid-1980s when the focus changed from separated and sequential activities of product development followed by production process development to an integrated product and process development (IPPD) or concurrent engineering (CE) approach—meaning that all planning, design, and development aspects occurred simultaneously in interactive collaboration—at least in the utopian model. Fine (1998) extends the concept of concurrent engineering in *Clockspeed* into what he calls 3-DCE (three dimensional concurrent engineering), where supply-chain development is added to the simultaneous activities of product and process development.

9. *Business Week* (1995), "Ryder's Rocky Road to the Bargaining Table," October 16, p. 44. In 1995, Ryder had 60 percent of GM's hauling business and 40 percent of Chrysler's; and sales at both companies were affected when the Teamsters struck Ryder in September.

10. *Business Week*, (1995), "The Glitch That Shut Ford's Plants," October 2, p. 70.

11. *Business Week* (1995), "Is Spindler a Survivor?" October 2, p. 62. This article noted that the part shortages plaguing all PC makers were hitting Apple the hardest because "many of its components are custom-designed and sourced from one supplier." Christmas demand was booming but remained unfilled because Apple lacked critical parts.

12. A heated discussion took place at the National Center for Manufacturing Science in 1986, where representatives from the U.S. machine tool industry rebutted a simplistic "You should have listened to the voice of the customer" comment made by a representative from Detroit's automakers. The essence of the rebuttal was that the machine tool industry had done extensive polling of the automakers to find what they wanted, then did exactly that and got no reward. Instead, the automakers began buying heavily from the Japanese machine toolmakers, who had developed superior control technology on their own initiative—something the automakers had not asked for but knew that they had to have once they saw it.

13. J. Martin (1995), "Ignore Your Customer," *Fortune,* May 1, pp. 121–126.

14. G. Hamel and C.K. Proholad (1994), "Seeing the Future First," *Fortune,* September 5, pp. 64–70.

15. Cahners (1996), "Business Trends," *Electronic Business Today,* July, p. 23.

16. D. Bank (1995), "The Java Saga," *Wired,* December, p. 245.

17. S. Alsop (1997), *Fortune,* April 14, pp. 169–171.

18. D. Kirkpatrick (1997), "Three Promising (Non-Intel) Chipmakers," *Fortune,* December 8, pp. 211–212.

19. P. Eng et al. (1995), "Microsoft Plays the Net," *Business Week,* December, p. 41.

20. B. Schlender (1998), "Gates' Crusade," *Fortune,* June 22, pp. 30–32.

Chapter 2

Change-Enabling Structure and Culture

In this chapter, we provide tangible examples for four kinds of adaptable manufacturing enterprise environments: product, process, practice, and people. The fundamental common pattern these examples share—reusable components reconfigurable in a scalable framework—is a suitable structural template for guiding improvement strategies.

If you are in a manufacturing business and responsible for management, strategy, or planning, you will discover here a common set of concepts applied across a full range of system design, from a machine on the production floor all the way up to an organizational structure of multiple divisions and plants. If you are responsible for operations or production, you will find specific models of response-able production that should either offer reasonable templates or readily adaptable concepts for implementation.

If you are in another part of the business, such as human resources, information technology, or product development, or are in a completely different business (perhaps a process industry or the service sector), the fundamentals of adaptable organization and system structure are plainly illustrated here for adoption into your environment. It may require a little more thought on your part, and you'll be the wiser for it . . . recipes don't turn a line cook into a chef.

■ ADAPTABLE STRUCTURE

Remember the child's round-peg, square-hole pounding toy? It has a wooden frame with 6 or 8 uniquely shaped holes and a matching set of wooden pegs. The trick is to hammer each peg into its only compatible hole. Although such toys teach valuable lessons about matching, the more valuable lesson may be about incompatibility. The frameworks have a fixed number of holes that demand filling. A missing peg renders the system incomplete. Spare pegs usually cannot be bought separately, and similar toys rarely use the same peg geometry.

Contrast that design with the adaptable Lego brand system that many children play with today. The framework has a simple repetition of identical sockets on a standard grid pattern and can be extended indefinitely simply by attaching additional framework sheets. The components come in various simple forms, all with an identical socket structure. Macrocomponents can be assembled from basic pieces and replicated as often as needed to build or expand complex systems quickly. Losing a few pieces is hardly noticeable. The framework is so simple that compatible components from competitors are readily available with special characteristics and pricing advantages. And the observed useful lifetime of the reconfigurable Lego set far exceeds that of the peg-pounder.

An RRS (*reusable* components, *reconfigurable* within a *scalable* framework) design strategy can engineer adaptability into a wide variety of systems. When we define a system as any group of units that work together to achieve a common purpose, we include such business systems as a collection of machines in a manufacturing process, a procedure in an assembly process, an integrated chain of suppliers, a contract full of clauses, a gaggle of partners, a team of people, an organization of departments, and so forth.

It should come as no surprise that we can find examples of adaptable operating techniques in the fast-change industries of electronics and software. In fact, we draw heavily on two aspects of semiconductor manufacturing in the detailed examples that follow. We also, however, use an equally instructive example from an automotive brake manufacturing operation. We chose the following three examples not because they are unique, but because they illustrate both adaptability and the application of RRS concepts at progressively higher levels of production: the machine level, the process level, and the organization level.

■ ADAPTABLE PRODUCTS

The United States lost the semiconductor market to Japan in the 1970s, and hopes for regaining leadership were hampered by a noncompetitive process equipment industry—the builders of the machine tools for semiconductor fabrication. In this high-paced industry, production technology advances significantly every three years or so, as every new generation of processing equipment crams significantly more transistors into the same space.

Semiconductor manufacturers build a completely new plant for each new generation, investing $250 million or more in equipment from various vendors, and twice that for environmentally conditioning the building to control microcontaminates.

For equipment vendors, each new generation of process equipment presses the understandings of applied physics and chemistry. Multimillion-dollar machines are developed to deposit thinner layers of atoms, etch narrower channels, imprint denser patterns, test higher complexities, and sculpt materials at new accuracies and precessions. Generally each machine carries out its work in a reaction chamber under high vacuum, with a sizable supporting cast of controls, valves, pipes, plumbing, material handling, and whatnot.

New equipment development is actually new invention, frequently taking longer than the three-year prime time of its life. And because the technology used in each generation is unique, market success with one generation of equipment has little to do with the next or the past generation. The industry's history is littered with small vendors that brought a single product-generation to market.

Single purpose, short-lived, complex machines. Long equipment development cycles. Repeatability and reliability problems. All targeted for a high volume, highly competitive production environment serving impatient, unforgiving markets. And every new generation requires a new plant with more stringent environmental conditioning to house the new machines. The learning curve in this industry is dominated by touchy equipment that takes half its product life to reveal its operating characteristics.

Getting product out the door is so critical, and mastering the process so tough, that no one has time to question the craziness. This is the way of semiconductors. Or rather, it was until something occurred in 1987: Applied Materials, Incorporated, a California-based company, brought a new machine structure to market based on reusable, reconfigurable, scalable concepts.

Depicted in Figure 2.1a, the AMI Precision 5000 machines decoupled the plumbing and utility infrastructure from the vacuum chamber physics, and introduced a multichamber structural concept. Instead of one dedicated processing chamber, these machines contained up to four independent processing modules serviced by a shared programmed robotic arm. Attached like outboard motors, process modules are mixed and matched for custom configured process requirements. A centralized chamber under partial vacuum houses a

Reusable

☐ Material interfaces, transfer robots, process modules, utility bases, docking modules, and user controls are independent units.

☐ Common human, mechanical, electrical, gas, and hydraulic framework.

☐ A growing variety of processing modules may be mixed or matched within a cluster.

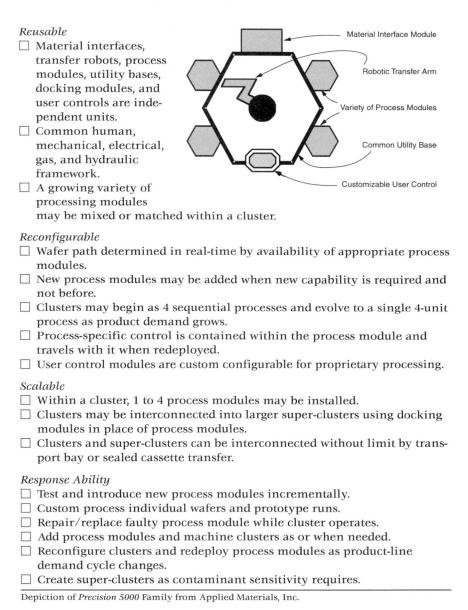

Material Interface Module

Robotic Transfer Arm

Variety of Process Modules

Common Utility Base

Customizable User Control

Reconfigurable

☐ Wafer path determined in real-time by availability of appropriate process modules.

☐ New process modules may be added when new capability is required and not before.

☐ Clusters may begin as 4 sequential processes and evolve to a single 4-unit process as product demand grows.

☐ Process-specific control is contained within the process module and travels with it when redeployed.

☐ User control modules are custom configurable for proprietary processing.

Scalable

☐ Within a cluster, 1 to 4 process modules may be installed.

☐ Clusters may be interconnected into larger super-clusters using docking modules in place of process modules.

☐ Clusters and super-clusters can be interconnected without limit by transport bay or sealed cassette transfer.

Response Ability

☐ Test and introduce new process modules incrementally.

☐ Custom process individual wafers and prototype runs.

☐ Repair/replace faulty process module while cluster operates.

☐ Add process modules and machine clusters as or when needed.

☐ Reconfigure clusters and redeploy process modules as product-line demand cycle changes.

☐ Create super-clusters as contaminant sensitivity requires.

Depiction of *Precision 5000* Family from Applied Materials, Inc.

Figure 2.1a   Semiconductor Wafer-Processing "Cluster" Machine

robotic arm for moving work-in-process wafers among the various workstations. The arm also services the transfer of wafer cassettes in and out of the machine's external material interface.

A single machine can integrate four sequential steps in semiconductor fabrication, decreasing the scrap caused by contamination during intermachine material transfer. Yield rate is everything in the competitive race down the learning curve; but this integrated modular approach pays other big dividends, too.

Applied Materials shortened equipment development time and cost significantly by separating the utility platform from the processing technology. They now focus development resources on process technology, reusing a utility base common across technology generations, which accounts for 60 percent of the machine. This eliminates a significant design effort for each additional process capability Applied brings to market, and shrinks the complexity and time of shakeout and debugging in prototyping stages. More importantly, perhaps, is the increased reliability that Applied's customers enjoy with a mature and stable machine foundation.

In process sequences with disparate time differences among the steps, a configuration might double up on two of the modules to optimize the work flow through a three-step process. A malfunction in a process module is isolated to that module alone. It can be taken offline and repaired while the remaining modules stay in service. The structure also facilitates rapid and affordable swap-out and replacement servicing if repair time impacts production schedules.

Semiconductor manufacturing is barraged with prototype run requests from product engineering. New products typically require new process setups and often require new process capability. When needed, redundant process modules can be dedicated to prototyping for test-analyze-adjust iterations it takes to establish process parameters. And if a new capability is required, a single new "outboard motor" is delivered quicker and at a lot less cost then a fully equipped and dedicated machine.

Cluster structure also achieves major savings in both time and cost when creating new fabrication facilities. The ultraclean environment needed for work-in-process can be reduced to controlled hallways rather than the entire building. People can attend and service the machines without elaborate decontamination procedures and special body suits.

Work-in-process is most vulnerable to contamination when it is brought in and out of high vacuum. The cluster machine structure reduces these occurrences by integrating multiple process steps in one machine. As depicted in Figure 2.1b, a docking module can directly interconnect these machines to increase the scale of integration.

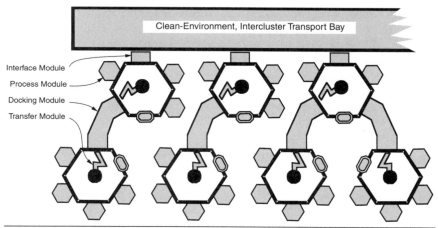

Using standardized docking modules to replace a process module allows multiple cluster machines to be assembled into larger, constant-vacuum clusters. This has particular value when a process sequence is sensitive to contamination, which is most likely to occur when wafers make the transition between the vacuum environment of the cluster machines and the atmospheric pressure of the intercluster transport bay. Process modules may be mixed or matched within a cluster.

Figure 2.1b   Scalable Machine Clusters

In 1989, the Modular Equipment Standards Committee of SEMI (Semiconductor Equipment and Materials International) started work on standards for mechanical, utility, and communications interfaces.[1] What started as a proprietary idea at Applied Materials started moving toward an industry open architecture, promising compatible modular process units from a variety of vendors.

Applied Materials revolutionized the semiconductor industry. Their cluster machines propelled them into global leadership as the largest semiconductor equipment supplier in the world. Leadership is defined by followers, and today, every major equipment supplier in the world has a cluster tool strategy.

The machine structure discussed in this section is sufficiently adaptable to enable a response-able production environment. Next we look at an equally adaptable metal-cutting production operation, with machines that are not themselves adaptable.

■ ADAPTABLE PROCESSES

Manufacturing cells in general and flexible machining cells specifically are not especially new concepts, though their use and deployment are still in an early stage. Machining centers involve expensive machine tools, and the economics of building cells from multiples of these machines is still beyond the vision and justification procedures for many. It is typical to expect benefits from these flexible machining cells in production operations with high part variety and low volume runs. This is understandable when justification and benefit values are based on flexible configurations and objectives.

Now, however, innovators are finding important values in quick market response: rapid new product introduction, accommodation to unpredictable demand, fast prototype turnaround, non-premium-priced preproduction runs, efficient engineering-change-order incorporation, longer equipment applicability, and the latitude to accept (or insource) atypical production contracts to improve facility utilization.

These new response-able system values challenge applications where transfer lines and dedicated machinery have traditionally reigned, and their applicability is based on concepts that push beyond the traditional flexible values. After examining these values, Kelsey-Hayes decided to build two entirely cellular plants for the production of ABS (automatic braking systems) and other braking systems. "We want to achieve a strategic advantage on product cost and delivery" was the vision voiced by Richard Allen, president of their Foundation Brake Operations.[2]

We are not talking mass customization here, with custom configured products. We are talking about fundamental change in the value structure of the high-volume-car/high-volume-brake markets. Technological advances in ABS systems have cut each succeeding product generation's lifetime in half. The trend to higher automotive-system integration and more technology promises even more change. Car companies want leadership in functionality and feature, and faster times to market; and can't afford to feature obsolete systems when competitors innovate. Kelsey-Hayes sees opportunity in this faster paced, less predictable market. To put the problem in perspective for evaluating solutions, we will look at some change issues first.

It is common in high-volume manufacturing to custom design and build an automated process that basically functions like one big multistage machine. Called transfer lines, these machines typically advance every part-in-process simultaneously through the sequence of workstations that make up the process. There is a high up-front investment in these single-purpose machines, justified by the high speeds and low unit costs this automated approach can deliver when producing standard parts in large quantities over time. The auto industry, for example, still makes extensive use of this approach for large machined items like engine blocks as well as for smaller machined and assembled components like automotive braking systems.

Product life cycle for ABS dropped from 10 years to 3 years over three generations of product, and continues to decline; therefore taking 4 to 6 months to retool a custom built, single-product, dedicated transfer line has become a significant part of the production life—not good. As automakers mine new niche markets and increase total systems integration in standard models, the frequency of ABS model-change increases. Within this shortened life of any model is the increasing frequency of modifications to add feature advantages and necessities. Nor do all these modifications and new models spring to life from pure design; each one needs prototypes and small preproduction runs.

Automakers, like most everyone else, have never been able to forecast demand accurately, and it's only getting worse. Because of new just-in-time material arrival requirements and reduced finished goods inventories, the automakers attempt to throttle production in concert with demand on a week-by-week basis. Suppliers must either be proficient at capacity variation or face increased costs in higher finished goods inventories and higher scrap at end-of-life obsolescence.

Earlier, we looked at how an adaptable semiconductor-production machine structure supports a response-able production operation. Now we look at how an adaptable cell structure (system of separate machines/processes) accomplishes that task. Both the cell (Figure 2.2a) and the production environment (Figure 2.2b) use capabilities and configurations possible with the LeBlond Makino A55 machining centers, and resemble actual installations. Other vendors can provide similar capabilities.[3]

Figure 2.2a includes a synopsis of some of the response abilities possible with this machining cell configuration. Flexible machining cells have been implemented in many places, but the response-able configuration here brings additional values. The configuration and the specific components were chosen to increase the responsiveness to identified types of change. The LeBlond Makino A55 horizontal machining centers do not require constructing special rigid foundations or digging pits underneath the machines to deliver cooling fluids and remove scrap, so they are (relatively speaking) readily movable. A cell can increase or decrease its machining capacity in the space of a day and never miss a lick in the process. The plant infrastructure facilitates a framework for reconfiguring components easily by providing common utility, coolant, mechanical, and human interfaces. These and other reusable-reconfigurable-scalable concepts are detailed in Figure 2.2a.

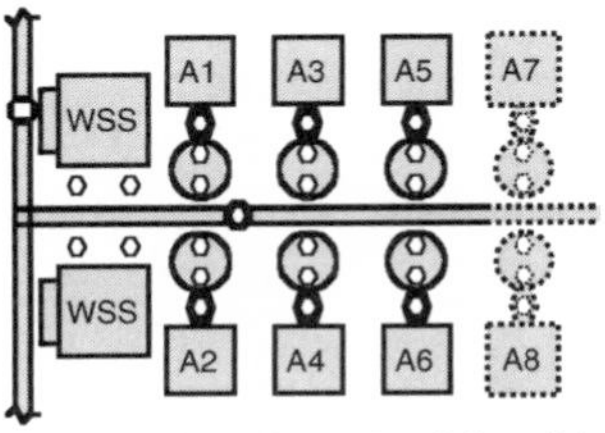

Reusable
- ☐ Machines, work setting stations, pallet changers, and fixtures are all standard, independent units.
- ☐ Common human, mechanical, electrical, and coolant framework.
- ☐ Machines do not require excavated pits or special foundations and are relatively light and easy to move from one cell to another.

Concept Based on LeBlond Makino A55 Cells at Kelsey-Hayes

Reconfigurable
- ☐ Cell control software dynamically changes work routing to accommodate unit status changes and new or removed units on the fly.
- ☐ Complete autonomous part machining, nonsequential.
- ☐ Machines and material transfers are scheduled by cell control software in real time according to current cell status.
- ☐ Part programs downloaded to accommodate work requirements when needed.
- ☐ A machine's life history stays with the machine as part of its controller.
- ☐ Machines ask for appropriate work when they are ready.

Scalable
- ☐ A cell may contain any number of machines and up to four work-setting stations.
- ☐ Cells may have multiple instances of each unit in operation.
- ☐ Machines are capable of duplicate work functionality.
- ☐ Utility services and vehicle tracks can be extended without restrictions imposed by the cell or its units.

Response Ability
- ☐ Install and set up a new cell in 4 to 8 weeks.
- ☐ Reconfigure a cell for an entirely new part in 1 to 4 weeks.
- ☐ Duplicate cell functionality in another cell in 1 to 2 days.
- ☐ Add/calibrate new machine in 1 to 2 days while cell operates.
- ☐ Remove or service machine without cell disruption.
- ☐ JIT part program download.
- ☐ Insert prototypes seamlessly.

Figure 2.2a Adaptable Machining Cell

It is accepted knowledge that replacement or massive retooling of a rigid production component is more expensive than transformation of a flexible production component. Response-able system configurations can further change the economics to overcome an initial investment that historically has been higher. "Has been" should be stressed.

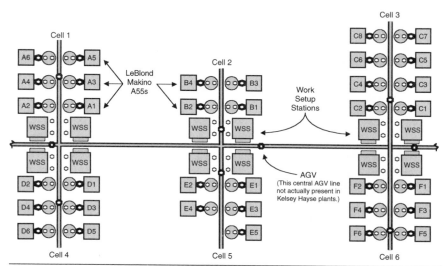

These horizontal machining centers do not require that pits be dug underneath the machines for delivery of cooling fluids and removal of scrap or that special rigid foundations be constructed, so they are readily movable. A cell can increase or decrease its machining capacity in a day. This is facilitated by a plant infrastructure that provides common utility, coolant, mechanical, and human interfaces that provide a framework for reconfiguring components easily.

Figure 2.2b   Adaptable Cells in Reconfigurable Factory

The price/performance ratios of modular production units are improving as increased demand increases their production quantities.

Don't let the previous examples lead you to a wrong conclusion. Response-able production requires neither response-able nor flexible machines: The response ability is a function of how the components of production are permitted to interact. The need for a response-able system to be readily reconfigurable can be accomplished simply by having a large variety of compatible but inconsistently or infrequently used production units.

This is a common approach in the toy industry. Not knowing from year to year what toys will be the hot items until a few months before they must make volume deliveries, toy manufacturers are either highly vertically integrated (with poor resource utilization) or broadly leveraged on outsourced manufacturing potential. Agility is a relative issue, and the toy industry has few alternatives to either outsourcing or just-in-case vertical integration. The just-in-case alternative does not have to be as onerous as it sounds if these practitioners become proficient at insourcing work from other companies to cover the costs of their insurance base.

From the organizational viewpoint, a response-able production capability can be built effectively from a seamless and reconfigurable network of outsources, which is what we look at next.

■ ADAPTABLE PRACTICES

LSI Logic was founded in 1981 as a "fabless" semiconductor company, meaning that they had no internal fabrication (manufacturing) capability. Though they were one of the first fabless suppliers, they are not unique: There were over 200 such companies in 1998.

The highly competitive, volatile, and cyclical semiconductor market often finds some manufacturers without enough capacity to meet demand while others have excess capacity. Initial speed to market, as well as speed-to-volume, are major factors in developing market share for products whose prime time may be only 12 months, 6 months, or even a single Christmas season.

LSI initially made a market in consolidating, managing, and delivering the industry's excess capacity to other semiconductor companies in need. It coupled this resource management capability with unique specialized services that featured faster initial speed to market. LSI has always been a leader in this area with front-runner process technology for semicustom ASICs (application-specific integrated circuits). In addition, a proprietary circuit-design tool called CoreWare[4] reduced new ASIC design time dramatically by reusing previously developed and tested subcircuits. Reusable subcircuitry also cut total time-to-volume significantly with "right-first-time" product.

Nintendo and PlayStation provide a useful example. At one time, Nintendo had a lock on the game-hardware market. They heavily promoted their next generation offering for the 1996 Christmas season, but then couldn't meet the demand. Meanwhile Sony had taken their new entry, the PlayStation, to LSI, which finished the design and took it to production in a mere 8 months rather than the traditional 18 months. Sony filled the demand that Nintendo created that season and PlayStation was catapulted overnight into a major market position. So much for brand loyalty: People went to the store looking for Nintendo and bought what was there—availability is what counted.

LSI is no longer a fabless operation, having added significant fabrication capability of their own over the years. They used the fabless strategy to enter the market without immense up-front capital requirements. The majority of companies in the fabless category specialize in proprietary chips, typically for specialty markets like communications, video, or military applications. LSI, on the other hand, provides manufacturing and design services for other semiconductor manufacturers that principally sell direct (e.g., Intel and the traditional fabless operations with proprietary designs) as well as other major semiconductor users that also have significant internal manufacturing capability (e.g., Sony and Motorola). Consequently, LSI competes not only with their customers' in-house capability but also with their other outsource options—companies such as Texas Instruments, Toshiba, Fujitsu, and Hyundai.

Although the structure of LSI's CoreWare design tool is instructive in its own right, our present focus is on their overall product realization services. To their customers, they are an outsource that incorporates other outsources into their resource pool.

The principal different feature that LSI introduces is a set of practices designed to nurture and manage a loosely coupled mixture of in- and outsources as a coherent entity. Since its founding in 1981, the corporate operational center has been a management group in Hong Kong, which builds and maintains this pool of outsources, and assigns and schedules both in- and outsources for specific customer orders (see Figure 2.3).

The resource assignation process is notable in that potential resources bid on specific jobs, offering both price and availability. A production resource path is then assembled from the best bids. Bids from a given resource are likely to change with each job, whether in- or outsource, depending on their available capacity and loading at the time required as well as their facility, process, and labor costs. Insources are not given any preferred status over outsources—the ability to deliver low cost on time is what produces a repeatable profit stream. If an inside resource cannot compete with outsource alternatives, it is a candidate for upgrade investment, divestiture, or retirement.

LSI's motivation for developing insourced fabrication capability was not primarily to gain an expected cost advantage but to guarantee capacity at the leading edge of process technology. Their addition of wafer testing/sorting capability was also a response to technology issues, and began with a program to test and refine new technology and then export it with training to their outsources. One benefit of this approach is now a common online interface that allows them to monitor the test results in real time at both in- and outsource locations. They continue to test and refine other critical backend production technologies as a prelude to helping their outsources adopt these leading capabilities.

A key element in the effective management of a loosely coupled resource pool is the standardization of the interresource interface. LSI has been evolving a system they call the Subcontractor Technical Network (STN) to accomplish this. In popular terms, STN is pioneering combined features of an interenterprise integration system and a

Reusable

☐ Individual insource and outsource resources are configured and assigned to an order on a bid-per-order basis.

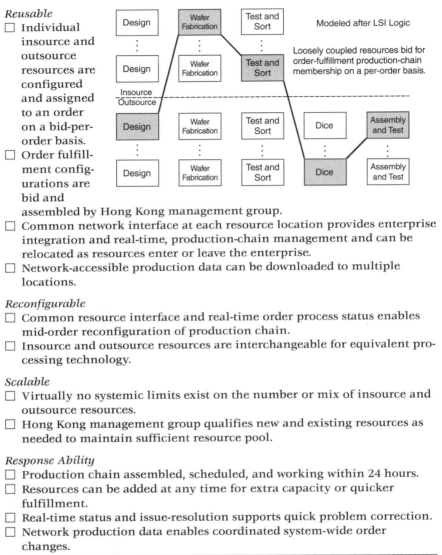

☐ Order fulfillment configurations are bid and assembled by Hong Kong management group.

☐ Common network interface at each resource location provides enterprise integration and real-time, production-chain management and can be relocated as resources enter or leave the enterprise.

☐ Network-accessible production data can be downloaded to multiple locations.

Reconfigurable

☐ Common resource interface and real-time order process status enables mid-order reconfiguration of production chain.

☐ Insource and outsource resources are interchangeable for equivalent processing technology.

Scalable

☐ Virtually no systemic limits exist on the number or mix of insource and outsource resources.

☐ Hong Kong management group qualifies new and existing resources as needed to maintain sufficient resource pool.

Response Ability

☐ Production chain assembled, scheduled, and working within 24 hours.

☐ Resources can be added at any time for extra capacity or quicker fulfillment.

☐ Real-time status and issue-resolution supports quick problem correction.

☐ Network production data enables coordinated system-wide order changes.

LSI has practices to nurture and manage a loosely coupled mixture of in- and outsources as a coherent entity. The corporate operational center is a management group in Hong Kong which builds and maintains the pool of outsources and assigns and schedules both in- and outsources for specific customer orders. Resources bid on specific jobs—offering both price and availability. A production resource path is then assembled from the best bids. Insources are not given preferred status.

Figure 2.3 Adaptable Organization

real-time electronic supply chain management system. STN comes packaged as a common hardware/software port for each of their principal production resources, with LSI providing installation, support, training, and upgrade services.

In addition to interresource communication protocol and transaction standards, STN provides design and manufacturing data and report transfer standards, a common set of databases accessible to all, real-time progress monitoring, some real-time process monitoring as in the example of test and sort, and importantly, an issue resolution capability.

LSI sells quick concept-to-design, speed of market entry, short time-to-volume production, and variable production capacity to its customers. It also sells leading-edge process technology as well as leading-edge design complexity, pioneering the system-on-a-chip concept. Sometimes it does the design work for its customer, sometimes it collaborates on the design with its customer, and sometimes the customer provides a design. In this highly competitive first-to-market environment, design effort often continues even after initial release to production. These are some of the principal change issues that LSI's organizational structure is designed to service.

The concept is similar to what Peter Drucker called the *flotilla* structure[5]; he contrasted it with the traditional factory, which he identified as a *battleship*. The flotilla is a collection of ships, each with its own command and control but also under an overall fleet-level command and control. Drucker likened each component to a ship, able to maneuver to another location in the process chain and able to develop new relationships with others in the flotilla. The organization provides a common set of operating standards for each component while giving greater flexibility to the total process. When his article appeared in 1990, he was suggesting the application of this flotilla concept to the subprocesses within an integral factory, and he believed that no such organizations existed as yet. Drucker reveals understated insight when he suggests that standardization and flexibility are no longer in opposition but tightly related, albeit in a different balance in these organizational structures. Though beyond the scope of this discussion, experience shows the line between standardization and autonomy to be the central design issue for response-able systems.

■ RRS STRUCTURE

The structures of response-able production systems, and even portions of the enterprise systems that encompass them, suggest that response ability is enabled by design. Engineers are responsible for each system's design—consciously or unconsciously, as the case may be. Structures for adaptable systems became a major focus with the advent of object-oriented software interests in the early 1980s. The progress of software technology and deployment of large integrated software systems has provided an interesting laboratory for the study of complex interacting systems in all parts of enterprise. The integrated software system, whether it's serving the accounting area, providing management decision support, or reaching countless factory computers and programmable logic controllers, is the creation of a team of programmers and system integrators with ongoing responsibility for maintenance and upgrade during the life of the system. Thus, the system is the product of intentional design, constant improvement, and eventual replacement, with the cycle repeating.

As engineering efforts, the design and the implementation of these integrated software systems proceed according to an architecture, whether planned or de facto. By the early 1980s, the size and complexity of these systems grew to a point that made traditional techniques ineffective. This awareness came from waiting in line for years to get necessary changes to the corporate accounting system; from living with the bugs in the production control system rather than risk the uncertainty of a software change; and from watching budgets, schedules, and design specifications have little or no impact on actual system integration efforts.

Software design and implementation techniques typically approached the activity as if a system would remain static and have a long and stable life. New techniques, based on *object-oriented* structures, recognize that systems must constantly change, that improvements and repairs must be made without risk, that portions of the system must take advantage of new subsystems when their advantages become compelling, and that interactions among subsystems must be partitioned to eliminate side effects.

These new approaches have been maturing for two decades now and have emerged most visibly into everyday employment under the name *client-server structure*. Though there are significant differences between systems concepts called client-server and those called object-oriented, they share the key concepts of modularity and independent module functionality. More to the point, information automation practitioners are now focusing attention on the structures of systems that accommodate change.

Though the RRS concepts have more depth than presented so far, the examples and abstractions convey the fundamental ideas. The theory and application of RRS design concepts are explored in greater depth in later chapters.

Component Management

Management Activities	Component Pool
Creation	
Classification	
Replication	
Modification	
Validation	

Framework

Applied's Machines	Kelsey-Hayes' Cells	LSI's Production Chains
Components	*Components*	*Components*
Processing Units	Machines	Insource Resources
Robot Transfer Arms	Work Setup Stations	Subcontractor Resources
User Controls	Pallet Changers	Network Interfaces
Framework	*Framework*	*Framework*
Standardized Utility Base	AGV Network Grid	Enterprise Network
	Cell Layout Standards	Qualification Standards
	Common Machines	

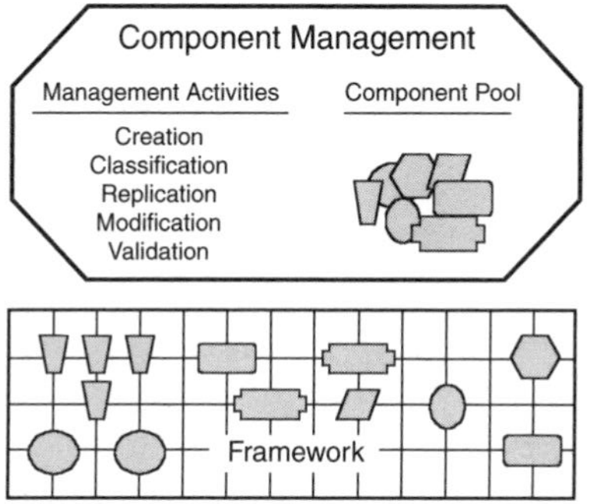

Figure 2.4 RRS Design Strategy—Reusable Components Reconfigurable within a Scalable Framework

The framework and component structure is central to the RRS design strategy and the maximization of change proficiency. The framework is a set of slowly evolving standards that establishes the limits on size and complexity of system configurations, we well as the speed with which components can be assembled into systems. The standards chosen for the framework define the system boundaries: too much standardization reduces size and complexity, not enough standardization increases component incompatibility—both conditions restrict system configuration and reconfiguration potential below the optimal. Finding the right point is the designer's art form.

You can observe the pattern (Figure 2.4) emerging here in the adaptable processes in your environment. By the same token, you can use this pattern to improve the areas you feel are in need. We have focused on hard, tangible examples of system/organization structures to illustrate important static design concepts that facilitate the implementation of change; but these structural concepts don't cause change—knowledge and people do that.

■ ADAPTABLE CULTURE

Isaac Asimov's robotic laws of science fiction fame employed three rules* to govern all robotic interaction with humans:

1. A robot may not injure a human being or, through inaction, allow a human being to come to harm.
2. A robot must obey orders given it by human beings except where such orders would conflict with the First Law.
3. A robot must protect its own existence as long as such protection does not conflict with the First or Second Law.

Asimov's many books repeatedly show how these three simple laws result in the best and safest response to all possible interactions with humankind. Interestingly, he didn't, instead, hand each of his thinking robots a policies and procedures manual at birth; perhaps he realized he could never finish such a manual sufficiently to give the first robot a name. Nor could that robot, no mater how wonderful its *positronic* brain, ever finish integrating the apparent but necessary contradictions. The brain would either loop among contradictory procedures or retreat into catatonia.

Another roboticist, Rodney Brooks, built autonomous robots at MIT's Artificial Intelligence Laboratory. One famous six-legger graced many magazine covers in the early 1990s, uncannily exhibiting behaviors of insect life when faced with obstacles and problems in the real world. What set the Brooks approach[6] apart from others was its lack of any overall worldview or hierarchical control—the behavior emerged from the combined interactions of many independent, simple-ruled decision mechanisms. There was no master control that understood how to coordinate six legs into forward motion, how to climb over or circumnavigate an obstacle, or how to

---

*Three Laws of Robotics," from *I, ROBOT* by Isaac Asimov. Copyright 1950 by Isaac Asimov. Used by permission of Doubleday, a division of Random House, Inc.

right itself after being turned upside down. Instead, there were independent controls for joints and other decision actuators, each with a set of goals, a set of simple rules, and the ability to sense its environment, including the actions of other controllers. Eventually, these independent decision makers learn which cooperative responses result in goal attainment. Again, simple rules are capable of complex behaviors and novel responses to unanticipated events.

A belief Brooks eventually expressed[7] was that the emergent behavior could not easily be determined in advance. That is, humans who designed the rule systems for the myriad autonomous control units could not predict the collective results. That makes it difficult to design such a system to a precise behavior specification. On the other hand, it makes it possible for the system to cope with unanticipated situations, and in fact to be innovative and come up with novel solutions.

Examples all around us demonstrate that we can design useful emergent systems purposefully. A free market economy is one, the stock market another. In the business world, we see experiments with empowerment, teaming, listening to the voice of the customer, organizational learning, and other concepts as movements toward self-organization—though not necessarily with that end in mind.

Fractal math has gained general exposure recently, and the *Mandelbrot*[8] set is the most famous fractal graphic. Named after the inventor of fractal geometry, the infinite complexity of the Mandelbrot graphic (Figure 2.5) is obtained from a simple equation with only three terms. Overlaid on that graphic is a quotation from *Built to Last,* by Collins and Porras,[9] that identifies a strong corporate ideology as the secret to long-term corporate viability. In their research comparing numerous well-known companies, they showed how those with a strong ideology consistently outperformed those without; and they suggested that having a clear corporate ideology is so overwhelmingly powerful that its specific content is not important. They see the ideology as the core values that guide the decisions of all employees, creating an organizational result that emerges from collective action.

Collins and Porras show that any ideology is better then none. But the content of an ideology does make a difference, and some ideologies are better than others. This is evident in *An Agile Enterprise Reference Model with a Case Study of Remmele Engineering,*[10] which examined 24 critical business practices for response ability. Remmele exhibited broad-based maturity at dealing with change.

The more practices analyzed at Remmele, the more it became apparent that they all owed their adaptability to a very few common ideological beliefs plainly stated in the corporate Guiding Principles.

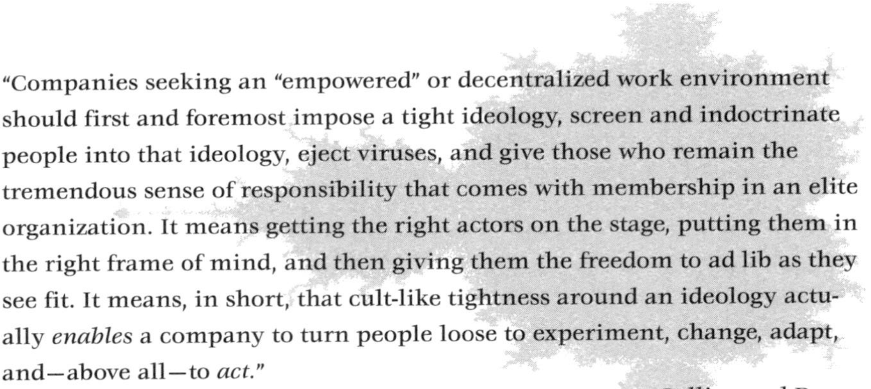

"Companies seeking an "empowered" or decentralized work environment should first and foremost impose a tight ideology, screen and indoctrinate people into that ideology, eject viruses, and give those who remain the tremendous sense of responsibility that comes with membership in an elite organization. It means getting the right actors on the stage, putting them in the right frame of mind, and then giving them the freedom to ad lib as they see fit. It means, in short, that cult-like tightness around an ideology actually *enables* a company to turn people loose to experiment, change, adapt, and—above all—to *act*."

Collins and Porras
Built to Last, pg. 139.

Fractals are one of the aspects of chaos math that have gained general exposure, and the *Mandelbrot set* is the most famous fractal graphic. Named after the inventor of fractal geometry, the infinite complexity of the Mandelbrot graphic is obtained from a simple equation with three terms. Overlaid on that graphic is a quotation from *Built to Last* (permission by HarperCollins) that identifies a strong corporate ideology as the secret to long-term corporate viability. From a few simple rules in a corporate ideology emerges a pattern of corporate behavior infinite in its complexity.

Figure 2.5 Infinite Response from a Small Set of Rules

Among those principles are the beliefs in constant change and continuous learning. These two, as well as a few others, form the generating function for the organizational entity called Remmele Engineering. Like Asimov's robotic laws and Brooks's distributed control, a simple set of ideological beliefs generates a highly successful response capability in the face of unanticipated change. And like the Mandelbrot set, infinite complexity emerges from a few simple terms.

■ REMMELE ENGINEERING—ENGINEERED FOR RESPONSE ABILITY

Remmele Engineering is in the machined-metal parts and custom-automation business, operating in Minnesota at a little over $100 million in 1999, growing at a sustained and comfortable 12 percent per year on average. They are abnormal in a market populated mainly by slow or no-growth family-owned regional businesses in the $5 to $25 million range.

They offer several advantages as a case study: They are small enough to analyze in deep and comprehensive detail, yet large enough to exhibit some complexity; their history spans enough decades to claim sustainability, yet not so many that the path is forgotten; their industry is not undergoing explosive growth that drags everyone along and masks true competency, yet it exhibits major changes in technology, markets, and skills; and the lessons they offer are readily transportable to companies of any size in other industry and service sectors.

Metal-parts machining may not be a high-growth market, but it is far from stable. Technology is having its way here as most everywhere. Programmed controls and robots introduced an abstract and indirect relationship between the skilled machinist and the part, and continue to shift more of the hands-on direct control into the abstract and procedural realm each year. On top of that, these control and robotic technologies continue to evolve with new capabilities and new service problems with each generation. CAD/CAM systems are changing the way parts are represented and the way they are introduced to the machining processes. Sophisticated process analysis is increasingly necessary as machine speeds and feeds increase, as materials become more exotic, and as parts are put into critical high-tech medical, aerospace, and defense applications. Accurate cost accounting is shifting as flexible automation changes the underlying traditional economics. Computers and the Internet are rapidly changing the relationships between customer and supplier both upstream and downstream with electronic drawing transmission, remote video real-time product/process design conferencing, remote quality-assurance buyoff, and the latest trend toward online real-time supply-chain status monitoring. And, there are major human resource problems: Increasing knowledge requirements and decreasing general interest in a manufacturing career conspire in tandem to reduce the potential workforce.

Management at Remmele has embraced change as both a comfortable business reality and a corporate strategy, and has engineered the organization for response ability. In our earlier examples, we looked at RRS structural design, but here we are focusing on Remmele's cultural enablers, looking at their ideology as formed by their mission and strategic policies.

➤ Adaptable People

At Remmele, they know what their competitors do, they know what their customers think, they know what technology has to offer, and they know what their capabilities are. They know—because they listen and continuously probe for the latest developments in all these areas, because they are genuinely curious and committed learners, and because they have a culture of communication, collaboration, and knowledge sharing. But you don't hear them talk about knowledge management. It isn't a phrase used in the company. They just do it. The Remmele Mission Statement expresses that commitment:

Remmele Mission Statement

Our Goal—Our goal is to be the BEST company in our industry.

Who We Are—We are a company which specializes in high quality, difficult and complex work requiring innovative technologically advanced processes in the areas of: (1) contract fabricating, machining, and assembly; (2) designing and building of tooling; and (3) designing and building custom equipment for automating a variety of manufacturing processes.

Contract machining services are primarily directed toward high value-added machining of complex, close tolerance parts. These services encompass small lot non-repetitive machining, repetitive-batch machining, and high volume continuous-run machining. Customers for our services consist primarily of manufacturing industries throughout the world.

Why We Want To Be The Best—We want the satisfaction and pride of achievement associated with being important, highly skilled members of an organization that is constantly working toward being the BEST in its industry and, with our families, to share the material rewards that this success brings.

When We Will Be The Best—To be the BEST in our industry, we will have a consistently growing number of loyal customers who recognize us as the leader in providing customer satisfaction. Our employees will demonstrate a high level of satisfaction with our company and their jobs. We will be recognized as a good corporate citizen by our employees and those people we impact in our communities, and our vendors will recognize us as an ethical and valuable customer. We will be at or among the top companies in our industry both in terms of sales and profitability, and we will maintain a record of consistent growth. As an aid in measuring our performance, we will compare ourselves annually to a select number of the top performing companies in our industry, and to the industry data available through our trade associations.

The company goal is to "Be the BEST," and the company people know how they stand in the industry. The sense of self-confidence is pervasive, but it is constantly earned and reaffirmed, not blindly taken for granted. This self-confidence stems from a shared ideology, the totally involved pursuit of objectives, and the active and open discourse that takes place among tightly aligned and highly competent teams—not from a sense of superiority. There is no arrogance here.

The goal is clearly and honestly stated. More importantly, the metrics for achievement are defined and tracked. In the machining industry, gross revenue and net profit percentage tend to move in opposite directions, so being the *best* for Remmele means being among the highest in both simultaneously. They also put meaningfulness into "meeting and exceeding customer expectations" without employing that trite and lazy phrase. Their mission statement doesn't sound like Madison Avenue wrote it; nor does it sound like it was the outcome of a consultant's project. There is truth in their words. They live and breathe them. The words reflect their culture.

"Pride in Quality" is on the company T-shirt, and the mission statement affirms: "We will have a consistently growing number of loyal customers who recognize us as the leader in providing customer satisfaction." That's the result and the measurement of producing a quality product, providing a quality service, and maintaining a quality relationship. Remmele turns away work, even when it's hungry, if the job demands a compromise on quality. This is not an issue of policy as much as the fact that nobody there will work on a job requiring such a compromise. That's how they feel. That's one of the reasons they are there.

The "why" part in the mission statement is important. It relates the company mission to each and every individual in the organization. It defines the common mental attitude of the Remmele employees. And it is a large part of the entrance attitude-exam for prospective employees.

In 1976, Remmele grossed $8 million in sales. At that point, it broke with tradition in its industry and set up a national sales rep organization. Within six years, in 1982, revenues exceeded $26 million, making it one of the few at the top end of its industry. It continued investing in equipment and people, typically committing to a promising technology before they found the business to support it; they based this policy on the belief that they should first understand and master the technology before seeking customers. In 1989, sales exceeded $60 million. By 1996, Remmele Engineering had more than 475 employees and annual revenues of approximately $90 million. Its customer base includes computer companies, automotive manufacturers, medical device manufacturers, heavy equipment manufacturers, and the aircraft/defense/space industry. In 1996, Remmele Engineering had grown to five plants grouped into four divisions—each serving a different type of market, each operating in a mode compatible to that market and different from the other divisions. It added a sixth plant in 1998.

➤ Guiding Principles

Remmele's guiding principles are both straightforward and fairly comprehensive:

Remmele Strategic Policy: A—Guiding Principles

We at Remmele Engineering believe that conducting our business with the following principles in mind will ensure the accomplishment of our goals and provide job security for all. Success in following these principles will result in an ever increasing number of satisfied customers, the retention and growth of our people, and increasing profitability to be shared with all employees.

1. *Customer Satisfaction*
   a. *By aspiring to excellence in quality, delivery, and productivity, which will assure competitive prices.*
   b. *By committing to continuous improvement in every service or product we provide a customer.*
   c. *By treating everyone with courtesy, integrity, and friendliness.*
2. *Employee Satisfaction*
   a. *By making Remmele an economically secure and personally rewarding place to work.*
   b. *By providing an atmosphere of trust and open communication where people can continue to grow in knowledge, skill, responsibility, and compensation.*
   c. *By maintaining high standards of concern for the needs of the individual and the community.*
   d. *By involving everyone in our organization to ensure we accomplish our goals.*
   e. *By maintaining a clean, orderly, well lighted, and safe working environment.*
3. *Growth*
   a. *By attracting and further training outstanding people who are intelligent, honest, hard-working, skilled, and self-motivated to excel.*
   b. *By maintaining an innovative environment through challenging the status quo, embracing change, and encouraging informed risk taking.*
   c. *By regularly investing in the best tools, systems, and equipment available to be effective and competitive.*
   d. *By following a strong, well planned, effective marketing program.*
   e. *By formulating detailed, specific action plans to aid in accomplishing our goals.*

4. *Community Service*
   a. *By being a good corporate citizen, protecting our environment and supporting worthwhile community activities.*
5. *Profits*
   a. *Sufficient to accomplish these goals and provide a fair return to our stockholders.*

As with the mission statement, Remmele does not stop with a simple list of objectives, but follows through on these guidelines with a set of strategic policies that detail how these guidelines are employed in the operations of business. These living, evolving statements are reviewed and refined annually to reflect changes in the business environment and deeper understandings of core values and beliefs.

They plan and follow through on their plans constantly—not just at annually triggered events. Everybody involved in implementing a plan is involved in the formulation or critical review of that plan. Critical review is a continuous process in this open communications environment, where the biggest sin appears to be making decisions without doing defensible homework. No one is penalized for decisions that turn out to be wrong as long as the decision is based on a diligent effort to assemble and interpret the available knowledge. *Informed risk taking* is an often-repeated phrase at Remmele, and a concept that everybody in the company understands.

Though descendents of Fred Remmele, the original family founder, still hold all shares and a few board positions including the chair, no family members are involved in company management. Profit targets and distribution are first concerned with the strategic needs for continued investment in technology, human resources, and knowledge development—the sustainability of the business. Shareholder dividends are considered after the investment decisions have been made.

Underneath it all, management recognizes that continued success is based on the people the company can attract and retain. They have a strong and directed recruitment and screening program that continuously trolls for thinking, curious people. And they maintain an environment that these kinds of people require and seek: honest communications, continuous learning and new knowledge application, a voice in the company decision-making dialogues, loyalty, and respect. That doesn't mean they have management by consensus, and it doesn't mean they have abdicated responsibility at the top. They practice accountable empowerment at all levels, with clear and differentiated responsibilities as well. Top management, after honestly listening to all who wish to be heard, is responsible for determining strategic objectives and investments, but not for dictating how to achieve or carry out those plans. And the decisions of top management come under the same open scrutiny and critical review as decisions made by any other employees.

➤ Customer Satisfaction

Remmele next focuses on its customers:

Remmele Strategic Policy: B—Customer Satisfaction

1. *Meeting customer expectations results in customer satisfaction. Customer satisfaction goes far beyond the products we manufacture and encompasses the total business relationship between our customers and all our people and activities within our company. Leadership in the marketplace can only be sustained by constantly meeting or exceeding the expectations of our customers and anticipating their future needs through continuous improvement of our products and services.*

2. *Consistent with our Guiding Principles, we will accomplish this through teamwork and employee involvement; by regularly investing in the best equipment, tools and systems available; and by investing in the ongoing training and development of our people to enable each of us to perform in a manner that meets or exceeds the expectations of our customers.*

Okay, there it is: "meeting or exceeding the expectations of our customers"—a vacuous phrase that all too often substitutes for actionable substance in company mission statements. Notice that this is not the mission statement, and it is not offered here as the objective. Meeting expectations is viewed here as a means to customer satisfaction, and exceeding expectations as a means to market leadership. And all of this is followed by specific guidelines on means for achievement, ultimately laid at the doorstep of continuous investment in process capability and knowledge development.

➤ Organization

At Remmele, organization is a critical aspect of company policy:

Remmele Strategic Policy: C—Organization

1. *To better serve our customers we will utilize small (200 people or less) focused plants to ensure good communication, maximize the involvement and commitment of our people, and ensure responsiveness.*

2. *In the interest of enhancing the psychological ownership of our business by all employees we will continue to (1) involve people in the process of making decisions which affect them, (2) provide for decision making and problem solving at the most appropriate level, (3) encourage risk taking, and (4) empower employees with the freedom and authority to make the decisions necessary for effective job performance.*
3. *Emphasize communication at all levels within the company so all our people will understand (1) what is going on in the business, (2) the issues the company is facing, and (3) how they can help.*
4. *During times when sufficient work is not available, we will implement a series of responses to try to cause additional business to happen while simultaneously reducing working hours to match the available workload. Recognizing that our people are our most valuable resource, we view layoffs as the last resort to be undertaken only during a sustained severe business downturn when the survival of the company may be at stake.*

Remmele believes real and effective communication is important for profitable growth, and that letting employment at any one plant get above 200 people makes this difficult. Small plants help maintain close working relationships with customers as well as with all employees and provide a nurturing environment that gives employees the opportunity for recognition and a sense of contribution. The size criterion is based on relationship management and the employee's view rather than the more typical management span of control arguments.

Keeping the plant small enables customers to know everyone involved in their job and helps the employees feel a sense of "ownership." For example, when a prospective customer visited one of Remmele's plants unannounced, he was referred, without hesitation, to the group supervisor and machine operator involved in the proposed work. The operator described to the prospect how he would approach the proposed project and showed his thought preparation with a software analysis of the tool path he had worked out. The prospect became a customer, impressed that Remmele's operators knew exactly what they were going to do from a technical perspective during the estimation and proposal stage.

When a plant grows too large, Remmele spins off one or a few of its capabilities into an independent operating unit. They do this to help maintain an entrepreneurial atmosphere, sense of excitement, and team spirit within the company. Employees said that a common question among them is: "When are we going to split off and become our own plant or division?"

➤ Management

The central importance of communication, along with the themes of learning and interpersonal respect, underscores management policy:

Remmele Strategic Policy: D—Management

1. *We will continue to develop a supervisory team that successfully plans and leads in reaching objectives that benefit our company and all of those associated with it.*
2. *We will continue to encourage all members of the supervisory team through various forms of education, to increase their managerial skills, such as:*
   a. *Enhancement of our interpersonal skills so that:*
      (1) *Our communications are candid and open;*
      (2) *We develop the trust of our peers and subordinates;*
      (3) *We constructively manage conflict;*
      (4) *We are aware of our use of, and do not abuse, power;*
      (5) *We develop competence through delegation;*
      (6) *We accept and support the need for change.*
   b. *Increase our verbal and written communication skills so that:*
      (1) *We eliminate "jargon" when talking with customers and others in the company;*
      (2) *Our written communications are clear and concise;*
      (3) *All of our communications reflect care and competence.*
   c. *Improvement of our group process skills so that:*
      (1) *Our communications are candid and open;*
      (2) *We accept the ideas and communications of others;*
      (3) *We are supportive and cooperative;*
      (4) *Our focus is on team building;*
      (5) *We have more productive meetings;*
      (6) *We accept and support the need for change.*
3. *We will continue to encourage all members of the supervisory team to increase their technical skills through various forms of education; i.e., college courses, seminars, in-house training, etc. In addition, we must develop a structured program of continuous technical training for each managerial and technical field, i.e., design engineer, designer, project manager, plant manager, etc.*
4. *We will continue to manage with honesty, thoughtfulness, compassion, humility, courage, and enthusiasm. We will demand of ourselves, and encourage from those with whom we work, the highest standards of performance, emotional stability and maturity, consulting supervision and leadership.*
5. *Continuous improvement of quality and productivity are an integral part of our management philosophy.*

Item 2.a.6, "We accept and support the need for change," is a recurring theme that appears to be an underlying driver for much of what is stated. In reading through these strategic principles, one develops the sense that the authors chose their words thoughtfully. It is revealing that they included "the need for" in this statement, rather than omitting these three words and simply acknowledging that change happens, and that people should make their peace with it. These three words transform an otherwise reactive approach into a proactive strategy.

Lists are just lists in many places, but at Remmele the Strategic Policy is a mission realization road map that is the evolving product of an annual review—a collaborative process involving a large percentage of the company. To know Remmele is to believe that these statements are their attempt to capture explicitly their implicit beliefs and values, and not a wish for what they ought to be, or a desire for how others should perceive them.

A large investment in maintaining and developing skill and knowledge resources was evident to our team as we conducted the Remmele analysis. Though their four-plus year apprenticeship program is an obvious major investment estimated at $100,000 for new employees, many other instances abound. A majority of the company's machinists are regularly sent to the annual machine tool show for several days each year—a heretical concept in an industry where income is generated by someone working at a machine, not off at a show. We asked President Tom Moore how he budgeted and measured this investment: as a percentage of payroll, as a percentage of gross revenue, as an annually decided target, what? He responded with words to the effect that he wanted no explicit performance measures of training and education for fear that they would become managed numbers rather than necessary and integral parts of the operating activity. Some amounts are obvious and easy to ascertain from the books if anyone wants to do so (e.g., sums spent on employee tuition subsidies); but they are not reported as separate performance metrics. Tuition, by the way, is covered 100 percent and paid up front by the company; it is not reimbursed partially or contingent on grades or other performance criteria; and studies toward any skill needed anywhere in the company are eligible without restricting a specific employee within his or her current or anticipated job function. The deeper you dig, the more committed is the philosophy you find here.

They do not mention the maintenance and evolution of a common culture in the list of centralized functions as this is not recognized as a direct product or responsibility of any particular function.

Under the centralization of human resource activities, however, are the management of the corporatewide apprenticeship program and the recruitment process, two activities that have a pronounced impact on the corporate culture.

During the recruitment and interviewing activities, lots of talk happens up front to fit people with the culture and weed out unsuitable matches. Common screening procedures test for like-minded people who expect serious work, a sense of family, and constant learning. Though the recruitment screening is formal and specific, the qualifications are for broad values and ethics rather than dogma and background. The company actively seeks self-motivated innovative problem-solvers who think for themselves. The Director of Human Resources described the process this way: "We discuss continuous learning as the job, commitment to continuous improvement, empowerment and the responsibility it brings, that getting ahead is attached to skill and ability, that people come to own their work very overtly, about access to information, about challenging people, and that the Remmele reputation is to solve tough manufacturing problems, so we need the best and the brightest." Recruitment efforts target top talent and gifted personnel with minds of their own; machinist apprentice candidates are screened for breadth of interest and world consciousness, as well as for values and value systems, rather than for specific beliefs.

The nature of Remmele's ideology and its consistency among employees have resulted in a decentralized self-organizing operation system. When three shop employees were asked: "What if somebody gets past the screening process and turns out to be on the lazy or less prideful side?" the individual answers were a progression of practice: (1) "It wouldn't happen"; (2) "We'd talk to them and help them get up to speed"; and (3) "Eventually they'd see that they didn't fit and leave voluntarily, but if all else failed, the supervisor would invite them to leave." These sentiments were echoed closely in another division, where the focused-factory cell teams made their own decisions about who would join the team, and then worked among themselves to develop the necessary complement of skills and responsibilities: "Nobody really hasn't fit in, but if all else fails, the pressure is raised on that person and eventually the supervisor will help if they don't move on voluntarily."

Remmele has an excellent and active internal collaborative network. Within plants, the family/team culture fosters this activity. Across plants, common-function forums convened for purchasing, accounting, technology, and marketing provide collaborative learning events and channels. Both marketing and technology conduct frequent and periodic cross-divisional meetings to look for potential innovations and new opportunities. Both groups engage in continuous and deep knowledge development: Red Heitkamp, director of advanced manufacturing-engineering, spearheads a dedicated world-search for technologies, engaging other personnel when promising process or equipment is discovered; and Bert Casper, director of marketing, spearheads classic research activities into markets targeted for investigation by the cross-divisional team and the management team. These knowledge development activities are continuous, structured, scheduled activities.

Learning is not insular at Remmele. Though they are not totally immune to hidden bias, their ability to embrace foreign concepts and their propensity to expose themselves to foreign ideas creates a broad pool of fresh ideas. They bet first on people and their passions to pursue a reasoned idea instead of first choosing a direction and then finding a person willing to follow it. Examples of strategies they employ that are uncommon in their industry include the use of manufacturers' representatives, a predominantly outside board of directors, significant growth as a goal, a major commitment to knowledge and skill development, accountable empowerment, finite shop scheduling, and activity-based costing for job estimation. And they do not hesitate to adopt useful strategic principles from other industries. An excellent example is the concept of "informed risk," which President Tom Moore credits to Intel's mission statement from the early 1990s.

■ STRUCTURE AND CULTURE IN PERSPECTIVE

In this chapter, we have looked closely at structures that enable change: static system structures that make change possible, and a dynamic organizational culture that makes change probable. Both the static and the dynamic parts are important.

Static structural views are comfortable for many as they are technological, hard-edged concepts that lend themselves well to factual examination and direct control. They are impersonal. The cultural side of change proficiency is another matter. It is about people, their beliefs, and their values. It is the soft side of the business, with contradictions, equivocations, and indirect control. It is personal.

Two different styles of system control are exhibited here. One employs a physical structural design that is easily changeable, and then puts a change master in charge of it. The other creates a set of boundary conditions and objectives and turns everyone loose. In these early days of agile competition, either of these stand-alone approaches can make almost any company a lot more adaptable than its competitors—in the land of the blind the one-eyed is king. Real competitive potential, however, is not realized until a company is strong in both the possible (greater range) and the probable (more likely to act) dimensions.

Harvard's David Upton wanted to understand why it was so difficult for companies to become more flexible, even when they saw it as a competitive advantage.[11] To accomplish this, he studied 61 factories that make fine papers in North America, and compared the ways in which each employed automation and computers in the factory. His answers showed little correlation between flexibility and the employment of technologies intended to make factories more flexible. Indeed, many common assumptions were proven incorrect: He found no relationship between size of plant and flexibility, and no relationship between workforce experience and flexibility. Instead, the flexibility of these plants was primarily determined by the people, and their personal interests and concerns for flexible operation. "Plants whose managers had not made flexibility a clearly understood goal were much less flexible than those whose managers had."

The corporate culture provides alignment among the employees and between the individual and the organization. Culture is a framework. It can promote or inhibit the reusableness and reconfigurableness of human resources. Simply having a culture is not enough to promote agility. The culture at Remmele embraces continuous learning and its application. People expect the nature of their jobs to change frequently. They look forward to personal growth and development. They anticipate the opportunity to help develop a new business and join it in a newly created plant. They know their markets have ups and downs, and expect to contribute however necessary during the downs and work overtime during the surges. If things didn't change, they would be disappointed.

But neither is embracing change alone enough. The culture provides a common set of standards for interaction, relationships, participation, and values. These standards facilitate the mobility of people within the organizations because they provide a common language, common objectives, and open communications that permit someone to enter into new relationships effectively.

The static-design examples described earlier were focused on specific well-bounded physical systems. Here in the dynamic cultural environment, where the systems that get built and reconfigured are the corporate operational strategies, and the components in those systems are the corporate resources, the cultural framework has a pervasive effect. In all cases, we want to quickly and effectively assemble appropriate resources into a purposeful system (see Figure 2.6).

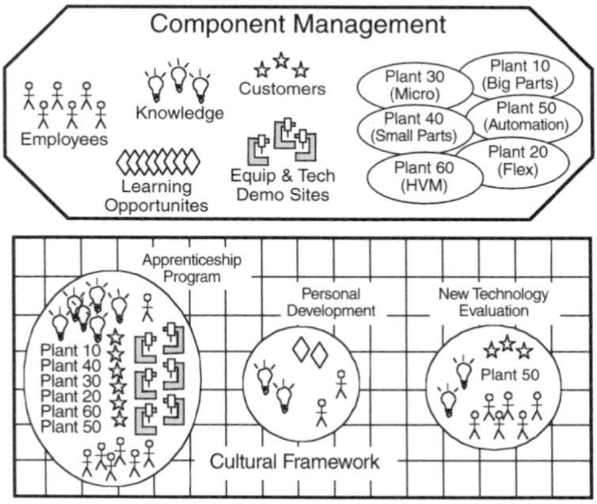

Reusable
☐ Common core knowledge and culture make people internally mobile.
☐ Continuous employee development keeps skills current and meaningful.
☐ Continuous search for new solutions to problems matches knowledge to opportunity.
☐ Common business-unit interface shields internal business-unit differences.

Reconfigurable
☐ Collaborative organizational learning is self-organizing.
☐ Knowledge and competency control, not rank.
☐ Apprentices do not select, or get assigned, to a home plant until after their multiyear apprenticeship is completed.
☐ Employees empowered to seek learning opportunities, plants empowered to educate and train without a budget cap.

Scalable
☐ Employees screened for curiosity rather than similar thinking.
☐ Common interest and competency at learning provides large capacity for massive and rapid knowledge diffusion when needed.
☐ Cultural framework continues to evolve.

Response Ability
☐ Maintain healthy margins and growth in a no-growth industry.
☐ Meet continuous growth needs in staff size and knowledge-base in an industry that isn't a major draw for graduates.
☐ Maintain continuous leadership in new technology introduction.
☐ Reorient plants and divisions when markets disappear.
☐ Absorb demand fluctuations without loosing resources.
☐ Continuously identify, create, and enter new markets.

Depicted here are three competency development system types that get constructed and reconfigured regularly at Remmele. All share a common framework defined by the corporate culture. The cultural framework at Remmele enables change especially well because it specifically embraces continuous learning and the continuous application of new learning as the expectation of all employees, as well as providing trust, respect, and opportunity factors to support a sense of family.

Figure 2.6 Remmele's Corporate Culture Provides the Framework for Highly Response-Able Competency Development

In the static examples, this system assembly and reconfiguration process is personally managed: Someone (or some group) is specifically responsible for reconfiguring a machine or a process or a production/supply chain to meet a need. Within the cultural framework, however, the human resources often play a direct role in self-organized system assembly and reconfiguration. Some degree of self-organization occurs in every peopled organization, no matter whether the cultural framework is designed to constrain or enable this process effectively to meet organizational goals. When a cultural framework does not recognize and address self-organization beneficially, it guarantees built-in productivity conflicts.

Remmele has an effective culture for dealing with the changing business environment. There are other ways perhaps more suited to other organizations in other industrial or service sectors. The important concept here is the need for a culture that can serve as an effective framework for assembling the necessary response systems. And these response systems must deal effectively with the nature of change in a specific operating environment. It is this nature of change that we look at next.

■ NOTES

1. SEMI, *Cluster Tool Module Interface and Wafer Transport Standard,* 1989.
2. Vasilash (1995), "On Cells at Kelsey-Hayes," p. 59.
3. "Transfer Lines Get Flexible" was the cover story in the January 1999 issue of *Manufacturing Engineering,* pp. 42–50. This article offers an overview of approaches from machine tool manufacturers that have modularized what they used to offer as stand-alone machining units; the individual reusable components can be reconfigured into customized flexible transfer lines. Transfer lines built this way have downloadable product flexibility not present in prior generations. The structural concept provides the machine tool manufacturers with an agile machine assembly capability. Some of the machine manufacturers were looking at mechanical component standards that would move some of this reconfiguration agility into the machine owner's domain. None were yet promoting the response ability that a Lego-like, reconfigure-on-site, structure would offer the user; but that is only a short move from where they are.
4. LSI Logic's proprietary CoreWare tool is a classic example of RRS structural concepts. The tool contains a library of popular and commonly needed subcircuits—some of which LSI has purchased rights to and some of which they have developed themselves—and assists the designer in stitching these into a total system-on-a-chip along with any new circuitry that is required. It is credited with a dramatic shortening of time

in new chip development, typically one-third the time it would take to develop a total circuit from scratch. The concept is a mirror of the subcontractor management concept reviewed in this chapter: there is a pool of circuit resources, there are people who obtain and standardize the circuits that enter the pool, there are people who access the pool and stitch together resources into a total solution, and there are people responsible for establishing and evolving the plug-compatibility framework standards that govern the compatibility of resource components. More can be learned about CoreWare at the LSI Logic Web site: www.lsilogic.com.

5. Drucker (1990), "The Emerging Theory of Manufacturing," p. 94.
6. Dewdney (1991), "Insectoids Invade a Field of Robots"; and Brooks (1990), "Elephants Don't Play Chess."
7. During a visit to the Santa Fe Institute in 1995, Chris Langton related this to the author.
8. Campbel (1993), p. 184.
9. Collins and Porras (1994), *Built to Last.*
10. Dove et al. (1996), *An Agile Enterprise Reference Model with a Case Study of Remmele Engineering,* Sue Hartman, a colleague in this research along with Steve Benson, had been to Remmele Engineering earlier for a single-practice analysis, and suggested that they would be an excellent candidate for a corporatewide analysis.
11. Upton (1995), "What Really Makes Factories Flexible?"

Part Two

Change Proficiency

The Language of Agile Enterprise

Part Two and Part Three of this book deal with two fundamental aspects of response ability: change proficiency and structural issues. In Part Two, the focus is on change proficiency as a language and as a competency. We deal with words, concepts, and metrics that allow us to communicate, categorize, measure, compare, and prioritize business strategies and issues concerned with adaptability in practices and processes, social and organizational structures, and even product and service configurations. We explore a common language for discussing adaptability in all aspects of business, and develop an appreciation for competency. Part Two offers tools as well as concepts to analyze and compare change proficiency, so that a map of possibilities and actualities can be drawn and goals and objectives can be established.

Chapter 3

Frameworks for Change Proficiency

In this chapter, we explore the two key aspects of change proficiency: the nature of change and the nature of proficiency. This chapter first establishes a metric framework for proficiency at change, and then introduces the notion that change comes in various types. A company's proficiency may exist in one or a few of these areas and not in others, and these *change domains,* as we prefer to call them, can form a structural framework for understanding current abilities and setting improvement and strategic priorities.

There is nothing arcane or radically new in the following conceptual discussion. The concepts should be a comfortable interpretation of what you already know because they stem from common sense and observation. What is new is the organization of these concepts and words into a body of thought and language focused on change proficiency.

■ CHANGE PROFICIENCY IN PERSPECTIVE

The decade of the 1990s started calmly enough. Electronic commerce wasn't on the radar screen. Knowledge workers were not recognized as a separate category, let alone a critically scarce resource. Remote workers were not real. Collaboration was unnatural. Communities of practice did it at the bowling alley. Suppliers weren't sharing information electronically, nor even with intimate working relationships.

Outsourcing was an anomaly. Customer relationship selling was not a concept. We knew nothing of learning organizations or virtual organizations. Lean manufacturing was just a suspicion, while agile manufacturing wasn't a thought. Knowledge management wasn't recognized, and chief knowledge officers (CKOs) did not exist. The North American Free Trade Agreement (NAFTA) and the European Union (EU) were pipe dreams. The cold war had just ended, and Russia and China were not on the business agenda. Japan thought they would forever lead, had become the teacher, and would benevolently tutor the United States. Personal computers and cell phones were for the few, and Palm Pilots and ubiquitous pagers weren't dreamed of. Help desks and call centers were isolated concepts. E-mail? What's that? Human Resource Management was not on an intranet. There was no intranet, nor the legions of support staff with critical knowledge incomprehensible to everyone else. Computer security was a defense firm concern. WWW, ERP, and Y2K only suggested alphabet soup. Companies had valuations based on P/E ratios, and obtained capital based on projected short-term earnings.

All of that and more changed during the 1990s, with profound effects on the conduct of business. Many companies survived those dramatic changes—not because they were change proficient, but because their competitors were not.

Change proficiency has both reactive and proactive modes (Figure 3.1). Reactive change is opportunistic and responds to a situation that threatens viability. Proactive change is innovative and responds to a possibility for leadership. An organization sufficiently proficient at reactive change to respond when prodded should be able to use that competency proactively and let others do the reacting.

The changes we read about in the business press are generally at the strategic and market-upheaval level: Microsoft got blindsided by Netscape's Web browser, Digital Equipment Corporation bet on semiconductors and lost the farm, IBM's unassailable reputation became irrelevant, GM's continual slide seems irreversible, AT&T is forced into competition, the entire U.S. defense industry is remapped at the end of the cold war, Sears loses its way, the U.S. steel industry comes back, Motorola goes from role-model star to goat, and Kodak is confused. All big, high-visibility, newsworthy companies. More diffuse but just as strategic are the corner CD stores that dried up when Amazon.com changed the market economics, and the stockbrokers who were put out of business by Web trading.

Most changes a company deals with, however, are hidden from public view in the ongoing operational activities: finding qualified

☐ *Viability:* The ability to meet minimum requirements of continued operation. Resilience. Ability to seize opportunity and follow another's lead.

☐ *Leadership:* The ability to shape the operating environment and set requirements of continued operation. Innovative. Marked by followers.

☐ *Agile:* RA state marked by high competence at both proactive and reactive change. Typically open minded, curious, experimental, interactive, sharing, and listening.

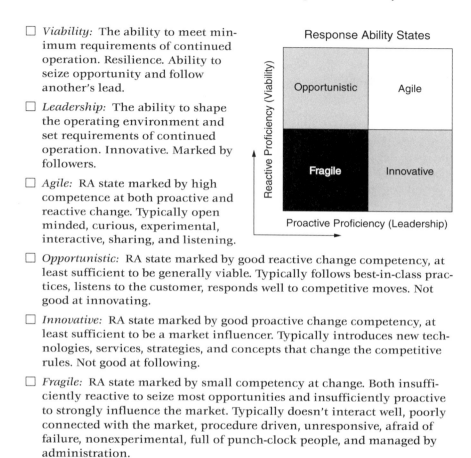

☐ *Opportunistic:* RA state marked by good reactive change competency, at least sufficient to be generally viable. Typically follows best-in-class practices, listens to the customer, responds well to competitive moves. Not good at innovating.

☐ *Innovative:* RA state marked by good proactive change competency, at least sufficient to be a market influencer. Typically introduces new technologies, services, strategies, and concepts that change the competitive rules. Not good at following.

☐ *Fragile:* RA state marked by small competency at change. Both insufficiently reactive to seize most opportunities and insufficiently proactive to strongly influence the market. Typically doesn't interact well, poorly connected with the market, procedure driven, unresponsive, afraid of failure, nonexperimental, full of punch-clock people, and managed by administration.

Change proficiency is a competency with both reactive and proactive modes. Reactive change is opportunistic and responds to a situation that threatens viability. Proactive change is innovative and responds to a possibility for leadership. An organization sufficiently proficient at reactive change to respond when prodded should be able to use that competency proactively and let others do the reacting.

Figure 3.1 Change Proficiency Benefits: Viability and Leadership

employees to maintain growth, gaining new competencies, sustaining competitive innovation, bringing a new product to market on time, meeting unexpected product demand, surviving Y2K problems, transforming the corporation with an ERP installation, recovering from computer virus and hacker attacks, absorbing an acquisition, and even changing the organizational culture.

■ MEASURING CHANGE PROFICIENCY

When agility was identified as a desirable enterprise characteristic, the immediate question turned to metrics. How do you measure it? How do you know when you are improving your agility, or losing ground? How do you know if you are less agile than your competition? How do you set improvement targets? Agility, as defined earlier, results from the combination of both response ability (RA) and knowledge management (KM). Here we are going to focus on ways to measure the RA component.

Webster says that *proficiency* means "highly competent." Competency is one of those umbrella words that we often use to encompass qualities that are hard to quantify. Nevertheless, a practical measure is needed before we can talk meaningfully about getting more of it, or even getting some of it. Keep in mind, however, that measuring competency is generally not unidimensional, nor likely to result in an absolute and unequivocal comparative metric.

Consider the competency of two accomplished hand-to-hand combat fighters picked at random from the vast range of the martial arts. No matter how competent they are, they are unlikely to have identical styles, skills, and training, nor identical physical resources. Under one set of circumstances, the larger of the two might leverage that advantage against the smaller, but under other circumstances the smaller, quicker one may consistently win. In any event, both will always outperform opponents with clearly lesser competency.

Naive discussions often confuse change proficiency with quickness, which reduces simply to cycle-time reduction. Time, as the metric here, shows its inadequacy when we test it and other candidates against extreme conditions. Would you call it proficient if a short-notice change was completed in the time required, but at a cost that eventually bankrupted the company? Or if the changed environment thereafter required the special wizardry and constant attention of a specific employee to keep it operational? Is it proficient if the change is virtually free and painless, but out-of-synch with market opportunity timing? Is it proficient if it can readily accommodate a broad latitude of change that is no longer needed, or too narrow for the latest tricks thrown at it by the business environment?

These questions let us tease apart change proficiency into four metric dimensions: time, cost, quality, and scope (Figure 3.2). Exploring the interrelations of these four shows a need to score sufficiently well in each.

Completing a change in a timely manner is the only effective way to respond at all in an environment of continuous and unrelenting

Change Proficiency—The competency available for accomplishing a transformation.

Change Proficiency Metric—A four dimensional performance indicator that quantifies a relative competency value for change proficiency:

1. Time [t]: A measure of elapsed time to complete a change.
   Fairly objective.
2. Cost [c]: A measure of monetary cost incurred in change.
   Somewhat objective.
3. Quality [q]: A measure of prediction quality in meeting change time, cost, and specification targets robustly.
   Somewhat subjective.
4. Scope [s]: A measure of the latitude or range of possible change, typically bounded by mission or charter.
   Fairly subjective.

Change Proficiency Issue—

1. A transformation considered of sufficient import to be included as an issue of concern that must be considered and addressed.
2. A transformation with sufficiently inadequate change proficiency that it is an issue of concern.
3. A transformation that the change proficiency metric is applied to, for example, formation of a partnership, expansion of plant capacity, replacement of a faulty supplier, changeover of a production plant, and so on.

Figure 3.2   Key Change Proficiency Definitions

change. After all, we need some time in between changes for a little value-added work. But the *time* of change alone does not provide a sufficient metric. You can change virtually anything if *cost* is no object. However, if your cost of change is too much relative to your competitor's costs, and changes happen with any frequency, there will be a steady erosion of working capital, or shareholder dividends, or both. Change at any cost is not viable, else we need not restructure anything ever: We can simply throw out the old and buy a new capability assuming, that we can bring something new to the operational level quick enough.

Quick, economical change, however, is still not a sufficient profile for proficiency. If after a change, the result is a house of cards that requires constant attention or repair to remain functional, the change process *quality* was insufficient. If we cut corners during the changing process to do it quickly and economically, we end up with a fragile result that lacks robustness. Encompassing robustness, quality requires predictability. Proficient change is accomplished on time, on budget, and on spec.

Change is a transitional term that implies a starting point and some new ending point. How far away can the ending point be from the starting point, and still be a quality, affordable, and timely change? The dimension of *scope* addresses this question. Are we change-proficient if we can accommodate any change that comes our way as long as it is within a narrow 10 percent of where we already are?

Scope is the principal difference between flexibility and response ability. Flexibility is a characteristic fixed at specification time. It is a range of planned response to anticipated contingencies. Response ability, on the other hand, is capable of dealing effectively with unanticipated change.

At the heart of scope is the architectural issue: Rather than design something that anticipates a defined range of requirements, or 10 or 12 contingencies, design it so it can be deconstructed and reconstructed as needed. Design it with a reusable, reconfigurable, scalable strategy—the subject of Part Three.

Scope is only a statement about the magnitude of change that can be accommodated. The amount of change that can be accommodated is useless if it can't be done in time to matter, at a cost that is reasonable, and with a surety of completeness. Thus, for any element to be truly proficient at change, it must have some effective capability across all four dimensions of time, cost, quality, and scope (see Figure 3.3).

► Measurement in Perspective

The purpose of taking measurements is to make comparisons. Are we better or worse than we thought we were? Are we better or worse than before? Are we better or worse than our competitors? Are we better or worse than our performance objectives? Methods for answering some of these questions directly are the subject of Chapter 9, where *change proficiency maturity* reduces the multidimensional change proficiency metric into a single comparative number. Here we are concerned with measuring the individual dimensions of time, cost, quality, and scope.

Measurements of any kind are not always unequivocal. A person measuring the length of a piece of raw lumber for a construction project generally arrives at an easy and unequivocal result, at least when the piece of lumber has square ends and is free of compromising knots

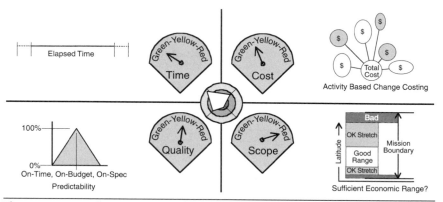

These measures can be numeric and reasonably unequivocal if time is taken to debate and research them; or they can simply be statements of good-green, okay-yellow, and bad-red based on collective knowledge and reason in order to set improvement priorities or performance objectives. A periodic exercise which develops a set of normalized perfection limits establishes a sense of competitive positioning and what is possible in each of the four dimensions. The principle value of such an exercise is the discussion and exploration that develops awareness and knowledge—embedding values and beliefs into the culture. Like litter, if a community talks about the values of a litter-free environment sufficiently, it sinks into the culture, making it difficult for anyone to cause or ignore a discarded bottle or can.

Figure 3.3   The Change Proficiency Metric Is a Four-Dimensional Balanced Scorecard

and splits. A measurer who knows that pieces will eventually be cut into 4-, 6-, and 8-foot lengths does not need to measure each piece of candidate lumber to the fraction of an inch, only to designate acceptability in at least one of the three categories. If there are split ends and knots, however, two different measurers may disagree; they might even dispute how to categorize the first or last piece of lumber.

In looking at measures for the four-dimensional change proficiency metric, we will find that some have more split ends than others, and none are unequivocal. Judgment is required.

In workshop-based analysis work conducted over many years, it was often impossible to come up with precise measures during the workshop. People associated with the process or practice under analysis, however, generally found no difficulty in categorizing the measure as low, medium, or high (or good, okay, and bad) in relationship to a desired target or presumed possibility. This eliminated the need to get precise measures on change issues that were *okay* and *good,* and was often a sufficient measure for immediate decisions about where to focus priorities.

➤ Time of Change

Time-to-market of a new product is a good way to look at the *time of change*. Sometimes time-to-market is satisfied when initial production quantities are shipped, even though they are far below planned production levels, while at other times it may mean the time it takes to reach full capacity production levels. This is a total elapsed time measure, not an integration of individual project hours or workhours. Time is the most unequivocal of the four metric dimensions, generally having clearly demarcated start and end points, but not always.

In the 1990s, the time to develop and produce a new car model was a major issue with auto companies around the world, primarily because the Japanese automakers had set embarrassing new records. Product development, the time to design and engineer a new car, had been reduced to about two years at most automakers by the mid to late 1990s, with product life cycles averaging about four years. As the product development portion of the total time became acceptable, the focus turned to the production *ramp-up* time of a new model *launch*. Ramp-up time is the time it takes a plant to return to full capacity production after introducing a new car model into the plant.

The University of Michigan's Transportation Research Institute examined 30 single car, single plant launches in North America during the 1992 to 1996 period.[1] The study found it necessary to define its interpretation of launch-start and launch-end times, as these may in fact be calculated differently by different automakers. For example: ". . . the authors choose to measure the new vehicle's launch from the time the facility stopped producing the old vehicle . . . [rather than] . . . from the month of when the first [new] vehicle was produced."[2] The spread in ramp-up times was dramatic: Honda's average was under a month and even completed one launch over a weekend, Toyota's rate was approximately two months; Ford's, four months; GM's, eight months; and Chrysler's, nine months. That's all history, of course, as these companies have continued to work on their launch times; and during much of the period under study new launch infrastructure was being put into place by the U.S. manufacturers. We'll follow this study through the discussion of change proficiency as it offers a consistent thread, but we'll also look at other business examples.

When the initial interest in agile enterprise arose, a major concern was the time it took to get a new contract created (drafted, modified, approved, and signed). Businesspeople and engineers found little difficulty in quickly reaching a handshake agreement on who was responsible for what in a prospective partnership, yet the subsequent interactions between legal departments often added many months of little apparent valued-added time to the process. Though making changes to an existing contract has its own difficulties, the time to create an operating contractual relationship was seen as a pressing problem impacting the ability to hit shrinking market windows. In one approach to shorten relationship-creation time, groups of companies in the 1990s (consortia, frequent project partners, regional supplier networks) established standard contract sets, approved once by the legal departments of each company and reused multiple times thereafter.[3] In a similar manner, the moviemaking and construction industries bind a team of independent operators together on a project with industry-standardized working agreements. The time to create a contractual working relationship is generally well demarcated: It starts when the informal "business agreement" is understood and turned over to the legal function for drafting, and ends when the final signatures are obtained.

Training people for new skills has become a major time issue, especially in jobs where the technology and tools change frequently. In the mid-1990s during a new-car product launch that I had the opportunity to analyze, the company chose to send fewer people to training sessions when the amount of new equipment and technology complexity raised the hours required for individual training. This trend of greater complexity and more frequent new technology introduction continues. The increased training time must be attacked directly rather than disguised by giving training to fewer people. It doesn't matter if the new technology is a word processor upgrade or a new piece of factory equipment, the training time required for both user/operator and service technician must become part of the vendor's product specification and objectives.

➤ Cost of Change

Time is money, goes the old saw; but more time to make a change doesn't always result in more cost. As shown earlier in the comparative times of new car launches, Chrysler's times were the poorest of the lot. Chrysler's vice president Frank Ewasyshyn was quoted as saying, "Everyone will remember a quality product, but few will remember a fast launch."[4] Chrysler learned the hard way that getting cars to market fast can dampen subsequent sales considerably if quality problems result. It used to be common knowledge among car aficionados that buying an early-production-run car from almost any manufacturer was sure to bring problems with it: the body panels might not fit well, the paint might peel, close examination might find reworked body panels, subsystems could have design problems, and unexplainable *lemons* would occur—cars with multiple problems that defied diagnosis and repair. Ewasyshyn also suggested that dealer inventory of the prior model would have to be discounted if new models appeared before older inventories were exhausted. Though some of this may well have been spin-doctoring, real economic factors are at work here, and they are all part of the cost of change.

At the beginning of the car launch study, it was postulated that an elastic model of launch costs existed in the automotive industry, where shortening the launch time would result in greater total cost; generally a counterintuitive expectation. The study concluded with a confirmation of this relationship: "It appears to be true that it is generally more expensive to shorten [new production] equipment installation periods of time within a company's launch cost curve (or paradigm). During the past several years, several companies appear to have attempted to shift their cost curves, when in fact what they have done is merely moved along their original line [to a higher cost-of-change point]."[5]

The cost of a slow change is not just associated with the money involved in the change process itself. In the case of new product launches, a slow launch may impact eventual market share heavily. The lost market share in late-to-market electronic or semiconductor products is a typical example. Compared with semiconductors, automobiles have a reasonably stable, or at least slow changing, customer base. Though car buyers may in fact buy something rather than the unavailable new model they had in mind, it may well be a model from the same manufacturer. A delayed car launch will not change market share to the effect that it will in semiconductors, which are not consumer products: They are used in another company's consumer product. Rather than risk sure loss of market share by late entry, these other companies will find a suitable substitute immediately, from a different supplier, and the late entry will be locked out of that opportunity, at least until the next generation of product is introduced. This lost market share is a cost of inadequate change proficiency.

In the case of new car launches, the profit contribution from lost sales spanning the time that the older model is no longer produced until the newer model is satisfying market demand is a real cost of change, as is the cost of lost market share because of a poor quality premature entry.

Employee turnover incurs a cost of change. A close look at the factors involved in the cost of employee turnover can make the point for retraining rather than layoffs followed by new hiring when new skills are needed. Table 3.1 lists factors that one human resource consultant suggests for consideration. All factors are not

---

Table 3.1   The Cost of Turnover: An Example of the Cost of Change

Costs Due to a Person Leaving

1. Calculate the cost of the person(s) who fills in while the position is vacant. This can be either the cost of a temporary or the cost of existing employees performing the vacant job as well as their own. Include the cost at overtime rates.

2. Calculate the cost of lost productivity at a minimum of 50% of the person's compensation and benefits cost for each week the position is vacant, even if there are people performing the work. Calculate the lost productivity at 100% if the position is completely vacant for any period of time.

3. Calculate the cost of conducting an exit interview to include the time of the person conducting the interview, the time of the person leaving, the administrative costs of stopping payroll, benefit deductions, benefit enrollments, COBRA notification and administration, and the cost of the various forms needed to process a resigning employee.

4. Calculate the cost of the manager who has to understand what work remains, and how to cover that work until a replacement is found. Calculate the cost of the manager who conducts their own version of the employee exit interview.

5. Calculate the cost of training your company has invested in this employee who is leaving. Include internal training, external programs and external academic education. Include licenses or certifications the company has helped the employee obtain to do their job effectively.

6. Calculate the impact on departmental productivity because the person is leaving. Who will pick up the work, whose work will suffer, what departmental deadlines will not be met or delivered late. Calculate the cost of department staff discussing their reactions to the vacancy.

7. Calculate the cost of severance and benefits continuation provided to employees who are leaving that are eligible for coverage under these programs.

8. Calculate the cost of lost knowledge, skills and contacts that the person who is leaving is taking with them out of your door. Use a formula of 50% of the person's annual salary for one year of service, increasing each year of service by 10%.

9. Calculate the cost impact of unemployment insurance premiums as well as the time spent to prepare for an unemployment hearing, or the cost paid to a third party to handle the unemployment claim process on your behalf.

10. Calculate the cost of losing customers that the employee is going to take with them, or the amount it will cost you to retain the customers of the sales person, or customer service representative who leaves.

11. Subtract the cost of the person who is leaving for the amount of time the position is vacant.

Recruitment Costs

1. The cost of advertisements (from a $200.00 classified to a $5,000.00 or more display advertisement); agency costs at 20–30% of annual compensation; employee referral costs of $500.00–$2,000.00 or more; Internet posting costs of $300.00–$500.00 per listing.

2. The cost of the internal recruiter's time to understand the position requirements, develop and implement a sourcing strategy, review candidates backgrounds, prepare for interviews, conduct interviews, prepare candidate assessments, conduct reference checks, make the employment offer and notify unsuccessful candidates. This can range from a minimum of 30 hours to over 100 hours per position.

(continued)

Table 3.1 *(Continued)*

---

3. Calculate the cost of a recruiter's assistant who will spend 20 or more hours in basic level review of resumes, developing candidate interview schedules and making any travel arrangements for out of town candidates.
4. The cost of the hiring department (immediate supervisor, next level manager, peers and other people on the selection list) time to review and explain position requirements, review candidates' background, conduct interviews, discuss their assessments and select a finalist. Also include their time to do their own sourcing of candidates from networks, contacts and other referrals. This can take upwards of 100 hours of total time.
5. Calculate the administrative cost of handling, processing and responding to the average number of resumes considered for each opening at $1.50 per resume.
6. Calculate the number of hours spent by the internal recruiter interviewing internal candidates along with the cost of those internal candidates to be away from their jobs while interviewing.
7. Calculate the cost of drug screens, educational and criminal background checks and other reference checks, especially if these tasks are outsourced. Don't forget to calculate the number of times these are done per open position as some companies conduct this process for the final 2 or 3 candidates.
8. Calculate the cost of the various candidate pre-employment tests to help assess a candidate's skills, abilities, aptitude, attitude, values and behaviors.

Training Costs
1. Calculate the cost of orientation in terms of the new person's salary and the cost of the person who conducts the orientation. Also include the cost of orientation materials.
2. Calculate the cost of departmental training as the actual development and delivery cost plus the cost of the salary of the new employee. Note that the cost will be significantly higher for some positions such as sales representatives and call center agents who require 4–6 weeks or more of classroom training.
3. Calculate the cost of the person(s) who conduct the training.
4. Calculate the cost of various training materials needed including company or product manuals, computer or other technology equipment used in the delivery of training.
5. Calculate the cost of supervisory time spent in assigning, explaining and reviewing work assignments and output. This represents lost productivity of the supervisor. Consider the amount of time spent at 7 hours per week for at least 8 weeks.

Lost Productivity Costs
1. Upon completion of whatever training is provided, the employee is contributing at a 25% productivity level for the first 2–4 weeks. The cost therefore is 75% of the new employees full salary during that time period.
2. During weeks 5–12, the employee is contributing at a 50% productivity level. The cost is therefore 50% of full salary during that time period.
3. During weeks 13–20, the employee is contributing at a 75% productivity level. The cost is therefore 25% of full salary during that time period.
4. Calculate the cost of coworkers and supervisory lost productivity due to their time spent on bringing the new employee "up to speed."
5. Calculate the cost of mistakes the new employee makes during this elongated indoctrination period.

Table 3.1 *(Continued)*

6. Calculate the cost of lost department productivity caused by a departing member of management who is no longer available to guide and direct the remaining staff.
7. Calculate the impact cost on the completion or delivery of a critical project where the departing employee is a key participant.
8. Calculate the cost of reduced productivity of a manager or director who loses a key staff member, such as an assistant who handled a great deal of routine, administrative tasks that the manager will now have to handle.

New Hire Costs
1. Calculate the cost of bring the new person on board including the cost to put the person on the payroll, establish computer and security passwords and identification cards, business cards, internal and external publicity announcements, telephone hookups, cost of establishing email accounts, costs of establishing credit card accounts, or leasing other equipment such as cell phones, automobiles, pagers.
2. Calculate the cost of a manager's time spent developing trust and building confidence in the new employee's work.

Lost Sales Costs
1. For sales staff, divide the budgeted revenue per sales territory into weekly amounts and multiply that amount for each week the territory is vacant, including training time. Also use the lost productivity calculations above to calculate the lost sales until the sales representative is fully productive. Can also be used for telemarketing and inside sales representatives.
2. For non-sales staff, calculate the revenue per employee by dividing total company revenue by the average number of employees in a given year. Whether an employee contributes directly or indirectly to the generation of revenue, their purpose is to provide some defined set of responsibilities that are necessary to the generation of revenue. Calculate the lost revenue by multiplying the number of weeks the position is vacant by the average weekly revenue per employee.

Reprinted with permission: © Bill Bliss, 1998, http://www.blissassociates.com.

applicable in all situations, but the range and size of the collection show how the costs associated with change can get involved and complex. Removing someone from a highly integrated employment relationship has many side effects that are not usually considered. In situations with high turnover, this list might usefully guide the design of employee relationships, staffing processes, and training practices away from the expensive areas.

■ QUALITY OF CHANGE

A quality job by a bank teller means closing out the cash drawer at the end of the day with neither a shortfall nor an overage. Overages do not offset underages over time. Both are considered equally unacceptable and prime grounds for termination if repeated with even small frequency and in small amounts. Both signify either inexcusable carelessness or lack of required skill. The issues affecting the bottom line are predictability and perfection, not dollars.

Measuring the quality of a change process is similar to measuring the quality of a product or a service. Generally we want to know how closely the end result conforms to specifications competitive in the market and consistent with customer expectations. You can measure the quality of a product in the amount of scrap, rework, and returns. You can generally measure the quality of a service in customer complaints—a more subjective measure since the customer may have unrealistic or unreasonable expectations. At times, measuring the quality of a change process may be even more subjective because specsmanship, the art of riskless promises, plays a real role, both intended and unintended.

The object of the quality dimension of change proficiency is to gauge process mastery. Is competency sufficient to predict an actual and competitive outcome? On completion, is the result on-time, on-budget, and on-spec? Taking the *absolute measures* of time and cost of change is different from measuring the *predictability* of time and cost of change. Time of change, for example, measured over three similar change events may have a respectable average result, yet fluctuate widely about the individual desired results—much like the bank teller losing $100 one day and making it up with an extra $50 each of the two following days.

Meeting the performance specification is just as important as meeting the time and cost targets. Performance can always be traded for time and cost, and often is when projects are defined as finished because they exhaust a budget or run out of time before meeting performance goals. Respecifying the finished result as a success is a common occurrence—and a telling indicator of a shortfall in the quality dimension.

Less telling is when a specification is met as a result of riskless specsmanship. The change-proficiency metric attempts to diagnose aspects of corporate health: Are you really fit to cope with this changing environment? Denial plays a role in both deliberate and ignorant forms. Listen to Chrysler in 1998 explain the success of their bottom-ranked rating for launch time:

> The real measure of a launch is "Did you meet your goals?" said Frank
> Ewasyshyn, vice president—Advanced Manufacturing Engineering at
> Chrysler. According to Ewasyshyn, the company sets goals for each

launch, yet they realize that trade-offs are required. Ewasyshyn identi-
fied quality [of product], quickness [time of change], and meeting the ob-
jectives [quality of change] all within the investment parameters [cost of
change] as the true measure of any launch. "You can throw money at a
launch, and get what appears to be a fast, great launch, but it probably
won't be cost effective.[6]

This is true. But predicting the ability to meet a noncompetitive goal is
not proficiency. Chrysler laudably appears to have known what they
could do with what they had, and the course they chose may well have
been the best under the circumstances. But that doesn't (or didn't
then) make them proficient at change—just safe and predictable.

As to unintended specsmanship, red flags should be raised, for example, when a company sees itself negotiating delivery dates while
using on-time delivery as a corporate performance metric. Though
this may sound like the intelligent thing to do, so as not to promise
something that can't be met, it is another form of defining away a
change-proficiency problem. Telling a customer who really wants the
goods tomorrow that next week is what you'll agree to may produce
an on-spec result but lose the market in the end.

Absolute single-quantity measures for change quality are elusive.
The predictability factors in a change process are generally multidimensional. If the change of interest is the creation of a new product,
the engineering process might be multidisciplinary, involving mechanical, electrical, and software engineering. Any or all of these dis-
ciplines may be working outside their established applications
experience, attempting an innovative stretch. Let's say the original
specification called for a certain set of features, some of which were
not developed in the time allowed, and some of which did not achieve
full performance expectations. When the business decision was made
to start the project, the performance specifications, the budget, and the
allowed time were all thought to be acceptable, at least by those making the business decision. Yet in the end, the original specification was
not achieved. Perhaps it would have been if the monetary budget had
been increased. Or perhaps it would have been if the time allowed had
been extended. Or perhaps it couldn't have been achieved no matter
what the cost and time involved.

Those intimately involved with such creative activities frequently suggest that innovation and creativity are not the results of
turning a crank. And therefore, the only measure of process quality
in these cases is something related to eventual success of the product.
I won't argue with that belief here. But I will argue that predictability
is valuable and that competency includes an understanding of the

difference between what can be done, and what might be attempted and explored.

More importantly, innovation and creativity play an increasing role in most of the critical changes that companies face. Leadership organizations are marked today by innovation in all aspects of business, not just product development, stretching the application of new knowledge in all functional areas. And then doing it again next year. Followers, though they may not be called innovative, generally find that most changes pioneered somewhere else can't be simply dropped in place without unique and creative alterations to fit the local culture and resource base.

The point: Transformation activities of all types will be done with increasingly less experience and less reference knowledge, they will face higher degrees of uncertainty when they are planned, and they will either be reasonably predictable by-and-large or the toll will be unaffordable.

Earlier, we saw how the cost of a change interacted with the time of a change. Now we see a similar interactive relationship with quality. It is the addition of the quality dimension to the change-proficiency metric that keeps time and cost "honest."

The quality measure is more subjective than either time or cost as it is subject to local definition. How you choose to define it will be a statement of where both your control and your improvement priorities lie. As a minimum, definition is required for the boundaries of *good, okay,* and *poor* predictability of time, budget, and specification attainment. Don't confuse this quality definition as a statement of "good-news" performance, and allow an underbudget, early-completion, or overfeatured result to be called good. You are measuring perhaps the most critical parameter for making sound business decisions— predictability.

➤ Scope of Change

Simply stated, this is a measure of how much latitude, or range, a potential change can accommodate (see Figure 3.4 for examples). When this range is small and finite, we typically have a flexible, rather than a response-able, capability. Though scope concerns are most readily associated with capacity range (how many cars could you build if demand skyrocketed?), capability range is often more meaningful (how many different types of car could you build in this plant?). With people, this distinction is perhaps more obvious: a person willing to work flex time ranging from 10 hours a week to 60 hours a week, as needed, versus a person capable of learning new skills when needed. Scope of

Product	Process	Practice	People
• Number of peripheral devices possible on PC • Max load on pickup truck while still offering good unloaded family ride • Web site hits per hour peak • Variety of desktop technology available on the corporate network • Working relationship defined by a contract • Amount of learning required to use a product effectively	• Economic production capacity, both upper and lower limits • Order entry fast ramp-up limits • Minimum economic limit on a service call • Range in counter customers serviceable within 60 seconds • Electricity available for delivery in the summer • Recruitment and hiring ramp-up rate limits	• Minimum/maximum economic volume by salesperson • Minimum/maximum effective training class size • New knowledge and thought leadership for consulting practice • Size of town required to support retail chain • Business quantity needed for local presence • Range of people productively applied to a project	• Effective intercorporate cultural interface range • Vision and mission in tune with market developments • Likelihood that a service tech can fix whatever the problem is • Breadth of available technological expertise to product development • Breadth of alternate use for employees already attuned to the culture • Effective knowledge reuse

Figure 3.4 Scope Examples

Scope is a measure of how much latitude, or range, a potential change can accommodate, and is closely associated with the concept of agility. When this range is small and finite we typically have a flexible, rather than a response-able capability. Though scope concerns are most readily associated with capacity range (How many cars could you build if demand skyrocketed?), capability range is often more meaningful (How many different types of cars could you build in this plant?). With people this distinction is perhaps more obvious: A person willing to work flex time ranging from 10 hours a week to 60 hours a week as needed versus a person capable of learning new skills when needed. Scope of change is not limited to capacity and capability changes and applies to the latitude of any type of change. Good scope, more than the other metric dimension, requires a conscious organizational design – one which specifically enables and facilitates wide latitude changes. It cannot be achieved meaningfully by working harder, smarter, or more working hours in the day.

change is not limited to capacity and capability changes; it applies to the latitude of any type of change, as shown later in this chapter. We explore scope somewhat more than the other dimensions as it is the least understood and the most important.

Scope has the effect of keeping all the measures before it honest. One way to get a good quality (predictability) score is to simply pass over anything that looks too difficult. Scope measurements counter this effect as they attempt to reflect both "opportunities lost" and "innovations achieved," though such measurements are better done by omnipotent eyes in the sky—a hypothetical position you should imagine for a moment. The discussion starts by using a customer/producer metaphor at the enterprise level, which should translate into any system (producer) of interest to you at any organizational (enterprise) level that serves a purpose (customer).

Scope has an outside useful boundary defined by the enterprise mission: If the plans call for controlled growth at a stated rate, or for maximum market share at a stated percent, failure to pursue additional opportunities outside these boundaries is not viewed as a scope problem, unless reduced viability is the result. If your market share or gross revenues are decreasing against your will it is a strong indicator of a scope problem, assuming you have a good strategy.

Opportunities are presented to producers by prospective customers. Lost opportunities are those occasions when a change could have provided some useful advantage but was declined. An opportunity must fit within the producer's mission (charter) to qualify as an opportunity. A refusal to go after an opportunity is akin to a no-bid. Going after an opportunity but failing to secure it is basically a bad-bid, and is equivalent here to a no-bid because the producer is unable to capitalize on the opportunity. It doesn't matter whether the reason for nonpursuit is "we are already at capacity," "we don't want/need any more business," "we are over committed at the moment," or "we don't have the resources." These are precisely the words uttered by an organization with a scope problem.

An innovation is a self-initiated change on the part of a producer, and has a meaningful and positive value to the customer in the context of the market. Innovations by definition go to market with a positive effect—they are not unimplemented ideas, nor are they new ideas that don't produce positive market-altering value. Catching up is not innovation. Duplicating best practices in your industry is not innovation.

Innovations are an indicator of good scope. Lost opportunities are an indicator of poor scope. Some of both is an indication of poor scope; they do not balance out. Poor scope is not a moral judgment. It is simply a statement that something within the mission wasn't done. Though at first blush, this may sometimes appear to be a wise priority choice, since you can't do everything, it is in fact an admission that you can't do everything, precisely what scope is all about. We are talking degrees here, and if you were in fact able to accommodate the first two opportunities that came along and not the third, that would demonstrate more scope than if you had only been able to accommodate the first one that came along, and had to ignore the next two.

Scope is a measurement of how much change a system can accommodate. In an absolute sense, it is bounded by *none* on the lower end and *infinite* on the upper end, and measured then as a unitless ratio ranging from 0 percent to 100 percent. Useful scope is generally bounded well short of infinity, and focused on specific units of latitude, like the range in car unit production that could be provided to a market at profit, or the maximum number of hits per hour that a Web site design could accommodate before needing a different architecture, or the range in both quantity and type of programming resources available on call to a product development department.

Establishing an actual (or estimated) scope measurement requires an understanding of mission beyond strategy. When Chrysler introduced the minivan concept and the demand exceeded their capacity to deliver, the production strategy had met its specification target, most likely couched as the ability to produce at some percentage above the original market forecast. However, the mission statement most likely had words like "meet or exceed customer expectations," a target unmet by the production capability. One insider pegged the principal factor as not enough engines, and no acceptable way to get more. That the true mission was to meet demand, rather than forecast, was evident in the chagrin expressed at the time, and in the moves subsequently taken by Chrysler to gain more latitude.

More than one Japanese automaker set a strategic target of *any car in any plant,* to meet uncertain demand. This entailed conscious plant design to permit a high-demand model, whatever it might be, to be inserted in additional plants along with whatever else they were producing. One U.S. automaker looked at the cost of such an open-ended strategy and decided the problem was bounded at a more reasonable level. Historical data showed that a car producable in three plants should be able to meet virtually any unexpected high demand, and that a plant able to produce three different cars should be able to stay profitable in the face of virtually any unexpected low demand. These probabilistic assumptions leave very little exposure, greatly increase the scope of potential change, and are affordable.

Scope is closely associated with the concept of agility and often is associated with the expectation that agility is costly. There was also a time when it was "known" that quality would be costly as well, until people realized that cost added to boost quality was more than recovered from reduced cost in other areas like scrap, warranty repairs, and sales (replacing lost customers). Designing plants for three cars and cars for three plants may well add a cost that would otherwise not occur, but this cost can be offset by the profits from meeting otherwise lost demand and by the elimination of losses in plants operating below breakeven. As discussed in Part Three, gaining scope is not necessarily an added cost, anymore than an enlightened design is necessarily more expensive than a naive design.

Sometimes scope does need to enter the virtually infinite realm. Consider the demands on enterprise-level systems from e-Commerce. As a first approximation, many companies are simply offering Web interfaces into their existing marketing, sales, and order entry processes. This defensive move confers no advantage on anyone. Then along comes a brand-new company that designs itself to take unique advantage of the Internet connectivity in place. Rather than build or invest in production or even warehousing facilities, it sets itself up as an electronic clearinghouse for matching orders with suppliers. This not only changes the economics in the market, it also changes the customer/supplier relationship values.

For example, today's question, as these words are being written: Will the bricks-and-mortar category killer, Toys "R" Us, change or sidestep its organizational infrastructure fast enough to effectively compete with the upstart eToys? That's not the real issue, though. E-Commerce is still young enough that whoever wins this first round, eToys or a new version of Toys"R"Us, hasn't won the war, just the first of many battles; with each battle played by a brand-new set of rules that turns Internet connectivity into customer value. E-Commerce will continue to surprise us for at least a decade, with new enterprise models coming out one after another. Companies that survive the rat race of new model testing and development will do so only because they have a large latitude in effectively accommodating unpredictable organizational change.

Apple's Macintosh computer lost out to the PC because of a scope failure. As a user, you could in fact add new peripherals and software much more quickly and predictably to a Macintosh than to a PC, but there simply wasn't enough variety by comparison.

Scope is not hard to measure once you select the important issues. You specify precisely *what* to measure (production capacity, rapid staffing ability) and *how* to measure it (units of product per month, hiring ramp-up). What may be difficult, however, is understanding where the important competitive issues lie, and where to set boundaries, and this is what strategy and mission are really all about.

■ CATEGORIZING CHANGE IN A FRAMEWORK

In the early work on agility, the most vocalized change issues were concerned with meeting production demand when it soared and hitting shrinking market windows with new products. The first was an issue of capacity, and the second one of creation—or so our research workshops called them at the time. With the realization that these were two distinctly different response situations, or domains of change, the obvious question was how many more might there be. From these workshops eventually emerged a framework of eight domains, subsequently refined and shown in Figure 3.5, which had proved sufficient and useful for discussing and analyzing adaptable business practices.

Change proficiency is now recognized in a variety of change domains. On the proactive side, we have creation (make something new), improvement (make it better), migration (move on to something completely different), and modification (change its capabilities). On the reactive side, we have correction (fix it), variation (deal with its variance), expansion (get more of it), and reconfiguration (reorganize it).

This framework offers more than just a vocabulary. At the corporate level, it is a way of categorizing the strategic issues faced by the company, seeing how they group, and sensing where difficulties clump together in certain domains but not others. This helps prioritize improvement strategies. Below the corporate level, in any of the various business systems, the framework provides a structure for focused measurement and analysis (see Figure 3.6). It also provides a structure for defining problems and opportunities in terms of their dynamic operational environment, and doing so from a consistent and comprehensive perspective. This establishes requirements for solutions and evaluation criteria for sorting among competing solutions and strategies.

Central to the discussion is the concept of a change issue. An *issue* is a question for which an answer is needed. It is a subproblem in need of a solution, an open item that must be dealt with. In a product or project specification, it is a requirement that must be met. The focus on change casts these issues in terms of a system's operating dynamics, forcing us to develop an understanding relative to

Change Domain	Definition and General Issues	General Characteristics
Proactive		
Creation (and elimination)	*Make or eliminate something.* Issues are generally involved with the development of something new where nothing was before or the elimination of something in use.	*Proactive* changes are generally triggered internally by the application of new knowledge to generate new value. They are still proactive changes even if the values generated are not positive and even if the knowledge applied is not new—self initiation is the distinguishing feature here. A proactive change is usually one that has effect rather than mere potential; thus, it is an application of knowledge rather than the invention or possession of unapplied knowledge. Proactive change proficiency is the wellspring of leadership and innovative activity.
Improvement	*Incremental improvement.* Issues are generally involved with competencies and performance factors and are often the focus of continual, open-ended campaigns.	
Migration	*Foreseen, eventual, and fundamental change.* Issues are generally associated with changes to supporting infrastructure or transitions to next generation replacements.	
Modification (add/sub capability)	*Addition or subtraction of unique capability.* Issues are generally involved with the inclusion of something unlike anything already present or the removal of something unique.	
Reactive		
Correction	*Rectify a dysfunction.* Issues are generally involved with the failure to perform as expected, recovery from malfunction and side effects, and the rectification of a problem.	*Reactive* changes are generally triggered by events which demand a response: problems that must be attended to or fixed and opportunities that must be addressed. There is little choice in the matter—a reaction is required. Reactive changes are often a response to competitive dynamics, for example, electronic commerce changes customer relationship expectations. They are also responses to customer demands, equipment malfunctions, legal and regulatory disasters, product failures, market restructuring, and other non-competitor-generated events. Reactive change proficiency is the foundation of viability and opportunistic activity.
Variation	*Real-time operating change within the mission.* Issues are generally associated with operational activity performance and interaction variances that must be accommodated	
Expansion (and contraction of capacity)	*Increase or decrease existing capacity.* Issues are generally involved with quantity and capacity changes when either more or less of something is demanded or desired.	
Reconfiguration	*Reorganize resource or process relationships.* Issues are generally involved with the reconfiguration of existing elements and their interactions, sometimes with added elements as well.	

Figure 3.5 Change Domains

The change domains provide a framework for describing a system in terms of its dynamic operational issues, rather than in terms of a tacitly assumed solution. When categorizing issues, don't get lost among the trees in the domain forest and wonder, for instance, why you can't modify something as a reactive change. If you are modifying it for reactive reasons, it is properly classed as a correction. Similarly, proactive reconfigurations are properly creations or improvements.

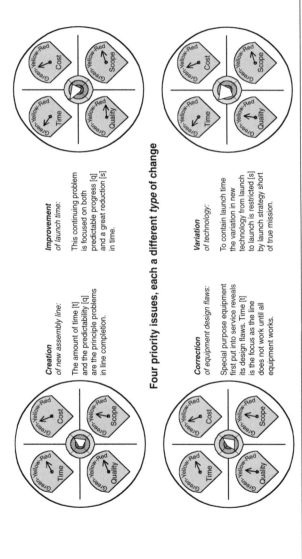

Creation
of new assembly line:

The amount of time [t] and the predictability [q] are the principle problems in line completion.

Improvement
of launch time:

This continuing problem is focused on both predictable progress [q] and a great reduction [s] in time.

Four priority issues, each a different *type of change*

Correction
of equipment design flaws:

Special purpose equipment first put into service reveals its design flaws. Time [t] is the focus as the line does not work until all equipment works.

Variation
of technology:

To contain launch time the variation in new technology from launch to launch is restricted [s] by launch strategy short of true mission.

The procedure for launching a new model car in an assembly facility is a study in change proficiency issues. Designing and refining this procedure is a major focus of all automakers, each with their own strategies and priorities. Shown here are four priority issues suggested from the examples in this chapter. Change proficiency meters might show the last measurable launch performance, some running average over the past few launches or perhaps just the gut-level guess of knowledgeable people about the current state of product launch, depending upon the data available. The purpose is to direct focus where it is most needed.

[t] = time, [c] = cost, [q] = quality, [s] = scope

Figure 3.6 Product Launch Change Proficiency at Acme Cars

Change Domain		1995–Motor Vehicles	1995–Electronics	1995–Aerospace/Defense	1999/2000–Amalgam
Creation (and elimination)	Proactive	• Opportunities • Strategy for change • Product realization • Buy-in, acceptance	• Product realization • Human resource forecast • Capital forecast • Innovative ideas	• Opportunities • Product realization • Innovative ideas • Core competency forecast	• Create unique, preemptive e-Commerce strategy [ts] • Create a learning organization [qs]
Improvement	Proactive	• Product quality • Product cost • Product cycle time	• Product quality • Product cycle time • Product cost • Continuous learning	• Product cost • Product quality • Product cycle time	• Increase innovation [qs] • Improve information system security [q]
Migration	Proactive	• Evolve the culture • Organizational learning • Time compression	• Empowerment and alignment	• Evolve the culture	• Preparation for Y2K [tcqs] • Transition to ERP [tq]
Modification (add/sub capability)	Proactive	• Customer relationship skills	• Customer relationship skills	• New core competencies • Customer relationship skills • Systems and processes	• Add knowledge management capability [s] • Add change proficiency to the existing culture [cqs]
Correction	Reactive	• Training by suppliers • Customer problems	• Quality problems • Customer problems • Training by suppliers	• Customer problems • Quality problems • Training by suppliers	• Attracting qualified knowledge workers [ts] • Information system security breech [tq]
Variation	Reactive	• Scheduling and execution	• Worker variation • Material availability	• Scheduling and execution	• Electronic integration of different suppliers [cs] • Customizable products [cs]
Expansion (and contraction of capacity)	Reactive	• Production quantities • Human resources	• Product development	• Product development	• Response-able downsizing [c] • Meeting unforecastable demand economically [cs]
Reconfiguration	Reactive	• Process technology • Teams	• Process technology • Adaptable worker	• Organizational structure • Process technology • Equipment and process	• Postmerger integration [qs] • Reorganization to meet e-Commerce needs [tcs]

The first three columns are from a study done at the Agility Forum. The fourth column is from the author's selected condensation from current business publications and shows the metric focus [tcqs]. Categorizing strategic issues within a specific enterprise places the problems in context, helping to focus strategy. Also, people with enterprise intuition can scan the profile to identify general domains of competency and confusion—one way to map improvement priorities for change proficiency.

[t] = time, [c] = cost, [q] = quality, [s] = scope

Figure 3.7 Typical High-Priority Corporate Change Issues at the Strategic Level

Change Domain	• Internal Network Service † Home Entertainment Center	• Assembly Operation † Order Entry Process	• Supply Chain Management † Product Development	• Knowledge Workers † Collaborative Culture
Proactive — Creation (and elimination)	• Security without isolationism [qs] † Encourage incremental add-on of options [tqs]	• Create comfort with, and proficiency at, change [s] † Create a knowledgeable OE customer interface [tc]	• Qualify new supplier for electronic compatibility [ts] † Create innovation culture and infrastructure [ts]	• Staff a new facility with scarce k-workers [tcqs] † Create commitment and understanding of values [t]
Proactive — Improvement	• Increase uptime of all shared components [s] † Reduce user learning time to zero [ts]	• On-time delivery [q] † Customer satisfaction with order-taker knowledge [ts]	• Supplier loyalty and trust relationship [tq] † Development cycle time [ts]	• Increase innovation among existing k-workers [s] † Increase rate and reach of knowledge transfer [s]
Proactive — Migration	• Next-generation user applications and desk/net technology [cs] † To system-on-a-chip technology [q]	• Collaborative work groups [qs] † Remote home workers [qs]	• Next-generation electronic supplier interface [t] † Development team is remote and separated [qs]	• Outsource knowledge work effectively [qs] † Become a learning organization [ts]
Proactive — Modification (add/sub capability)	• Customer/user sensitivity as added technician skill [s] † Expand options with latest technology [ts]	• Add custom electronic WIP interface for customer [cs] † New-product knowledge [tq]	• Add new class of shared information [tc] † Contract k-workers side by side with employees [s]	• Add special contractor talent to project team [qs] † Collaborate with competitors [q]
Reactive — Correction	• Virus loose in the network [t] † Automatic local and remote immediate diagnosis [tqs]	• Labor strike [c] † e-Commerce interface goes down [t]	• Failure of critical supplier [tc] † Insufficient talent on development project [t]	• Company not attractive to k-workers [cs] † Intellectual property loss [cq]
Reactive — Variation	• Wide range of user configurations [cs] † High configuration variety [qs]	• Accommodate high number of options [tc] † Customer dialog range of breadth and depth [qs]	• Supplier cultures vary widely [s] † Required talent/innovation varies by project [qs]	• Quality and productivity of individual k-workers [q] † Dealing with diversity among individuals [t]
Reactive — Expansion (and contraction of capacity)	• Help desk volume when new applications installed [cs] † Space/power needs when many options present [c]	• Dealing with lower than expected demand [cs] † Meeting demand surge caused by e-Commerce [ts]	• Hot multiple sources with low volume [cs] † Obtaining additional k-workers resources [qs]	• Critical general shortage of qualified resources [tcqs] † Involving the majority of employees [qs]
Reactive — Reconfiguration	• Redeploy older generation resources [qs] † Frequent reconfiguration and upgrade by customer [q]	• Outsource and insource allocations [qs] † Fallback alternatives when support automation fails [t]	• Items and destinations for core suppliers [s] † Redeploy development resources to production urgency [t]	• Redeploy existing k-workers in other areas [ts] † Collaborative group membership [ts]

Figure 3.8 Change Issues in Product, Process, Practice, and People Examples

Mapping change issues illuminates the operational dynamics of a situation, providing a set of solution requirements and evaluation criteria. Only one issue is shown in each category here, and all show an issue whether they deserve equal consideration or not. Shaded cells are expanded in the chapter text.

[tcqs] = metric focus, [t] = time, [c] = cost, [q] = quality, [s] = scope

the real operating environment, as opposed to the hypothetical ideal environment where everything works as planned. An automotive assembly process can be designed to meet forecast; or it can be designed to adjust gracefully when forecasts don't materialize, accommodate transparent next-model launch tests and transitions, and even weather a no-warning major supplier failure.

Figure 3.7 shows typical high-priority change issues at the strategic level, cataloged in separate domains. The three leftmost columns are from a 1995 industry-sector study done at the Agility Forum.[7] The column on the right, a selected condensation from year-2000 business publications, shows a generalized metric focus for each issue as well, and is expanded in the following discussion. Categorizing strategic issues by change domain within a specific enterprise places the problems and opportunities in context, helping to focus subsequent strategy. Also, people with enterprise intuition can then scan the profile to identify general domains of competency and confusion—one way to map improvement priorities for change proficiency.

Figure 3.8 profiles eight examples in four types of business systems: people, practices, processes, and products. Products and services, as designed systems, exist in a dynamic environment just as do business process, practices, and people. Identifying the change issues in the product usage environment, for example, can orient a response-able design strategy and extend useful life, or form the foundation of a product or service business strategy. The first column in Figure 3.8 profiles change issues for both a home entertainment center product and an internal infrastructure service concerned with the corporate desktop computing network. Only one representative issue is listed under each category, and for illustrative purposes all categories have an issue listed, regardless of whether they deserve equal consideration. Issues and metrics are amalgamated from real situations and could be different in other specific situations.

Half of the issues in Figure 3.8 (those that are shaded) are expanded in the discussion that follows. The issues populating these change domain frameworks are representative and are not meant as a focused profile. Later chapters explore technique and employment of this tool. Here the intent is simply to develop the language and concepts of change domains, and provide some familiarity with their use.

■ PROACTIVE DYNAMICS

Proactive change proficiency is the wellspring of leadership and innovative activity. Proactive changes are generally triggered internally by the application of new knowledge to generate new value. They are still proactive changes even if the values generated are not positive and even if the knowledge applied is not new—self-initiation is the distinguishing feature. A proactive change is usually one that has effect rather than mere potential; thus, it is an application of knowledge rather than the invention or possession of unapplied knowledge. In some cases, however, a seemingly unapplied invention may in fact have an effect—such as an atomic bomb invented and tested but not dropped might have had. Proactive changes typically introduce new approaches; and especially effective ones make existing approaches obsolete, change the rules for everyone, and may even disrupt markets. The four proactive change domains are creation, improvement, migration, and modification.

➤ Creation

To make or eliminate something generally involves developing something new where nothing was before, or dispensing with something in use. Creation issues often use words like develop, acquire, identify, or cause in their first articulation, as each in its own way is trying to create an event, a situation, a thing, a resource, an idea, some knowledge, a skill or competency, or something else that wasn't already present. Many of the change domains have mirror images, and the mirror of creation is elimination; in some instances, this can be equally or even more difficult to accomplish (e.g., eliminating product liability when a product is discontinued, or dealing with old and excess nuclear weapons).

Probing Questions

What is it that must be created? What supporting factors also require creation? Is the eventual elimination of the created item or its supporting elements potentially difficult or of concern? What about elimination of items being replaced by the newly created item?

Corporate Level Examples (Figure 3.7, Column 4)

➤ An almost universal panic is presently being reported in the business press: Virtually every type of business in every business sector feels it must develop an e-Commerce strategy quickly or watch as it becomes disconnected from, and irrelevant to, its market. Though time is the primary vocalized concern, it is also evident the scope plays a major role: Many strategies require a fundamental change in the business structure and are not simply an electronic portal to sales and marketing.

➤ Though the concept of the learning organization is not quite as new, it, too, is another core structural issue for which most of business is waking up late. Without the same sense of time panic, however, creating this new culture and its supporting infrastructure is more focused on quality and scope.

Product/Service Examples (Figure 3.8, Column 1)

➤ *Internal network service.* Creating a secure computing and in-formation infrastructure is a big issue everywhere, with scope (how close to perfect security) and quality (known and pre-dictable) the prime, though maybe elusive, objectives.

➤ *Home entertainment center.* For the home entertainment center product, with a component-stereolike architecture, en-couragement (to the customer) to expand the center with more components can be created by the product design strat-egy. In this issue, the focus is on creating the customer en-couragement quickly (time) and to a high enough degree (scope) to predictably cause (quality) frequent and additional purchasing actions.

Process Examples (Figure 3.8, Column 2)

➤ *Assembly operation.* With product life in general getting shorter, process technology changing faster, and the busi-ness strategy exploring the opportunities of e-Commerce, assembly operations in many industries experience are moving toward continuous change in parallel with assembly production. Creating comfort with, and proficiency at, this continuous change is an issue focused on scope—a little bit more is not enough.

➤ *Order entry process.* E-Commerce is accelerating the move-ment toward remote ordering introduced with mail order, and removing limits on the breadth of applicable product selec-tion. For many products, customers ordering remotely need more information about the product and its fit to their needs than can be effectively anticipated in catalog entries and Web-page descriptions. Order entry (OE) people are increasingly involved in a dialogue approaching the traditional sales engineer's knowledge base. Creating a knowledgeable OE customer interface, especially as new product churn increases, is focused on the time and cost this takes.

➤ Improvement

Incremental improvement generally involves issues with competencies and performance factors and is often the focus of continual, open-ended campaigns.

Probing Questions

What is it that must/should undergo sporadic or continuous improvement during operational life? What performance factors will be expected to improve with time?

Corporate Level Examples (Figure 3.7, Column 4)

➤ At the strategic level, innovation is a prime improvement issue in almost all types of business and has moved in front of the more traditional cost and quality improvement priorities in many companies. The focus here tends to be on innovation quality and scope.

➤ Another common corporate level improvement issue is the quality of information systems security. With an increasing dependence on electronic connectivity in all aspects of business, the vulnerability and potential for major disruptions and damage increase.

Process Examples (Figure 3.8, Column 2)

➤ *Assembly operation.* The processes in a company, especially in manufacturing, are where traditional continuous improvement programs have the most procedural history. On-time delivery is a common performance metric in many industries and often is the target of improvement programs. In some companies, like Amazon and Dell, delivery performance is part of their image and positioning. As customer expectations get molded by more Amazon and Dell-like companies, programs to improve delivery time focus on predictable (quality) performance results with firm target dates.

➤ *Order entry process.* Processes outside manufacturing, such as order entry, may also find on-time delivery a common improvement issue. The order-entry process example in Figure 3.8, however, recognizes the increase in telephone and Internet ordering, and the subsequent need for order takers to supply knowledgeable product information. The company in the example has a large catalog (scope), and wants to be first (time) among their competitors with broadly knowledgeable order takers.

Practice Examples (Figure 3.8, Column 3)

➤ *Supply chain management.* Some industries and companies are integrating suppliers closely with the production and next generation development processes. With this dependence approaching what was traditionally expected and exclusive with employee relationships, the improvement of trust and loyalty is focused on both the speed (time) of accomplishment and the surety (quality) that it will occur.

➤ *Product development.* Improving development cycle time is an old issue everywhere that continues on the front burner. Pushed by competitive pressures, how fast (time) the product can be improved and how much improvement is possible are the two focal points.

➤ Migration

Foreseen, eventual, and fundamental change is categorized as migration. Issues are generally associated with changes to supporting infrastructure, or transitions to next generation replacements. Change issues in the migration category get there because there is plenty of advance warning. Good migration proficiency makes use of the advance notice, and if necessary, institutes incremental and digestible change in advance of the event so that the event looks more like a nonevent.

Probing Questions

What in the future will replace (not simply modify) what we have? What support structures are likely to change with time? What changes would be likely to invalidate some current and basic assumptions?

Corporate Level Examples (Figure 3.7, Column 4)

➤ At the corporate level, Y2K is a prime recent example. Crossing the millennium was an anticipated event with plenty of warning, a firm transition date, and lots of preparation and disruption in advance. The issues receiving most of the early attention were time and cost of preparation, with quality and scope gaining equal recognition only as time ran out.

➤ The transition to ERP (enterprise resource planning) is another corporate level migration issue. It has far-reaching effects throughout the enterprise, may take many years to complete, can be a disruptive transition, and never comes as a surprise, but rather after lots of planning and decision making. Time and quality are generally the major focus for ERP transitions.

Practice Examples (Figure 3.8, Column 3)

➤ *Supply chain management.* As the Intranet and e-Commerce reshape buyer-seller relationships, supply chain management will see a succession of new ideas play out as experience is gained. Companies with a large supplier base may be planning for the next generation electronic interface while still rolling out the prior generation. Time becomes the focus on this migration issue as new features support the business strategy.

➤ *Product development.* Meanwhile, product development, with its need for scarce knowledge workers, is migrating naturally toward development teams whose members are chosen for availability and applicability, rather than geographic coincidence. Whether globally scattered employees, outside mercenaries, or both, the Internet, groupware applications, and virtual reality environments are removing the barriers to product remote teaming. With development projects so critical to business success, the issue's focus is on predictable (quality) capability far beyond (scope) productivity impediments caused by a technology-mediated interpersonal interface.

People Examples (Figure 3.8, Column 4)

➤ *Knowledge workers.* Finding enough knowledge workers to go around is only getting worse, and many of the best ones in high demand are going freelance. Outsourcing knowledge work, even for the sensitive areas of developing new product and intellectual property, is an alternative whose time has come. The issue focuses on both the quality match of the outsource to the task, and broadening (scope) the types of task that can be effectively outsourced.

➤ *Collaborative culture.* Behind the interest in collaborative culture is the belief that it is a required step to becoming a learning organization—a concept that has moved from theoretical interest to practical necessity on many agendas. Committed organizations are focusing on how long this migration takes and how close it gets to the theoretical.

➤ Modification

The addition or subtraction of unique capability generally involves the inclusion of something unlike anything already present, or the removal of something unique. Change issues here are often concerned with compatibility and the breadth of potentially compatible additions. As to removals, common issues are concerned with interdependencies and intimately integrated capabilities.

Probing Questions

What new capabilities will we (might we) need to add with time? What capabilities present might be candidates for removal if operating conditions change? How unique and exclusive is the compatibility framework? What interdependencies are there among the existing capabilities?

Corporate Level Examples (Figure 3.7, Column 4)

➤ At the corporate level, knowledge management is a new competency receiving lots of attention, and most of it is initially focused on scope. Whether added as a new functional area, a new performance criterion, or a new management responsibility, it comes in as a new corporate capability.

➤ Change proficiency is another new competency gaining recognition and respect at the corporate strategic level, and the focus here appears to be on cost, quality, and scope. Adding either or both of these capabilities into the corporate competencies can be difficult if the cultural framework isn't prepared or compatible.

Product/Service Examples (Figure 3.8, Column 1)

➤ *Internal network service.* Maintaining and upgrading the internal network resources brings extremely knowledgeable technicians in contact with barely knowledgeable computer users constantly. Frustration on both sides is common in communications; it is difficult for the technician to imagine the working knowledge possessed by the user, let alone appreciate the differences among users. Adding the social skill of empathy to the technician's repertoire is a modification issue focused on scope—generally a long stretch from the values of technical competency.

➤ *Home entertainment center.* The marketing strategy behind this product calls for continual upgrade and add-on, and succeeds only if the company is among the first to offer the latest technology-enabling features. The product itself is actually a platform that must accommodate optional components spanning generations of technology as well as feature concepts. The platform-design issue of adding as yet undesigned components must ensure that the compatibility standards will not slow down (time) new market introductions while accommodating an indeterminate variety (scope) of future possibilities.

People Examples (Figure 3.8, Column 4)

➤ *Knowledge workers.* With many companies unable to get sufficient knowledge workers as employees, contract workers are increasingly used in mixed project teams, especially where a unique talent or skill is required. Adding a unique capability to team with outside talent, and doing so without impairing the team or setting it back, is an issue focused on predictable (quality) effectiveness across a breadth (scope) of resource choices.

➤ *Collaborative culture.* Collaborative corporate cultures are relatively new operating concepts and still unnatural or uncomfortable to many people. The idea of collaborating with competitors or personnel employed by competitors is difficult for most. Yet in these times of cooperative product and market development, megaprojects like satellite nets and space commercialization, and just plain old knowledge-worker scarcity, collaboration with competitors is hard to avoid. Learning how to do it effectively and safely is a focus on the quality of the change.

■ REACTIVE DYNAMICS

Reactive change proficiency is the foundation of viability and opportunistic activity. Reactive changes are generally triggered by events that, once recognized, demand a response. Maybe they are problems that must be attended to or fixed, or maybe they are opportunities that must be addressed. The principal differentiation is that there is little if any choice in the matter—a reaction is required. Reactive changes are often a response to competitive dynamics: Japan makes car quality an issue, electronic commerce changes customer relationship expectations. They can also be responses to customer demands, order fulfillment requirements, equipment malfunctions, legal and regulatory disasters, product failures, market restructuring, and other self-induced or non-competitor-generated events. Reactive changes typically respond to the voice of the customer, say yes to opportunity, mitigate the downside of problems, and provide general resiliency. The four reactive change domains are correction, variation, expansion, and reconfiguration.

➤ Correction

A correction rectifies a dysfunction. Issues are generally involved with the failure to perform as expected, recovery from malfunction and side effects, and the remedy of a problem. Corrections may be concerned with diagnosis and repair as well as recall, upgrade, and swap-out situations. Issues of correction can apply to relationships, strategies, processes, practices, and people as well as to broken equipment, poorly designed product, and inadequate services.

Probing Questions

What can break or fail? How can a relationship become dysfunctional? What assumptions may become invalid? Are recalls and upgrades a concern? Will location or accessibility make correction difficult? Can slow correction be catastrophic? Is diagnosis easy and sure?

Corporate Level Examples (Figure 3.7, Column 4)

➤ From the corporate perspective, the inability to attract and keep enough qualified knowledge workers is one of the biggest concerns today. Whether it's the recruiting process, a mismatched corporate culture, the educational system, a supply-demand imbalance, or the bell-shaped intelligence distribution, something's broken and needs to be fixed. For most, the focus is on time—the shortage is stunting corporate growth, and on scope—the shortage is occurring in more and more functional areas.

➤ Another major issue that has risen to strategic proportions is the ability to correct an information system security breach. With more of the business dependent on electronic connectivity, more of the business is at risk. Recovering from a damaging breach is both time and quality critical: Though customers may wait a while for restored functionality, they have less tolerance for unpredictable durations.

Product/Service Examples (Figure 3.8, Column 1)

➤ *Internal network service.* A virus-infected computer is bad enough, but one loose in the corporate network can shut down the operating support infrastructure. The correction issue is focused intensely on how fast (time) detection, diagnosis, and recovery can be accomplished.

➤ *Home entertainment center.* An important part of the business strategy here is customer-effected maintenance—no service calls to the home, negligible inconvenience to the customer, and minimal, if any, downtime. Product design deals with both local and remote automatic diagnosis as a prime issue and is focused on immediate (time), accurate (quality) diagnosis regardless of what has gone wrong (scope).

People Examples (Figure 3.8, Column 4)

➤ *Knowledge workers.* Not being able to attract affordable critical resources to the company is a problem that needs to be fixed; it is a major issue on the HR agenda if not on the corporate strategic agenda. Everyone has their price, but escalating compensation is a losing game in this apparent inelastic market. For companies in undesirable locations or industries, the focus is on affordable (cost) resources with sufficient (scope) skills.

➤ *Collaborative culture.* Whether collaboration is limited to employees or includes outsiders in various relationships, the potential risk of intellectual property (IP) loss increases as more people know more about more things. Recovery after an IP loss focuses on minimizing total costs and knowing (quality) the extent and end of damage.

➤ Variation

Real-time operating change within the mission falls in the category of variation. Issues are generally associated with accommodating operational activity, performance, and interaction variances. Issues may be concerned with the variety of relationships to maintain, the variety of options and customization to accommodate, the variance on raw materials and among resources, and the sure-to-happen operational anomalies that typically go unrecognized but always get accommodated.

Probing Questions

What types of scheduling changes are typical? What latitude is possible/typical in order arrival, product features, supplier performance, employee skills? How big are the variations likely to be? Where have surprises come from before, especially repeatedly? What range of relationship cultures and individual diversity can be expected?

Corporate Level Examples (Figure 3.7, Column 4)

➤ Upstream supply chain integration and management through the Internet is just as critical today as downstream e-Commerce. The variation among supplier readiness, competency, and internal infrastructures raises issues focused on cost, where compatibility lowers the real cost of doing business, and scope, where a broader range means more potential suppliers and alternates.

➤ Variety plays a big role in the product and production strategies. Mass customization and product configuration options have become customer expectations, requiring high speed, real-time (time) variation in production processes with a simultaneous emphasis on cost containment (cost) and broad latitude (scope).

Practice Examples (Figure 3.8, Column 3)

➤ *Supply chain management.* Closer working relationships between customer and supplier accentuates the cultural differences among suppliers, and between each supplier and the customer. Rather than have cultural differences get in the way of otherwise helpful relationships, this issue focuses on scope and benefits from maximizing the potential suppliers that could have compatible relationships.

➤ *Product development.* All development projects do not require the same degree of innovation, nor the same degree of talent from the project participants. With both innovation and knowledge workers in short supply, dealing with this variation focuses on the scope of variance, and the ability to closely match (quality) resource capabilities with real project needs.

People Examples (Figure 3.8, Column 4)

➤ *Knowledge workers.* Knowledge workers vary more in productivity and skills than workers in all other categories. The fact that they can perform at all is of sufficient value to secure a position. Most would be valued though not called talented, in the sense that we apply the term to gifted people, and among the talented there is wide variation. Among all, both valued and talented, there is a wide range of productivity. As seen in the prior discussion on product development, regardless of functional area, dealing with this variation successfully focuses on matching resources to tasks appropriately (quality).

➤ *Collaborative culture.* Collaboration gains its greatest benefits from diversity, in the experiences, perspectives, knowledge, and individual collaborative styles of active participants. It also has its greatest hurdle to overcome in this essential diversity: the wider the variations among participants, the more time it can take for a collaborative group to become effective.

➤ Expansion

The existing capacity may increase or decrease. Issues are generally involved with quantity and capacity changes, when either more or less of something is demanded or desired. Expansion issues are often concerned with meeting rapidly increasing demands on resources economically, such as production capacity, service people, Web site access, or help desk traffic. Contraction issues are often concerned with downside limits imposed by fixed costs, minimum critical mass, regulations, or social obligations in cases like downsizing.

Probing Questions

What does capacity mean in this situation? Where are the upper and lower capacity limits, and how would they become a problem? What forms might expansion take? Are there minimal fixed costs or times involved? What kinds and amounts of additional resources are available? What are the time limits in which increased capacity must take effect? Do unit costs increase or decrease with additional capacity?

Corporate Level Examples (Figure 3.7, Column 4)

➤ Though downsizing to reduce costs and become lean was a common trauma in many corporations during the 1900s, it will continue as an operational strategy independent of becoming lean, at least for postmerger rationalization, and increasingly for containing costs in volatile markets. Cost is the driving focus.

➤ On the upside, meeting unforecastable demand becomes an even more major issue as both e-Commerce and the global information network add the capability for dramatic and impatient demand ramps on new products. Though the primary focus here is on scope, cost plays an important role as rapid ramp-up is often an expensive trade-off.

Process Examples (Figure 3.8, Column 2)

➤ *Assembly operation.* Assembly operations with fixed costs can cause a low demand period to fall below breakeven for an assembly facility. Dealing with this issue effectively focuses on reducing the cost of changing to a lower rate than expected, and moving the lower break-even limits as low as possible (scope).

➤ *Order entry process.* Unexpected e-Commerce demand surge isn't just an issue for production or stock replenishment, it can also affect the order entry department if order processing requires any human intervention such as customer interaction, account initiation, or credit verification. This issue focuses on rapid (time) resource expansion and subsequent contraction, and wide accommodation potential (scope).

Practice Examples (Figure 3.8, Column 3)

➤ *Supply chain management.* Maintaining active multiple sources that are prepared to ramp up (scope) delivery rates or services is a necessary hedge against supplier failure, market opportunity, and demand surge in certain critical markets. This can be costly (cost) for parts or services with relatively low volume (e.g., aerospace/defense markets), as there is not enough to spread around.

➤ *Product development.* With product life shrinking and technology developments happening more frequently, product development activities increase, at least they do if development resources can increase. People are still central in the innovation and design process and knowledge workers are what we call them. To increase the amount of development work beyond what productivity increases might bring is an issue of increasing the available knowledge workers in a scarce market. The focus here is on gaining sufficient quantity (scope) with the required skills on schedule (quality).

➤ Reconfiguration

Reorganize resource or process relationships. Issues are generally involved with the reconfiguration of existing elements and their interactions, sometimes with added elements as well. Reconfiguration issues might arise with corporate reorganizations, project team, personnel transfers, supply networks, product configurations, assembly sequences, or customer relationship management.

Probing Questions

What relationships might change with time or need? What sequences will change? What resources or subprocesses might be moved to another location? When could some resources offer value if they were moved? Might a process or procedure need to be reconfigured later?

Corporate Level Examples (Figure 3.7, Column 4)

➤ At the corporate level, postmerger restructuring is one of the biggest and most difficult issues, too often resulting in damage rather than synergy. Completing the restructuring on schedule with the promised results is the typical quality focus, with scope equally important, as cultural differences are often the cause of failure.

➤ A new strategic issue with little history arises from the rapid development of e-Commerce. The best strategies leverage synergy from a match of the e-Commerce opportunities and market interface with the organizational structure and re-sources. Early stage e-Commerce is still exploratory, reveal-ing new opportunities and market interfaces that need reconfigured organizations and resources. Though time ap-pears to be the principal focus, as new entries quickly make older ones obsolete and irrelevant, cost and scope are equally important because the magnitude of the restructur-ing is often cost prohibitive.

Product/Service Examples (Figure 3.8, Column 1)

➤ *Internal network service.* It happens. A new generation of PC finally demands deployment, and a new generation of soft-ware applications finally compels a switch. The older equip-ment and applications are still useful to someone, maybe in another department or division, or maybe just lower on the tool performance-requirements ladder. Redeploying these resources is focused on predictable resource involvement and beneficial results (quality), as well as on finding a suffi-cient demand (scope) to absorb the assets.

➤ *Home entertainment center.* When a marketing strategy is based on upgrades and incremental options added by the cus-tomer, the design issue will focus on ease of accomplishment by the customer, and make or break the strategy for meeting this objective (quality).

Process Examples (Figure 3.8, Column 2)

➤ *Assembly operation.* Large production operations, like those in the auto industry, as well as some smaller operations, are ex-ploring the benefits of blending outsource and insource as-sembly, some of it under the "modular" movement. In the electronics field with each new generation moving last genera-tion's assembly onto this generation's chip, a seemingly differ-ent form of insource/outsource reconfiguration occurs. In common is the issue of changing both the mix and the part-ners in this dance as the opportunities and economics change. The reconfiguration focus is on predictable outcomes (qual-ity) and the freedom (scope) to take advantage of unantici-pated opportunity.

➤ *Order entry process.* Remote order entry relies on a support infrastructure of Web sites, telephones, product knowledge bases, and the basic automation of the order entry and payment verification action. When an automated support system fails, customers are less likely to postpone their gratification and try again later if they have other options for buying now. The objective of reconfiguration to fallback alternatives is immediate (time), or as close as possible.

■ THE LANGUAGE OF CHANGE PROFICIENCY

Change proficiency is a competency. Regardless of what it is called, or how narrowly it might be focused, it is fostered, nurtured, and developed in organizations by people who recognize its value. It is practiced, refined, talked about, debated, and taught. It seeps into the culture though this frequent exercise of language. But generally the language and the application focus are different in different companies—even in different parts of the same company.

This chapter has introduced a general framework and language that should complement most initiatives in most places, provide a common foundation for cross-pollination among separate initiatives, and help broaden the application of change proficiency within an organization that already has a beachhead. For organizations that are only starting to build this competency, all the better.

Change domains and proficiency metrics are only part of the language, more will come in other chapters, but they are the means for "typing" and comparing, the foundation of any language.

A 1998 publication[8] outlined the Chrysler operating system, which is basically the cultural infrastructure behind the way they do things. The article described it as consisting of three core beliefs and values, made possible by four enablers, with four key subsystems sharing a systemic relationship. The system is backed up by support processes and tools. The article stated:

> *While all this may sound rather complex, [vice president] Ewasyshyn explains that it is really a means by which people in the organization focus on what's going on and then begin to ask the questions. . . . "You start to look at things in an entirely different way," he says. "In the past when we'd visit other companies' plants, we used to look for the latest technology that they were using. We weren't looking at the right things. The hardware you can buy. The trick is how the business operates. How is the technology applied? What is the people side of the business? . . . Although some people might dismiss this as touchy-feely stuff, know that regardless what it is, it is providing big returns to Chrysler."*

Not the whole story, perhaps, but Chrysler is a front-runner on the agility track. They have their own language. They have a simple set of concepts. And the conversations spoken in this language are sinking into the culture.

■ NOTES

1. A six-part series published in *Automotive Manufacturing & Production* during 1998 examined the performance of single-car, single-plant new vehicle launches among Chrysler, Ford, General Motors, Toyota, and Honda in North American plants during the period 1992–1996. See McAlinden (1998) and Smith (1998) references for magazine issues in the months of February, March, June, July, October, November.
2. Smith (1998), "World Class Launch: Chrysler Corporation," p. 71.
3. The National Center for Manufacturing Sciences, a consortia headquartered in Ann Arbor, Michigan, with a few hundred members, facilitated the development and approval of standard contracts for binding its members together in cooperative technology and intellectual property development projects. Lockheed Martin, Rockwell, and Texas Instruments developed standardized preapproved contracts in anticipation of forming virtual enterprises repeatedly, under a DARPA-funded development project called AIMS. The Agile Web (www.agileweb.com) in eastern Pennsylvania facilitates the development of virtual enterprise relationships among a region of Pennsylvania suppliers with standardized contract forms.
4. Smith (1998), "World Class Launch: Chrysler Corporation," p. 72.
5. Smith and Swiecki (1998), "World Class Launch: The Conclusion," p. 69.
6. Smith (1998), "World Class Launch: Chrysler Corporation," p. 71.
7. DARPA and NSF, the funding source and channel behind the Agility Forum, raised a question in 1994 about the potential for different agility priorities in different industry sectors. We first polled a small group of executives from a cross-industry selection of organizations associated with the Forum, and developed a likely list of possibilities in each of the eight change domains. A survey was then mailed out in early 1995 to all organizations associated with both the Agility Forum and the National Center for Manufacturing Sciences. The results showed clear differences between auto, aerospace/defense, and electronic sectors, but none were surprising in retrospect; based on the different conditions each of those sectors was facing at the time. A synopsis of the findings appeared in "The Voice of Industry Speaks on Agility Priorities," Dove (1996), pp. 16–17.
8. Vasilash (1998), "The Chrysler Operating System," pp. 63–64.

Chapter 4

Response Situation Analysis

In Chapter 3, we introduced a set of metrics for measuring change proficiency, and a structural framework for describing a situation in terms of its dynamic operating requirements. In this chapter, we show how to apply these tools to develop profiles of situations and problems in need of understanding and solution. We are building a language of change proficiency in this second part of the book, and now begin to exercise this language and show how it is employed.

■ THE PROBLEM WITH PROBLEMS

Americans are known to be solution oriented. They go for the bottom line quickly. Americans feel measured by, and prideful of, how quickly they can arrive at a solution. It is a part of the culture. Non-Americans see it plainly. It's the water Americans swim in, so they live with it, unquestioningly.

Unquestioningly. Therein lies the issue that we will look at first. Ask two questions, get two answers, connect the dots, and extrapolate an end point. You can't get to a reasoned solution quicker. Okay—ask a third question, get a third answer, and verify that your line of reasoning is reasonably straight. That adds carefulness to speed, especially if you choose the question carefully so it won't kink the line too badly. Don't ask a fourth question; it might screw up the picture. In between *a* solution and *the* solution to a problem lie a lot of questions—mostly never asked.

Though this may be a typical American stereotype, it is not an exclusive American failing. It is a human failing although different cultures manifest the symptoms in different ways, and to different degrees. We are knowing people. We know the answers. That's important to us. Our kids believe it. We learned as children that as adults we would have the answers. This, and other common difficulties for understanding a problem clearly, are depicted in Figure 4.1.

In the world of science, we dream up an hypothesis, then we search for proof that it is true. Scientific communities employ peer review to weed out this natural bias to justify an answer. It works well there (sometimes too well) as another natural force is at work that seeks to discredit anything new.

In the world of business—on the production floor, in product development planning, at organizational strategy meetings—we have answers first as well. But the business objectives and the political environment often conspire to support a suggested solution, rather than question its achievement potential or discredit it. The driving objectives are things like increased production yield, more innovative ideas, or higher purchasing leverage, not optimal problem solving or absolute truth. There is a job to do and this problem-solving stuff gets in the way.

What would help is a discipline that objectively defines a problem before considering solutions, better yet, a discipline that defines

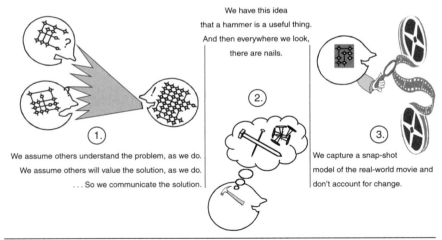

(1) Assuming incorrectly a common problem perception, (2) Knowledge of a solution, which shapes the image of the problem, (3) Defining a static situation, when in fact the problem continues to change.

Figure 4.1 Common Problems with Problem Perception

the criteria for evaluating potential solutions. The operative word here is discipline.

Research into agile enterprise and agile manufacturing has been done by analyzing business practices and processes that exhibit high adaptability. The analysis procedure employs a discipline that asks, "How does this system respond to changes of type X?" and "Specifically what changes must this system deal with of type X?" This is called *response situation analysis* (RS analysis).

This structured analysis activity defines the system's response requirements in terms of four categories of reactive change and four categories of proactive change (Figure 4.2). This important initial step creates an objective profile of the problem to be solved by the design and builds unbiased evaluation criteria for subsequent design solutions. It also provides a foundation of "assumptions" to guide later evolution when conditions affecting these assumptions change. The change-issue profile provides both the justification for, and the verification of, the eventual system design—and does so in terms of the dynamics of the system's operating environment throughout its life cycle.

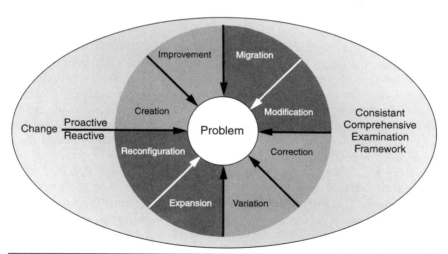

Defining a problem completely in terms of its operational dynamics means asking the right questions and asking enough questions. A structured questioning process that employs the eight change domains can be used to accomplish this. The structure provides consistency and comprehensiveness, while the focus on change provides a definition in dynamic terms.

Figure 4.2 Response Situation (RS) Analysis Looks at Problem Dynamics from All Angles before Evaluating Solutions

■ ESTABLISHING RESPONSE-ABLE DESIGN REQUIREMENTS—FOUR DIVERSE EXAMPLES

In Chapter 2, we introduced four examples of highly adaptable system configurations: a machine architecture, a process architecture, a business practice architecture, and a competency development architecture. Each of these was designed specifically to address dynamic situations to advantage. In this chapter, we briefly show the supporting thought behind the issues shown in Figures 4.3 and 4.4, which encapsulate the analysis of the four systems introduced in Chapter 2.

The life-cycle situation instigating the original design of these four systems is profiled across the eight change domains, with the metric focus for each issue shown explicitly as time [t], cost [c], quality [q] and scope [s] of change. Once these new system designs became the established norm, a new life cycle was created in which these original issues would not necessarily be the same. The issues listed in Figures 4.3 and 4.4 are not meant to be exhaustive, and are chosen to illustrate results of the analysis process.

➤ Design Issues for a Product—Applied Materials' Cluster Machines

In Chapter 2 (Figure 2.1), we described the cluster architecture introduced by Applied Materials for their semiconductor fabrication machines. At the time this architecture was introduced, this industry developed a new technology of machines approximately every three years, many companies only existed for a single generation, and new technology took considerable time to master in both machine development and machine operation. The architecture was quickly mimicked by Applied's competitors as it fit the real situation better than previous approaches.

Here we look at some of the product-design issues faced by a company that wished to remain in the fabrication machinery market across multiple technology generations, and amplify the points made in Figure 4.3. Each issue is worded as a situation statement devoid of the solution eventually manifested in the cluster machine design. Perhaps another design approach could accommodate these issues just as well:

> ➤ Create new product family [tcs]. Approximately every three years the industry creates an entirely new generation of machinery based on new technology. Creating a broad family of machines, rather than one for a single process step, requires

Change Domain		Applied Materials' Cluster Machine	Kelsey Hayes' Matching Cell
Proactive	**Creation**	• New product family [tcs]	• Design/install new-part production capability [tcq]
Proactive	**Improvement**	• Manufacturing cost [s] • Calibration time [s] • Customer yield curve [s]	• Short run costs are high [t]
Proactive	**Migration**	• Across technology generations [ts]	• Next generation of machining technology [cs]
Proactive	**Modification**	• Other process within technology generation [s]	• Engineering change order needs process change, and new product cannot wait for replacement process [tcs]
Reactive	**Correction**	• Malfunctioning equipment [t]	• Cost of lost production due to equipment malfunction/repair [tc]
Reactive	**Variation**	• Product family process capability [cs]	• Prototype runs require process variations [tcs]
Reactive	**Expansion**	• Process-step capacity to meet different product mix [ts]	• Increase or decrease planned production [tcs]
Reactive	**Reconfiguration**	• Meet international local-content needs optimally [qs]	• Salvage and reuse production stages for new parts [cs]

The column on the left is concerned with life-cycle issues of a new product family within a generation of technology and is viewed from the perspective of the precluster design situation. The column on the right is concerned with life-cycle issues of a plant's process architecture and is viewed from the perspective of the previous approach situation. Once a new design concept becomes established, each of these systems is faced with a new and different situation, and subsequent analysis would produce a different set of issues.

[t] = time, [c] = cost, [q] = quality, [s] = scope

Figure 4.3 Product and Process Examples

Change Domain		LSI Logic's JIT Order Fulfillment Chains	Remmele's Competency Acquisition
Proactive	Creation	• Custom production chain for each order [t]	• Develop new technical/market knowledge and skill [tqs]
	Improvement	• Outsource quality [s] • Outsource cycle time [s] • Outsource on-time delivery [q	• Application knowledge development is slow [s]
	Migration	• Move from fabless to foundry, with a leadership strategy in successive technology generations [tq]	• Move to new markets and new technologies [tqs]
	Modification	• Add new capability for packaging as needed [tqs] • Move final test into assembly houses [q]	• Add nontraditional capability and adjust the company self-image [s]
Reactive	Correction	• WIP scheduling-problem resolution [t]	• Traveled down the wrong path [t]
	Variation	• Popular packaging options number over a hundred [s]	• Employee interests and background knowledge necessary to grasp diverse new technologies [s]
	Expansion	• Increase/decrease capacity with market/customer cycles [tqs]	• Increase the number of employees who share a body of knowledge [tcs]
	Reconfiguration	• Switch resources scheduled to fill an order [tq]	• Reconfigure corporate resources and business units to pursue expertise and business development [ts]

Figure 4.4 Practice and People Examples

The column on the left is concerned with operating issues of a business practice that configures production-chain resources just-in-time, from a pool of inside and outsource resources and is viewed from the perspective of the early-stage design situation. The column on the right reflects issues concerned with developing a new core competency concurrent with the expectation of an emerging market. The perspective is of the system that generates an initial competency knowledge and skill base, rather than the strategic system that chooses which paths of knowledge development to pursue.

[t] = time, [c] = cost, [q] = quality, [s] = scope

large resources working in parallel, and often more elapsed time than a product's prime selling life.

➤ Improve manufacturing cost [s], calibration time [s], and customer yield curve [s]. As with most new products, manufacturing cost is expected to improve over time, especially where high ticket items can gain market share if they have significant cost advantage. On the customer side, two major issues exist: the time it takes to calibrate a new machine before it can be turned over to production, and the time it takes to get acceptably high yields from the total process that the machine process-step is a part of. All improvements are looking for major gains (scope metric).

➤ Migrate across technology generations [ts]. The needed expertise and knowledge in development engineering and service changes with technology generations, and often little is transferable.

➤ Modify product capability to address additional process steps [s]. Process-dedicated machine designs are highly specific and difficult to modify within the technology generation.

➤ Correct malfunctioning equipment [tcqs]. Returning dedicated-process machines to service quickly requires maintaining large inventories of spare parts and having broad and knowledgeable expertise readily available. Repairs can stop the entire process flow for the duration of the malfunction.

➤ Vary the process alternatives available within a product family [cs]. Typical semiconductor fabrication involves some 120 different process steps. Some steps are repeated processes, some steps are processes that share some characteristics with others, and some steps are processes that are totally unique; and all steps share certain common and highly critical material handling needs.

➤ Expand process-step capacity to meet different product mix [ts]. This is a customer product issue, and recognizes that product mix in the fabrication facility may change and require incrementally increased capacity for certain process steps.

➤ Reconfigure the manufacturing process to meet international local-content needs optimally [qs]. International contracts often require some local content in the machines. Dedicated-process machines leave few options for partial manufacturing and assembly of critical versus noncritical machine subsystems.

➤ Design Issues for a Process—The Manufacturing Cells of Kelsey-Hayes

Figure 2.2, in Chapter 2, depicts a cellular process design for manufacturing automatic braking systems (ABS) at Kelsey-Hayes. This design broke with tradition by employing collections of identical flexible machining centers grouped into cells, rather than perpetuate the previous approach of specially designed and dedicated transfer lines. The investment justification for such an approach took into account that the equipment could be reused across successive generations of ABS product design and deliver a longer useful lifetime as well as greater customer responsiveness and new customer benefits. The change issues faced at the time that the new design was conceived shaped the result:

➤ Create and install new-part production capability [tcq]. Higher frequency of new-part introductions, shorter part lifetimes, and less tolerance for missed production start dates put a new focus on the development of new production capability quickly, cost-effectively, and on schedule.

➤ Improve short-run costs [t]. Short-run costs are dominated by high fixed costs of transfer line acquisition.

➤ Migrate to next generation of machining technology [cs]. Acquisition costs of flexible machine technology are higher than transfer line, and very different, especially with the use of downloadable software technology and optional routings.

➤ Modify machining process to accommodate engineering change orders and new product designs [tcs]. Modifying a process can be a difficult and costly interference with production, while the increased frequency of new product can no longer wait for a new replacement process.

➤ Correct a malfunctioning process stage [tc]. When a single stage in the transfer line is down, the entire transfer line is down; making a high cost of downtime as well as the time to correct a priority.

➤ Vary the machining options to meet the needs of prototype runs [tcs]. Prototype runs disrupt production processing, generally require machining difficult to accommodate on the standard production line, and are on the increase.

➤ Expand and contract planned production capacity [tcs]. Transfer line technology takes too much time and cost to accommodate increases over upside of planned production rates, and add to the per unit cost when operated below downside of planned rates.

➤ Reconfiguring production stages for new parts [cs]. Trying to salvage a transfer line and reuse its production stages for different part production is costly and limited in possibility.

➤ Design Issues for a Business Practice—LSI Logic's JIT Order Fulfillment Chains

Figure 2.3, in Chapter 2, depicts the production organizational practice employed by LSI Logic to fill semiconductor orders. Recall that they began as a fabless (no manufacturing facility) company and assembled a group of outsource capabilities to fill orders for other semiconductor companies that lacked sufficient capacity. Eventually they built some of their own wafer fabrication facilities and now augment this inside fabrication capability with some outsource, while continuing to outsource all backend production processes. When an order is received by LSI, they custom configure a production chain from a pool of inside and outsource resources chosen for applicable process, capacity availability, and cost. The issues listed here are those that might have been some of the design drivers for this loosely coupled, highly adaptable, production organization:

➤ Create a production chain for an order [t]. Customers want a fast commitment for short-cycle order fulfillment, regardless of the process and packaging options. Resources need to be available and scheduled quickly.

➤ Improve outsource cycle time [s], production quality [s], and on-time delivery [q]. Outsourcing backend lead application and packaging necessitates shipping finished wafers from one facility to another, usually to another country, and can add 3 days or more to critical order fulfillment time, especially when final test is done at another facility before shipment to the customer. Quality problems that surface in a final test facility 3 days after shipment from the packaging outsource can cause 3 days of production scrap.

➤ Migrate from fabless to foundry, with a leadership strategy in successive technology generations [tq]. Corporate strategy is to lead the industry with new wafer production technology, requiring significant investment in expertise development and processing facilities to have early and predictable capability.

➤ Modify capabilities for backend packaging [tqs] and location of final test [q]. With over a hundred packaging styles, customer opportunities hinge on specific styles that may not be in the existing stable; also, there is value in moving final test capability into the assembly houses.

➤ Correct a work-in-process scheduling problem [t]. Anything that holds up the continuous flow of work-in-process must be corrected quickly.

➤ Vary the packaging options across the hundred-plus different popular types [s]. Popular packaging is spread across a number of basic family styles, each with many variations. Basic family styles require unique equipment and process.

➤ Expand and contract production capacity to meet market and customer cycles [tqs]. The semiconductor industry is notoriously cyclical, with good times causing firms to build new production capacity, which then becomes overcapacity for the industry until the market catches up. Customer cycles are also noticeable as semiconductor usage increases in consumer products popular as seasonal gifts.

➤ Reconfigure the production chain scheduled to complete an order [tq]. When a customer places or removes a hold on work-in-process, or changes the quantity and delivery dates, resources must be rescheduled immediately. Sometimes this may mean configuring a different production chain than originally committed, to meet new schedules.

➤ **Design Issues for a Peopled System—Remmele Engineering's Competency Acquisition**

Remmele's strategy is to position themselves at the high end of technology leadership in metal machining growth areas—with the understanding that metal may evolve to other materials, and machining may evolve to other formation processes. They want to be the first to develop real skills with new technology, and to maintain a reputation for not only having the latest capability, but for also having leadership in knowledge and expertise on applying it effectively. They recognize that new markets can emerge from nontraditional areas, that last year's growth market may be next year's history, and that new technologies are being introduced at an increasing frequency. This pursuit has led them to machining parts as small as the period at the end of this sentence, as large as 747 wings, as heavy as the large parts in earthmoving behemoths, and as delicate as spiderwebs. They have unattended lights-out machining, team-based part production, medical-parts clean-room precision work, high velocity machining, electronic customer connections to testing equipment, video engineering collaboration on the Internet, and most everything else on the leading edge. And they continue to search for, and learn about, what's next.

Built into the Remmele culture is the need to master a new technology before they take it to market. The important metrics on most issues associated with competency acquisition are early timeliness [t], real and deep understanding [q], and a broad, open outlook [s]. The proactive issues are generally about discovery, and the reactive issues are generally about growth and diffusion.

The perspective here is of the system that generates an initial competency knowledge and skill base, rather than the strategic system that chooses which paths of knowledge development to pursue:

➤ Create new technical/market knowledge and skill [tqs]. To stay on the leading edge requires discovering new markets and new technologies in their early stages, developing deep competency before others, and considering a broad and open interpretation of the future. New markets and technologies may not be at all like their predecessors: Marketing knowledge and production requirements for medical microprecision parts are not at all like those relied on for automotive part machining.

➤ Improve the development of technology-application knowledge in emerging markets [ts]. Knowledge of new technology typically precedes knowledge of how broadly and beneficially it can be applied. Generally slow adoption indicates considerable room for improvement.

➤ Migrate to new markets and new technologies [tqs]. As new competency is developed and new markets emerge with demand, new knowledge and skills must replace existing knowledge and skills as the capability matures into a prime line of business.

➤ Modify the self-image of what the company does to accommodate new nontraditional capability [s]. Micromachining of precision medical parts utilizes processes and tools so different from previous machining concepts that the self-image of what the company is and does had to be adjusted. Similar adjustments are anticipated with technologies still in research or pregrowth phases, like atomic deposition or powdered metals.

➤ Stop journeys down fruitless paths quickly [t]. Timing is everything, and often the pursuit of a new technology turns out to be insufficiently matched with market emergence. Recognizing such situations early is important.

➤ Vary the pool of background knowledge and interest among employees [s]. The exploration of new technologies and the development of new competencies is performed best by people with related background knowledge and skills, and personal interest and curiosity in the direction of pursuit. The diversity of technology potentially important to a metal machining business is on the increase, and calls for an increased diversity among employee interests.

➤ Expand skill and knowledge base among employees [tqs]. Once a small initial team develops a new competency and a matching market appears to be emerging, this knowledge and skill base must be spread effectively to a wider population of employees in concert with opportunity growth demands.

➤ Reconfigure corporate resources and business units to pursue expertise and business development [ts]. When a market for new competency exhibits real business growth potential, serious resources and business unit attention need to be applied, without displacing or detracting from existing good business activities.

■ METHODOLOGY—DEFINING PROBLEMS AND OPPORTUNITIES WITH RESPONSE SITUATION ANALYSIS

The analysis process described here employs the fundamental tools and language developed in Chapter 3. It is a basic pro forma approach, proven in both individual and workshop-based analysis activities. A more extensive process called Realsearch is described later, which employs this analysis process as a subset activity in the creation of response-able solutions and insights.

The objective of RS analysis is to define a problem or opportunity as a comprehensive set of *change issues* that should be addressed by any as-is or to-be solution. In a product or project specification, these issues are typically called *requirements*. In addition to defining requirements, we also use the analysis process tools to introduce and spread the concepts and language of change proficiency, which aids the development of a cultural understanding, as described in later chapters.

The principal tool of the analysis process is the change domain (Figure 3.5) introduced in Chapter 3. This structural tool provides both a language and a framework of change types, four in the proactive category and four in the reactive category. The *language* aspect is critical—our understandings are formed by how we express things. The *framework* aspect provides a questioning structure that surrounds the problem, shedding light on its nature from various angles, as we look for issues in eight different *change domains.*

The seven steps depicted in Figure 4.5 form a structured analysis exercise. Though a single individual may well use this or a modified version to arrive at a result, we look at it as a workshop exercise for valuable reasons discussed shortly. We also assume in our discussion that a person or small team of people have the responsibility of achieving a result, and convene a workshop of additional participants to gain a larger perspective.

As a workshop exercise, a facilitator is needed who knows the process and will provide the process training and discipline. The facilitator may be simply that, or may also be the person responsible for the analysis result.

Step 1 *Assemble a collaborative analysis team, choosing participants with diverse perspectives and a genuine interest in or knowledge about the subject.*

Though a single person can do this analysis process, it is preferable to use a collaborative group. The purpose of the analysis exercise is to develop a comprehensive understanding of a problem, and different minds will have different perspectives. Probing for issues by asking a question often gets a result multiplied by the number of people who respond to it. With fewer people in a group, more thought-stimulating questions need to be asked.

Obtaining a group of participants is not difficult if you seek those who would value a perspective on the problem for their own related purposes. Perhaps they are people who are affected by the problem, people who will be the customers of a solution, or people from somewhere else with a related problem of their own. In any event, secure an agreement from all participants to use the RS analysis process and tools.

With a small group, all can work together through all the steps. A larger group offers the advantage of parallel breakout groups during

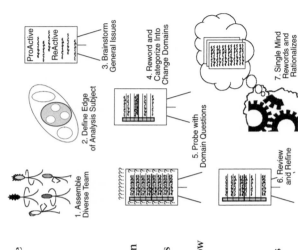

1. Assemble Diverse Team

2. Define Edge of Analysis Subject

3. Brainstorm General Issues

ProActive
ReActive

4. Reword and Categorize Into Change Domains

5. Probe with Domain Questions

6. Review and Refine

7. Single Mind Rewords and Rationalizes

1. Assemble a collaborative analysis team; choosing participants with diverse perspectives and genuine interest or knowledge in the subject.

2. Define the boundaries of the system to be analyzed, establishing a clear perimeter understood by all participants.

3. Brainstorm for general issues, putting them into proactive and reactive categories if and when readily possible.

4. Review change domain definitions and sort brainstormed issues into the eight domains; rewording as appropriate. Disagreement over categorization indicates that an issue should be rearticulated as multiple issues.

5. Probe with questions specific to each change domain, adding new issues as they surface.

6. Review all issues: eliminate obvious mistakes, combine redundancies, throw out the trivial, remove those that belong to higher/lower or successor/predecessor systems, and where not already done, specify metric(s) of primary interest: time, cost, quality, scope [t,c,q,s].

7. Finally, delegate one person to reword and rationalize the list of issues for clarity of meaning, completeness, and uniqueness. Change-domain names and categories may no longer be important at this point.

Optional: it is often useful to analyze higher/lower or predecessor/successor systems to help put the subject system in context.

The seven steps depicted above form a structured analysis exercise. Though a single individual may use this or a modified version to arrive at a result, it is presented here as a workshop exercise with collaborative participants, chosen for their ability to provide a broadened perspective. A workshop can take as little as half a day, or as long as two days, depending upon the purpose of the group participation and the experience of the participants. If the purpose is principally to help broaden the perspective of a single person or a small team (and the participants have had some prior experience in the process), a half a day can be quite fruitful.

Figure 4.5 The RS Analysis Process

some of the steps, which is often surprisingly fruitful when different breakouts take completely different perspectives. Steps 3 and 5 are good candidates for parallel activity.

Step 2 *Define the boundaries of the system to be analyzed, establishing a clear perimeter that all participants understand.*

It is important to establish the boundaries of the system under analysis, so that all participants focus on the same thing. For example, the process for introducing a new product into production is different from the process for ongoing production. The practice for finding and qualifying new suppliers is different from the practice employed in managing them. These are examples of predecessor-successor systems (processes or practices), occurring in sequence; yet it is common for issues from one to be attributed to the other in preliminary analysis work when understandings are not yet crisp.

Another common early-stage confusion occurs when subsystem issues are attributed to the higher level system to which the subsystem belongs, or vice versa. For example, if analysis is being used to establish requirements for a response-able production capability from the business perspective, issues associated with the response-able design of flow-manufacturing (a specific approach to manufacturing) are those of a lower level subprocess. In analysis work, this partitioning of nested system/subsystems is not always as clear as the predecessor/successor partitioning; but it becomes easier to see when you understand the system design principles introduced in Chapter 5.

These confusions are not necessarily important when analysis is being used to initiate and sensitize a group of people to the language and concepts of change proficiency. They become important when analysis results will form the basis for synthesizing subsequent design or establishing acquisition specification and evaluation criteria.

Step 3 *Brainstorm for general issues, putting them into proactive and reactive categories if and when readily possible.*

Unless all participants in a group are well versed in RS analysis, it is best to start the process by brainstorming for general issues of any type. With this approach, several issues can be developed quickly without distracting discussion of what a change domain is, or debates over categories that bog down the generation process.

With experienced groups, the facilitator might separate these issues into proactive and reactive categories as they are offered, or do so at the end of the brainstorming session with group assistance.

Frequently a brainstormed issue is not stated in a way that makes its proactive or reactive status clear, and the clarification often stimulates additional issues. The facilitator might review the definitions of proactive and reactive change with the group to clarify the difference. It also helps for everyone to have preprinted forms that allow them to take notes, develop ideas, and refer to the definitions of proactive and reactive change, as well as the eight change domains.

It is useful to wordsmith brainstormed issues so that the operating dynamic is obvious. The facilitator might accomplish this either during or subsequent to the brainstorming activity by rewording the suggestion to include the name of the change domain to which it appears to belong. If a brainstormer suggests "Competency of an outsource is hard to assess in advance," the facilitator might reword that statement as "Creating an assessment of outsource competency in advance." The purpose of this word work is to focus more precisely on the dynamic that makes the statement an issue, which again often results in generating additional issues as people see variants in more than one domain.

Step 4 *Review change domain definitions and sort brainstormed issues into the eight domains, rewording as appropriate. Disagreement over categorization indicates that an issue should be rearticulated as multiple issues.*

Categorization is sometimes problematic with inexperienced groups but has the advantage of clarifying what is meant, and often expands the list of issues. Different people may attach different and equally valid meanings to the same statement. These conflicting interpretations surface when you categorize an issue to the satisfaction of one person and the dissatisfaction of another.

The facilitator should be an active participant and help develop a clearer statement by using a flip chart, or other group display mechanism. This free interpretation is a thought stimulator and either captures the essence of an issue or elicits debate that often results in identifying additional issues. If the issues have not yet been reworded to include a specific reference word from one of the eight change domains, now is the time to do that.

Step 5 *Probe with questions specific to each change domain, adding new issues as they surface.*

This is the point in the process where the easy issues have surfaced, and people have exhausted their personal experiences. Now it is time to help the group think of the situations that they may not have directly experienced but can imagine as reasonable probabilities.

Do this slowly, by probing with questions through each of the eight domains of change. As each domain is explored, allow enough time for people to change their frame of mind and imagine the situation. Typical probing questions for each of the domains were suggested in Chapter 3 and provide a good starting point; but the facilitator should probe well beyond these typical questions, attempting to trigger latent and tacit knowledge among the participants.

As a language, these eight change domains help us categorize and discuss concepts. At times in group settings, there may be heated debate about which domain properly classifies a specific issue. This generally indicates that an initially stated issue is in fact more than one issue, or at least the debaters obviously think so. In any event, the discussion and debate can be a healthy way to expand the understanding of the essence of the issue. This is a positive factor when evaluating subsequent potential solutions.

Step 6 *Review all issues: Eliminate obvious mistakes, combine redundancies, throw out the trivial, remove those that belong to higher/lower or successor/predecessor systems; and where not already done, specify metric(s) of primary interest—time, cost, quality, scope [tcqs].*

Up until this point the list of issues has been growing with little thought to relative importance, redundancy, or even real relevancy. In this final task, the group reflects on the total list and refines it into a *short list* of key issues.

It is also important to review the final issues to see if they are isolated to the system under analysis, or are contaminated with issues from the next higher or lower systems, or from predecessor or successor systems. There is a limit to how much of this can be done well in camera, but a start here prepares the participants for Step 7.

Often a group narrows a sizable list down to a few that dominate in priority. Sometimes there is value in keeping at least one issue in each of the eight categories, even though all areas may not carry the same weight. This might be the case when a problem is going to be attacked in prioritized phases, when the evolutionary nature of a problem is clear, or when the display of issues is intended to carry some insightful or instructional value.

The facilitator should ensure that the list indicates which change proficiency metrics are important for each issue: time, cost, quality, scope, or some combination. The process of designating the important metrics spreads a common understanding of the issue among

the group, and often results in a debate that generates additional issues. More importantly, the metrics focus the subsequent solution to
the issue.

When selecting the metric focus for a change issue, inexperienced groups make some common mistakes. An improvement in
cycle time does not necessarily mean that the issue's focus is on
time, unless the interest is in how fast the improvement can be completed. It is more likely that the issue's focus would be on scope—
where a large change in cycle time is desired. The point here is that
the metric focus relates to the *process or action* of changing. Thus,
had [t] been selected rather than [s] as the metric focus, the statement would be a need for an improvement in cycle time quickly,
though the improvement might only be minor. This confusion
arises from the words used to describe the issue. It can happen in the
other domains as well. For example, an issue may be to *create* a sense
of urgency in a service group's response. Again, time might appear
to be the focus, when in fact it is scope: How much closer to immediate can the service response be made? Had the focus been on time,
the issue would be satisfied with some token response quickening
accomplished after a 30-minute sensitivity talk. Question: Do you really care how long this change will take, or how big the change can
be, or both?

Let's say the issue is improving *on-time delivery*. Is the change metric predictability (quality), scope, or both? In some circumstances, the
correct focus might be on [q]—where a spec is already developed for
what constitutes acceptable on-time delivery performance and a commitment is made to achieve the improvement within three months.
Under these circumstances, the focus is on the ability to meet the spec
on time (within 3 months), which is [q]. It might also be [s] if the
change is going to be sufficiently different from past performance that
it may be a real stretch to achieve.

Questions that can help sort out these differences:

➤ Is the time it takes to make this change critical?
➤ Is the cost of this change critical?
➤ Is a successful change in high doubt?
➤ Are the limits of change being stretched quite far?

The focused metrics should be whittled down to as small a number as possible. One focus is not sacrificed to another. Thus, if [s] is
the single focus, it doesn't imply that it is unimportant how long it
takes to get the job done, it simply means that making progress is

more important than the amount of time it takes to reach an end point. When a company sets a goal of six sigma quality to be achieved within five years, it doesn't stop at the end of five years if the company is making progress but has not yet reached six sigma. Its focus is on the scope of change.

Before the group is disbanded, make sure they understand that Step 7 will rationalize the material, and significant changes can be expected, especially if the workshop was rushed.

Step 7 *Finally, delegate one person to reword and rationalize the list of issues for clarity of meaning, completeness, and uniqueness. Change domain names and categories may no longer be important at this point.*

Analysis by groups of people in condensed workshops is generally incomplete and never fully rationalized: Inconsistencies and redundancies remain, some real issues never surface, metrics are incomplete, and wording is imprecise. This is not really a problem; it is just to be expected. The value of the workshop is in developing a broad appreciation for the nature of the problem. Once this is accomplished, a single mind needs to rationalize the problem description using the information gained from the workshop. This is best done with an attitude of agentship; that is, the person who does it feels he or she is the agent for the participants, and knows that any additions or subtractions will be acceptable to the group and are consistent with the group's understanding of the problem.

Typical errors to look for and correct at this point include:

➤ *Mixed systems.* Differentiate predecessor/successor, system/subsystem.

➤ *Issues stated as solutions in disguise.* State the issues as objectives, and let the solution proposers or designers decide how to achieve them.

➤ *Too much detail.* Single root issues are itemized as multiple separate issues distinguished by individual nuance. The difficulty here is that overly detailed itemization tends to focus the solution designers on a punch list of specifics, rather than on a more inclusive general class of problem issues.

If the group's subsequent buy-in is necessary, the facilitator should schedule time after doing Step 7, before making the results public, to review these results with the participants—either individually or in a final review session, as appropriate.

It is often useful to analyze higher/lower or predecessor/successor systems to help put the subject system in context. Predecessor/successor relationship analysis can be especially beneficial when developing strategies or plans. The customer for the predecessor process of production start-up, for example, is the successor process of production operation. Analyzing one often benefits from a simultaneous, if only brief, analysis of the other; it helps establish context and also clarifies the system boundaries.

■ FINAL NOTES ON THE ANALYSIS PROCESS

Productive group analysis work can take as little as half a day, or as long as two days, depending on the purpose of the group participation and the experience of the participants. If the purpose is principally to help broaden the perspective of a single person or small team, and the participants have had some prior experience in the process, a half-day workshop can be fruitful.

If the objectives include gaining deep understanding and ownership by the participants, however, a process that lets the participants sleep on initial work before reaching final conclusions can be beneficial, even among experienced analyzers. With an inexperienced group, a 1.5 to 2-day agenda is appropriate, while an experienced group may take the afternoon of one day followed by the morning of the next.

If the subject under analysis is an existing system, rather than a situation in search of a future solution, a word of caution is in order. The task at hand is not to observe and identify the issues being addressed by the system, but rather to identify the issues of the situation faced by the system. It is a mistake to only ask the system what it is dealing with, as it will define itself a success by being mute on the things it is ignoring. In analysis work, the first objective is to know what the real problem is. If a solution is already in place, then the second objective is to evaluate how well the solution addresses the problem. Thus, the perspective of the analyzers is not "What is this system addressing?" but "What should this system be addressing?"

The purpose of this process is to make people think, to broaden the thinking process to include as much relevant material as possible, and especially to bring a problem life-cycle perspective. It is a tool. Like any tool, it can be used improperly or inadequately. And like any tool, the more it is used the more proficient the user becomes, assuming the user focuses on the desired outcome instead of simply traveling through the sequence of steps.

The analysis process described here was from the individual point of view, rather than the group point of view. Chapter 10 discusses a more inclusive process involving a group of people who develop the conclusions.

■ CONCLUSION

This chapter introduced the notion that situations, problems, and opportunities are often perceived in terms of potential solutions, resulting in biased or highly filtered definitions. To counter this tendency, a structured analysis process based on the eight change domains was shown to aid in developing a more comprehensive and more objective understanding. At the same time, this change-based analysis provides an understanding in terms of the dynamic situation faced by the problem or opportunity, providing a set of operational requirements and life-cycle evaluation criteria for would-be solutions and strategies.

The analysis technique can be used to develop a common understanding among a group of people and might be employed to:

➤ Reach an objective understanding of business opportunities, market trends, competitive position, operating practices, technology needs.

➤ Kick-start strategic planning teams.

➤ Kick-start committed reengineering planners.

➤ Kick-start committed technology planners.

The functional departments and varied activities in a business have great differences in their objectives, professional knowledge bases, and jargons. The four examples from product, process, practice, and people situations, however, showed a common descriptive method for discussing and communicating dynamic situations. This common language helps form the core of a corporate cultural platform sensitive to change and the need to respond.

Part Three

Adaptable Structure

The Enabler of Agile Enterprise

Part Three of this book reveals the core concepts of how to build enterprise systems so that they can be changed when they should be changed. Adaptable enterprise systems are shown to be collections of components whose interactions are constrained and enabled by a common framework. Here we will examine the nature of acceptable frameworks, ten design principles for enabling high adaptability, real examples of these principles at work, and methodologies for creating response-able systems.

Chapter 5

Enabling Response Ability

The agile enterprise can respond to opportunity and threat with the immediacy and grace of a cat prowling its territory. This *response-able* competency is accentuated or inhibited by the design of key enterprise systems. In eight years of analytical research, I have observed 10 common system design principles that enable an enterprise to reconfigure its product designs, production processes, business practices, and organizational structures. This chapter introduces these principles.

The examples present defining aspects of the principles and provide a platform for discussing how the framework/component structure produces systems of *reusable* components *reconfigurable* in a *scalable* framework. The dynamics of adaptable enterprise systems come in two forms: directed and self-organizing. Directed dynamics are generally used where the components of the system are inanimate such as the workstations in an automated assembly process. Self-organizing dynamics are possible when the principal resource components are goal seeking and empowered such as the people in a company.

■ CONTROL IN RESPONSE-ABLE SYSTEMS

A personal story will illustrate the difference between directed and self-organizing systems. I feel most comfortable when I am directly involved in all the decisions and most of the execution of any project I am responsible for. I know from long experience that nothing's likely to turn out the way I envision it if I don't actually do it myself. And I have little natural patience for communicating infinite nuance to someone else so that person can do it the way I want it done. I'm old enough to know better, but I don't really want to change the way I am—I get too much joy from creating exactly what I want to see, and nothing short.

In moments of deep truth, I suspect I have little confidence in my skills for perfect static planning. I can't play the chess game 47 moves in advance so I want my hands on the controls as the creation takes form. I know things will happen that I haven't foreseen or would fail to convey to someone else, and that I'll need to be there to make the corrections and guide the result to the end I envision.

One of my creations is now a well-adjusted and quite capable grown-up daughter. Yet the management style that brought this creation to the "operating" mode was completely different. There was no micromanaged hands-on control here. Her mother and I rarely *told* her what to do, and never what to think. Instead, we showed her how to reach her own decisions and how to think, and suffered quietly as she learned. Today, she is more than we envisioned, and we don't have to stand at the controls to keep her that way.

Two completely different management styles. One builds things that are static and lifeless, requiring constant attention and energy to remain useful and relevant over time. The other builds a self-organizing system capable of dealing with unforeseen challenges; able to adjust, correct, and augment its own capabilities to meet the needs of new environments—it evolves. From the designer/builder's perspective, one is under control and the other is out of control.

Out of Control is the name of a book written by Kevin Kelly.[1] The flyleaf says, "[It] chronicles the dawn of a new era in which the robust adaptability and autonomy of living organisms becomes the model for human-made systems, for everything from telecommunications to movie-making technology, from the global economy to manufacturing processes and drug design." Kelly's book explores adaptable natural systems like beehives, prairie ecologies, and the evolution of species; and also looks at human-made systems like computer viruses, the Internet, and artificial life in the computer domain.

Most business systems and most businesses are not ready for autonomous self-organization akin to that in nature, yet they must become more adaptable; and I don't like using words like *ecology* to explain in shorthand a rich and useful organizational concept for business. For one, these soft-edged metaphors turn off a lot of hard-edged businesspeople who occupy a large portion of the organizational power structures, especially in operations and manufacturing where monthly shipping targets are expected to be met regardless of the circumstances. For another, nature has the patience and resilience to absorb a lot of failed or marginal experiments that would terminate a business enterprise. And besides, nature doesn't care who wins. Many parallels are being drawn between business and biological organisms, business and ecology, business and chaos theory, business and anthills, business and neurological nets, and other complex, adaptive, self-organizing systems. Simply referencing the metaphorical links and then postulating a new business paradigm doesn't appear successful in communicating with most people who have operational concerns.

■ RESPONSE-ABLE STRUCTURE

Our research indicates that a business-system structure consisting of reusable components reconfigurable in a scalable framework can be an effective base model for creating adaptable systems. The nature of the framework appears to be a critical factor. To illustrate this point and introduce the framework/component concept, we will look at three types of construction toys and observe how they are used in practice rather than consider what might be done with them in theory. Construction toys offer a useful metaphor because the enterprise systems we are concerned with must be configured and reconfigured constantly, precisely the objective of most, though not all, construction toys.

I grew up in the age of the Erector Set. I watched my daughter grow up with Lego. Both dominated the construction-toy market of their eras (Lego's era continues). Though my construction experience with Erector Sets goes back to childhood, seeing one on someone's living room rug doesn't call for hands-on action the way Lego does. You can build virtually anything over and over again with either; but fundamental differences in their structures give each system unique dynamic characteristics. Both consist of a basic set of core construction components, and both have a structural framework that enables connecting the components into an unbounded variety of configurations.

One popular Erector Set kit featured a picture of a 2-foot-high Ferris wheel on the box cover. A current day collector/reseller suggests on his Web site that few people ever completed or even attempted this pictured construction, though the complexity was alluring. By (unfair) contrast, massive whole-town reproductions have been made from Lego. Perhaps it is the tedium of using nuts and bolts to connect the construction components of Erector Set that inhibits large construction. Whatever the cause, the Erector Set is not as scalable in practice as Lego.

Modern-day Erector Set kits can be purchased for constructing specific models, such as a small airplane that can be assembled in many different configurations. Lego offers similar kits, and both toys include a few necessary special parts, like wheels and cowlings, to augment the core construction components. Watch a child work with either and you'll see the Lego construction undergoes constant metamorphosis; the child may start with one of the pictured configurations, but then reconfigures the pieces into all manner of other imagined styles. With the Erector Set kit, the first built model is likely to remain as originally configured in any one play session. Erector Set, for all its modular structure, is just not as reconfigurable in practice as Lego.

Lego components are plug compatible with each other, containing the connectivity framework as an integral feature of the component. A standard grid of bumps and cavities on component surfaces allow them to snap together into a larger configuration. The Erector Set connectivity framework, by contrast, employs a special-purpose intermediate subsystem used solely to attach one part to another—a nut-and-bolt pair and a 90-degree elbow. The components in the system all have many holes through which the bolts may pass to connect one component with another. When a nut is lost, a bolt is useless, and vice versa. When all the nuts and bolts remaining in a set have been used, any remaining construction components are useless, and vice versa. All the parts in a Lego set can always be used and reused, but the Erector Set, for all its modularity, is not as reusable in practice as Lego.

In contrast to both of these construction toys is the model builder's kit. You can get one of these for an airplane, too. The finished glued-construction, or maybe snapped-together, model will have a lot more esthetic appeal than the Lego or Erector Set versions; but it will remain what it is for all time. The parts are not reusable, the construction cannot be reconfigured, and one intended size precludes any scalability. A highly integrated system, this construction kit offers maximum esthetic appeal for one-time construction use. Figure 5.1 depicts the essential characteristics of all three kinds of toys.

Complex adaptive systems theorists speak of the vibrancy and adaptability that exists between the borders of chaos and order. Too much order and nothing much happens in response to an environmental change. Too much chaos and nothing much happens with coherency and purpose. In our construction-toy examples, the model builder's glued-together kit is highly ordered with a single purpose in mind. Although the Erector Set's nuts-and-bolts connectivity allows connection to almost anything with a hole, it makes

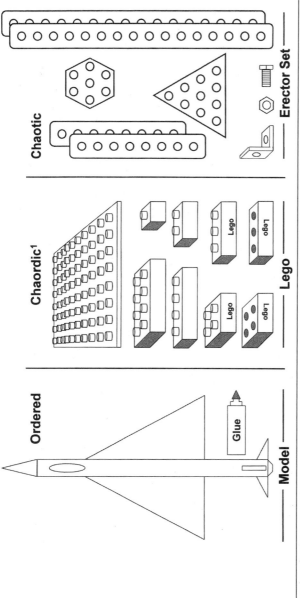

Figure 5.1   Three Types of Construction Toy Systems

Complex adaptive systems theorists speak of the vibrancy and adaptability that exists between the borders of chaos and order. Too much order and nothing much happens in response to an environmental change. Too much chaos and nothing much happens with coherency and purpose. In these examples the glued-together model kit is highly ordered with a single purpose in mind. The Erector Set, with its nuts and bolts connectivity, allows connection to almost anything with a hole, while simultaneously making the connection/part-interaction process tedious—often resulting in simple constructions with novel appendages—a chaotic result. Lego accommodates the moment-to-moment whim and imagination of the user with a readily adaptable system. The model building kit has a tight framework: a precise construction sequence, no part interchangeability, and highly integrated. Erector Set has a loose framework that doesn't encourage interaction among parts and insufficiently discriminates among compatible parts. Each module in the Lego system carries all it needs to interact with other modules, and the interaction framework rejects most unintended parts.

Note: [1]Dee Hock (Hock 1997) coined the word *chaord* for organisms, organizations, and systems that harmoniously exhibit characteristics of both order and chaos.

the connection/part-interaction process tedious and often leads to simple constructions with novel appendages—chaos is the result. Lego walks between, accommodating the moment-to-moment whim and imagination of the user with a readily adaptable system.

The model building kit has a tight framework: a precise construction sequence, no part interchangeability, and high integration. Erector Set has a loose framework that doesn't encourage interaction among parts and insufficiently discriminates among compatible parts. Each component in the Lego system carries all it needs to interact with other components, and the interaction framework rejects most unintended parts.

These construction toys are all "good" systems. But Lego is the more adaptable. Lego is also the dominant construction toy of choice among our preteen builders—who appear to value experimentation and innovation.

■ GENERAL PRINCIPLES OF RESPONSE-ABLE SYSTEMS

We call any organization of common-purpose interacting components a "system": a team of people, a cell of workstations, a network of controllers, a chain of suppliers, a corporation of functional departments, even a contract of clauses. Figure 5.2 provides our working definitions for *system, component,* and the *framework* that binds the two.

Figure 5.3 provides a brief synopsis of each of the 10 RRS principles. The following discussion includes many examples for each principle to help develop an intuitive understanding from a bombardment of similar patterns. The examples also show these principles at work in various types of systems, such as those that contain people and those that contain machines, those that have software intelligence and those that don't, those at the high organizational level and those among the organization's minutia. Many of the examples, in fact, exemplify more than one principle, though this point is generally not made in the interest of immediate focus.

➤ Self-Contained Units (Components)

Components of response-able systems are distinct, separable, self-sufficient units cooperating toward a shared common purpose.

The sense of unit and component carries some specific additional meaning with the words *self-contained* beyond that of just a separable item. In the information technology (IT) field, we might

Stereo System of Components

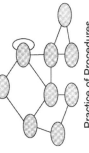

Practice of Procedures

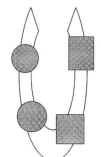

Team of People

System

A group of components

sharing a common interaction framework

and serving a common purpose.

Framework

A set of standards

constraining and enabling the interactions

of compatible system components.

Component

A separable system subunit

with a self-contained capability/purpose/identity,

and capable of interaction with other components.

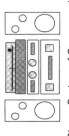

Company of Divisions

Chain of Suppliers

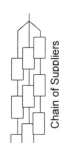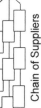

Cell of Workstations

Figure 5.2 Basic Definitions

The reconfigurability of component systems is familiar to us from the ease with which we can add, change, or upgrade units in our home stereo and entertainment centers, even when different brand names are involved. We call any organization of common-purpose interacting components a system: an entertainment center of components, a team of people, a cell of workstations, a network of controllers, a chain of suppliers, a corporation of functional departments, even a contract of clauses.

139

Reusable / Scalable

Self-Contained Units (Components) – Components of *Response-able* systems are distinct, separable, self-sufficient units cooperating toward a shared common purpose.	**Evolving Standards (Framework)** – Frameworks of *response-able* systems standardize intercomponent communication and interaction; define component compatibility; and are monitored/updated to accommodate old, current, and new components.
Plug Compatibility – Components of *response-able* systems share defined interaction and interface standards; and are easily inserted or removed.	**Redundancy and Diversity** – Duplicate components are employed in *response-able* systems to provide capacity right-sizing options and fail-soft tolerance; and diversity among similar components employing different methods is exploited.
Facilitated Reuse – Components of *response-able* systems are reusable/replicable; and responsibilities for ready reuse/replication and for management, maintenance, and upgrade of component inventory is specifically designated.	**Elastic Capacity** – Component populations in *response-able* systems may be increased and decreased widely within the existing framework.

Reconfigurable

Flat Interaction – Components within a *response-able* system communicate directly on a peer-to-peer relationship; and parallel rather than sequential relationships are favored.	**Distributed Control and Information** – Components in *response-able* systems are directed by objective rather than method; decisions are made at point of maximum knowledge; information is associated locally, accessible globally, and freely disseminated.
Deferred Commitment – Component relationships in a *response-able* system are transient when possible; decisions and fixed bindings are postponed until immediately necessary; and relationships are scheduled and bound in real time.	**Self-Organization** – Component relationships in *response-able* systems are self-determined; and component interaction is self-adjusting or negotiated.

These principles have been observed in both natural and man-made highly adaptable systems and organizations. They can be employed effectively in both inanimate directed configurations and in thinking/deciding self-organizing configurations. These are synergistic design guidelines which accommodate innovative interpretation and have greatly amplified value when employed as a complete set. Much more can be usefully understood about all principles than that which is contained in this table, most especially about components and frameworks—the fundamental system structural elements.

Figure 5.3 Response-Able System Principles (RRS Principles)

use the phrase *encapsulated modularity,* indicating that the perimeter of the component is *opaque.* In essence, what a component can do is known, but how it carries out its tasks should not be known, or at least should not be interfered with or taken advantage of by another component. This concept is extremely important for response-able systems because it permits internal change without unintended side effects rippling throughout the rest of the system.

The phrase self-contained was suggested by non-IT people, who found the word encapsulation too foreign. For similar reasons, the word *unit* rather than *component* is featured initially. Human resources people, for example, had difficulty equating a component to a person comfortably. I generally use the word component, however, and will now attempt to impart an important appreciation for the concept expressed by *encapsulation.*

Encapsulation of components in a system enables safe, risk-free change. The values of component systems are familiar to us from the ease with which we can add, change, or upgrade units in our home stereo and entertainment centers, even when different brand names are involved. We think nothing of incrementally upgrading these systems when we see a new set of speakers that we just have to have, or when we want to add that new 240-disk CD carousel. Information systems, production floor software, and desktop computer applications are typically modularized as well; but they have rarely supported the same cavalier attitude toward component swapping and upgrade. The difference here is the concept of encapsulation, which simply means that modules are black boxes that accept inputs and deliver outputs without making their inner workings directly accessible to any other module. Software development has a long tradition of violating modular boundaries in the interest of "special" features, reduced storage requirements, and faster operation. The resultant level of intimate integration among a collection of modules makes simple changes likely to cause unexplainable systemwide side effects.

This concept of encapsulation is powerful. A cell on the factory floor that needs material can send a message to the "material manager" component, and ask it to get part "A" and bring it to location "B" in time "C." Over the course of years, the component responding to this message might be upgraded through successive technology generations from a boy with a pushcart to a full-blown automated guided vehicle system; yet the cell sends the same message, and no side effects ripple unexplainably through the production system from the technology upgrades.

A Navy seal team meets together for the first time at midnight on the top of a desolate hill in a place none have been to before. Each knows the objective, and each knows his own role as well as that of the others on the team. They do not sit down and interrogate each other to decide about individual trustworthiness and competency. They don't have a debate on the moral or ethical position of dispatching the objective. The team leader may in fact choose the tactical targets for demolition, but the demolitions expert will determine how to accomplish the task. And any one of them could have been any one of many others.

➤ Plug Compatibility

Components of response-able systems share defined interaction and interface standards; and they are easily inserted or removed.

Plug compatibility for response-able systems means more than a physical interface match between a component and its place in a system, whether it's a new printer for a desktop computer, a new machine for a factory, or a new team member for a development group.

Manufacturing semiconductors is a multistage process that involves many types of discrete process machinery, made by different vendors, from different countries. Controlling a factory with mixed vendor machinery, or even monitoring the work in process, was typically a manual hands-on and record-to-clipboard job, even after factory data collection networks were common in other industries. At least that was true until a machine communications protocol called SECS (Semiconductor Equipment Communication Standard) was established as an industry standard. Within a short while, virtually all new semiconductor machinery spoke this language (interaction standard) through a common standardized connector (interface standard). This spurred the installation of factorywide *Manufacturing Execution Systems* that automated the manual work-in-process data collection and machine setup. Previously, such systems required expensive special purpose custom designed electronic interfaces for each machine on the network. Machines from mixed vendors and new machines from new vendors are now plug compatible with the SECS communication framework, and are immediate participants in the factorywide network.

In contrast, an attempt by General Motors in the 1980s to establish a standard communication language called MMS (Manufacturing Messaging Specification) for general manufacturing environments succeeded, but failed to gain wide acceptance among machine vendors and users. General factory floor systems have remained difficult to implement as a result.

As to the ease of insertion: A friend of mine had occasion to spend some time in France back in the 1970s, directing the development of a minicomputer product line. His wife accompanied him and they rented a home in Grenoble for the two years they were there. He learned to speak French quite fluently in the process and practiced many of the more colorful phrases with each successive purchase of a home appliance. As he tells the story, every appliance came with a new and different plug configuration totally incompatible with any plug socket in the house. A novice in the culture, he felt that keeping the appliance as bought would make it easier to dispose of when their tour of duty was up; so he opted to install a matching plug socket. This entailed a trip to the hardware store, the purchase of a compatible socket, the selection of the outlet in the home to be dedicated to this appliance, and the installation of the matching socket. Changing the plug might have been easier, but was no less an unexpected and unappreciated incompatibility to one familiar with the universal electrical standards in the United States. In venting his frustration at the lack of standards to someone at work, he was quickly informed that he was mistaken, there was no lack of standards at all, there were plenty of standards. And eventually there was plug compatibility for his appliances, but not with ease.

As to ease of removal: In the 1990s, the auto industry got closer to its suppliers, paring down the number of multiple sources and developing close and even exclusive relationships with many. Then they began integrating some suppliers into the production process by having them take up residence near or on the production campus. This was not a radically new concept: Beer companies learned a long time ago the advantages of sharing a common wall with their glass producer. Toward the end of the 1990s, automakers were experimenting with suppliers in the assembly plant, actually installing the parts and subsystems they produced. When highly integrated systems like this work well, they can provide excellent advantages, especially in collaborative improvement areas. But when these systems get the hiccups, the suppliers are so highly integrated with the company that they are difficult to remove and replace. Better to have the suppliers partitioned as components, readily swapped out for repair or retirement when they suffer severe malfunction.

➤ Flat Interaction

Components within a response-able system communicate directly on a peer-to-peer relationship; and parallel rather than sequential relationships are favored.

Gatekeepers that select, approve, censure, or otherwise gate the communications of a system component are stealth[2] members of the system. Take the gumball machine, for example. You put in your quarter and expect a gumball. There are generally two reasons for failure: The machine is out of gumballs, or the selection mechanism that allows a gumball to fall from the pool into your hand does not do so. If you know gumballs are present and really want one, you may spend another quarter and try again. Again the selection (approval) mechanism may or may not allow one to pass through. A second failure (if you are that patient) will probably result in your indictment of the gumball machine as broken. Maybe the gumballs in this batch are slightly too large or out of round; or maybe the selection mechanism has something stuck in it. The fact that the selection mechanism is failing while the gumballs are present is not important to you, it is all just one system and it is broken. Similarly, any person in the approval chain for a new product, say in the finance department, is part of the product development component, and not external to it serving some other component as they often believe or are told. Flat interaction in a response-able version of this case puts the gatekeeper in direct communication and real-time interaction with the rest of the team.

Peer-to-peer communications imply that components within a system may initiate communications in any direction at any time. In the IT world, where we employ client-server networks predominantly, a client—by convention—may initiate a dialogue with a server but the server cannot initiate a dialogue with a client. Thus, the print server connected to your desktop computer at work may respond that the color printer you requested is not available. It will not, however, initiate a message later informing you that the color printer has been returned to service. In the response-able world of people, someone involved in a situation that has just changed may well send an e-mail to the president of the company asking for reconsideration of some prior decision affecting the pursuit of current work. This is desirable when both of these people are components of the same system responsible for an activity affected by the changed situation.

An example of flat interaction in a product design can be seen in many after-market CD players for use in an automobile. The ones I'm speaking of communicate directly to your installed radio by broadcasting the CD material on some preselected fm frequency. Some radios come equipped with a socket on the front panel to accept a wired CD input, but most don't today. Those that do may discriminate among acceptable CD players by the socket (gatekeeper). The wireless interface gives the CD player a great deal of mobility and reuse in any car with a radio, and any car with a radio can instantly have output from a CD player.

More and more today, we are seeing machinery of various kinds come equipped with a direct communications link back to its manufacturer. For years, Mack Truck has offered the option of monitoring and even diagnosing problems with the truck's engine from the factory where the best expertise exists, cutting out all the middlemen with lesser knowledge, and eliminating the so-called telephone effect where a message repeated through a sequential line of people doesn't come out the other end the same way it started.

Business went through a strong process reengineering focus in the 1990s. A lot of that effort was directed at changing sequential processes into unitized or parallel processes. Processing insurance claims was drastically improved by making one person responsible for all processing steps rather than passing the claim from person to person, each of whom was responsible for only one step. Similarly in many areas of manufacturing, the concept of cellular processes took favor over sequential processes, partly because the process that created the problem had the ability to attend to it immediately and directly.

➤ Deferred Commitment

Component relationships in a response-able system are transient when possible; decisions and fixed bindings are postponed until immediately necessary; and relationships are scheduled and bound in real time.

Deferred commitment basically keeps your options open as long as possible. The underlying wisdom here says don't make a decision until it is necessary, knowing that more information arrives with time and decisions should take advantage of that flow. This is a two-edged sword for response ability: (1) It configures things at the last possible moment to avoid the possibility of unproductive change and rechange, and (2) it reserves otherwise early-committed resources for alternative use if a greater need arises. The concept of decoupling otherwise integrated units into separate components is often what provides the ability to defer commitments.

Hewlett-Packard has a classic story here.[3] In the early days of their laser printer product line, when they were getting ready to replace one generation with its successor, they found a major problem with unbalanced global inventories. After they ceased production on the old printer, they found that the demand for exhausting the inventory in the United States was not the same as in Europe and Asia. Printers that had been configured at the factory with power suppliers, and packaged with destination documentation could not be moved from one country to another effectively. In some countries, they had demand and no inventory, while in others they had more inventory than demand. Now such destination-specific items are either reconfigurable or multipurpose. With their DeskJet printers, they designed external power supplies and chose to have the final commitment made by their local distribution centers rather than at the factory. These centers purchase power suppliers, manuals, and packaging specific to the customer country, and configure the packed deliverable when shipping to the customer. The customer plugs the accompanying power supply component into the printer during setup.

Mass customization[4] is another classic story of deferred commitment. This production capability custom configures each product at the last minute on the production line. Generally this capability comes from a combination of process and product design features that enable last-minute product configuration. Motorola got a lot of publicity in the 1980s for its pager production line that configured each pager for its intended customer. Highly automated, this line had robotic assemblers that worked according to a download program for each pager. In addition, the pager had features that were enabled by internal firmware which was downloaded into the product. In another arena, Huffy bicycles sells through mass merchandisers, often with the merchandiser's brand name on the products. They have 55,000 possible permutations, and a custom configuration is negotiated with the merchandiser for their unique brand differentiation.

Some commitments can be deferred indefinitely. When LSI Logic built its Gresham, Oregon, semiconductor fabrication facility in 1998, they decided to use people instead of automation to move wafer cassettes from one process machine to another. People were more flexible than the best automated guided vehicle system available then, and they anticipate reconfiguring the factory from time to time to optimize production areas and match changing markets and product mix. Any form of automated conveyance would have limited their machine relocation options.

➤ Distributed Control and Information

Components in response-able systems are directed by objective rather than method; decisions are made at point of maximum knowledge; information is associated locally, accessible globally, and freely disseminated.

A classic example of distributed control exists in the Internet. Messages and data sent through the Internet are first cut into small uniform-size packets, each with some header information that includes its destination address and its proper place in a reconstructed data sequence. These packets are then sent off to their eventual destination as a disconnected series of independent uniform-length data streams. As they travel, they are sent through the global network, re-layed from one station to another, until they eventually arrive where they are supposed to be, and reconstructed into the original se-quence. Every packet may well take a different path as each relay sta-tion decides in real time the most expeditious relay station to send this one to next. Each relay station is connected to some relatively small number of other relay stations, any one of which may become unavailable at any moment for reasons impossible to predict. The control of the routing is distributed throughout the entire network, not centrally located. Messages that cannot reach their destination because access to a critical network leg may be down at the moment are parked for awhile at whatever relay station detects the temporary dead end. When the path is again open, they resume their travels. If the path doesn't open after some preset time limit (typically a num-ber of days), the packet is returned to the sender to free up the storage space in the relay station. This distributed routing control has en-abled the rapid and awesome growth in the size of this global net-work. It is something that could not have occurred if routing was under a centralized controller, which would have had to grow large enough, fast enough to keep up with the new route possibilities from each new point and old point to all other new points and old points. Also, trying to balance traffic on the network by choosing in advance how one Internet node will be connected to all other possible desti-nations would literally be impossible. Instead, each relay station reroutes messages in real time around other relay stations that are overtaxed or otherwise unable to provide service at the moment.

Empowerment at the team and the individual level is the classic example when people and organizations are involved. One example of empowerment at work in a command-and-control culture was re-flected in the statements of one CNN reporter during the 1990 Gulf War. This reporter was commenting on different responses available to the U.S. and Iraqi militaries in the face of severed communica-tions, and offered that the Iraqi army was modeled in the Russian army mold, which required a direct order from the Kremlin before any field action was permitted. During that war, the U.S. Air Force severed the communications links between the Iraqi field forces and Baghdad almost immediately. The field forces dug in and adopted a defensive posture. The reporter capped these statements by offering that a U.S. unit, out of touch with its command structure, is specifi-cally expected to take the initiative and pursue the objective in what-ever way it feels is appropriate.

Distributed information is often a reinforcement of the self-contained unit principle. Remmele Engineering was a pioneer in the use of what we now call *Activity Based Costing*. For job estimation, they utilize costing information for specific processes on specific machines. When they have to estimate a complex job and its various alternatives, they can construct a total cost from each of the processes in any given proposal alternative by simply adding up the component costs. As their plants bring in new equipment and new technology, new components are made available and represented to the estimation activity as a process cost associated with a specific machine. Their estimation system is simply an Excel spreadsheet, which provides more cost justification detail and accuracy in less time than methods that attempt to estimate a multistage job by some standard characterization and rules of thumb. Also, the Remmele approach readily lends itself to reconfigured or innovative process alternatives when cost constraints or job characteristics require something new and different. Though costing information is not physically kept within the associated machine, it is distributed in the sense that it is separable and mobile, and can easily accompany the machine to a new home in another division or even another company should that be desirable.

Usually we think of distributed information as being physically distributed throughout the components of a system. Data distributed in this way is more robust than when it is centrally located and subject to a single point failure. In the absence of an overwhelming concerted effort, like that which occurred in Serbia's 1999 Kosovar offensive, citizens holding copies of their own identity and property documents are not at risk to municipal or other governmental record-keeping problems. Also, residents in California can readily move to New York, or even New Delhi, and take with them the information necessary to directly reestablish identity and substance.

A final and different interpretation of distributed information is also implied by this principle. In this case, it is the distribution of information useful to people in pursuit of organizational goals. At Remmele Engineering, the president visits every division each quarter and holds an all-hands, no-holds-barred question and answer session after he shares the company's results for the prior period. This sharing of financial and competitive performance along with the candid information flow is a strong contributing factor to the loyalty, dedication, and competency shown by the employees. The concept of sharing financial performance information and the overwhelming advantages that can be gained as a result have been largely documented under the category of *open book management*.[5] Useful information is not limited to financial data, however, and should include whatever can channel employees toward organizational goals, engage them as supporters of organizational change, and help them weather and understand difficult times.

➤ **Elastic Capacity**

Component populations in response-able systems may be increased and decreased widely within the existing framework.

Earlier in this chapter, we looked at the Lego toy system to lay some groundwork for framework concepts. A Lego block is completely self-contained and wrapped in its framework, and can simply plug into any other Lego block with unused sockets, anywhere; or onto a Lego framework sheet, which can be extended forever by cojoining additional sheets. There is no inherent limit to the number of Lego components one can use in a construction imposed by the Lego framework.

The Internet example introduced under the distributed control principle shows a virtually unbounded framework. Much like the Lego toy system, each component in the Internet system is basically wrapped in the plug-compatible system framework (almost but not quite, as we'll see). Similar to the Lego toy, a new self-contained Internet relay station simply plugs into another relay station (or a few) with available ports. In a fractal sense, new self-contained Internet Service Providers (ISPs) simply plug into any available relay station, and new Internet users simply plug into any desirable and available ISP.

In all these Internet cases, plugging-in involves a communication channel of some sort, be it a telephone line link, a cable link, a satellite link, or a wireless radio link. In this sense, we have the Erector Set equivalent of a component acting as a framework intermediary piece, the weakest link in the system. Other parts of the framework ensure component compatibility through registration and authentication procedures, thus avoiding the chaos of Erector Set's inability to distinguish among compatible components.

When outsourcing became a strategic discussion point in the early 1990s, the focus was generally on core competency issues: Concentrate on your strategic differentiations, and farm out the rest to others who make a competency from what you consider to be supporting functions. That may have been the verbal debate, but the concept got its implementation push from companies that needed rapid capacity fluctuation options. In the electronics market, typical product life cycles were then slipping under 18 months. Timely market entry determines both market share and market growth rate in this industry. Solectron Corporation, a Baldrige Quality award winner in both 1991 and 1997, specializes in contract electronic board production. They were founded in 1977 in California's Silicon Valley specifically to handle the local manufacturers' overflow. In 1992, their revenues were $400 million, and by the end of the decade they had reached $6 billion in revenue from operations in 21 manufacturing facilities worldwide. This was not because Hewlett-Packard and others like them abandoned internal board production, but because these companies did not find it economically feasible to maintain internal rapid surge production and capacity fluctuation options.

Making outsource capacity-fluctuation options work seamlessly is a matter of production placement framework design. As described in earlier chapters, LSI Logic set up a management group and procedures for qualifying and maintaining outsource plug-compatible production resources that would be transparently interchangeable with equivalent internal production resources. Greater detail on their framework and system operational procedures is provided in Chapter 6.

Remmele Engineering's apprenticeship program is set up to accommodate virtually any number of apprentices. When the company is expanding and candidates are available, two factors in particular enable this seamless expansion. First, apprentices are matched with personal mentors during their apprenticeship. Rather than restrict the population of potential mentors, Remmele values the mentoring concept for employee growth as much as for the apprenticeship concept, and views every accomplished machinist as a mentor candidate. With a much larger population of accomplished machinists than apprentices, this requirement imposes no restriction. Second, apprentices learn by doing real work. Though they are not as productive as an accomplished machinist and take some production time away from mentoring machinists, they are not a pure expense. Their impact on profits is minimal enough that a large expansion in their number is generally affordable. On the downside, there is no negative impact when the number of apprentices drops below normal, assuming that this is not caused by a lack of suitable candidates to meet forecasted growth. In times of reduced apprenticeship activity, the mentoring values are not lost as all employees exist in an active collaborative learning culture.

➤ Redundancy and Diversity

Duplicate components are employed in response-able systems to provide capacity right-sizing options and fail-soft tolerance; and diversity among similar components employing different methods is exploited.

It is often better to have two machines that each do half the work then one that does it all, if being completely out of service is impossible. As a customer, I have been in retail outlets with one cash register that goes down and have been told, "come back another time," and in banks with one central processor and told to come back later because "the system is down," and in delicatessens with one scale and told "that product can't be weighed." The customer-supplier relationship was jeopardized in each case, and immediately terminated in more than one.

Currently, Mobil Oil Company offers a little sensor that you can carry on a key ring or paste on the back window of your car. When the sensor is in the proximity of a gas pump, it activates the pump and the gas purchase is charged to the credit card you designated. Very convenient. Except at 11:45 P.M. when the computer is down. Then customers have to wait for several minutes or go to a competitor. Better to have another computer take on the current load while the first is out of service.

Sometimes it is advantageous to have two six-station assembly lines instead of one 12-station line, if demand rate fluctuates. An automotive Maquiladora plant in Juarez, Mexico, found it advantageous to break up its long wiring harness assembly lines into multiple, fewer-station lines, with more responsibility at each station. When demand slacked off, an entire line could be shut down and the few people redeployed to other jobs. With the single large line, this often resulted in poor productivity on the line or a half-time run followed by a difficult attempt to redeploy a larger number of people for a shorter period.

In some cases, it is a good idea to have options for getting a task done rather than relying on a single optimal approach. The Internet would be a disaster if communications between two points had only one dedicated path: Malfunctions in the network would frequently black out whole portions of the Net. LSI Logic maintains a pool of resources capable of fabricating semiconductor wafers; some are wholly owned and some are qualified outsources. When an order arrives, a production chain can be assembled immediately from these pooled resources without waiting for some single resource or some resource with a unique capability that must finish its current commitment.

Frequently, it is more useful to have multipurpose people than dedicated experts. Cross-training in teams is often justified by the need to always have someone covering every need, regardless of who is absent for whatever reason. This obvious point is violated more often than not, especially in control cultures where single-point approvals rob momentum, stop activities, or put the customer on hold while the gatekeeper is out of town, on vacation, out-to-lunch, ill, or otherwise unavailable.

Collaborative learning and collaborative work have better results in a group with mixed backgrounds and mixed points of view. Women have a different perspective than men, easterners see things differently than westerners, financial people consider different aspects than do marketing people, technical people don't see what human relations people see, and so on. Diversity in a group of people trying to reach conclusions will broaden the problem understanding and consequently broaden the solution applicability.

There are usually multiple and diverse ways to accomplish the same ends. For example, Y2K brought home the value of alternative sources of energy to many people, a rural fire department is likely to have pond and lake pumping capability as well as hydrant hookup, a person who uses a calculator for arithmetic is inconvenienced or in trouble frequently if that is the only way he or she can do arithmetic, and the company that cannot operate when its main computer system goes down is likely to be out of business. Keeping older generations of technology employed or employable can be a hedge against new failure modes with new technology, and can also be a source of extra capacity.

Expect diversity and design for it, instead of designing a system with "oneness" in mind.

Don't design a framework strictly to fit a specific problem at hand. Instead, accommodate the general situation for which the immediate problem is simply a particular case. Thus, an accounting system that must do a periodic P&L rollup should not expect that period to always be a calendar month, a stored calendar date should not assume that the first two digits of the year will always be 19, a data modem should not assume that it will always converse with other modems of similar speed and capability, Microsoft should not assume that everyone will upgrade to the new version of their software, management should not assume that there is only one way to get a job done acceptably, and team members should not assume that there is only one correct point of view.

➤ Self-Organization

Component relationships in response-able systems are self-determined; and component interaction is self-adjusting or negotiated.

Self-organization is typically related to natural systems such as ecologies, societies, and beehives, where seemingly intelligent, or at least purposeful behavior, emerges from the total system even though no central direction or control is evident. Artificial systems with this same emergent behavior and no central control also exist, with classic examples such as a free market economy, the stock market, certain aspects of the Internet, and even the artificial life one does battle with in popular computer games. More traditional artificial systems, like products, processes, and practices can also exhibit self-organizing behavior, but typically to a lessor extent and mixed with various degrees of centralized control and direction. Empowered teams, for example, may exercise a fair amount of self-organization while still having leadership both within the team and above the team, directing and changing its priorities, resources, and allowable activities. Response-able systems generally make good use of some degree of self-organization, but the spectrum is wide.

At the business organizational level, we have well-known examples like VISA Corporation and the personal selling companies like Amway and Mary Kay Cosmetics. These companies have a minimal set of core rules that provide a growth framework. The personal selling company generally employs a multitier field operation that allows a salesperson to enlist other salespeople at their own discretion, making a commission on their own sales and an override on revenues generated by their enlistments as long as their own sales exceed some minimum. In turn, their enlistments can build subnetworks of salespeople under the same rules. Growth is not directed and scheduled from the top, but rather emerges from a framework that encourages self-initiative among the system's components.

VISA Corporation's explosive global growth occurred from a different mechanism of simple rules. Growth for VISA comes from banks and other organizations that issue and promote VISA cards under their own marketing programs. To be a card issuer in the VISA system, you must abide by the rules for trademark use, interact with the central clearinghouse according to a standard transaction protocol, and be able to stand behind the credit extended to your customers. Virtually any organization that wants to issue a VISA card may do so within these rules. The predominant growth experienced by the company was the result not of a massive field sales force cold-calling and signing up card issuers, but of requests from would-be card issuers that contacted VISA and self-qualified themselves. It is a product with appeal, a nonintrusive relationship, and a self-engagement process.

In the business world, empowerment, teaming, listening to the voice of the customer, organizational learning, and other concepts are movements toward more self-organization—though not always with that end in mind. The principle of self-organization basically means that the components of a system have some discretion in deciding how to accomplish the goals established for them: what processes to employ, what priorities to set, and when to use which resources. In even more advanced systems, the component can choose what to do, when to do it, and with whom to do it. In large systems, the resulting behavior typically reflects many individual decisions or actions, and is often called *emergent behavior* because no one entity is solely responsible for the result. Collectively, it means that a perturbation to the system will cause an automatic adjustment—like an ecosystem reacting to a new predator. In most small artificial (human-made) systems, the degree of discretionary decision making by the components is limited, but nonetheless an important enabler for response ability.

Consider the case of two modems trying to handle a data connection between two desktop computers. When you use your desktop computer to communicate over the Internet or send an e-mail message to someone not on your office or home network, the modem on your end translates the data into something acceptable for the communications system. Whoever or whatever you connect with on the other end uses a modem to retranslate this data back into something understandable by the receiving device. In the early 1980s, a typical modem for a stand-alone computer transmitted and received data at 110 baud, about 10 typewritten characters per second. Each new generation of modems found ways to increase that speed and still use existing telephone lines, which were never installed with high-speed, error-free data traffic in mind. My personal modem purchases for home use have mirrored the new technology introductions almost step for step, and include individual top speeds of 110, 300, 1200, 2400, 4800, 9600, 33k, and 56k baud, so far. That represents a technology upgrade approximately every two years. When modems with new capabilities are introduced in this market, they must be prepared to communicate successfully with any and all of the prior generations. At the same time, communication over telephone lines will run through a variety of different telephone-exchange technology and telephone-line quality, in urban areas as well as in forgotten rural areas. Modems succeed in this complex environment precisely because they negotiate between themselves how they will communicate during a given session, before they begin transmitting data. They try to find the maximum speed compatible with both the quality of the transmission line between them and with their own respective capabilities. This is self-organization at the component interaction level.

Self-organization works in the mechanical world as well. In the mid-1990s, I visited with a scientist at Sandia National Laboratories who was concerned about putting a part into a fixture correctly, especially if a robot was going to do it. In this problem, a part picked up from a bin of jumbled-up parts must first be oriented in alignment with the fixture, and then placed into the fixture to a very high repeatable positioning precision. People don't usually have difficulty doing this when they are paying close attention, but robots do. Rather than approach the problem with artificial intelligence and better-than-available vision systems, this scientist looked at the mechanical design of the part and the fixture. The object was to find design tricks for part geometry and fixture geometry that would self-guide the two components into a perfect mating—conceptually like a solid cone being pushed deeper into a hollow cone socket until their centerlines match perfectly, but for a variety of more complex shapes. In this case, the example is of self-organizing mechanical components.

An everyday example of self-organizing mechanical components is the universal socket wrench. More than one design is on the market, but the basic concept is that a single self-contained wrench can be placed on any size or any shape nut, within limits, and the user simply tightens or loosens without making any overt socket selection or adjustment. Bringing this back to the bigger picture of response to changing conditions, these adaptable wrenches can remove an abused and out-of-shape nut, whereas the special purpose socket set will fail. Limited as it may be on occasion, self-organization has a place and a benefit in almost any system.

➤ Facilitated Reuse

Components of response-able systems are reusable/replicable; and responsibilities for ready reuse/replication and for management, maintenance, and upgrade of component inventory are specifically designated.

Can a duplicate of an existing component be readily created if another is needed? Can a necessary component be readily deployed when a new system must be constructed? Can a component be readily replaced or re-created if it is lost, stolen, or destroyed? As we are concerned with effective response to dynamic needs, someone or some mechanism is specifically charged with the responsibility for each activity involved in preparedness.

Reusability can mean one component is reused in multiple systems over time, and it can also mean that the design or template of one component is reused to make duplicate units on demand. A software component is not exhausted from the component pool when it is used in a new software program. The act of reuse occurs when another copy of it is created. The analog in the mechanical world occurs when another welding cell, say, is needed in addition to the two that were originally ordered from the vendor. In this case, all the necessary information needed for ready generation of a duplicate welding cell is inventoried in the component pool.

As to the *facilitation* of reusability, even in self-organizing systems with high degrees of autonomous activity, there are centralized functions that require attention and responsibility. At VISA, there is the centralized clearinghouse for transactions, a gatekeeper for admitting new card issuers to the family, and a procedure for changing the framework rules; in the stock market there is the New York Stock Exchange, the Tokyo Stock Exchange, and others like them matching buyers and sellers and maintaining the rules of listing membership and trading membership; and in the beehive the queen lays the eggs. In general, once the initial framework and components are created, operational response ability is maintained and managed by specific mechanisms and responsible entities that attend to the dynamic needs of framework and component pool evolution. The continuing viability of the system is determined by the extent to which these responsibilities are attended to. In Chapter 6, a formal means for designating this systems integrity management function is discussed.

With a Lego toy, if someone (a parent perhaps) does not actively maintain the inventory of components available to the user in an orderly fashion, replenishing lost components and perhaps adding new components from time to time, the range of construction possibilities slowly diminishes and eventually vanishes. On another level, someone at the Lego company functioning as a product manager is responsible for adding new specialized components, such as airplane propellers and roadster steering wheels, that broaden the range of construction possibilities and maintain the system's appeal in the face of competitors' toy innovations.

Defense contractors who are unable to ramp up quickly when the military wishes additional cruise missiles have failed the *readiness* part of this principle. Instead of viewing each contract as a standalone business transaction, a larger production-on-demand system designed with response ability in mind would view contracts as a triggering event to re-create a production capability (component) and would have designated responsibilities for ready re-creation of whatever is required. This doesn't necessarily mean 24-hour response, but it definitely doesn't mean 24-month response. Texas Instruments consolidated its various missile manufacturing operations into a single multimissile plant when the cold war ended and the Defense Department reduced the size and frequency of missile production orders. This plant could effectively respond to small quantity and even single unit orders for any of a variety of missiles made by TI.[6] From a different perspective, this concept doesn't necessarily require that a defense contractor maintain the inventory of production components. The military customer could very well design a framework for a system of contractors with (relatively speaking) generic production capabilities; utilizing management concepts like those employed by LSI Logic for subcontracted production resources, combined with the workstations and layout concepts employed by Texas Instruments in its multimissile manufacturing facility.

Say you're going to acquire a production welding cell from an outside vendor. The spec you provide to this vendor includes the framework within which it must work. This is principally an interface spec: mechanical, physical, electronic, electrical, informational, and emissional (limits on emissions of radio waves, heat, sound, fluids, etc.). As part of the informational interface, you specify the messages it must respond to and the expected response: start, stop, operating priorities, status request; and you specify the messages it may send to the system for response: material request, transport request, maintenance request, alarm. You also specify the performance requirements of the cell in terms of duty cycle, product throughput and surge capacity, product quality, and product variety. At this point, the system builder has all the necessary information to build a plug-compatible process component that is reusable/replaceable as a unit. To *facilitate* reusability, however, you want ready replication that could handle the possible need for more or different versions. To accomplish this, you maintain the design spec and a template of the design in the component inventory/library, and designate someone in charge of that library.

Attempts at formalized knowledge management are actually classic examples of facilitated reusability. New knowledge generation aside, the principal focus of knowledge management is the mobilization of existing knowledge: moving it from where it is to where it is needed, and doing this effectively by reusing knowledge in new applications. Business started looking into knowledge management when it became evident that no one was really responsible for making and keeping this activity effective. A typical first step in most organizations is to capture and inventory existing knowledge in a repository, designating processes and people responsible for these activities. The packaging and nature of access to this captured knowledge also gets early focus and designated responsibilities with search engines, intranet web masters, and knowledge librarians. Facilitation in many cases has even addressed user behavioral changes, with designated responsibilities for creating and maintaining collaborative cultures and communities of practice, and the infrastructures that support them.

This principle ensures that responsibilities for ongoing operational effectiveness are recognized, designated, and dispatched. Response-able systems are by definition concerned with ongoing system dynamics and not simply the construction of the first version of a system.

➤ **Evolving Standards (Framework)**

Frameworks of response-able systems standardize intercomponent communication and interaction; define component compatibility; and are monitored/updated to accommodate old, current, and new components.

The reconfigurableness we seek with response-able systems relies on *framework* interface standards that may consider electrical, informational, mechanical, weight, shape, human factors, beliefs, values, goals, or other elements that facilitate the utilization and interaction of components, without violating the concept of self-contained encapsulation. Though component entertainment systems offer an almost limitless catalog of boxes that can work together, there are in fact families of components that share plug-compatible standards. Trying to plug a four ohm speaker into an amplifier expecting an eight ohm load doesn't work any better than trying to play a PAL (European format) videotape cartridge in an NTST (USA format) VHS player. Plug compatibility works as a family of interface standards.

It is useful for the framework to contain standards that tend to self-select plug-compatible components. For example, it is not so good that you can take a small nine-volt transformer intended for use as a battery eliminator with a calculator and plug it into your laptop battery eliminator connector which wants six volts. It would be helpful if stereo speaker components used connectors that physically distinguished between eight ohm and four ohm speakers—fewer blown speakers would be the result. Erector Set pieces will mate with anything that has a fairly common hole through which the set's bolts will fit, while Lego toys utilize a fairly distinctive framework that is unlikely to mate with anything non-Lego.

The purpose of the framework in a response-able system is to facilitate reconfiguration, reuse, and scalability. A framework should both constrain and enable these characteristics, bounding the set of potential configurations of an acceptable system while encouraging full exploration of the possibilities. In discussing the concepts and methods for "control in an age of empowerment,"[7] Robert Simmons includes beliefs and boundaries as two of the four mechanisms used to control the modern corporation, and refers to them as the "yin and yang that together create a dynamic tension . . . these systems translate limitless opportunity into a focused domain that employees and managers are encouraged to exploit actively. In combination, they establish direction, motivate and inspire, and protect against potentially damaging opportunistic behavior."

The framework for an organization is its culture, providing both constraints and enablers to guide the organization as it develops. A reasoned and articulate culture provides constraints that guide the organization away from behavior it wants to avoid and away from becoming something it does not want to be; and it provides enablers toward behaviors it wants to exhibit and toward the things it wants to become.

In a cultural framework, the values and beliefs that form the backbone are descriptions of the ties that bind the people together. Generally a strong cultural framework will attract and hold compatible members while rejecting people who don't fit. People are willful beings, however, and there is always the potential for transient alignment, good intentions, and self-delusion to mask an incompatibility for a while. Though plug compatibility with a cultural framework may not be as immediately obvious as in a physical framework like that of the Lego toy, once established it is highly robust and tenacious in the face of hostile environmental conditions. Where a Lego construction might lose some blocks when subjected to a fall or intense vibration, cultural bindings tend to increase their hold when the organization is attacked.

In the world of mergers and acquisitions, the failure rate is considered high. The general suspicion is that cultural mismatch is the problem, and that this problem generally remains unattended. Chrysler and Daimler merged in 1998 with the idea that success was likely since they had a strong cultural overlap: engineering excellence. On the surface, they both looked like a competency-focused culture—the external image that products from both companies had created in the market. Internally, however, Daimler operated as a control culture while Chrysler, relatively speaking, operated as a collaborative culture. Must one convert the other for harmony? Should the vanquisher convert the vanquished? Is there really a merger possibility or is it always acquisition underneath?

As to evolving a framework: part of the success of the Lego toy is a good initial framework design that required virtually no evolution for many years. Recently, however, a product manager equivalent saw fit to incorporate changes that brought motion and computer-programmed microprocessor control to Lego constructions, a move sure to extend its popularity and use beyond what it would have been otherwise. The framework now includes an additional interface very different from the physical bumps on the blocks: a radio link to a computer and a specification for downloading codes into a construction's microprocessor controller. Without someone responsible for this evolution possibility, Lego would diminish in relevance. In Chapter 6, a formal means for designating this *systems integrity management* function is discussed.

■ CONCLUSION

Our focus is on response-able systems. The design principles introduced in this chapter can enable this, sometimes with the sacrifice of seemingly optimal efficiency, but really only illustrating the trade-off between efficiency and the latitude to make a later decision. Adaptability is not the only performance factor to consider when designing products, business practices, processes, and organizational structures; but you should weigh it carefully because the cost of a nonresponsive system in an uncertain and dynamic operating environment can be very large, and even terminal.

These principles have been extracted from observations of systems that exhibit high adaptability. Applying them, however, doesn't guarantee an adaptable system. How each is used and how all are combined in any specific system is the designer's art form, and the source of competitive advantage. Developing good art form comes from study and practice. In Chapter 6, we examine how these principles are employed in a few systems, and Chapter 10 presents methods for developing this art form while attending to the business at hand.

■ NOTES

1. Kelly (1994), *Out of Control*.
2. In Kanter's classic, *The Change Masters* (1983), the first few chapters show in real case examples how people in the hierarchy, who make whimsical decisions about projects, without participating or communicating directly with the project personnel, in fact rob the organization of innovative thinkers and thinking, and push it toward riskless, safe, and lackluster project results. This lack of direct contact and involvement is what I label *stealth participation*.
3. Fitzinger and Lee (1997).
4. Pine (1993).
5. Stack (1992) and Case (1995), and (1997).
6. Texas Instruments sold off its defense segment to Raytheon in 1997. Reconfiguration and consolidation by Raytheon moved much of the TI production responsibilities. It is not known at this writing if the multimissile production concepts designed and operated by TI will be duplicated by Raytheon as they move responsibility for missile production in 1999 to another location.
7. Simons (1995), p. 86.

Chapter

Response-Able
Enterprise Systems

This chapter pulls together all the preceding material and depicts numerous system examples with a repetitive graphic format. These graphics establish a common pattern of reusable, reconfigurable, scalable (RRS) principles at work—a pattern that will be an important element of knowledge transfer concepts discussed in Chapter 10.

Building a response-able system has little value if it is not continuously managed to remain response able as the environment changes. The concept of *systems integrity management* is designed to achieve this goal.

■ WHO'S IN CHARGE?

➤ Directed and Self-Organized Dynamics

Self-organizing systems are receiving a lot of attention today, with a strong focus on business organizational systems, especially in the areas of teaming and organizational learning. At the root of successful self-organizing systems is a framework consisting of rules that govern interactions among the systems modules. Isaac Asimov, in his science fiction, enforced three rules to govern all interactions a thinking robot could have with a human being: (1) You must never harm a human being, (2) you must obey human beings unless this conflicts with rule one, and (3) you must protect yourself unless this conflicts with rules one or two. These three simple rules precluded the need for a policy and procedures manual and successfully addressed unanticipated situations.

Dee Hock is well known for his *chaordic* design of the VISA corporation,[1] which rapidly grew this company to the largest credit card entity in the world. The mechanism he employed was a framework of rules that encouraged virtually self-appointed membership and application innovation, instead of outlining the practices, procedures, and prices a card issuer must employ. Collins and Porras, in their landmark book *Companies Built to Last,*[2] focus on the role played by a well-defined yet simple corporate ideology in liberating employees to pursue corporate goals effectively under uncertain conditions.

In business systems whose modules include purposefully thinking/deciding people, the framework encourages and enables adaptability. It amounts to an ideological or cultural set of rules that establish boundaries and encourage the achievement of valued objectives—rules that cause undetermined things to happen and naturally select those that are right. However, when these people-based systems decide to make a change in one of the enterprise's inanimate systems, the design of that inanimate system will determine the ease or difficulty of that transformation, and the transformation will be directed by a person external to the inanimate system.

Response-able inanimate systems have people responsible for maintaining and directing that adaptability. Creating an RRS-based inanimate system involves three principal activities: (1) designing the framework standards, (2) defining the categories and nature of reusable modules, and (3) designating the responsibilities of "business-system engineers" charged with the creation and maintenance of pooled modules, the evolution of the framework standards, and the creation or reconfiguration of opportunity-triggered system solutions from pooled modules.

My expectations are that directed systems are the first approach for adaptability concepts within companies, across all four types of systems (product, process, practice, people). With time, more companies will experiment with, and feel comfortable with, self-organized autonomous module approaches.

➤ Systems Integrity Management

The RRS principle called *facilitated reuse* stated: Components of *response-able* systems are reusable/replicable; and responsibilities for ready reuse/replication and for management, maintenance, and upgrade of component inventory is specifically designated. Also recall that the RRS principle called *evolving standards (framework)* stated: Frameworks of response-able systems standardize intercomponent communication and interaction; define component compatibility; and are monitored/updated to accommodate old, current, and new components.

The key concept here is that frameworks and components of response-able systems can be no more static than the environment that they address. They must evolve and change at least in synch with, if not in anticipation of, the pace of environmental evolution and change.

The people or mechanisms responsible for the maintenance and evolution of components and frameworks are collectively called *systems integrity management*. When people are formally involved, descriptive titles such as business engineer, business operations engineer, business system engineer, and such, are suggested.

Ongoing systems integrity management involves four specific responsibilities:

1. *Framework Evolution Management.* The persons/groups/ mechanisms responsible for enforcing adherence to the architectural framework, for reviewing its continued effectiveness, and for changing its design when appropriate.

2. *Component Evolution Management.* The persons/groups/ mechanisms responsible for defining, developing, acquiring, and modifying reusable components plug compatible with the evolving framework.

3. *Component Inventory Management.* The persons/groups/ mechanisms responsible for cataloging and delivering reusable components, and for maintaining the repository from which they are drawn when needed.

4. *System Configuration Management.* The persons/groups/ mechanisms responsible for configuring/reconfiguring reusable components into functioning systems.

■ EXAMPLES OF RESPONSE-ABLE ENTERPRISE SYSTEMS

Our interest is in the full range of business systems, and in a design for these systems that will enable them to remain at least viable (if not dominant) in a constantly changing business environment. We are not concerned if their adaptation to the environment is caused by an internally self-organized response or an externally directed or manipulated reconfiguration. Our focus in this chapter is on an architecture and a set of design principles that enable adaptation regardless of how it occurs. Thus, we are not focused on complex *adaptive* systems, but on complex *adaptable* systems. This distinction is important in our realm of interest because business systems include those that are composed of thinking/deciding subsystems (a team of people) as well as those composed of unthinking/undeciding subsystems (a car configured from options for a specific customer).

We call any organization of interacting units a *system,* whether it is a product composed of options, a manufacturing process composed of workstations, a business practice composed of procedures, or an enterprise composed of functional departments. Table 6.1 includes additional examples from the four system categories.

The 10 RRS adaptable-design principles have been observed in both natural and human-made highly adaptable systems and organizations. They can be employed effectively in both inanimate directed configurations and in thinking/deciding self-organizing configurations. These are synergistic design guidelines that accommodate innovative interpretation and have amplified value when employed as a complete set.

➤ Response-Able Product

It is untrue that product confers benefits on its producers simply by virtue of an adaptable design. The change in Coca-Cola's formula, easily accomplished, did not prove beneficial as a successor to the original formula even after positive test marketing. One place where product design adaptability counts big is in markets where innovation happens frequently and market demand shifts to the latest innovation.

Table 6.1 Typical Systems in the Enterprise Environment

Product Systems	Process Systems	Practice Systems	People Systems
Machine tool	Manufacturing cell	Supply chain management	Knowledge management
Lego toy	Chemical production		
IT network	Purchasing	Project management	Company of departments
Legal contract	Auto assembly plant	Product development	
Personal computer			Community of practice
	Bank draft processing	Sales process	
		Strategic planning	Market of customers
			Team of people

The IBM Personal Computer is a classic example of real benefit deriving from a highly adaptable product design; with the Apple Macintosh as the contrast. The PC got its lead when the universally available Intel chip was chosen and the back plane (framework) specification was published. Any company could design and build compatible devices and interfaces (components), which led quickly to a much wider variety of product features being available in the PC world than in the closed Mac world. Microsoft's early encouragement and support of third-party application development had a similar effect on the range of software available for the PC. The PC's open framework eventually led to companies like Dell Computer and Gateway offering complete and custom systems assembled from readily available components produced by a large variety of vendors. And as Intel marched through its progression of faster/better chips, the framework evolved, but remained backward compatible. New machines could be purchased and older generation displays, modems, sound cards, scanners, and printers could be reused. Machines with problems could be stripped of their reusable parts for incorporation in other machines. Parts from an IBM machine could be used in a Gateway machine and vice versa. The customer benefited from reconfigurable machines and reusable parts, and the suppliers benefited from a larger and vibrant market. Scalability was a recognized problem, however, until the Universal Serial Bus (USB)[3] was introduced in 1999, finally lifting the frustrating limitation on the number of devices a single PC could connect with.

A major problem for aerospace and defense companies serving the U.S. government is the time it takes them to reach production after the technology design is frozen, while technology continues to advance. In many cases, a framework-based product design could permit new technology insertion almost up to production time. Perhaps even more useful, products designed this way would permit technology upgrade quickly and relatively inexpensively.

With more and more product features determined by software, reconfigurable product is likely to move heavily into real-time personalization. Think about walking up to a PC in the airport lounge, or at a customer's facility, or at your neighbor's house; and simply inserting a smart card that instantly configures all of its application-program human interfaces to be identical with your personal preferences. Or renting a car at the airport and having all of its programmable features conform to the ride and comfort and stored cell-phone numbers you expect. Or having a 55-mph maximum restriction on the activation card you give your teenager for the family car, and a warning message that announces at 11:30 P.M. that the car will cease to function in 30 minutes.

The Applied Materials' semiconductor-fabrication cluster machines introduced in earlier chapters employ an RRS product design. In Chapter 2, we reviewed key benefits of this design, and in Chapter 4 we looked at the critical types of change that this machine accommodates. Figure 6.1 graphically depicts this machine as a response-able system, showing how components can be combined for different needs. The depiction also lists critical change issues, identifies who is responsible for maintaining the system's reconfiguration integrity, and calls out a representative employment of the RRS principles. The comments in the RRS examples may not reflect actual usage of Applied's product, but rather what is possible with the product capability. This diagrammatic format, which we call a *response ability model,* captures and communicates the interesting characteristics of highly adaptable systems. The use of response ability models as knowledge transfer mechanisms is discussed later.

Applied's cluster tool approach recognizes that a fairly common set of utilities are required to support almost any of the various processes used in semiconductor fabrication. The cost and time to design a new generation of process machinery is cut considerably when all processes can reuse a single common utility base. This benefits both customer and vendor. Applied also gains useful production options when international sales require local content: The base unit can be manufactured locally without jeopardizing the quality issues associated with the high precision reaction chambers. Applied's customers can incrementally upgrade any platform one chamber at a time any time, mix or match chambers on a platform for redundancy and custom processing needs, reconfigure platforms to add new capability or pace growing demand, and swap-out dysfunctional units for fast malfunction recovery.

The RRS examples in Figure 6.1 are reasonably straightforward, but two merit discussion. The *Self-Organization* principle is satisfied with local real-time determination of the wafer path within a cluster. This may sound more like an example of distributed control, and a weak example of self-organizing behavior. It is not uncommon for system characteristics to satisfy more than one principle—there is some overlap among many of them. These are conceptual guidelines and subject to the interpretation of the designer or analyzer. I chose to envision the wafer (through an agent in the cluster controller, perhaps) deciding where to go next when it finishes one process in the cluster. Under these conditions, with a variety of wafers in a cassette, the path streams of all wafers through a cluster are indeterminate beforehand and emergent in real time. Stronger versions of self-organizing behavior will be evident in *practice and people* systems, where system units are thinking/deciding entities.

The other example to discuss is listed under *Evolving Standards*. It is clear here that the framework standards pertain only to individual intermodule interaction and not to larger configurations of modules. For example, the standardization rules do not restrict what modules must be grouped together, does not require that four process modules be present or active, nor do they impose any path sequence through a specified series of modules. The *evolving* part isn't reasonably applicable here—we are looking at a product family that is based on a technology generation. From one generation to another, the mechanical standards for a family of products are quite likely different to accommodate a different wafer size; while the mechanical standards within a product family are unlikely to accommodate process modules from different generations. Communication standards are eligible for some evolution within a product family's lifetime, but not anticipated. This example points out again that the principles are guidelines that may or may not be applicable under specific circumstances.

➤ Response-Able Process

The dies used to stamp auto body panels are a long lead item for automakers, often taking six months to a year to make, and even more sometimes. Designers try to release drawings as soon as possible to get a jump on this process. When the push to shorten car design time came in the 1990s, die makers at one auto company discovered something interesting—just because you can respond quickly doesn't mean you should. Early drawing release often leads to multiple engineering change orders (ECOs) while the die making is still in process. The die makers had been responding immediately, postponing additional work on the die until prior work was reworked in conformance with the latest ECO. Two steps forward, one step back. Pressure to speed up the process led to some historical analysis that prompted a different approach. Except in radical cases, ECOs are now stockpiled while the die continues through the entire process as originally planned, uninterrupted. Then the collected ECOs are analyzed and a single rework pass is made. The result saves months in the average total time. No more changing the changes.

Processes that give benefit from high response ability are typically those which must frequently produce a new or different product in an existing plant, or frequently produce a current product at a new location.

An interesting location example arises when a sale requires local content or regional production. The producer either needs to subcontract or partner out some or all of the production, or set up what I call a *Point of Delivery* (PoD) plant. Companies in the food service

Key Proactive Issues

Creation

- Create a new broad product family approximately every three years [tcs]

Improvement

- Manufacturing costs [s]
- Machine calibration time [s]
- Customer yield curve [s]

Migration

- Develop expertise in a new generation of science/technology approximately every three years [ts]

Modification

- Include new process capabilities in a machine when it becomes available [s]

Key Reactive Issues

Correction

- Time to return malfunctioning equipment to service, and effect that equipment outage has on total throughput [t]

Variation

- Equipment configurations and process options [cs]

Expansion

- Selectively expand/contract process-step capacity to meet (relative) long-term product mix changes [ts]

Reconfiguration

- Optional assembly procedures must meet local content needs of international contracts [qs]

Components

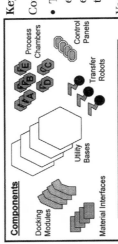

Process Chambers

Control Panels

Transfer Robots

Docking Modules

Utility Bases

Material Interfaces

Systems Integrity Management

Framework: Product manager
Components: Engineering
Inventory: Product manager
Configuration: Installation crew

System Examples

Dedicated Parallel Processing Step

Variable Steps Under Constant Vacuum

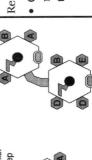

	Scalable / Reusable	
Self-Contained Units (Components) – Material interfaces, transfer robots, process modules, utility bases, docking modules, and user controls are independent units.		**Evolving Standards (Framework)** – Standardization focused on individual module interconnect only: mechanical coupling, communication protocols, and utility connections.
Plug Compatibility – Common human, mechanical, electrical, gas, vacuum, hydraulic, and control system interfaces.		**Redundancy and Diversity** – Machine utility bases are all identical, duplicate processing chambers can be mounted on same base or different bases.
Facilitated Reuse – Processing modules may be mixed or matched within a cluster. Machine manufacturer extends/replicates process module family. Customer manages reuse of all modules.		**Elastic Capacity** – 1–4 process modules per cluster. Docking modules can interconnect clusters into super-clusters. Transport bay can interconnect clusters and super-clusters without limit.
	Reconfigurable	
Flat Interaction – Scheduler in one base unit may access process history data for a process module on another base—perhaps to correct for a wafer's prior process steps		**Distributed Control and Information** – Process history and tight-loop control located in process module, traveling with it when redeployed. Cluster controller manages macro-process and material transfer.
Deferred Commitment – Process modules custom configured when installed. New process modules added when new capability required. User control modules are custom configurable for proprietary processing.		**Self-Organization** – Wafer path within cluster determined in real time according to the availability of appropriate process modules.

We use this diagrammatic format, which we call a response ability model, to capture and communicate the interesting characteristics of highly adaptable systems. More is said about the use of response ability models as knowledge transfer mechanisms in Chapter 10. Comments made under the ten RRS principles above are representative examples of what is possible as a result of the actual Applied Materials Cluster Machine system design.

(Metric focus legend: t = time of change, c = cost of change, q = quality of change, s = scope of change)

Figure 6.1   Product System Response Ability Model: Cluster Machine

business with flexible product options (e.g., those involved in the "designer" bread business) have pioneered interesting techniques here. Empire Bakery Equipment,[4] a large-line bakery equipment seller, features multipurpose equipment and reconfigurable process plans for making anything from bagels to rolls to breads by reusing or reconfiguring much the same equipment.

The Kelsey-Hayes production process discussed in earlier chapters employs an RRS design. Chapter 2 reviewed key benefits of this design, and Chapter 4 looked at the critical types of change that this process accommodates. Figure 6.2 depicts the process as a *response ability model,* showing how process components are combined for different needs and identifying representative usage of the RRS principles. The comments in the RRS examples reflect potential made possible by the process design, and don't necessarily reflect current operating practice at Kelsey-Hayes.

Servicing the automotive automatic braking system (ABS) market, Kelsey-Hayes saw the value in responding faster to customer new-product needs, the necessity to handle shorter production runs, and the disparity between forecast and actual product demand. The old custom-made transfer-line approach could not meet the needs of a shrinking product life cycle and uncertain production quantities. They analyzed the general nature of ABS design and determined that general purpose flexible machining capability could satisfy the manufacturing requirements and provide an ability to reconfigure production capacities in real time.

That you could manufacture ABS with flexible machines came as no surprise. That you could do it economically was the new twist. One of the principal reasons the economics became favorable, besides the increasing difficulty in gaining transfer-line ROI, was the ability to resize production capacity, either up or down, to match uncertain and changing customer production demands. This was achieved primarily by using identical machines throughout the factory and by being able to move them quickly from one customer's cell to another's.

It is difficult to single out one or only a few of the RRS principles that provide the response ability enjoyed by Kelsey-Hayes. The restriction to a single common machine type as a framework standard is key, as is the high redundancy of all components and the elastic capacity of a cell's configuration. Programmed self-organizing controls that defer resource commitments until a part is ready for machining facilitate changing configurations and having cells accept or lose resources gracefully and quickly.

Systems integrity management, in principle, involves three different and specific people: the general manager, the operations manager, and the customer account manager, though Kelsey-Hayes may not recognize these assignments explicitly. Because the system is in fact the entire production facility, the responsibility for evolving the framework falls on the general manager, regardless of how it may be delegated. Though a customer account engineer may need to negotiate with various operations people to have a cell resized, the responsibility for a suitable configuration lies with the general manager. And again, regardless of delegation, operations management is responsible for the maintenance and availability of usable components.

➤ Response-Able Practice

Some things that sound highly adaptable at first blush turn out to be woeful disasters in the end. In 1993, Jay Chiat of Chiat/Day, a top-of-the-line advertising agency, embarked on a grand idea to tear down the walls of the workplace and usher in the era of the virtual office.[5] This was an idea whose time had come. The press touted it loudly, and many of us knew he had hit on something compelling. The idea was superb: Eliminate the personal cubicle and office, and eliminate single-person dedicated equipment like phones, laptops, and desks. Observation showed that these dedicated resources were too often idle, especially in the emerging road warrior business environment. Better to tear down the walls and build some really interesting group spaces, private nooks, and meeting rooms that could be occupied by anyone at whim. Everyone got a locker to store personal stuff. The computer eliminated the need for filing cabinets and paper of any kind. When people needed to be at the office, they would check out a laptop that could be plugged into any one of the copious data ports, and a portable phone that was radio linked through a ceiling grid.

Jay Chiat was the keeper of the framework and systems integrity for this RRS business practice, but somehow he didn't think to evolve it as difficulties became evident with this experiment. While declaring and strongly enforcing the requirement for a paperless office, he made no accommodation for the fact that the creative staff worked with story boards and the client contracts came on paper. When too many people showed up at the office too many times, an acute shortage of phones and laptops became evident—which went unresolved to the point that people would come in before 6:00 A.M. to check out and hide equipment before returning home for another few hours of shut-eye. Eventually people used the trunks of their cars as filing cabinets, and the parking lot became an extension of the office. Turf wars erupted as some homesteaded the few closed-door meeting rooms. The disaster was evident to all but Chiat himself, who sold the company and walked away as it quickly returned to the old comfortable

Key Proactive Issues

Creation

- Design/install new-part production capability frequently and quickly [tcq]

Improvement

- Customers are demanding a reduction in short run costs [t]

Migration

- Moving from transfer line technology to next generation flexible machines brings different concepts [cs]

Modification

- Higher product change frequency requires production process modification rather than replacement [tcs]

Key Reactive Issues

Correction

- Cost of lost production due to equipment malfunction and repair time [tc]

Variation

- Prototype runs are more frequent, and require more varied machining options [tcs]

Expansion

- Expansion and contraction of production capacity must accommodate unforecastable demand [tcs]

Reconfiguration

- Salvage and reuse old production stages in new production configurations [cs]

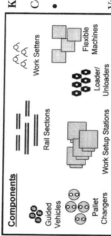

Components

Guided Vehicles · Rail Sections · Work Setters
Pallet Changers · Work Setup Stations · Flexible Machines
Loader/Unloaders

Systems Integrity Management

Framework: General manager
Components: Operations manager
Inventory: Operations manager
Configuration: Customer account engineer

System Examples

3 Station Cell

6-8 Station Seasonal Cell

Reusable / Scalable	
Self-Contained Units (Components) – Flexible machines, rail sections, work-setting stations, loader/unloaders, pallet changers.	**Evolving Standards (Framework)** – General manager responsible for component commonality, and interconnect standards for mechanical coupling, communication protocols, and utility connections.
Plug Compatibility – Common human, mechanical, electrical, and coolant system interfaces. Common intermodule mechanical interfaces.	**Unit Redundancy and Diversity** – Cells have multiples of each component, all cells made from same types of components, machines have full work functionality.
Facilitated Reuse – Machines do not require pits or special foundations, and are easy to move. Account managers with P&L responsibility add/subtract resources as needed. Operations manager maintains resource pool.	**Elastic Capacity** – Cell can accommodate any number of machines limited only by physical space for rail extension. A part can be made in multiple cells. One cell can make multiple parts.

Reconfigurable	
Flat Interaction – Complete autonomous part machining, direct machine-repository program download negotiation.	**Distributed Control and Information** – Part programs downloaded to machines, machine history kept in machine controller and accompanies machine as it changes location, machines ask for work when ready.
Deferred Commitment – Machines and material scheduled in real time, downloaded part programs serve individual work requirements.	**Self-Organization** – Cell control software dynamically changes work routing for status changes and for new, removed, or down machines on the fly.

Figure 6.2 Process System Response Ability Model: Machining Cell

The representative reactive/proactive change issues are those perceived by the process owner/user making an initial transition from a fixed transfer-line configuration to a flexible cellular configuration. In time, a different set of issues emerge once the cellular configuration is the base perspective and the user expectations change. The examples of RRS system principles do not necessarily reflect actual usage of the Kelsey Hayes machining cells, but rather what is possible with the cellular configuration design.

(Metric focus legend: t = time of change, c = cost of change, q = quality of change, s = scope of change)

173

tradition. Perhaps some good could have come from this experiment if the kinks had been attended to.

The LSI Logic practice discussed in Chapter 2 employs an RRS design, and is depicted in Figure 6.3. Most of the operational aspects of the order fulfillment system are managed by LSI's logistics planning group in Hong Kong—a location convenient to many of the subcontractors employed as system components. LSI's resources bid on order fulfillment work, and they may well bid a different price and delivery ability each time even if the work is identical. Their bids may vary based on their own plant loading at the requested time. Planners in the Hong Kong then configure order fulfillment systems based on the price and availability offered in the bids.

Another form of self-organization is present as well. Subcontractor improved performance is self-motivated as they all see the performance metrics for everyone in the group and know that a low index will cost them work and price concessions. Self-organizing quality improvement programs among subcontractors is encouraged by a set of de facto rules on how LSI allocates work and values costs. These improvement programs also benefit from final test equipment that LSI provides to the subcontractors for free. These expensive machines provide immediate feedback at the end of the line.

In the beginning, LSI handled testing the traditional way: Final product was shipped from the assembly house to an LSI facility that tested for quality. The three days involved in shipping and receiving finished product insured that any systemic problems discovered at final test would have at least three days of bad product in the test queue. The principle of distributed control was employed to put both the information and the control at the point of maximum knowledge, sensitizing the subcontractor to quality improvement. Though LSI pays for the machines used in final test at the subcontractor's plant, it allows the subcontractor to use the machine free of charge on non-LSI work—all in the interest of encouraging good practice habits.

► **Response-Able People**

In the early 1990s, Motorola was in high demand as a benchmark example of new teaming concepts. Not only were they a committed leader in teaming implementation, but a showcase of success as well. Underneath it all were some very evident RRS principles at work, hallmarks of teaming: *self-contained units, distributed control,* and *self-organization.* People at Motorola had read the book on teaming and taken it to heart, or so it seemed.

This strong control culture company appeared to have transitioned into a collaborative culture (Figure 1.3) almost overnight. One showcase example was the way the company encouraged teams to improve their teaming effectiveness—a mandate for *self-organization*. There was even a clear responsibility for *evolving standards* that dreamed up ways to spread good concepts among teams, the ultimate in team sharing.

Motorola, like most companies, employed a recognition incentive program in sales, sending salespeople with the best results to an annual conference in some resortish part of the world. Why not recognize and reward good teaming—results in a similar fashion, no matter what part of the company they come from show the company's commitment to new organizational practices, provide a self-organizing improvement program, and give engineers and production people an opportunity for recognition and reward?

Motorola is a large company, and lots of teams had good ideas to share. The teaming framework evolved to include a set of annual elimination events, where teams with hot ideas would present them in local, regional, national, and global runoffs, vying for the highest recognition from their peers. The competition to encourage self-development of good ideas sounded good, but then, according to one HR team specialist at Motorola, the competition became the focus— and the very intent of teaming was contradicted and destroyed. And according to one engineering manager, when times started getting tough for Motorola in the later 1990s, things reverted back to the traditional command-and-control culture that flatly ignored empowerment concepts.

What happened at Motorola was not a failure of empowerment and teaming concepts, but rather a failure to fit the concepts to the underlying culture,[6] or to move the culture successfully from the control quadrant into the collaborative quadrant, finishing the business practice design. Teams can deal with adversity if they are designed to do so. Motorola was forging ahead in the late 1980s and early 1990s, and team practice design never employed anything like an RS Analysis that considered the possibility of reactionary times.

The Motorola example can be contrasted with Great Harvest, a bakery franchiser that has added a new model to the world of franchising.[7] Unlike McDonald's, no two Great Harvest bakeries are likely to be the same in architecture or product list. What you will find are dedicated, friendly people with a distinctive enjoyment-of-life style, a commitment to produce healthy and wholesome bakery products while having fun at it, a commitment to local community service, and most likely a high percentage of whole wheat products. Behind the scenes is an active community of practice fostered by the franchiser and nurtured with an Internet infrastructure. Once a bakery can demonstrate its commitment to common values and mastery of

Key Proactive Issues

Creation
• Quickly configure production chain for each order customized for required cycle time [t]

Improvement
• Outsource quality [s]
• Outsource cycle time [s]
• Outsource on-time [q]

Migration
• Move from fabless to foundry production, with a technology leadership strategy [tq]

Modification
• Add new packaging styles as needed [tqs]
• Combine final testing with assembly location [q]

Key Reactive Issues

Correction
• Work-in-process problems at handoff to next outsource that lengthen total cycle time [t]

Variation
• Packaging families and styles within families provide over 100 popular options [s]

Expansion
• Cyclical market increases and decreases need for capacity greatly [tqs]

Reconfiguration
• Reconfigure a committed production chain when customer holds make an alternate chain more desirable [tq]

Components

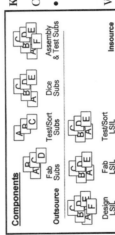

Outsource: Fab Subs, Test/Sort Subs, Dice Subs, Assembly & Test Subs

Insource: Design LSIL, Fab LSIL, Test/Sort LSIL

Systems Integrity Management

Framework: HQ planning group
Components: Hong Kong subcontractor group
Inventory: Hong Kong subcontractor group
Configuration: Hong Kong subcontractor group

System Examples

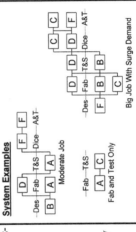

Des–Fab–T&S–Dice–A&T
Moderate Job

Fab–T&S
Fab and Test Only

Big Job With Surge Demand

Self-Contained Units (Components) – Fabrication, assembly, and test capabilities are distinct, separable organizations, some internal, some external.	**Reusable** / **Scalable**	**Evolving Standards (Framework)** – Planning group establishes/maintains guidelines and strategies for compatible resources; evolving, for instance, requirement for on-site LSI test engineers.
Plug Compatibility – Outsources meet common qualification standards, have common electronic "supplier technical network" interface, and test with common test equipment.		**Unit Redundancy and Diversity** – Resource pool contains multiple resources for each individual order fulfillment requirement.
Facilitated Reuse – Hong Kong management group qualifies new resources as needed, maintains qualified pool, and assembles fulfillment chains on a per order basis.		**Elastic Capacity** – Virtually no systemic limits exist on the number or mix of insource and outsource resource options.
Flat Interaction – An electronic "supplier technical network" encourages direct interaction among resources to resolve mutual problems.	**Reconfigurable**	**Distributed Control and Information** – Testing done at outsource by outsource, and data used for outsource-directed improvement programs.
Deferred Commitment – Resources in an order fulfillment chain are not committed until the order is received.		**Self-Organization** – Order fulfillment chains are established with an open bidding process that considers capacity availability, quality record, and cost optimization.

Figure 6.3   Practice System Response Ability Model: JIT Order Fulfillment Chains

The LSI order fulfillment chain concept has evolved over the years with some change in guiding principles. Early use saw more outsourced fabrication, more diversity among outsources, and larger numbers of resources in the pool; while recent use relies on more internal fabrication, testing located at assembly houses, and fewer outsources with tighter predictability of capacity availability, quality, and on-time delivery.

(Metric focus legend: t = time of change, c = cost of change, q = quality of change, s = scope of change)

Key Proactive Issues

Creation

- Develop new knowledge and skills of continuously emerging technologies and markets [tqs]

Improvement

- Leadership in emerging markets requires faster knowledge development [s]

Migration

- Replace knowledge and skills of existing markets/technology with new knowledge and skills [tqs]

Modification

- Add nontraditional capability and adjust the company self-image [s]

Key Reactive Issues

Correction

- Early recognition that new markets/technologies are not the right ones to pursue [t]

Variation

- Employee interests and background knowledge necessary to grasp diverse new technologies [s]

Expansion

- Increase the number of employees who share a body of knowledge [tcs]

Reconfiguration

- Reconfigure resources and business units to pursue new business development [ts]

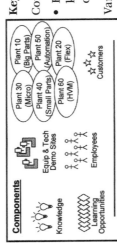

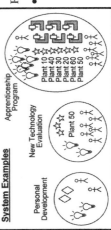

	Scalable / Reusable	
Self-Contained Units (Components)—Employees, knowledge, learning opportunities, and equipment are highly mobile among business units; and customers of one often become customers of another.		**Evolving Standards (Framework)**—Strategic (cultural) guidelines and HR programs reviewed yearly by president and executive strategic group.
Plug Compatibility—Different business units share common corporate culture, common HR department and programs, and common apprenticeship training.		**Unit Redundancy and Diversity**—Employees screened for general curiosity and breadth of interests, not for like-mindedness.
Facilitated Reuse—CTO for technology/knowledge; HR for employees and learning opportunities; marketing for customers; president and strategy group for plant focus.		**Elastic Capacity**—Inherent employee interest in learning provides large pool of eligible and competent learners when knowledge must be deployed wide scale rapidly.
Reconfigurable		
Flat Interaction—Direct collaboration in pursuit of knowledge and competency is unrestricted by rank or hierarchical bounds.		**Distributed Control and Information**—Employees empowered to seek learning opportunities, tuition reimbursed w/o conditions, business units empowered to educate/train w/o budget limitations.
Deferred Commitment—Employees enter apprenticeship program without selecting home-plant until multiyear cross-plant program is completed.		**Self-Organization**—Employees typically take the initiative for determining what skills and knowledge to seek next.

The competency acquisition system at Remmele includes a lot of sub-systems, and is difficult to represent comprehensively within the graphic format constraints here. For instance, the employee is not always the only factor involved in configuring a knowledge development program, sometimes management and/or the HR director is responsible for the configuration management activity; and components of the apprenticeship program might be shown as well if space permitted. The intent here is to show the nature of response-able system representation in a consistent format across many types of systems, so that common patterns contributing to the response ability become evident.

(Metric focus legend: t = time of change, c = cost of change, q = quality of change, s = scope of change)

Figure 6.4 Peopled System Response Ability Model: Competency Acquisition

fundamental business and production concepts, it is encouraged to experiment and collaborate with the other bakery owners. They find alternate sources of raw materials, they invent new business operating practices, they discover new process and equipment opportunities, they collaborate on new product ideas, and they reinvent the business constantly. Great Harvest screens for compatible candidates, gets them started with the fundamentals, supports an active collaborative community of practice infrastructure, and gets the hell out of the way.

Teaming at Remmele, the company we introduced in Chapter 2, comes from even less overt planning than that at Great Harvest. At Remmele, you won't find infrastructure in place to foster and nurture teaming, yet you will find the strongest and most effective teams, based on unmitigated trust and shared values, emerging as a result of corporate culture.

You'll also find high competency at Remmele. They are generally the first and always one of the best at whatever the latest machining markets demand in the way of technology. Though this owes much to the cultural environment, it is also very much dependent on a focused infrastructure. The RRS examples shown in Figure 6.4 depict Remmele's system for acquiring competency.

■ CASE STORIES AS MODELS

What follows is a very real story of a highly adaptable business system. This story, coupled with its accompanying response ability model (Figure 6.5), forms what is called a *metaphor model*—a means for conveying knowledge and insight about RRS principles to others through analogy and pattern. When those *others* are people who work close enough to the system to be aware of its value and performance, this metaphor model carries the additional distinction of being a *local metaphor.* The value and use of local metaphors is discussed in Chapter 10.

➤ Assembly Lines—Built Just in Time

Look through Fred Mauck's eyes for a moment. You work in a GM stamping plant outside Pittsburgh that specializes in after-model-year body parts.* Your principal customer is GM's Service Parts Organization. They might order '73 Chevelle hoods quantity 50, '84 Chevy

---

* Portions of the description of GM's JIT assembly process appear in the 2001 issue of Maynard's *Industrial Engineering Handbook.*

Impala right fenders quantity 100, or '89 Cutlass Supreme right front doors quantity 300. Your plant stamps the sheet metal and then assembles a deliverable product. Small lots, high variety, hard-to-make-a-buck stuff.

Every new part that the plant takes on came from a production process at an original equipment manufacturer (OEM) plant that occupied some thousands of square feet on the average; and the part was made with specialized equipment optimized for high-volume runs and custom built for that part geometry. To stamp a new deck lid (trunk door) part you bring in a new die set—maybe six or seven dies, each the size of a full grown automobile, but weighing considerably more. And you bring in assembly equipment from an OEM line that might consist of a hemmer to fold the edges of the stamped metal, perhaps a prehemmer for a two-stage process, dedicated welding apparatus for joining the inner lid to the outer lid, adhesive equipment for applying mastic at part-specific locations, piercer units for part-specific holes, and automated custom material-handling equipment for moving work between process workstations.

You got a call a few weeks ago that said your plant will start making the Celebrity deck lids, and production has to start in 21 days. Not too bad; sometimes you only have four days. For new business like this, your job is to get the necessary assembly equipment from the OEM plant, reconfigure the equipment and process to fit your plant, and have people ready to produce quality parts in the next three weeks. Others are responsible for the die sets and stamping end of the production process.

In the past five years, you've recycled some 800,000 square feet of floor space in OEM plants for new model production. At this point, you have assembly equipment and process for some 1,000 different parts—but no extra floor space ever came with any of it.

And no extra floor space materialized in your plant either. Good thing you haven't needed it—the core competency here is rapid new-part starts, and small-lot, high-variety production—in a business that is traditionally based on high-volume economics, and you've learned to do it without the usual capital budget. Eight years at this has evolved some unique techniques, and a pretty unique culture as well.

You don't do this by yourself. You're a team leader who may use almost anyone from anywhere in the plant. At this point, almost everyone is qualified to help bring in new work. Surviving under these conditions has developed a can-do/let-me-at-it attitude almost everywhere, and a shared understanding of how to do it.

Eight years ago, the plant went to a single job classification in production, cross-training everyone on everything: A press operator

Key Proactive Issues

Creation

• Designing short-run assembly lines for new parts that come with long-run tooling [t]

Improvement

• Productivity of limited space while increasing part variety [s]

Migration

• Production of non-GM parts with non-GM tooling [qs]

Modification

• Absorb employees from closed/downsized GM plants with different union work rules into cross-trained Production Team Member positions [ts]

Key Reactive Issues

Correction

• Union refusals to accommodate necessary work rule changes [cs]

Variation

• High part production variety [s]
• Time available for new line design [t]
• New parts to accommodate with the JIT system [s]

Expansion

• Absorb growing part variety [s]
• Absorb growing inventory of tooling [s]

Reconfiguration

• Short-run assembly line construction/tear-down [t]

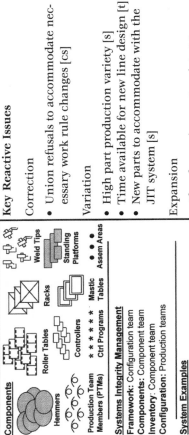

Components

Production Team Members (PTMs) — Hemmers — Roller Tables — Controllers — ★ ★ ★ ★ ★ ★ Ctrl Programs — Racks — Mastic Tables — Weld Tips — Standing Platforms — ● ● ● Assem Areas

Systems Integrity Management

Framework: Configuration team
Components: Component team
Inventory: Component team
Configuration: Production teams

System Examples

P41 Deck Lid System

Area B

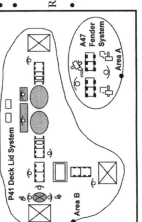

A47 Fender System

Area A

Reusable / Scalable	
Self-Contained Units (Components) • Hemmers • Racks • PTMs • Roller tables • Weld tips • Programs • Mastic tables • Controllers	**Evolving Standards (Framework)**—The framework configuration team eventually decided to strip unused legacy items from hemmers, and to add TDA lifters to Area A utility grid.
Plug Compatibility—Everything carry/roll/fork portable, common piping/wiring, quick disconnect fittings, no integrated controllers, standard controller interface/programs.	**Unit Redundancy and Diversity**—Eight identical controllers, cross-trained production team, diversity in roller/mastic tables, weld guns, standing platforms, racks, weld tips, and assembly areas.
Facilitated Reuse • Management and Union manage PTM cross-training • Component team manages all other components • Production teams manage system configurations	**Elastic Capacity**—Frequently used components are pooled locally, with separate warehousing available for unlimited inventory growth and rarely used components.

Reconfigurable

Flat Interaction • PTMs free to make real time process changes • Communication encouraged among tradesmen, engineers, supervisors, and customers	**Distributed Control and Information** • PTMs make real time decisions on process configuration improvements and changes • Operation sequence sheet attached to hemmer
Deferred Commitment • Assembly lines configured just-in-time for production • New-part acquisition/transfer team is not designated until a transfer opportunity requires an action	**Self-Organization**—People take initiative in solving problems and making operating improvements because risk is encouraged and failure expected/accepted.

Figure 6.5 Response Ability Model: JIT Assembly Systems

This example is taken from GM's Pittsburgh metal fabrication plant, where after-model-year auto-body service parts are stamped and assembled in a high-variety, small-quantity production environment. They might get an order for 1973 Chevelle hoods quantity 50, 1984 Chevy Impala right fenders quantity 100, or 1989 Cutlass Supreme right front doors quantity 300. The production economics and volumes are very different than that of model-year high volume plant processes, requiring a different production technique. Even more unique are the problems caused by the high variety and quantity of production fixtures and equipment inherited from the original production lines.

(Metric focus legend: t = time of change, c = cost of change, q = quality of change, s = scope of change)

one day might change dies as well, the next day work in the assembly area building hoods in the morning and fenders in the afternoon — and the following day visit another plant to review a piece of equipment or part to determine how to bring it back.

For this new business, Jim Lesniewski wanted to do the initial recon. He went on the last trip, too, experimenting with his video camera. Now he thinks he's ready to do a perfect taping job. He got the idea himself while trying to bring several jobs at once back from another GM facility. This environment encourages self-initiative.

In addition to taping the operational assembly process, this time he added close-ups of key equipment pieces. In the debrief review, everyone saw the same thing at the same time, there was almost no debate over what to bring back and what to ignore, and you got a jump on the equipment modifications by seeing what was needed in advance. Some time ago, the value of having a good cross section represented in these reviews became evident: Nobody gets surprised; everyone shares their knowledge; and when the equipment arrives, the modification team is prepared.

There are two keys at this stage: knowing what to bring back and knowing what modifications to make.

This new deck lid would be handled by bringing back the hemmer only; while ignoring the mastic application machine, two welding robots, the welding fixtures, two press piercers, the shuttles, the press welders, and the three automated material handling fixtures. Basically, it would mean bringing back a footprint of 200 square feet from a process that covered 2,500 square feet. The rest would go to salvage disposition while the hemmer would go to "hemmer heaven" — that place in your plant where some 200 different hemmers hang out until needed.

That you only need the hemmer is where a key part of the plant's unique core competency comes to play. Rather than build a growing variety of product on some sort of omnipotent universal assembly line that grows to accommodate next year's unpredictable new business as well as the last 10-to-20 years of legacy parts, this plant builds a custom assembly line for each product — and builds that assembly line just before it runs a batch of, say, 300 hoods. When the hoods are done, you tear down the assembly line and build another one for fenders, perhaps, on the same floor space, and then run 500 or so fenders. Tear that down and build the next, and so forth. The same people that built the hoods build the fenders, and the deck lids, and the doors, and the . . . and tomorrow some of them will be running a press, changing press dies, or running off to evaluate the next incoming equipment opportunity.

Necessity is the mother of invention, and the driving force here is the unrelenting requirement to increase product variety, without increasing costs or making capital investments. But fundamentally, for assembly, the scarcest resource is floor space.

Yes—a newly built customized assembly line for each and every small-batch run, every time, just in time.

The plant has six assembly areas, and can build any part in any of those areas. Usually you like to do the deck lids in the "A" area, though, as it has the most flexibility for welding.

While you were waiting for that new hemmer to arrive, you designed the process system configuration. Betty Garrison and Denny Hanko usually do this as a team. Once they figure out which assembly modules are best and how they should be spaced, Betty and Denny put together a configuration sheet for the assembly system by cutting and pasting standard icons for each module and running it through the copy machine. It wasn't always this easy, but you've learned a lot over the years. You build these assembly systems according to the one-page configuration diagram in Betty's three-ring binder, in real-time from reusable components. Components are easily moved into place, and they share common interface standards and quick disconnects. On the average, it takes about 15 minutes to break down the last assembly system and configure the next one.

Rule 1: Nothing is attached to the floor permanently. If it can't be lifted and carried easily by anybody, it will have wheels on it, or as a last resort, fork-lift notches.

A typical deck lid assembly sequence might hem the outer skin, mastic some cushioning material to the inner skin, then weld a brace into place, and finally weld the inner skin to the outer skin in 30 places. In the process, the material has to be turned over once and some gauging is done. The assembly system configuration might call for two three-foot roller tables in the front to receive the inner and outer pieces—think of these as hospital gurneys, on wheels, with rollers on top so the "patient" can be rolled across the table to the next station when the designated operation is complete. Next in line for the outer skin is the hemmer—it's on wheels, too, and it's quick-connected to a standard controller off on the side out of the way. Yes, the controller is on wheels too. The outer skin is lifted into the hemmer with the aid of an overhead TDA Buddy, one advantage of doing lids in the "A" area: Two TDA Buddies hang from the ceiling grid. When deck lids are assembled in another area, a variant of the roller table is used that includes lifting aids. After hemming, inner and outer skins move to four-foot roller tables under the welding guns. The configuration sheet shows how many guns are active, where to position them, and which tip variant to install. All told there might be 12 simple icons on the sheet positioned in a *suggested* geometry.

A hemmer is a specialized piece of machinery. When it comes to this plant, it loses most of its specialness, and becomes plug compatible with all the other modules in the just-in-time assembly family. Importantly, the integrated controls are removed and quick-connect ports are installed to interface with the one standard electronic/hydraulic controller used for all hemmers. It is modified if necessary to work with one of the six standard control programs. Maybe a seventh will be added some day, but six has covered all needs so far. Finally, the setup sequence for the hemmer is typed up and attached to its side. Better there than in a file drawer.

Hemmers are pooled awaiting their time in the assembly area, each one being part specific. Other pools hold variants of standardized modules that have use in multiple assembly systems: There are 12 types of roller tables, 2 types of quick-connect weld guns, 3 types of weld tips, 1 standard controller type, 6 standard downloadable controller programs, and other reusable standardized items.

Whatever the configuration sheet shows is quickly carried, rolled, or forked into place, quick-connected or downloaded if required, and ready for action. The assembly area has an overhead utility framework that enables the adaptability below; by providing tracked weld-gun hookups, quick-connect power and air, light, and water. The operating atmosphere is not unlike the hospital operating room, except patient throughput is a lot faster, fast enough in this case to satisfy service parts economics.

It is common for production team members to make real-time changes to the configuration when they find a better way—better is better, and everyone knows what that means.

Rule 2: People rule. These assembly systems take advantage of the fact that people think better and adjust better than automated positioning devices, cast-in-stone configuration sheets, and ivory-tower industrial engineers. People bring flexibility when they are enabled and supported, but not constrained, by mechanical and electronic aids.

■ CONCLUSION

This chapter introduced a graphic representation for conveying the essence of responsible systems as repeatable patterns, and built that graphic into a metaphor model. Though this pattern representation may in fact be a simplistic communication of a response-able system, it focuses those who are often exposed to it on the essence of the design principles and develops understanding at the insightful level.

■ NOTES

1. See Hock (1997). Dee Hock is responsible for the *chaordic* organizational structure of VISA, which propelled it into the largest credit card company in the world. He has since become both a student and mentor of this organizational architecture, and is one of 30 living laureates of the Business Hall of Fame. Hock coined the word *chaord* for organisms, organizations, and systems that harmoniously exhibit characteristics of both order and chaos.
2. See Collins (1994).
3. Texas Instruments had a 1999 copyrighted USB (Universal Serial Bus) specification available for download in early 2000 from www.ti.com/sc/docs/msp/usb/mainpage.htm.
4. Empire Bakery Equipment, Hempstead, New York, www.empirebake.com, info@empirebake.com.
5. Berger (1999), "Lost in Space."
6. The concept of fitting would-be new corporate practices to the corporate culture was discussed in Chapter 1 in terms of the work presented in Schneider (1994).
7. Great Harvest Franchising, Inc., 28 South Montana, Dillon, Montana 59725, http://www.greatharvest.com.

Chapter 7

Systematic Design of Response-Able Systems

This chapter shows what RRS design principles look like when they are applied, and teaches methodologies for learning and employing these principles. Here we employ the concepts and tools introduced earlier in the book to design a core competency knowledge management practice. This systematic approach introduces a new tool for framework development that explicitly highlights the activities which manage system integrity.

■ SYSTEMATIC DESIGN

Now we outline a systematic design process that provides guidelines for new designers. With experience comes a more intuitive approach, an example of which we explore later. We will walk through the systematic process first, and summarize the steps when we are finished.

As described earlier, GM's Pittsburgh plant has a strong, unique, and evident competency at designing highly reconfigurable, highly flexible production systems. A workshop team of approximately 10 people interested in discovering and applying RRS principles visited there in 1997, joined by an equal number of people from plant management.[1] The purpose of the workshop was to understand the key design rules used by plant personnel for constructing highly adaptable systems, and relate them to the RRS principles; and then develop a method for articulating and packaging the plant's design rules for effective communication to all employees. When the plant manager invited us in, he told us that he wanted a training program—for both new hires and existing employees—that would spread this competency quickly and effectively throughout the entire workforce at the insightful visceral level rather than as a rote response to a fixed set of rules.

The General Motors metal-fabrication plant stamps and assembles after-model-year auto body parts, but we aren't concerned about things unique to metal fabrication, or even small-lot, high-variety production—our business practice design is generally applicable anywhere. For unrelated reasons unimportant here, the design was never put into practice at GM; but the process discussed next was employed to create the design. Early parts of the process occurred during the collaborative workshop generating key design ideas that were later refined and detailed.

➤ Preparation Prior to Design Work

In preparation for the design task, all participants were asked to read three papers beforehand, two of which proved instrumental: "What Really Makes Factories Flexible" by David Upton, and "How Bell Labs Creates Star Performers" by Robert Kelley and Janet Caplan.[2] The purpose of this reading assignment was to stimulate relevant discussion and develop some common knowledge among a highly diverse set of participants.

The Upton paper reported on a study that had shown factory flexibility most strongly correlated to employee appreciation for the values of flexibility, rather than to automation technology of any kind. The Kelly and Caplan paper described a two-stage process Bell Labs had successfully employed to (1) identify and capture what it was that made some engineers highly productive, and then (2) to transfer this knowledge to other engineers in such a way that many developed a new and lasting productivity competency. These papers were reviewed at the beginning of the workshop in group discussion, developing a shared understanding of the content of the papers as background group knowledge. During the review, no attempt was made to relate these papers to the upcoming design effort.

Next, the group analyzed two highly adaptable in-plant processes that exhibited the core competency of interest. Analysis of one of those produced the JIT assembly example in Chapter 6, complete with identified change issues and the employment of RRS principles. The purpose of the analysis work was to develop and exercise a common understanding of the tools and concepts that would then be employed in the design activity. Importantly, the GM plant participants gained new insight into the practices they knew and respected; they could see the fundamental principles that were responsible for delivering that characteristic of high adaptability.

➤ Establishing the Issues

"When we look at a production system we look to see how it can be taken apart—not how it can be built up." An insightful statement by one of the GM participants of their design rules. They automatically look for ways to modularize a production configuration so that subunits can be easily swapped or reconfigured for different assembly purposes.

That is a good principle—you could teach others to wield that concept as a productive design tool. But most of the other things the GM participants credited for their unique abilities are less instructive. "We'll do anything it takes to keep the doors open" is not very specific and not really true. "Time is always questioned," "everything can always be improved," and "presume that anything can be done—just find out how" are inspirational but not helpful with design direction.

These quotations are from a group of very competent people thoughtfully describing the principles they follow when exercising that competency.

"People are our most flexible tool," is another concept full of insightful value that can be employed effectively as a design rule. They won't consider automation if high variability is required and a person can do the task. A practical example: assembly people move and position the work piece because they'll set it right every time, even though their modular assembly systems are reconfigured somewhat differently every time. This concept can make sense beyond their unique high-variety, low-volume operation: It is used in a high-volume semiconductor plant, where people transport work-in-process wafer cassettes from machine to machine to keep options open that automated conveyance would otherwise close; these important options let them add or relocate production machinery to accommodate demand fluctuation and new technology.

"Enjoy people, make them feel like winners," "teaming at all levels is key," and "recognize accomplishment" are less instructive people-related guidelines. They are important in the background of core values, but not helpful in the engineering design sense.

So the main issue has reveled itself: Those with the competency can't seem to articulate it instructively. They employ tacit knowledge at the intuitive level that even they are unaware of. That's pretty common everywhere, and only becomes an issue when you decide it is time to explicitly inventory this kind of knowledge and spread it around.

Other issues must be addressed by the business practice we are designing. First and foremost, the knowledge management process itself must be highly adaptable—able to evolve and accept deeper and better competency understandings over time, able to accommodate new applications for that competency, and able to incorporate new knowledge developed elsewhere. A perfect application for the *issue-focused, principle-based* design methodology we are exploring.

Issue-focused design means we want to understand our requirements objectively before we commit to a solution. On the proactive side, additional key issues, along with some solution direction, include:

➤ To learn effectively, people must be interested and perceive value.

➤ The accuracy of knowledge, once it is captured, and the effectiveness of communicating it are both prime areas for constant improvement.

➤ With time, product and process technology will change, as will the nature of the knowledge and the knowledge focus.

➤ Some knowledge pays dividends when understood by different types of employees—engineers, skilled trades, accountants, personnel, management—each requiring a modified learning approach.

➤ Insular knowledge is dangerous. An effective core competency renewal process must be aware of, and able to incorporate, relevant developments outside the plant-local and greater-corporate environments.

On the reactive side, some key issues and solution direction include:

➤ All knowledge is not necessarily good (e.g., knowing how to make a process highly adaptable when doing so provides no value to the company). A self-healing process is needed to eliminate both incorrect and poor-value knowledge.

➤ People in training are employees with front-line jobs, and business priorities change daily. There's no longer a "time-out" for training. Key points: flexible scheduling; training time should look like job time.

➤ A training procedure must accommodate large and small groups, from a few new hires to large groups of existing employees.

➤ Technology and applications change with time, so fundamental knowledge must be reinterpreted.

■ A PRELIMINARY FRAMEWORK/ COMPONENT ARCHITECTURE

This is the point where our solution begins to take shape. Some might say it is where the magic happens, for it appears to be the least systematized step, yet all steps hereafter refine what is developed here. But there are tricks to help the magic. The GM workshop relied heavily on the Bell Labs article at this point, letting it give general shape to the design, as there were similarities in the problem being attacked. The workshop also benefited from having about 20 collaborators with diverse experience, knowledge, and preferences bounce ideas around. The synopsized reasoning that follows doesn't reflect the few hours of chaotic groping that led to the result, but that is when the ideas took shape.

Any knowledge management system must deal with rapid change in knowledge value, and provide means for evolving the knowledge base under management. Even leadership core competency becomes irrelevant in the churning competitive environment. The design requirements just reviewed focus on the dynamic nature of knowledge capture, dissemination, renewal, and creation; and recognize the need for transparent training that does not interfere with daily employee productivity.

For starters, we need a process to capture the knowledge and insight that a few people possess, and another process to diffuse that knowledge and insight effectively to other minds. Since the value of knowledge and the nature of its application change constantly, these processes must be response able. Consider the alternative: If we succeed in capturing and packaging the insights of a few people today, and also feed this boxed wisdom to everyone else, we risk both that the contents are incomplete and that they may become stale—better to let things compete for acceptance than to institutionalize rigor mortis.

Management sage Tom Peters says it well: "I'm totally opposed to the learning organization idea. I argue for the forgetting organization. You get droids when you have too much training and too many people thinking and learning in the same way."[3]

So we need a process that captures wisdom from those who have it, even if they can't articulate what it is; that seeks wisdom wherever it may be at the moment; that actively renews (improves, upgrades) its content; that creates and accepts new knowledge when it is appropriate.

With this reasoning, our knowledge capture process has grown into a capture, renewal, and creation process—the activities that identify and package the right stuff. But we're still going to have problems if this stuff is simply put in a box and handed over to a separate and dedicated "training" process: For one it'll go stale, for another the trainers will not be quick to change what they teach.

A little more reasoning is needed. New employees come in the door and existing employees change job functions constantly throughout the year, frequent events that trigger a need for training. Meanwhile, deliberate knowledge generation typically relies on the slow-to-admit-failure of existing knowledge as its triggering event. This tells us that the knowledge generation activities are better tied to the training triggers, and leads us to conclude that we don't want separate generation and dissemination processes, but rather an integrated system that generates and reaffirms knowledge in the process of teaching it. The implication is that the people being trained will be the agents of knowledge generation as well as the triggers of new knowledge need.

In this case of core competency knowledge management, we don't want off-the-shelf knowledge that we simply feed to people; but rather a training process for discovering and reinterpreting appropriate knowledge and its application.

At this point, we have addressed the stale knowledge problem and the stuck-in-a-rut teacher problem. Now reality bites: Performance pressures preempt time-off for training and postpone dollar commitments for training resources.

Actually these are blessings in disguise. We don't want dedicated training resources; they institutionalize the rigor mortis. Instead, we want a rotating mentor-student relationship that exposes the wisdom of real workers and challenges them to explain their insights explicitly. And we don't want time-off for training that encourages the wrong knowledge focus. Instead, we want training to occur during the process of solving real problems, with solutions that provide real value in real time to the organization. In a later chapter, we call this employment of real people solving real problems in real time *Realsearch,* and formalize the process further.

Next we define the architectural framework as a set of evolving standards that both constrain and enable the interactions of compatible system components; and note that there is both an implicit and an explicit framework.

The implicit framework is present whether we design it or not: the local corporate culture, global corporate policies and strategic plan, regulatory constraints, union contract and work rules, communication infrastructure (e.g., electronic distance learning technology), and skill sets and workforce capabilities. Though these are all parts of the framework, practically speaking we can have no immediately effective hand in their redesign. They are the *givens* of the framework, and for the most part are the constraining portion—they limit what is possible.

Our framework design effort is focused on the portion that enables the adaptability to changing knowledge values and application requirements, as well as to changing personnel priorities and profiles.

➤ Framework Standards

Having first established a set of change issues (requirements) that the system must accommodate, we then went through a reasoning process that fleshed out a preliminary solution approach; and from that reasoning five strategic themes emerge as our key framework standards. Figure 7.1 shows these framework standards as darker-shaded bubbles, connected to each other as well as to functional activities, the lighter-shaded bubbles, that constitute the implementation of these themes. The connecting lines convey a mutual support relationship that is neither unidirectional nor strictly hierarchical. Thus we have standards supporting standards as well as activities supporting standards and activities supporting activities. More connectivity indicates a tighter weave of mutual support, leading to a more consistent, more compatible, and higher leveraged set of elements.

Focus on Change Issues

Response-able production-process design is the core competency knowledge of interest here. A strong focus is therefore on identifying the change issues addressed by a design. Knowing how to analyze or develop a highly adaptable process is not necessarily good if no value accrues to the company. To this end, all process analysis and design work reflects on the relative value of the change issues being considered as design requirements. A more formal process for determining the value of flexibility could be obtained with *real options*[4] value analysis, but that is a subject for highly advanced work and well beyond our needs and interests here.

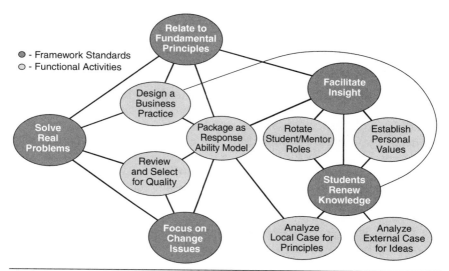

The darker-shaded *framework standards* are architectural rules/themes/strategies employed by the lighter-shaded *functional activities* as constraints/enablers/objectives. The representational notation, called a *framework activity diagram*, is modeled after Michael Porter's activity-system maps in "What Is Strategy," *Harvard Business Review*, Nov/Dec 1996. Connecting lines are nondirectional (sans arrowhead) as they imply a mutually reinforcing/defining relationship. Functional activities breathe life into a system of components and framework standards by defining a specific implementation of system purpose.

Figure 7.1   Framework/Activity Diagram: Core Competency Knowledge Management

Value is also important to the student. Developing new knowledge is not easy, and developing knowledge at the depth of insight is tougher yet. Some student preparatory work might be aimed at relating mastery of the fundamental principles to personal values.

Relate to Fundamental Principles

The problems associated with static knowledge are greater to the extent that knowledge is specific and narrow, and lesser to the extent that knowledge is fundamental and broad: In physics, the theory of general relativity is less likely to change than the accuracy with which we can measure the speed of light. Thus, we focus on principle-based knowledge. In the GM core competency knowledge context, the RRS principles themselves are appropriate, since the competency GM wants to manage is about adaptable systems. We can make the RRS principles more accessible than dry theory by translating them into "local rules" using the vernacular of the plant, its processes, and its people; and we can build a library of *local cases* depicting well-known plant processes as graphic *response ability models.*

Students Renew Knowledge

We want to keep taking a fresh look at the knowledge base. Students can provide this when they build and refine new *response ability model* "candidates." The models remain candidates until the QA *committee* (consisting of mentors and prior students) decides that they are worthy of entry into the official case example library. Students are also responsible for identifying and adding applicable *external cases* to the review library as literature references or other reviewable documentation. With less historical vestment in the status quo, students are more aggressive in their external information considerations.

Earlier, we reasoned for the need of an integrated process that utilizes those being trained to develop the very substance of the training material. The capture of core competency knowledge is the same act that also disseminates it.

Solve Real Problems

When learning time is focused on solving a real problem for the business, the time spent has direct and immediate payback, and the relevancy of the knowledge is self-ensuring. In our core competency knowledge context, topics for analysis and solution work are chosen for their abilities to shed new light on existing processes and/or develop new processes with superior characteristics.

Facilitate Insight

The real aim of all of this is to build a workforce highly competent in what this plant perceives to be a preemptive strategic advantage. Competency comes in varying degrees, and when accompanied by true insight, it is formidable. The three supporting functional activities shown in Figure 7.1, as well as the two connected framework standards, are organized to facilitate the development of personal insight.

Next we employ the RRS principles to design the functional activities that support the framework themes.

➤ Functional Activities

We have established and discussed (1) the contextual focus for this core-competency knowledge management system, (2) the major issues faced by it, (3) its key system modules, and (4) the framework that will constrain and enable module interaction.

In this discussion of the seven *functional activities* that are the heart of this business practice, keep in mind that the objective of this exercise is to employ RRS design principles that ensure the practice remains highly adaptable in a continually changing knowledge-value environment.

Activities define the interactions among system modules, the actions of the parties responsible for system reconfiguration, and the interactions between elements of the system and the external world. These activities fill in the framework/module architecture we've built.

Figure 7.1 depicts *systems integrity management* in action. The functional activities include the acquisition, modification, maintenance, and inventorying of the system components. *Design a business practice* is a "case example" if the QA committee accepts the result. In general, at least one activity is clearly responsible for generating the "output" of the system, and may then become itself a system component so that the system need only reproduce it the next time it is called for (rather than recreate it).

Establish Personal Values

You can lead a horse to water, but if he's not thirsty you can't make him drink. Jack Stack at Springfield Remanufacturing[5] taught his people to read the corporate balance sheet by showing them how this skill could help them manage their personal finances better; maybe even start a home-based jelly or muffin business. Learning happens when the mind is interested.

These core competency training workshops focus on what makes production processes highly adaptable. To create personal value from this knowledge, the workshop first looks at some of the adaptability issues that people face in their personal lives. Major purchases like a home computer to grow with the kids or a new entertainment system lose value quickly if they cannot be upgraded or adapted to technological change. Or, school and curriculum choices for children can either dead-end or maximize the options in a fast-changing world, as can continuing education and skill-training choices for adults.

Workshop students lead here, each choosing a personal interest area to examine for change issues and potential benefits if change-proficiency is realized. The library contains examples and analyses by past students to help in making a choice. Workshop mentors guide the selection process and the subsequent analysis exercise, which focuses on change-proficiency performance metrics; for example, how valuable is it to extend the useful life of your sound and video system by five additional years, to be able to accommodate DAT and DVD without replacing the entire system, to grow into 3D sound? What features of a base system maximize the options for someone with minimal technical expertise?

Students present their examples to each other and solicit suggestions for greater flexibility and identification of cost/value issues. Mentors guide the group through an exercise that helps each individual capture the key points of their example in a simplified (top half) *RA model* format, preparation for more formal modeling later. These early personal-value-examples are improved later in the workshop as homework; and after final presentations, students decide which ones get libraried as case examples to help future students.

Analyze External Case for Ideas

Students lead this activity by identifying pertinent candidate case stories in the existing library of external cases, in the general literature, and in potential plant tours within a day's drive. Mentors assist in the final selection to ensure that cases chosen for analysis will shed light on the application problem the workshop will attack later. A student-led discussion informally analyzes and identifies salient and novel features of what has been seen or read about. To the extent that a case deals explicitly with change, a more formal analysis will catalog the change issues, the enabling factors for response ability, and any readily available change-proficiency performance metrics. New cases that prove to be instructive are added to the library for future students to reuse.

Analyze Local Case for Principles

This is the primary mechanism for capturing core-competency knowledge and uses the students to analyze and describe the features and underlying principles of an existing highly adaptable system. Typically, the original designers of these existing systems have employed techniques that they cannot articulate sufficiently for others to duplicate the expertise. The purpose of this analysis is twofold: First, it turns tacit knowledge into explicit knowledge, and second, it is a warm-up exercise for the group members, who subsequently use what they have learned to solve the workshop application problem. Students choose the subject for analysis from candidates suggested by mentors. The fact that the subject may have been analyzed by previous workshops and already exists in the library as a case model is of no consequence, a new perspective may well result. Mentors provide process guidance, aiming the group toward the eventual descriptive requirements for consistent knowledge representation.

Design a Business Practice

Here is the crux of the workshop. The problem being attacked may well have been worked on by prior workshop groups who failed to gain an implementation recommendation. When possible, the workshop group is broken into small teams to have multiple perspectives vie for group appreciation. Mentors schedule periodic group reviews and provide process guidance. Student teams schedule their own team and individual task assignments over four to eight weeks, interspersed with frequent group progress review meetings. They remain employed at a reduced time commitment in their normal job function during this period. This activity culminates when the group, with mentor guidance, agrees on a comprehensive design approach and is ready to package the result as an RA model.

Package Knowledge as Response Ability Models

The metaphor model (Chapter 6) is used to capture and convey the salient features of both the analyzed local case and the designed problem solution, as well as the individual personal value examples developed by each student. It is both a descriptive discipline and an effective insight conveyance tool. It ensures that adaptable systems are consistently described in terms of the RRS principles and framework/module architecture that enable their adaptability, and catalogs the key change issues addressed by the system. These models are built by the students as a group while mentors provide process guidance. When a workshop group is large, it is broken into subgroups for collective work.

Rotate Student and Mentor Roles

The HR/OD function at the plant is responsible for scheduling workshops and designating the mentor and student roles. Individuals may be mentors in one workshop and students in another. Mentoring is process-guidance focused, studenting is workshop-product focused, and an individual gains knowledge and insight in both roles. Mentors assist in the identification of issues and in the interpretation of principles by exposing students to past work and by guiding students through a process, not by providing or judging answers. Every application exercise is a chance for a student to solve an important problem in a valuable way, and every mentoring opportunity is a chance to improve one's understanding of the tools and the concepts.

Review and Select for Quality

Although students are developing new knowledge, low or no value may result on occasion. A QA committee ensures that real problems of real value get targeted by workshop groups, and also ensures that marginal value results do not become institutionalized as part of the corporate long-term memory. The QA committee plays an important role by providing the ultimate value judgment on both old and new knowledge. They do not, however, interfere in the process of new knowledge development; but rather provide the objective up front and the evaluation in the end. In this way, the plant reaps the benefit of new thinking and new perspectives. The committee offers worthy candidate problems to a workshop and may also approve a problem suggested by a workshop group. At workshop completion, the QA committee evaluates the results of key workshop deliverables: the RA model developed while analyzing something that already exists, and the suggested solution to the application problem. Instructive local RA models are both admitted into the library and published within the plant, and good problem solutions are recommended for implementation.

There is another important committee as well. It has ownership of the entire knowledge management process and the evolution of the process framework. It is staffed by selected top management in recognition of the strategic importance of the plant's core competency, and staff members are personally accountable for maintaining an effective system at all times.

Next we look at the explicit relationship between the RRS design principles and the functional activities, and the relationship between the activities and the change issues identified as design requirements.

➤ Issue-Focused Design

Questions: Do the proposed functional activities actually address the issues we are concerned with? Are any of them superfluous? Are they sufficient to dispatch all the issues successfully? These questions must be answered for each of the 12 issues that constitute the design requirements specification.

The closure matrix in Figure 7.2 is a design tool that is used to relate the seven functional activities to the issues that they address, and to the RRS design principles that they employ. First we will focus on the issues, and discuss the employment of RRS principles next. The discussion will refer to the correlation between activities and issues shown in Figure 7.2's vertical shaded column. On the passive side, this tool displays after-the-fact proof that the solution activities actually address the original issues that defined the problem. On the active side, the act of thinking about what should be entered into each cell of this tool is what takes a preliminary design into a finished detail state.

Capturing Hidden Tacit Knowledge

Like butterfly collectors, we don't want to put our captured specimens in a box, but rather display them side by side in a similar format so that their individual merits and uniqueness are immediately obvious. To this end, a key activity is to *package as response ability model* (5) the knowledge we find. This RA model format also channels the activity that *analyzes a local case for principles* (3) into the tacit knowledge areas with explicit probing questions. The structured analysis process uses a template of eight change-issue areas and a template of 10 fundamental RRS principles to probe for hidden tacit knowledge, and to help relate that tacit knowledge and its personal representation to common fundamental principles. The third contributing activity is the *rotation of student and mentor roles* (6). Mentors attempt to cast their tacit knowledge into communicable terms, and in the process develop an appreciation for what they don't know about what they know. Students develop and exercise a communication mechanism and vocabulary that helps cast what they don't know into a coherent knowledge representation. A few times through loop develops highly mobile insight patterns. Finally, having a QA committee *review and select for quality* (7) the captured tacit knowledge ensures that something of real value was obtained.

Creating Student Interest and Value

This issue is hit square on the head with the activity to *establish personal values* (1), the lead-off exercise for every workshop. Two other activities play important roles here as well. Having to *design a business practice* (4) arouses interest in people affected by that practice, and gets a ho hum from people only indirectly affected. Similarly, choosing which case to use when you *analyze an external case for*

RRS Principles

Activities

1. Establish personal values
2. Analyze external case for ideas
3. Analyze local case for principles
4. Design a business practice
5. Package as response ability models
6. Rotate student/mentor roles
7. Review and select for quality

Issues	Principle-Based Activities and Issues Served	Self-Contained Units	Plug Compatibility	Facilitated Reuse	Flat Interaction	Deferred Commitment	Distributed Control & Info	Self-Organization	Elastic Capacity	Redundancy & Diversity	Evolving Standards
Proactive											
Capturing hidden tacit knowledge	3567	35	356	57	3	37	6	3		3	37
Creating student interest and value	124	1	1	1	12	124		124	1	1	
Improving knowledge accuracy	367		6	45	3	37	6	3		3	7
Improving knowledge effectiveness	1245	45	245	45	1			12	5	2	
Migrating the knowledge focus	247	27	4	2		4	7	247		4	47
Accommodating different student types	(all)	25	6			347	2	12345	1	17	2
Injecting fresh outside knowledge	26	26	26		2		6	2		3	
Reactive											
Finding and fixing incorrect knowledge	367	7		7	3	3	6	3		3	7
Excising poor value knowledge	2357	7		7	3	3	2	23		35	257
Allowing flexible student schedules	34	34			34			34			
Accommodating any size group	2345	2345	234				2	25	34	234	
Reinterpreting rules for new applications	23457	27		5		2	357	34			23457

Figure 7.2 Closure Matrix

The closure matrix is used to relate the functional activities to the issues that they address (vertical shaded column), and to the RRS design principles that they employ. The act of thinking about what should be entered into each cell of this tool is what transforms a preliminary conceptual design into a finished detail state.

ideas (2) lets you put your time where your interests lie. Passionate minds will do a much better job of analysis and design, but more importantly, they will do a better job of learning. If the company is faced with a pressing problem that the next workshop must deal with, then populate that workshop with people who care about that problem. If other students are waiting in the wings, run them in a parallel workshop. Let the workshop group decide from among management suggestions as well as their own candidates which problem to attack and what external cases look interesting. Remember, going to the movies is always enjoyable when you get to pick the movie, but if you're dragged off to someone else's choice it's often just that—a drag.

Improving Knowledge Accuracy

Three of the seven activities contribute to this issue. When the group *analyzes a local case for principles* (3), it may well be a case that has been analyzed in that past, producing different and more learned perspectives with time. *Rotating student and mentor roles* (6) on a re-analysis brings different depths of insight to bear as well. And the QA committee plays a vital role here in its *review and selection for quality* (7) of all results.

Improving Knowledge Effectiveness

The issue here refers to the breadth of both knowledge and communication among the employees; four activities play a role. By first *establishing personal values* (1), we have increased the receptivity of the audience. By *analyzing external cases for ideas* (2), we guard against narrow insular knowledge. When this knowledge is used to *design a business practice* (4), we broaden the collective application experience and develop personal competency. Finally, communicating newly developed knowledge throughout the employee base is easy when it is *packaged as a response ability model* (5) of similar format to past knowledge.

Migrating the Knowledge Focus

Knowledge based on fundamental principles has long life, but the focus of application changes much quicker. *Analyzing external cases for ideas* will explore new frontiers as often as it looks at current alternatives. When the group *designs a business practice*, or redesigns one, the opportunity to redefine leadership exists—especially in strategic practices. Our third contribution comes when the QA committee reviews and selects for quality those workshop results best aligned with the organization's strategic future.

Accommodating Different Student Types

Every activity contributes here, as they must. These workshops are fairly self-organizing, accepting objectives and guidelines but not repetitive rote learning. Students are responsible for choosing the *external case studies* (2), *local cases for analysis* (3), *business practices* for (re)design (4), and the individual *personal value* exercises (1). External guidance *rotates students and mentors* (6) and selects candidate business practice problems *and results* (7) with the group constituency in mind. Finally, the *response ability model packaging* (5) is a fundamental template that can model virtually any part of the business from the special perspective of any employee group.

Injecting Fresh Outside Knowledge

This issue is hit head on by *analyzing external cases for ideas* (2). But an even stronger contribution comes by *rotating student and mentor roles* (6), which breaks the chain of enforced old-think.

Finding and Fixing Incorrect Knowledge

When different student workshops are allowed to *analyze local cases for principles* (3) multiple times, a different perspective is inevitable, and with time, incorrect knowledge from prior work becomes evident. *Rotate student/mentor roles* (6) has a similar diverse perspective effect. Over time, these diverse results are *reviewed and selected for quality* (7) by the QA committee, with the effect of a continuous upgrade of the knowledge.

Excising Poor Value Knowledge

Purposely seeking and *analyzing external cases for ideas* (2) has the effect of broadening local perspectives, as well as providing a mechanism for tracking changing values in the industry. R*eanalyzing local cases for principles* (3) across multiple workshops brings diversity to bear on internal perspectives much as seen in the previous issue discussion. When these analysis results are commonly *packaged as response ability models* (5), the relative value weights of duplicate analysis subjects are easier to compare, and as previously seen, *review and selection for quality* (7) by the QA committee will continuously upgrade the value of the knowledge.

Allowing Flexible Student Schedules

There is no time-out for learning here, so people have to continue doing their normal jobs, though perhaps at a reduced capacity. When choosing which *local case to analyze for principles* (3) and what *business practice to design* (4), the nature and job needs of the student group can be accommodated to minimize schedule conflict.

Accommodating Any Size Group

Group size will vary depending on whether the purpose is to immediately train a few new hires or to diffuse some new knowledge among a larger group of existing workers. The flexibility in *analyzing external cases for ideas* (2) permits any number manageable by the group, and can consist of reading, guest presentations, and/or actual site tours as appropriate. When *analyzing local cases for principles* (3), a small group could all analyze the same case, while a larger group could do likewise or analyze additional cases. Splitting larger groups into working subgroups provides multiple viewpoints when *designing a business practice* (4), which are easily comparable when commonly *packaged as response ability models* (5).

Reinterpret Rules for New Applications

Though core competency design rules are expected to be fundamental and fairly unchanging, and begin as local variants of the 10 RRS principles, it is also expected that they will evolve with time. In some cases, this evolution may simply be a different articulation or emphasis on a basic principle; in other cases, it may be additional principles deemed appropriate for maturing knowledge or changing local conditions. This evolution will usually come from *analyzing external cases for ideas* (2) and *analyzing local cases for principles* (3), but can also emerge from a very new and different *business practice design* (4). In any event, once evolved, new rules will be reflected in new *response ability model packaging* (5) and in the QA committee's *review and selection for quality* (7) work.

➤ Principle-Based Design

Thinking is hard stuff and we all like to avoid it, especially if we believe we already know what's needed and don't need to think any further. I'm not talking about that fun spontaneous thinking we all get off on, where flashes of inspiration keep coming because we're in the mood and on a roll. I'm talking about that problem we are faced with that lives in a space we are not sufficiently familiar with. We know if we try to search that dark place, it's going to hurt the head. This kind of thinking is hard work. The typical motivation when faced with such a task is to get it over with asap. That is one reason we are satisfied with cheap solutions—those that look good at the high planning level but never deliver on the promise. Cheap solutions lose it when the details relegated to others and added later lack coherence and synergy.

Tools can help a lot here, especially tools that move the smoky abstract things into the tangible world where we can see what the concepts really are and how they fit with everything else. Good tools will transform a cheap solution into a robust solution.

One purpose of the closure matrix tool is to ensure that the final design actually addresses real issues, and isn't simply an implementation of faddish notions or personal management philosophies. Design elements we *felt* were important in our preliminary solution formulation all of a sudden declare how that importance will be realized. Applying the tool generally alters the vague activity descriptions we start with.

So much for the *issue-focused* part. Now we will employ the same tool to refine the *principle-based* part of the design. The methodology uses 10 RRS principles to make the design robust in a constantly changing environment, especially important where knowledge is involved.

Referring to Figure 7.2 again, but this time at the cell entries under the heading *Principle-Based Activities and Issues Served,* we will look at one (only) of the seven activities, *analyze local case for principles,* to see how the 10 principles are employed. Using the tool makes us think much deeper about how the activity would actually function, and what parts of it would keep it flexible. We are training a broad existing employee group, as well as new hires, on the core competencies exercised by a few—and also renewing and evolving that competency. These workshop training groups first analyze an existing process that exhibits this competency in its operational design, then they extract the essence of the underlying design that accounts for its excellence, and later they apply what they have learned to the design of a new process in need of similar characteristics.

The analysis activity is done in parallel by multiple workshop subgroups, and spans many weeks of part-time work. It produces the raw material for the subsequent *package as response ability model* activity and also trains the workshop group in the use of tools, concepts, and principles needed for subsequent business practice design activity. It is a cornerstone among the seven activities in our knowledge management practice. Table 7.1 shows the sequence for this activity as a series

Table 7.1   Analyze Local Case for Principles—Functional Activity
Work Flow

1. Explain in presentation/tour the local case under analysis.
2. Full group Q&A and discussion.
3. Breakout subgroups *identify the case's problem issues.*
4. There is full group discussion on subgroup results.
5. Breakouts *build framework/activity diagram* and *identify framework, modules,* and *system responsibilities.*
6. There is full group discussion on subgroup results.
7. Breakouts build *closure matrix* with *RRS examples.*
8. There is full group discussion on subgroup results.
9. Where possible, mentors lead consensus making among subgroup differences as a transition into the next activity: *response ability model packaging.*

of full group meetings and subgroup analysis periods. This table makes it evident that the process and tools we are using to design the knowledge management practice are reflected strongly in the practice design itself—the two have similar knowledge management aims and issues.

Using our closure matrix tool, we will again approach our effort with an issue focus, and look individually at each of the 9 issues (of 12) that the functional activity addresses; and explore which of the 10 principles play key roles in satisfying each issue. Because the issues are all change-proficiency oriented, and the principles are all change-enabling design concepts, there should be a good correlation here.

Capturing Hidden Tacit Knowledge

Employing the *flat interaction* principle, we encourage the subgroups to independently question and probe the people involved in designing or operating the system under analysis without restricting this to a full group discussion and Q&A activity. Importantly, *deferred commitment* is at work by first examining issues and activities before identifying the underlying important principles. This tends to broaden the perspective while focusing it on priorities at the same time. *Unit redundancy* is employed by purposely having multiple subgroups go after the same analysis independently so that if one gets in a hole another will surely succeed. By the same token, we let these subgroups exercise a high degree of *self-organization* as to how they will schedule their analysis activity, how they will interpret the principles, what libraried cases they will study for guidance, and how they will arrive at a *self-contained unit* conclusion requiring no dependence on other sub-groups. Of course, their conclusion is going to be *plug compatible* with the full group because the analysis structure is a given: The metaphor model is the template. This independent work by multiple groups will develop a broader and deeper set of alternative views, guard against single-view dogma, and generally make progress even if some of the people in the group are confused and lost. Finally, *evolving standards* will modify our understandings of the principles and their usage, and the change issue/value focus to keep up with new learnings and perspectives.

In general, a lot of principles were employed in satisfying that first issue. We are only looking for the important applications of principles here—the ones that would compromise our result if they were removed as design elements. It turns out that this first issue is the principal focus of the practice we are designing—so the strong employment of many principles is natural.

Improving Knowledge Accuracy

Redundant subgroups and even duplicate analyses by whole groups re-fine the knowledge. *Self-organization* of the subgroups and direct *flat interaction* between teams and sources increase the likelihood that some teams will uncover knowledge overlooked by others who approach the process differently. As before, *deferring* the close look at principles fo-cuses the priorities. And allowing direct team/source interaction broadens the total perspective.

Improving Knowledge Effectiveness

Chartering each subgroup as a *self-contained unit* means that they must build a complete stand-alone analysis, and not split up the ef-fort with another. This approach helps them learn a full system with all its checks and balances and not simply a few odds and ends about something that appears to work.

Accommodating Different Student Types

This issue is resolved by *deferring* the selection of the local case until the participant profile is known letting the group *self-decide* what the case shall be from among their own candidates as well as those of-fered by mentors.

Finding and Fixing Incorrect Knowledge; Excising Poor Value Knowledge

Both issues are achieved identically in our case here, and in a manner similar to improving knowledge accuracy. *Redundant* subgroups and even duplicate analyses by whole groups are bound to produce differing points of view and even expose a sacred cow now and then. *Self-organization* of the subgroups and *flat interaction* increase the likelihood that some teams will look at things differently than others. Finally, *deferring* the close look at principles until a sound set of issues and values is developed is likely to ferret out bad assumptions.

Allowing Flexible Student Schedules

This is enabled by *self-organizing* subgroups that stand alone as *self-contained* teams and are able to interact peer-to-peer (*flat interaction*) in their analysis work. Though there are times when an entire workshop group must meet together, the bulk of the time-consuming work is spread over weeks and can occur asynchronously.

Accommodating Any Size Group

Flexible capacity, ranging from a few new hires to a large retraining class, is achieved by splitting a total group into any number of subgroup teams, chartering these teams as independent *self-contained units* that work to a common *plug-compatible* process structure, and having them all work *redundantly* on the same objectives.

Reinterpreting Rules for New Applications

Technology and applications change with time, as do corporate strategies. By *distributing control* of this total process to the points of maximum knowledge we vest *evolving standards* responsibility in the hands of the *knowledge management committee,* for they have the current strategies and future goals of the organization in sight. Two strategic framework items in particular must evolve apace: the understandings of fundamental principles and the values of change proficiency. By definition, fundamental principles are expected to be true for all time, but in reality our grasp of these principles and how best to apply them is affected by time-deepening understandings, by shifting strategic priorities, and by changing technology. Deeper understanding, for example, a well split one of the 10 principles into two distinct concepts when finer distinctions prove useful. By the same token, values for change may move up the maturity scale as the competency knowledge is spread throughout the organization. The

Key Proactive Issues

Creation

- Capture tacit knowledge and make it explicit [ts]

Improvement

- Create student interest [tq]
- Accuracy of cataloged case models [s]
- Effectiveness of knowledge diffusion [qs]

Migration

- Knowledge competency focus changes over time [tq]

Modification

- Add nontechnical participants to development groups [s]
- Continually incorporate fresh outside knowledge [s]

Key Reactive Issues

Correction

- Repair incorrect embedded knowledge [t]
- Identify and excise poor value knowledge [t]

Variation

- Flexible student schedule to accommodate continued work requirements [s]

Expansion

- Accommodate any size group, from a few new hires to a large group retraining [s]

Reconfiguration

- Reinterpret rules for new applications [ts]

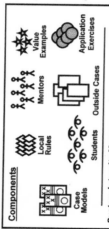

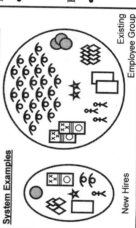

Reusable	
Self-Contained Units (Components) • Local Cases (Knowledge) • Mentors • Students • Local Rules (Knowledge) • Value Examples • External Cases (Knowledge) • Application Exercises	**Evolving Standards (Framework)** – Top management staffs the Knowledge Management Committee, which reviews effectiveness periodically and evolves the framework as appropriate.
Plug Compatibility • Fundamental-principle based • Change issue focus • Solve real problem • Insight facilitation • Students renew knowledge	**Unit Redundancy and Diversity** – Different workshop groups bringing new perspectives revisit identical problems in order to improve existing knowledge or identify incorrect knowledge.
Facilitated Reuse • QA committee manages rules/exercises/models • Students manage outside cases and value examples • HR/OD manages students and mentors	**Elastic Capacity** – Accommodate any size student group by splitting into subgroup teams of manageable size, which work independently during break-out sessions.
Scalable	
Reconfigurable	
Flat Interaction – Students are encouraged and expected to interact directly with all sources of knowledge, regardless of rank, when analyzing systems.	**Distributed Control and Information** – Systems integrity management is distributed among four groups: KM Committee, QA Committee, students, and the HR/OD people.
Deferred Commitment – Each class has a different student-interest makeup, so to optimize the fit, internal cases for analysis are not selected until all participants are identified.	**Self-Organization** – Participants must generate a result within the bounds of the process, but are otherwise responsible for study cases, work scheduling, and the final result.

Figure 6.5 shows strong, unique, and evident competency in GM's Pittsburgh plant at designing highly response-able production systems. A workshop team visited there in 1997, intending to understand the key design rules employed for constructing highly adaptable systems, relate them to the RRS principles, and then design a method for articulating and packaging the plant's design rules for effective communication to all employees. Specifically, the plant manager wanted a training program for new hires, as well as existing employees, that would spread this competency quickly and effectively throughout the entire workforce—at the insightful visceral level rather than as a fixed set of rules to blindly follow. This figure is based on the results of that 1997 workshop effort.

(Metric focus legend: t = time of change, c = cost of change, q = quality of change, s = scope of change)

Figure 7.3 Core Competency Development and Diffusion

Design Step	Objective	Example	Tools
1. Review external informa-tion relevant to the problem	• Introduce fresh relevant thinking	• Bell Labs engineer pro-ductivity paper	• External case literature
2. Analyze a known thing and build an RA model	• Build/refresh the pattern of principles and insight	• GM JIT assembly	• RA model template
3. Identify and define the problem issues	• Define the problem and solution valuation criteria	• See chapter text and Fig-ure 7.4 change issues	• Change domain template
4. Reason out a preliminary framework/component/integrity architecture	• Shape the general solution	• See chapter text	• External case literature • Diverse collaborators
5. Develop framework stan-dards and activities	• Establish the enabling architecture	• Figure 7.1 framework/activity diagram	• Framework activity dia-gram template
6. Design critical activities and validate solution	• Focus on the issues and employ the principles	• See chapter text and Fig-ure 7.2 closure matrix	• Closure matrix template • RRS principles template
7. Build solution response ability model	• Identify the main points of the solution model	• Figure 7.4	• RA model template

Figure 7.4 Systematic Design of Response-Able Systems

The steps and tools shown here have been employed successfully in workshop design efforts. Workshops generally produce sparsely populated templates that are later fleshed out by a dedicated design team focusing on the closure matrix tool. As in virtually all design efforts, good designs emerge from a spiral/it-erative pattern of activities, where the designer learns and returns to earlier stages frequently in order to steer the final result to the best possible outcome. Nevertheless, there is generally a linear progression through a sequence of stages, though experienced designers may well pursue different sequences to fit their own personal style.

possibility of adding or modifying strategic framework themes is always possible once operating experience makes the *knowledge management committee* wiser.

■ CONCLUSION

A workshop design effort, which was the origin of much of the design reviewed here, cannot get as detailed as the eventual real design efforts must go. Workshop efforts are used to develop broad buy-in as well as to jump-start a subsequent deeper design effort by a dedicated design team. Workshop design results are typically sparsely populated tool and model templates, but generally provide rich ideas. A small dedicated design team then works the closure matrix process to put flesh on the bones, and something like Figure 7.3 takes shape.

Figure 7.4 summarizes the sequence we just walked through. As in virtually all design efforts, good designs emerge from a spiral/iterative pattern of activities, where the designer learns and returns to earlier stages frequently in steering the final result to the best possible outcome. Nevertheless, there is generally a linear progression through a sequence of stages, though experienced designers may well pursue different sequences to fit their own personal style.

■ NOTES

1. This workshop approach and focus is described in Dove (1998), "Realsearch: A Framework for Knowledge Management and Continuing Education." Participants from General Motors included Leon Agnew, Al Beam, Jim Cook, Al Hall, Joe Leone, James Pazehoski, Dan Praschan, Guy Volponi. From other companies: Steve Benson, LSI logic; Lisa Bogusz, Rockwell Collins; John Bricklemyer, Eastman Kodak; Mark Correll, Rockwell Collins; Bob Dove, Lyceum Group; Bill Drake, Motorola; Sue Hartman, The Hartman Group; Jim Hughes, Agility Forum; Howard Kuhn, Concurrent Technologies Corp.; Joe Lichwalla, DuPont Automotive; Jack Ring, Innovation Management; Joe Rutledge, LSI logic; Dave Schmidt, Rockwell Collins.
2. Upton (1995); Kelly and Caplan (1993).
3. Kelly (1997), "Peters Provocations."
4. Luehrman, (1998), "Strategy as a Portfolio of Real Options." Real options is a method for placing a value on an investment, like discounted cash flow analysis, but places a valuation on an investment in options (flexibility) that may only have some probability of being exercised.
5. Stack (1992).

Chapter 8

Intuitive Design of Response-Able Systems

This chapter presents the design of an enterprise resource planning (ERP) implementation process, and an ERP architecture. Chapter 7 detailed a methodology for designing enterprise systems according to the RRS design principles. Such a methodology is useful as both an initial means to develop experience and mastery, and as a longer term design discipline. Experienced designers rarely follow such a methodology, however. For them the concepts and principles have become embedded in their thought processes, and conformal designs emerge with little conscious effort. This chapter relates such an intuitive design project.

■ INTUITIVE DESIGN

As I finish writing this book, I am engaged in the design, development, and implementation of the IT/ERM/B2B infrastructure and applications for a new semiconductor company called Silterra. The IT (information technology) infrastructure, the ERM (enterprise resource management, also known as enterprise resource planning or ERP) applications, and the B2B (business-to-business integration) applications are all expected to be fully e-enabled—meaning they must take advantage of electronic online/Web technology and support whatever business model the new e-World demands at the moment. Silterra will provide outsourced production services to the semiconductor marketplace, turning a design into a deliverable integrated circuit for the growing number of fabless companies, as well as the

214

established integrated device manufacturers looking for new or extra capacity.

Cy Hannon, president of Silterra, is building this enterprise to thrive in the new environment he sees: one of turbulence and uncertainty that the Internet is ushering in, of a growing market for seamless virtual enterprise, of attitudes and impatience shaped by retail e-Commerce experiences, of instant and open information access, and of rapid continuous change in knowledge, technology, and business models. He'll spend a billion-plus dollars in 2000 building Silterra's first fabrication facility in Malaysia, and end the year with a production facility running test product and 600 employees ready to start the new year with Q1 production deliveries.

Hannon knows he'll also have to spend tens of millions for development and implementation of IT/ERM support for the company, and he is concerned that even leading edge IT/ERM approaches are still clueless about the real need to thrive under high-change conditions. He didn't figure he'd find an appropriate, let alone differentiated, approach from any of the large established consultancies that design and implement these systems: Their business model requires reusable business strategies and implementations that they can reconfigure for many clients. What he wanted instead was something uniquely fit to Silterra's opportunity, something sustainable, and something that wouldn't be reoffered a week later to a world full of big-consultancy clients.

Here we briefly review the preimplementation phases of this project, focusing on the architectural design of both the IT infrastructure and of the ERM implementation process. We also review a bit of the process used to arrive at these architectural designs. The end of this story cannot be told until after this book goes to press. There is, of course, a business strategy, operating context, and corporate culture that IT/ERM is meant to serve, and that must be equally response able. In Chapter 10, we discuss some of the larger strategy and cultural issues.

This project began in November 1999 when Cy Hannon laid out his objectives and vision, and said that one year later the company needed fully functional IT/ERM support. Importantly, he wanted an architecture that would enable continuous and timely evolution to support whatever the business strategy decided was appropriate . . . whenever. The pace of change he envisions for business models and operational strategy is not at all in synch with the word evolution in the ERM arena. Nor is it typical to expect a custom-designed ERM system to functionally support a semiconductor manufacturing company within one year of first wish.

Cy figured our response-able systems knowledge offered a quick-start foundation for the architecture he needed. Then, believing that the greenfield lack-of-legacy situation would remove a lot of the usual ERM implementation time, we allocated six months for design and vendor selection, and six months for implementation.

Legacy, as we learned later, comes in many forms. A start-up company that pulls together a management team and 500 employees in the space of 18 months doesn't have an explicit integrated legacy— neither cultural nor infrastructural. Instead, it has a tacit distributed legacy hidden in the minds of management people coming from incompatible environments. Each person has a myopic version of what worked where he or she came from, and virtually none have experienced creating a company from scratch. Not an insurmountable problem, as will be seen.

The objectives for the IT/ERM infrastructure were quickly established:

➤ Enable, rather than constrain, the business model and operating strategies, whatever they might be.

➤ Support continuous change in the business model, operating strategies, and infrastructure technology.

➤ Put sufficient functionality in place within 12 months to run the company and enable an aggressive B2B Internet strategy.

Establishing the first two objectives did not require much thought. Though they may have appeared to be innovative and proactive, a simple observation of the business environment in the new millennium made them reactionary requirements for sustainable viability. Anything less for a company starting up business in these times would put the fitness of management in question.

In some sense, the objectives offered a first approximation to an RS analysis: They provided a problem definition couched in terms of change issues that must be addressed by any design solution.

Next, we began a furious survey of both the state-of-practice and the state-of-the-art in the IT infrastructure and ERM worlds, looking for natural occurrences of RRS frameworks and components. Initial returns on the state-of-practice were pretty dismal: Chaotic, expensive implementation and locked-in rigidity is the reality of ERM, and most vendors and integrators stood by dumbstruck by the Internet change. My own suspicion has always been that the nonvalue-added portion of ERM implementation projects has cost industry more than the billions spent on non-value-added Y2K work, but that is another story for another time.

Hope for a state-of-the-art solution appeared in a relatively new technology consisting of things variously called message buses, middleware, and enterprise application integration (EAI). The concept of the *enterprise* bus gained its foothold as a backbone integration network for factory MES (manufacturing execution systems), then gained recognition as middleware for connecting legacy systems to the World Wide Web, and subsequently became an expedient way to interconnect businesses as virtual enterprises or as integrated acquisitions. In concept, these buses are similar to e-mail systems, providing an infrastructure for reliable transmission of asynchronous messages between addressable components. We thought the concept had potential far beyond its typical deployment, however, for providing a response-able plug-and-play framework for enterprise (and cross-enterprise) infrastructure.

At the same time, among the ERM vendors, Oracle showed some promise with its development of a new enterprise application family called 11i, which appeared at first blush to consist of reasonably componentized application chunks, which were both plug compatible with the various middleware vendors, and directly Web oriented, as opposed to old stuff dressed up in a Web wrapper.

The architectural model began to take conceptual shape: an enterprise bus that forms the physical part of the framework, with independent plug-compatible enterprise applications that communicate with each other, the corporate database, and other applications through the enterprise bus. As a framework, the bus provides the physical portion. Response-able plug compatibility also requires standardization on corporate-data definitions, transmission protocols, interface rules, and operating principles.

Concurrent with this technology exploration, a deeper understanding of change issues began to take shape as an intuitive (rather than disciplined) problem definition (RS analysis). The enterprise bus should be vendor independent, meaning the framework architecture should accommodate a variety of existing bus vendors, as well as new offerings likely to emerge. By the same token, the choice of corporate database and individual enterprise applications should also be vendor neutral permitting a *best-of-fit* choice initially, as well as a better-of-fit replacement whenever it becomes advantageous.

Some strategic principles also help. For one, enterprise applications are there to support the business strategy and all its changes to accommodate a changing environment, not the other way round (as stated in our first objective). For another, enterprise application components should be off-the-shelf and never customized so that vendor upgrades and improvements are quickly and inexpensively installed (time and cost of change). Current ERM applications set these two principles in conflict, unless, as one independent consultant put it, you are happy letting the work from some programmer in Germany 15 years ago dictate how you should run your company today.

Armed with a conceptual approach that fit the needs of the times, the next stop was at a variety of middleware and ERM vendors to see how close a match their latest software could provide. That was when the first hints of deep-rooted cultural mismatch appeared. Both the ERM vendors and the middleware vendors present themselves as the center of the enterprise universe. The initial conflict we experienced with ERM views is depicted in Figure 8.1.

■ DEFINING THE PROBLEM

On the first of December, 30 days after the project began, we issued an RFI (request for information) to a variety of ERM and middleware vendors. This RFI embodied our intuitive problem definition, outlining the situation Silterra envisioned and the requirements that would have to be addressed by any solution.

> *What follows is a description of a new semiconductor manufacturing company, Silterra, its projected growth environment over the next few years, and its concerns for remaining highly adaptable. Some of the description is fact, and some is the potential situation the company believes it must be capable of dealing with. The purpose of the description is to paint a picture which must be addressed by the company's information technology (IT) infrastructure and eCommerce/eBusiness/eMIS applications. Here, Internet/intranet facilitation of customer relationships we call eCommerce, of all external relationships we call eBusiness, and of total enterprise operation we call eMIS—each successively inclusive of the other.*

> *The Company and the Business*

> *Silterra is a new company entering the semiconductor manufacturing field as an outsource. Its customers are other companies which either have no manufacturing facilities of their own (fabless companies) or do, but need extra production capacity, or need the latest in production and packaging technology. Construction of its first production facility is underway in Malaysia, and is expected to produce deliverable product by end of Q4 2000. The company is funded by the Government of Malaysia, which views the investment as a strategic national move, and expects to grow the company considerably with additional production facilities in a relatively short period of time.*

> *A semiconductor fabrication facility typically costs in excess of a billion U.S. dollars to bring up. Annual revenue from such a facility*

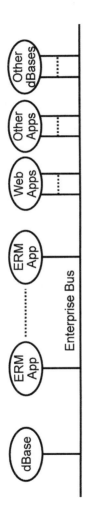

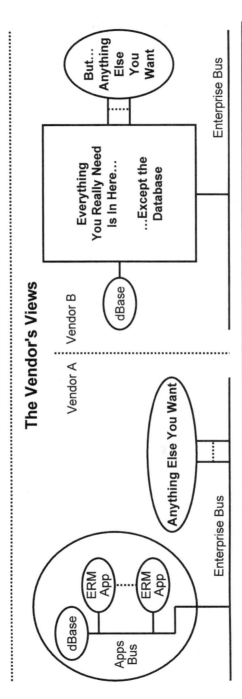

Vendors were approached with the diagram at the top, and told that their best opportunity to have Silterra as a long-term customer was to show Silterra how they were free to mix and match applications from whatever vendors had the best fit for Silterra's strategy at any time. In other words, the way to lock-in Silterra relationally is to show them that they are not locked-in systemically. Vendor B, with an aging patched-over architecture, but dominant installed base, offered a cloud of tightly integrated applications that could communicate (somehow) with any external applications that might be wanted. Vendor A, with a data-base-centric view, had a more enlightened and effective internal architecture, but still had a one-size-fits-all, why-would-you-want-to-go-anywhere-else attitude.

Figure 8.1 Silterra's Initial Chalk Talks with ERM Vendors

219

operating at capacity approaches the same number. Silterra expects its first plant to be operating at capacity before the end of 2001.

Currently Silterra has its first manufacturing facility under construction, production employees in training, and sales activities underway. It can begin filling orders in Q2 2000 from another company's production facilities, and then will fill orders from its own production capability by the end of Q4 2000.

As a new company Silterra as yet has no IT legacy to contend with. Now, however, is the time for Silterra to commit to an IT strategy, and to begin implementation. Implementation schedules will be driven by the company's emerging needs as they progressively awaken throughout the year of 2000. The strategy is still in the stage of initial formulation, and will in fact always be in a stage of re-formulation. The cornerstone of the strategy, throughout its evolution, will be an architecture that enables and facilitates constant change—in all dimensions.

It is anticipated that multiple vendors will participate in the creation of the IT infrastructure and applications; if for no other reason than to approach a guarantee that the resultant system will in fact accommodate software and hardware from multiple vendors as time unfolds. We intend to build an infrastructure that is independent of any software vendor, hardware vendor, or systems integrator; one that facilitates the quick inclusion of new applications, the replacement of any in-place applications or infrastructure element, and even the replumbing of the underlying structures and concepts.

This request for information seeks to help us understand how well you can help us address this intent of independence and adaptability, while providing elements of infrastructure and application necessary to support the enterprise IT and eMIS needs.

Some Issues of Adaptability

We are looking for an adaptive ability beyond what the term flexibility generally implies, an ability more in line with what some call "agility." The adaptive ability we seek encompasses the ability to change quickly, change inexpensively, change robustly, and change without limit.

As in most industrial sectors today, the onrush of eCommerce has the semiconductor industry madly searching for new forms of electronic relationships with customers, suppliers, partners, and employees. At the same time many companies have just completed, or expect to soon, a multi-year ERM mega-project implementation, a highly disruptive process in itself, and now one that threatens to limit the potential for eCommerce exploitation by the very nature of its business-model-defining framework.

Silterra believes that eCommerce/eBusiness means a lot more than a web view of the traditional business model, and also believes that a state of turmoil is likely to exist for the indefinite future, before successively newer business models eventually converge, if ever.

Silterra plans to grow relatively rapidly, both by addition of new internal production capability and by acquisition of other companies with frontend and/or backend capabilities. Local sales and customer support operations will exist wherever in the world reasonable markets exist, with active offices in the United States, Europe, and Japan by the end of the year 2000. Acquired organizations will have legacy systems installed which are unlike Silterra systems.

Though growth is expected, so is the unexpected, as are the cyclical fluctuations which have historically characterized this industry. Relative to change associated with volume, the IT infrastructure and applications should facilitate a contracting environment as well as an expanding environment.

Users of the company's IT systems and applications may be located anywhere at any time, may be connected with a variety of current and future data devices, be of virtually any national origin, and may have any of a variety of relationships to the company, including but not limited to employee, customer, supplier, and partner. Some will be heavy and repeat users of one or a few applications, while others may be occasional or one-time users of many, such as a manager making use of a financial planning application, an employee seeking information from corporate data, or a customer trying to resolve a problem. Users at customer locations may be large in number, diverse in nature, and change frequently. The ease and speed of becoming an effective user, as well as gaining appropriate and authorized access, is an issue for all types of users.

Recovery in the face of malfunction, dysfunction, and disaster is an adaptability aspect of some importance. The IT infrastructure and its applications should be both fail soft and fail safe as appropriate to the risk and penalties. The eCommerce user shows little tolerance for inaccessible or slow response, the eBusiness user can be expected to follow suit, and the eMIS user cannot afford to have the "dashboard" of the company disappear.

Security issues, always important, become even more so with the advent of eMIS; especially when this term includes the ability to control as well as monitor. If a customer, for instance, is to have a web-enabled ability to enter orders and change or reschedule existing orders, fail-safe, yet minimally intrusive, procedures must insure that only authorized persons may exercise these abilities. Security is a necessity, and so is a way to accomplish this end without unnecessarily intrusive procedures.

eCommerce/eBusiness has the potential to introduce unexpected surges and explosive increases in activity within the IT infrastructure. Computing platform choices are typically based on volume expectations. With the uncertainty associated with eCommerce/eBusiness, scalability is a concern.

Expressing our business as applications or executable models requires time, knowledge of the methods for expression, and knowledge of the business rules, processes, and practices. The nature and availability

*of the knowledge expertise, and the amount of time to capture and ex-
press the knowledge in applications or models are concerns.*

*Though Silterra is characterized as a semiconductor company be-
cause it addresses that market, it can also be viewed as a plant building
company, considering a scenario of two new plants built each year for
the next five years on the average. Reuse, reconfiguration, scalability,
and evolvability of all supporting IT infrastructure elements and applications becomes a concern in this light.*

Things to Address

*If they are applicable to what you are presenting, you should address the
following questions in addition to whatever else you wish us to know:*

➤ *What products, services, and/or approaches have you got that can
help us achieve any of our needs for functionality and adaptability?*
➤ *How do these address the situations and concerns we have raised in
his document?*
➤ *What else can these address that we should be concerned about?*
➤ *What would be the process that takes these and turns them into op-
erational functionality for us?*
➤ *What standards do these adhere to that give them interoperability,
and how strict are those standards followed?*
➤ *How do these relate to XML, CORBA, and eJB?*
➤ *What portions of these require what other portions of these?*
➤ *What portions of these are completely independent of all other por-
tions of these?*

Companies invited to present unfailingly addressed the first half
of the first bullet in the preceding list, and virtually ignored the rest.
Our clearly stated intentions to focus on adaptability fell on resound-
ingly deaf ears. Nevertheless, the RFI document served as a solid problem definition that provided guidance throughout the project.

Though we intended to stretch the envelope well beyond commonly available system solutions, a cornerstone decision was to go
with state-of-practice products, rather than state-of-the-art concepts.
We felt strongly that the IT/ERM strategy had to be based on COTS
(common-off-the-shelf) components and not employ custom-made
software components that we would have to maintain. Strategic advantage was going to come from architecture, not from unique application packages.

To ensure our architecture would accommodate the future art-to-
practice evolution in enterprise software, however, it was important
to have some visibility of how that evolution might unfold. It was
also important to understand where the edges of the state-of-practice
were. To this end, we invited Jack Ring[1] to assemble a presentation of

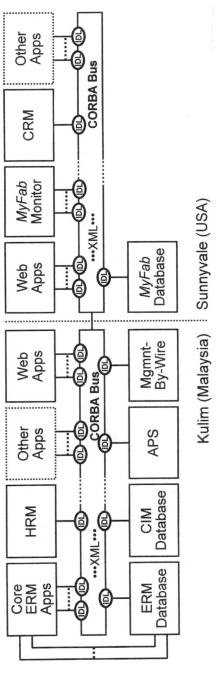

Kulim (Malaysia)   Sunnyvale (USA)

- The architecture is based on a set of functional components interconnected via a CORBA enterprise bus to enable application interoperability in a plug-and-play environment. All bus traffic is XML, and all bus interfaces employ CORBA IDL–to enable asynchronous addition and upgrade of applications.
- ERM applications may provide proprietary GUIs and interfaces to proprietary databases, but these ERM applications and databases must also provide external programmatic APIs to allow CORBA IDL object services direct access to their functionality.

The concept of the enterprise bus gained its foothold as a backbone for manufacturing execution systems (MES), then gained recognition as middleware for connecting legacy systems to the world wide web, and subsequently became an expedient way to interconnect businesses as virtual enterprises or as integrated acquisitions. The concept has potential far beyond its typical deployment, however, for providing a response-able plug-and-play framework for enterprise (and cross enterprise) infrastructure. This is enabled with a standard interface and protocol discipline, such as CORBA IDL and XML, and a metadata dictionary for XML tags.

ERM = Enterprise Resource Management, HRM = Human Resource Management, CRM = Customer Relationship Management, APS = Advanced Planning and Scheduling, CIM = Computer Integrated Manufacturing, IDL = Interface Definition Language, *MyFab* is a B2B trademark of Silterra, Management-by-Wire is Silterra's implementation of *Enterprise Strategist*, a trademark of Enterprise Software, Inc.

Figure 8.2   Semiconductor Foundry Silterra's IT Infrastructure Architecture

223

224

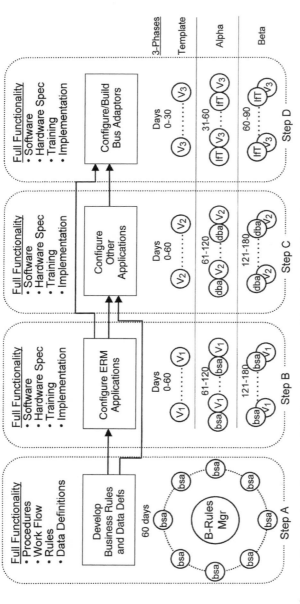

Figure 8.3 IT/ERM Implementation Strategy and Architecture

- Implementation strategy "encapsulates" each team, making them solely and totally responsible for functionality.
- Encapsulation of projects promotes plugable encapsulation of functional components.

Encapsulation allows teams to work toward stable objectives under conditions which they control. Three phase approach permits iterative improvement under stable conditions: Template is vendor out-of-box best-practice functionality, alpha is first iteration of corporate business rules, beta is second iteration. Day 0 is relative to a specific application. Steps B, C, and D are led by vendor project leaders. A program management office sits over top of the projects, and consists of a program manager, the IT infrastructure manager, the chief corporate business system analyst, the business rules project manager, and the three vendor project leaders.

bsa = business systems analyst, $V_1/V_2/V_3$ = different vendors, dba = database administrator, IfT = IT infrastructure technician.

next generation enterprise support concepts. Some few years earlier, Jack had joined our exploration for principles of highly adaptable enterprise, and had since gone on to focus on executable enterprise models and concepts of post-ERM enterprise support. The thrust and content of the day's education Jack brought to Silterra is not the subject of this book, but some of the team he assembled immediately became part of Silterra's team: Charan Lohara[2] and Gene Guglielmo.[3]

Gene Guglielmo, as timely luck would have it, gave us a seminar on enterprise bus architecture and specifically addressed concepts that focused on ease of component replacement as well as bus independence. He had been one of the developers of BEA's Tuxedo middleware, and had since become interested in next generation concepts of enterprise IT infrastructures. Though his ideas could not be called state-of-practice, they fit the needs of our architecture perfectly and were simply architecture and interface principles, not yet-to-be-proven software. The plug-compatibility framework began to take real shape.

With our principal homework done, it was time to issue an RFQ (request for quotation). Eleven pages issued in mid-January perhaps set a record for the shortest ERM RFQ, and this included specifications for enterprise bus and Web portal software as well. We didn't bother to specify functionality detail, figuring there was nothing strategic in the applications—a financial package from one company was going to be as good as one from another, and any lead one might have for the moment in Web implementations for CRM (customer relationship management) or SCM (supply chain management) would be short lived in the rapid development frenzy going on in the market.

Purchasable software applications were not going to be a source of strategic advantage for us, but an architecture (Figure 8.2) that permitted us to always have the best fit to a changing business strategy would be. Uniquely, the RFQ focused on architectural issues, not application features. Also uniquely, the RFQ specified an implementation process (Figure 8.3) with similar architectural principles.

Six weeks later, at the beginning of March, our evaluations were completed and the vendors were chosen. BEA won the bus and Web portal portions, Oracle got the bulk of the ERM award with their newly released 11i Applications, and PeopleSoft won the Human Resource Management application. April was spent in implementation planning and negotiation, and work began on the first of May.

■ ENCAPSULATED IMPLEMENTATION

Referring to Figure 8.3, Silterra planned a four-step, three-phase implementation. Each step and each phase is encapsulated, with clear, unambiguous, stable objectives and goals. Early steps provides information required by later steps, and act as driving functions. Phases within the major implementation activities for ERM and bus interfaces are divided into three phases:

➤ Step 1, Days 1–60: Vendor implements application best-practice templates out-of-the-box, resulting in "generic" operational functionality.

➤ Step 2, Days 61–120: Vendor reconfigures applications to Silterra "Alpha" Business Rules, resulting in a first cut at desired functionality.

➤ Step 3: Days 121–180: Vendor reconfigures applications to Silterra "Beta" Business Rules, resulting in final cut of desired functionality.

Vendors received the following instructions:

Silterra BSAs (business system analysts—see below) will provide alpha and beta business rules from an independent business rules generation project. Silterra realizes that it may have to compromise on desired business rules to fit that which is configurable within each application package's standard configurability. Alpha and Beta configuration activities will be done with a Silterra BSA and a vendor resource working in tandem, and be the major vehicle for ownership transfer and self-sufficiency. Ideally, the beta version will be done principally by Silterra BSAs with only occasional advisement needed from the Vendor.

Silterra BSAs report directly to a departmental manager, and are dedicated full time to the introduction, support and continuous evolution of business processes within a specific department, and to the introduction, support and evolution of IT tools employed to support the department in pursuit of its objectives.

We realize that there will be likely deviations from this ideal scenario as some applications may be scheduled to start and finish this process later than others. The implementation concept is predicated on the following principles:

1. Our business desires will drive the application software functionality, not the other way around. Thus, we will have a completely independent activity to generate our business rules, which will then be implemented in the applications (alpha and beta versions). If the applications cannot accommodate our desires, we will probably compromise in the short run and consider alternative solutions in the long run.

2. The Vendor implementation process will begin with a functional implementation of out-of-the-box best practice as recommended by the Vendor for semiconductor manufacturing. This occurs in the first 60-days of application implementation and will have very little direct involvement by Silterra "process owners" (known as BSA), other than to choose perhaps from a simple list of recommended alternatives and provide necessary data such as a chart of accounts, as they will be involved in a parallel process to generate "desired" business rules, and also perhaps in vendor application configuration training classes.

3. At day 61 there will exist a generic best practice functional capability, and also a set of "desired" alpha business rules. The second phase of implementation begins, and is expected to last 60 days. Process owners will begin to use the "generic" implementation and compare its functionality to the alpha set of desired rules, learning from both. At the same time, process owners with Vendor personnel will reconfigure the implementation for the alpha rule set, compromising when necessary in order to maintain standard off-the-shelf configurability. This reconfiguration will ideally be integrated with their self-sufficiency training.

4. At day 121 there will exist alpha functionality, perhaps with some compromise and perhaps with some willing modification influenced by the generic functionality. Now begins a 60 day period of alpha operation and beta implementation. Beta implementation will consist of new rules determined as desirable during the alpha period but not implemented in the alpha version, plus new rules which become desirable during the alpha 60-day functionality period. It is hoped that process owners will be sufficiently trained at the end of the alpha functionality period to accomplish most if not all of the beta reconfiguration self sufficiently.

5. A "clean" and unambiguous interface will exist between the application Vendor and all other technology and Vendors involved with the overall project. Each vendor involved in the various aspects of the total project will take responsibility for total functionality of the items they are supplying. Thus, they will provide the software, the hardware (or at least the hardware specification), the general training, the out-of-box generic best practice implementation, and the subsequent implementation reconfiguration leadership—guiding and assisting Silterra employees and BSAs one-on-one as they develop self-sufficiency.

6. There will be a program manager and a program management team. The program management team will include the responsible project lead from each Vendor as well as Silterra's IT manager and Business Rules project manager.

7. Silterra realizes that this process (as described above) may not be familiar to the Vendor. It is designed to "encapsulate" each vendor's responsibilities and authorities clearly so that each vendor is empowered and independently capable of meeting their objectives. One of its principal purposes is to ensure that the Vendor's work remains independently encapsulated from other vendor's work—so that all components of the overall project remain independently "pluggable," and don't become inseparably integrated. We hope that you will join with us in the spirit of this purpose, and together learn how to eliminate the confusion and inefficiency that typically accompanies projects of this complexity.

The vendors did not meet these plans with initial appreciation. In retrospect, after ignoring the tendency for business-as-usual, the comprehension and acceptance difficulty appeared to lie principally in the concepts of clean business rule development, dedicated BSAs, truly encapsulated functional responsibility, and clear intent on our part to make it happen this way—foreign ideas without role models in prior experience. Repeatedly, we had to say "Don't tell us it can't be done; tell us what the impediments are and we will eliminate them."

■ UNIQUE IT APPROACH PROVIDES UNIQUE COMPETITIVE ADVANTAGE

Silterra's approach to the design, implementation, and operation of its IT infrastructure and business support technology is expected to provide both significant competitive advantage and sustainable strategic differentiation. It is believed that this is the first instance of an IT infrastructure purposely, and effectively, designed to facilitate continuous change in a company's business model and its companion IT support technology. This capability provides Silterra with the unique ability to continuously employ the most effective information technology support available across successive generations of technological development—a competitive necessity now that the Internet is shaping and reshaping the expectations of business relationships and the effectiveness of business models.

This unique strategic approach stemmed from the reasoning that follows.

➤ Business Situation

Turbulence and uncertainty in the business environment is now expected as the norm, due principally to a continuously increasing rate of general and broad-based technological advancement, amplified by the discontinuity in business model evolution introduced by the current Internet onslaught.

➤ Implication

New opportunities will arise frequently in the first one or two decades of the millennium as new markets and business models emerge. At the same time, business risks will increase for companies impeded by traditional rigid infrastructures, and for companies that realign themselves for what may prove to be a momentary experiment in the market.

➤ Trends

ERM vendors were reengineering their applications for Web connectivity and highly integrated centralized control. New best-of-breed vendors for customer relationship management (CRM) and supply chain management (SCM) applications were focusing on customer self-service models while quietly migrating into other ERM areas. New middleware-market vendors were promising integrated connectivity between traditional back-office ERM core functions and new best-of-breed CRM and SCM applications while quietly migrating the implementation of business rules from the core ERM layer into this new middleware layer. Each expected (expects?) to be the center of the corporate IT strategy, and each promoted tightly integrated approaches steadily encroaching on the other's application turf. The result is simply a new form of locked-in infrastructure rigidity. Established companies began embracing middleware as a quick bolt-on answer for immediate connectivity to the new Internet world, eschewing costly reengineering of the fundamental infrastructure for total and continuous change.

➤ Assessment

Technology deployment decisions and methods must exhibit high and effective adaptability. On the cusp of the millennium, Internet technology was taking the business world by storm, and business-to-business (B2B) connectivity between supplier and customer was perhaps the most intense area of technological development, new business entries, IPOs, and proud acquisition announcements. Selecting technology for supply chain management (SCM) or customer relationship management (CRM) was a necessary crapshoot, like finally buying a laptop computer that fills a need instead of waiting for next month's ever-better promise.

The benefits of pervasive Internet-time communications are not limited to customer and supplier relations, however, and extend with at least equal impact into the employee and management ranks of an organization. The opportunity to manage knowledge, connect opportunity with decision, and respond to unforeseen events in very short times brings the potential to coordinate the efforts and resources of the organization like a concert, or have it respond with the grace of a flock of birds to obstacles in the flight path.

Old operating patterns, however, die slowly. At the dawn of a new business era, companies that tout Internet-enabled open communications didn't realize that customer expectations were being reshaped for more access, not just faster access. ERM and IT suppliers still expected (expect?) to control their customers—but Internet attitudes, technology, and access to information make the customer more impatient with less than the best, and more able to change.

With great flux in new Internet technologies, and slow change in implementation relationships and methods, it is unwise to get locked into one day's best offering if the next day's means customer defection to something better. This was clear in the highly visible areas of customer relationship management and supply chain management technology, and equally true in the deeper rooted advanced planning systems (APS) and production control and monitoring areas.

➤ Objective

It is necessary to be competitively proficient at continuous change, sufficiently to take advantage of new market opportunities, new business models, and new infrastructure technology whenever preemptively advantageous, or reactively necessary. Though there are multiple strategies within Silterra for achieving this, the one employed by the IT/ERM infrastructure was seen as fundamental, as this pervasive operating infrastructure would either enable or inhibit the implementation of strategic decisions involving changes in the business model and customer value proposition.

➤ IT/ERM Strategy

The business model must be able to drive the IT infrastructure and support applications, not the other way round, as is the traditional ERM legacy. The infrastructure must enable rather then inhibit constant change. This is accomplished with a plug-and-play, best-of-fit (to the business strategy), common-off-the-shelf (COTS) component architecture. It is built on an enterprise bus-centric infrastructure framework, with an implementation strategy that recognizes infrastructure change as a continuous process activity requiring core competency and company ownership, not third-party system integrators.

All enterprise applications, databases, Web portals, and other IT business support technology are able to communicate with each other as needed through a standard enterprise middleware bus. This plug-and-play functionality was enabled by adopting and enforcing certain interface standards that enjoy general acceptance throughout the technology-supplier community. The new Oracle 11i enterprise application suite, with its unique semiconductor-specific shop-floor-management (OSFM) option, and its front-running Internet implementation, offered best-of-fit ERM applications for Silterra's business needs in all core ERM applications (finance, manufacturing, materials management, etc.), supply chain management, and customer relationship management.

PeopleSoft's human resource management application was viewed as best-of-fit in that area, and plug compatibility with the architecture allowed us to include this choice without compromise. The choice of middleware vendor was of little technical consequence as at least three could provide the requisite physical framework. Advanced planning and scheduling systems were the remaining enterprise applications; and like CRM and SCM applications, were a hotbed of furious technological development and independent vendor focus. The architecture allowed us to defer a decision here until the need arose later in the year and to choose the best-of-fit at that time, which turned out to be Oracle's APS for planning and Adexa's (manufacturing capacity planning) for factory scheduling.

The upper bound of sound quality producible by a musical instrument is determined by the instrument's design and construction, but the quality of the music is determined by the performer's competency and artistry. This highly adaptable IT infrastructure could easily ossify over time if fundamental architectural principles are not maintained with religious zeal as the business needs and technologies evolve. To this end, the implementation and operation of the infrastructure is of equal strategic importance. From the start, Silterra took responsibility for the implementation and evolution of this infrastructure, building a core competency and studied discipline in continuous IT transformation. The same fundamental principles employed in the IT architecture were employed in the implementation and maintenance process—encapsulating transformation activities much like enterprise application components and reusing these methodologies in a plug-compatible framework of process. This process is expected to develop discipline, responsibility, and competency for employing continuous change as a competitive differentiating factor.

➤ Value-Generating Sustainable Differentiation

Though we refer to the architecture as bus-centric, the fact that the architecture employs an enterprise bus is not what provides value-generating sustainable differentiation, nor does this come from installing the best-fit enterprise application components available at the moment. Many of Silterra's competitors had or were installing enterprise buses, and they also had the opportunity, though perhaps at prohibitive costs, to update their enterprise applications as well.

Value comes from the fundamental architectural principles used to maintain and employ the bus, and all of its companion components, to a specific end: that of facilitating continuous system transformations. These principles are those explained in this book, and are employed in the continuous maintenance and evolution of the infrastructure. The result is an ability to easily and quickly incorporate new technology, or replace outdated technology with the next generation, independent of the vendor and the in-place legacy. And this applies to everything: the individual enterprise applications, the databases, the Web portals, and even the bus itself.

Sustainability comes from a collection of interrelated organizational activities difficult to duplicate elsewhere (without duplicating the entire interrelated set): an office of business process and IT architecture evolution, departmental business system analysts (BSAs; see following section) responsible for tooling their department with the most effective technology, pervasive operating objectives that value change proficiency as a core competency, and a learning culture that seeks and demands best-of-fit operating practices and tools.

■ SYSTEMS INTEGRITY MANAGEMENT

The *systems integrity management* functions for the IT infrastructure emerge from a new approach to corporate IT responsibility. As this is being written, Silterra is redefining the traditional concepts of CIO and IT responsibility. Cy Hannon believes that information today is a key logistics function, and has made the logistics department the seat of IT functionality for the organization. The new concept puts what might otherwise have been a CIO in the responsibility seat for purchasing, shipping, vendor relationships, supply chain management, and capacity planning . . . as well as the IT infrastructure. This is the first of three IT-related functions that are being separated from the traditional CIO model, with the result that there may not be a CIO title in the company.

The second functional change establishes a position called *Business Systems Analyst* (BSA) within each functional/departmental area of the company. Some functional areas may have more than one, as needed. A BSA is part of the department he or she serves (no dotted line to IT) and reports to the department head. A BSA's responsibility is to know the business processes within the department and to match their needs with advantageous IT tools. In this capacity, they must bring promising new business process concepts as well as promising new IT tools to the department for review, while also being the immediate source for all IT functionality support . . . but their job is to empower the user to be self-sufficient, not to make users dependent on support. Within the corporate IT strategy framework, they are free (and expected) to bring in any tools that will improve the department's ability to perform. These people form an important and formal part of the continuous "business engineering" activity at Silterra.

The third functional change establishes an office of corporate business systems, which has the systems integrity management responsibilities for the IT framework, among other things, and is similar to the BSA position at a higher level. This office must be on top of both marketplace and business model changes (proactive and reactive) and on top of emerging technology support for these emerging models. This office is also responsible for maintaining and evolving the corporate IT architecture framework rules that constrain the work of the departmental BSAs. As such, it has a strong understanding of framework theory as being grounded in minimal-but-sufficient standards imposed on the organization. This office is the owner/evolver of the architecture for the IT/ERM infrastructure and plays a leadership role in continuous business engineering activity. It is likely that this office will also act as the program management seat for certain special strategic development projects that are mismatched with the capabilities of the IT group in Logistics.

■ CONCLUSION

Accomplished engineers and designers have a mastery of the tools and principles of their trade, and rarely resort to rote design methodologies except where matters of safety or due diligence are paramount. Nevertheless, there is great value in revisiting an intuitive design with more formal procedures. For one, the design will generally be refined to produce better response ability. For another, it is an excellent way to spread ownership and appreciation for the important elements of the design, especially among those who inherit systems integrity management responsibilities. Figure 8.4 summarizes the change issues and design principles that shaped the IT infrastructure and its implementation process.

IT Infrastructure

Change Issues

- Continuously evolving business model
- Best-fit-to-strategy application replacement freedom
- Vendor and application independence
- Cost of change cannot be inhibitive
- Seamless upgrade/replacement (no downtime)
- Fast, effective user training
- Scalability in all dimensions
- All employees and customers as wired users eventually
- Variable and sufficient security
- Fail safe where needed

RRS Principles

- Components: dBs, ERM apps, Web apps, other apps
- Plug compatibility: bus, XML, CORBA/IDL, data defs, cots only, rules rule
- Facilitated reuse: bsa group
- Flat Interaction: Direct application-to-application dialogue
- Deferred commitment: XML permits asynchronous change
- Self-organization: Individual application
- Distributed: Application separation
- Elastic capacity: Virtually unlimited bus extendability
- Redundancy/diversity: PeopleSoft HRM, multiple app versions
- Evolving standards: Office of corporate business systems

Implementation Process

Change Issues (Key—look at it as a recurring process)

- Training and transfer
- Obtaining/creating the bsa group
- Time to go-live
- Cost to go-live
- Improvement/refinement
- People don't like to change once they learn a system

RRS Principles

- Components: bsa, vendor, dba, IfT, rules, cots software
- Plug compatibility: data defs, rules rule, stable input, stable objective, 3-phase, full responsibility for functionality, bsa CoP
- Facilitated reuse: bsa, chief bsa, program mgr, infrastructure mgr
- Flat Interaction: Program management style, bsa access to anyone
- Deferred commitment: Separated implementation phases take configuration when needed
- Self-organization: bsa cross-function interaction
- Distributed: bsa allegiance, functional responsibility
- Elastic capacity: Numbers of bsa, simultaneous application implementation projects
- Redundancy/diversity: bsa CoP
- Evolving standards: Office of corporate business systems, systematic design workshops among bsa group

Figure 8.4 Synopsis of Silterra's Intuitive Approach

The intuitive approach is the one that populates an empty sheet of paper quickly with concepts that leap to mind. Like the shopping mall artist who quickly develops a caricature sketch that looks pretty good even though there hasn't been enough time to get to know the nuances and personality of the subject. With the luxury of time, the artist would undoubtedly accentuate some features differently, capturing the essence of personality; and given time, the artist would use the first sketch as a valuable first-impressions study to help keep a more studied approach honest. The intuitive approach can be a very useful and valid way to get a project started quickly on the right track, and it will usually benefit from a subsequent studied approach that refines and augments the first impressions with some of the systematic steps discussed earlier. Also, a subsequent systematic refinement process is an excellent way to gain ownership and insight among a larger community.

bsa = business systems analyst, cots = common of the shelf, CoP = Community of Practice, dba = database administrator, IfT = IT infrastructure technician, mgr = manager.

■ NOTES

1. Jack Ring is the owner of Innovation Management in Scottsdale, AZ jring@amug.org. See Ring (1999), "Current Enterprise Models are *In Conflict* with Mass Customization," "When Enterprise = System," and "Toward the Intelligent Enterprise."
2. Charanjit Lohara is president and CEO of Enterprise Software, Inc., www.esistrategist.com, cslohara@worldnet.att.net. See Lohara (1999), "The Living Enterprise" and "System Engineering the Enterprise: Experience with Enterprise Frameworks."
3. Gene Guglielmo is developing software for Object Stream, in Pleasanton CA geneg@acm.org. See Guglielmo (1999), "Enterprise Integration in the Web Era."

Part Four

Knowledge and Culture

The Way of the Agile Enterprise

Chapters 9 and 10 offer techniques for altering a current corporate culture and mobilizing it down the path toward enterprise agility. These powerful knowledge management techniques very much manage the creation of knowledge that embeds itself in the culture during the process. Though these techniques manage the creation of knowledge, they do not dictate what that knowledge will be, only what it will be about. Thus, the knowledge forms compatibly with the existing culture, complementing as it transforms.

The first of the two techniques develops motivation, ownership, and objectives as it attempts to characterize the competitive maturity of an organization's response ability. The second develops skills and insights for reaching these objectives. Both are problem-solving techniques, not turn-the-crank transformation recipes. Thinking is required. Notably, each can be used to reach real, valued, and immediate objectives, teaching new concepts as a by-product rather than as an abstract or righteous exercise that must be pursued on faith.

Chapter

Waking Up
the Enterprise

Maturity is a word we often use to mean the wisdom that comes from time and experience, as opposed to knowledge that comes from information and understanding. It is a quality of knowledge that develops over time. If you think of skill as the degree of knowledge, and maturity as the facility to apply that knowledge, it is possible for one to be more skilled yet less effective, or more effective yet less skilled than another. Maturity is a quality that can be evident to an observer, though often difficult to measure in unequivocal linear terms. We have little difficulty in comparing the maturity of teenagers we know, and don't at all confuse this quality with their academic standing or intellect.

Applying the concept of maturity to an organization's knowledge, as opposed to an individual's knowledge, is no different.

This chapter introduces methods for gauging the maturity of an organization at change proficiency. In themselves, these are powerful tools for developing as-is and to-be models; and they provide a foundation and direction for both strategic programs and improvement projects. More important, however, is the by-product of cultural transformation that the use of these tools leaves behind. They present corporate thought with new values and insights that take root because they make sense, and because they yield actionable and valuable results.

■ CHANGE PROFICIENCY MATURITY PROFILES

How capable is your enterprise at dealing with the kinds of change that determine sustainable competitive success in your industry? An

Change Proficiency Maturity Model (CpMM)	A scale for gauging change proficiency maturity across five stages of development: accidental, repeatable, defined, managed, mastered.
Change Proficiency Maturity Profile (CpMP)	A critical evaluation framework of change proficiency maturity, encompassing both a maturity conclusion and a description of the change issues and observed responses which support that conclusion.
Business Practice Maturity Profile	A CpMP for a specific business practice.
Enterprise Maturity Profile	A summary radar chart of maturity conclusions and the supporting comprehensive collection of critical business practice maturity profiles for a single enterprise.
Industry Maturity Profile	Similar to an *enterprise maturity profile*, but with a range across multiple companies, choosing individual *business practice maturity profiles* from the best known cases in the industry.
Best-in-Class Maturity Profile	Similar to an *industry maturity profile*, but with a range across multiple companies, choosing individual *business practice maturity profiles* from the best known cases anywhere.
Maturity Reference Model	Any specific maturity profile employed as an instructive tool or benchmark.

Figure 9.1   Change Proficiency Maturity Definitions

How capable is an enterprise at dealing with the kinds of change that determine sustainable competitive success in an industry? An *enterprise maturity profile* answers that question with a collection of *business practice maturity profiles* for all "critical" business practice in the enterprise. Each of these business practice maturity profiles identifies a real and representative sample of key change issues facing the practice, shows by anecdotal and representative observation how the organization responds to these issues, and then measures the level of maturity painted by this stimulus-response story against a generic *change proficiency maturity model*. A business practice carries the "critical" distinction if it is part of an enterprise's strategic differentiation, or part of the industry's competitive differentiation.

Maturity Stage	General Characteristics	Example: Obtaining and Maintaining Skilled Human Resources
0: Accidental	Stumble through change, with recognition but no awareness.	Hire what's available, and hope they work out.
1: Repeatable	A set of rules for achieving change become understood.	Common hiring ritual to obtain new skills.
2: Defined	Rules broadened, performance metrics put in place.	Knowledge-based recruitment screening and testing.
3: Managed	Objectives clarified, rules refined, accountability in place.	Individualized employee development program.
4: Mastered	No longer rule based—actions guided by principles and ideology.	Environment enables and encourages self-development.

Figure 9.2   Pro Forma Example—Human Resources Skill Acquisition

This is a simplified example to show a progression of enlightenment that is not too atypical of young companies that start out without a professionally staffed human resources department. It assumes new skills are needed in the organization, and that there are only two ways to get them: either hire new people who will bring the necessary skills with them, or provide an environment that encourages employees to develop new skills—outsourcing or spot-market contracting is not considered here. Prior to the nineties it was not uncommon among large established companies to replace employees rather than consider retraining when skill needs changed.

241

enterprise maturity profile can answer that question. It does so with a collection of *business practice maturity profiles* for all critical business practices in the enterprise. Each of these business practice maturity profiles identifies a real and representative sample of key change issues facing the practice, shows by anecdotal and representative observation how the organization responds to these issues, and then measures the level of maturity painted by this stimulus-response story against a generic *change proficiency maturity model*. A business practice carries the "critical" distinction if it is part of an enterprise's strategic differentiation, or part of the industry's competitive differentiation.

The same technique can be used to build profiles across companies that show state-of-practice in an industry, or across industries that show best-in-class potentials. Figure 9.1 provides definitions for change proficiency maturity.

Analysis of hundreds of business practices and process with collaborative learning groups eventually revealed a natural order in the way change proficiency matured. Figure 9.2 shows the basic progression through five stages.

■ AN INTRODUCTION TO THE REFERENCE MODEL

In 1996, the Agility Forum sponsored the development of *An Agile Enterprise Reference Model with a Case Study of Remmele Engineering,*[1] with two principal goals in mind: (1) Provide a reference case of agile enterprise, capturing and displaying the essence of enterprisewide competency at both proactive and reactive change; and (2) provide a model for evaluating relative competency at change proficiency for any enterprise. The intent was to provide an instructive profile and a tool set with examples of usage to business managers and executives responsible for strategic planning, operational management, and reengineering.

The reference model spanned 24 interrelated critical business practices in six categories shown in Figure 9.3. Each of the 24 practices was presented in a 3- to 5-page structure that provided a generic business practice definition, the architecture (framework and components) of a case-study practice that fits that definition, a set of representative proactive and reactive change issues, case-study responses for each issue, and finally, a change-proficiency maturity statement that evaluated and measured the competency displayed by the case example.

The case study providing the examples is of Remmele Engineering in 1996—a $100 million, 4-division, 5-plant, Minnesota-based machin-

Strategic Planning

1 Strategic Plan Vision

2 Strategic Plan Dissemination

3 Strategic Plan Buy-In

Business Case Justification

4 Capital Investment Justification

5 Infrastructure Investment Justification

6 Business Engineering Investment Justification

Organizational Relationship Management

7 Business Unit Relationships

8 Employee Relationships

9 Partner Relationships

10 Supplier Relationships

11 Customer Relationships

12 Information System Unit Relationships

13 Production Unit Relationships

Innovation Management

14 Product Innovation Management

15 Process Innovation Management

16 Practice/Procedure Innovation Management

17 Strategy Innovation Management

Knowledge Management

18 Knowledge-Portfolio Strategy

19 Knowledge Generation

20 Knowledge Capture

21 Knowledge Mobilization

Performance Metrics

22 Leading Indicator Metrics

23 Operating Metrics

24 Valuation Metrics

These 24 practices were chosen in a series of 1995/1996 workshops, and reflect the realities and concerns of that time in sectors that included electronics, autos/trucks, aerospace/defense, chemicals/process, computers, software, business reengineering, and management consulting. Business practices were deemed "critical" if they met three criteria: (1) they dealt specifically with important competitive change proficiency competencies, (2) instances of good implementation and usage were relatively rare and not well understood, and (3) industry in general appeared prepared to tackle these areas as a natural step in transformation to broader-based change proficiency. Though these "critical" practices were appropriate in a pre-Internet business environment, many remain critical in today's environment, and can act as a starting point for an enterprise maturity profile armature.

Figure 9.3   Twenty-Four Critical Business Practices

ing company that serves aerospace, defense, electronic, medical, automotive, and electronic industries. Remmele was chosen very carefully for its observable broad proficiencies at change. It owes this competency to procedures that are instructive and exportable to companies of any size and in any business sector.

This reference model serves a twofold purpose: (1) Its employment of the change proficiency maturity model allows us to describe this tool and see how it is used, and (2) the structure of the reference model can provide a default model for your own employment. Excerpts from the reference model help establish techniques for employing the tool, as well as offering a strong dose of reality—corporate enterprise is a real and complex system, and the manifestations of response-able operation are not as pretty or as neatly described as the abstract concepts attributed to them.

A company's progress toward timeless mastery of change proficiency is not gauged by accumulating points for the existence of practices like teaming, mass customization, virtual partnering, integrated product/process development, and other important concepts of the day. Instead, we look for more fundamental capabilities that allow a company to adopt and integrate whatever operating concepts are important today as well as those yet undefined that will become important tomorrow. Implementing today's competitive practices says nothing about the ability to implement tomorrow's.

The five stages of maturity provide a metric for measuring a company's proficiency on the two axes of interest: proactive and reactive change proficiency. The key change issues for each critical business practice are developed using *response situation (RS)* analysis. The five-stage framework moves from "accidental" to "mastery" as the business practice under examination develops more competency at adaptation.

■ TWENTY-FOUR CRITICAL BUSINESS PRACTICES— THE REFERENCE MODEL ARMATURE

The reference model employed a framework of 24 business practices, and built a change proficiency maturity profile for each. The purpose of the business practice framework was to establish a corporate skeleton that would span the critical areas of the enterprise. The 24 practices were chosen in a series of 1995/1996 workshops,[2] and reflect the realities and concerns of that time in sectors that included electronics, autos/trucks, aerospace/defense, chemicals/process, computers, software, business reengineering, and management consulting (see Figure 9.3). The framework focused on those areas that lacked sufficient attention, yet were timely and critical in the pre-Internet competitive environment. At the same time, it ignored practices such as "listening to the voice of the customer" and "integrated product and process development" that already enjoyed high visibility and significant implementation examples. Instead, it illuminated items that met three specific criteria: (1) They dealt specifically with important competitive change proficiency competencies, (2) Instances of good implementation and usage were relatively rare and not well understood, and (3) Industry in general appeared prepared to tackle those elements as a natural next step in its transformation to broader-based change proficiency.

This was meant to capture a picture of the edge of a constantly advancing front. It was what industry was ready to do next. On reflection, you may find that many parts of it remain a reasonable representation of what industry is still ready to do next. This business practice framework was not meant as a comprehensive taxonomy of business practices, nor were the category groupings a suggested decomposition of a business model; the intent was to provide a map of actionable and necessary next steps for general progress. Here it is offered as an example, as these practices were identified in another time and across industries, rather than chosen for a specific company.

■ THE MATURITY MODEL

The *change proficiency maturity model* assumes that a progression through increasing stages of general competency will parallel a progression through specific competencies and characteristics (see Figure 9.4).

As a company progresses through these maturity stages, there is a specific and different emphasis on change proficiency metrics at each stage. These metrics are associated with the change process itself and refer to the *time* to affect a change, the *cost* of making a change, the *quality* of the change process, and the *scope* (breadth) of the change capability (see Figure 9.5).

All these metrics are interrelated, and all are important when evaluating any specific change capability, such as creating a new product or doubling plant capacity to meet unexpected demand; but the process of maturity places special emphasis on individual metrics at each stage. Being able to take advantage of an opportunity while the opportunity is meaningful makes time the initial focus, even if you have to pay a premium. After the "cycle time" of instituting a change is sufficiently under control to hit the "market window," the cost of making these changes enters the spotlight. When both time and cost are acceptable, the focus turns to predictability and consistency, or the quality of the change process. Finally, when good sound change proficiency capabilities are understood and managed, an organization gains competitive advantage in broadening the range of application.

Competency at specific types of change also tends to develop in a sequence: Some competencies are needed before others (just to be a contender); there is a pairwise synergy with the metric focus; and there is a difference in difficulty. Notice the pairwise synergy of

Stage 0: Accidental — Characterized by:
☐ The lack of any change-process recognition, yet change manages to occur.
☐ The process is ad hoc: exhibiting false starts and retries, unpredictable completion dates and costs, surprising results and side effects, and undesirable reactions from, and effects on, the personnel involved.
☐ Examples: Downsizing, management fad-of-the-day, grueling overtime, firefighting, multiple reengineering attempts, expediting.

Stage 1: Repeatable — Characterized by:
☐ Anecdotal "lessons learned" from past change activities.
☐ The time it takes to make a change is under control.
☐ Specific individuals and teams are recognized for repeatable success with effective change projects.

Stage 2: Defined — Characterized by:
☐ The emergence of formal change processes with documented procedures.
☐ The base of practitioners is broadened as process rather than intuitive talent becomes appreciated.
☐ Metrics for the change process are identified, cost of change is under control, and predictability becomes a known but elusive desire.
☐ Typically, procedures at this stage are rigid and based on studied experience and analysis.

Stage 3: Managed — Characterized by:
☐ The appointment of change managers (business engineers) with established responsibilities, though they may neither be called such nor recognized as such.
☐ An evolving knowledge base of change process fundamentals and rules begins to emerge.
☐ Rigid procedures are loosened, and predictable change processes are the norm.
☐ Appreciation for and participation in the corporate change process is widespread.

Stage 4: Mastered — Characterized by:
☐ A principle-based, deep appreciation of adaptability.
☐ An understanding that process alone is not sufficient.
☐ A conscious engineering and manipulation of the business practice structures and organizational infrastructures.
☐ Like a flock of birds swooping and turning as a unit, corporate change loses its event status and takes on a constant fluid motion.

Some level of change competency emphasized in stages 1 and 2 is required of virtually all companies today. The more advanced stages 3 and 4 are where preemptive competitive capabilities emerge. As yet, few companies have much to show in this rarefied area. Moving to a more mature stage doesn't mean abandoning the procedures in place at prior stages, it simply means that judgment plays a greater role in the applicability and application of rule-based procedures.

Figure 9.4 Change Proficiency Maturity Stages

Maturity	Critical Business Practice
4.0	1 Strategic Plan Vision
4.0	2 Strategic Plan Dissemination
4.0	3 Strategic Plan Buy-In
3.0	4 Capital Investment Justification
3.0	5 Infrastructure Investment Justification
3.5	6 Business Eng. Investment Justification
2.5	7 Business Unit Relationships
4.0	8 Employee Relationships
0.0	9 Partner Relationships
1.0	10 Supplier Relationships
3.0	11 Customer Relationships
0.5	12 Information System Relationships
2.0	13 Production Unit Relationships
4.0	14 Product Innovation Management
4.0	15 Process Innovation Management
4.0	16 Procedure Innovation Management
4.0	17 Strategy Innovation Management
4.0	18 Knowledge-Portfolio Strategy
3.0	19 Knowledge Generation
2.0	20 Knowledge Capture
4.0	21 Knowledge Mobilization
3.0	22 Leading Indicator Metrics
1.5	23 Operating Metrics
3.0	24 Valuation Metrics

Maturity Stage	Working Knowledge	Metric Focus	Change Competencies	
			Proactive	Reactive
0 Accidental	Examples	Pass/fail	None	None
1 Repeatable	Concepts	Time	Creation	Correction
2 Defined	Metrics	Cost	Improvement	Variation
3 Managed	Rules	Quality	Migration	Expansion
4 Mastered	Principles	Scope	Modification	Reconfiguration

Figure 9.5 Profiling Enterprise Change Proficiency Maturity

As a company progresses through maturity stages there is a specific and different emphasis on change proficiency metrics at each stage. These metrics are associated with the change process itself and refer to the *time* to affect a change, the *cost* of making a change, the *quality* of the change process, and the *scope* (breadth) of the change capability. Competency at specific types of change also tends to develop in a sequence; probably because there are clearly some competencies that are needed before others (just to be a contender), there is a pair-wise synergy with the metric focus, and there is a difference in difficulty. Notice the pair-wise synergy of *creation* with *time*, *improvement* with *cost*, *migration* with *quality* (being prepared in advance), and *modification* with *scope* (getting broader utility from a modifiable design). This profile is taken from *An Agile Enterprise Reference Model with a Case Study of Remmele Engineering*, Agility Forum, 1996.

247

creation with *time, improvement* with *cost, migration* with *quality* (being prepared in advance), and *modification* with *scope* (getting broader utility from a modifiable design).

Some level of change competency emphasized in stages 1 and 2 is required of virtually all companies today. On the proactive side, creation (e.g., product realization time) and improvement (e.g., development-cost reduction) are change capabilities that became the focus of competitiveness in the 1900s. Likewise on the reactive side, correction (e.g., fixing/replacing broken resources quickly) and variation (e.g., accommodating customer preferences afford-ably) were equally at the entry level for playing the game. The more advanced stages 3 and 4 are where preemptive competitive capabili-ties emerge. As yet, few companies have much to show in this rar-efied area.

Moving to a more mature stage doesn't mean abandoning the procedures in place at prior stages, it simply means that judgment plays a greater role in the applicability and application of rule-based procedures.

➤ Stage 0: Accidental

The *Accidental* stage is characterized by the lack of any change-process recognition, yet change manages to occur. The actual process is ad hoc: typically exhibiting false starts and retries, unpredictable completion dates and costs, surprising results and side effects, and undesirable reactions from, and effects on, the personnel involved. On the obvious bad side: grueling overtime, downsizing, multiple reengineering attempts, management fad-of-the-day, firefighting, ex-pediting. The seemingly good side also has its accidental successes: Sun Microsystems is in the limelight today for changing the network computer market with its Java product; but it stumbled there through missed opportunities, false starts, and sleepy competitors.[3]

> ➤ *Examples Knowledge Base.* Instances where something was changed successfully are recognized, and there is a small cat-alog of such experiences; but there is no explicit awareness that such successes could be controllably influenced by the way in which they were done rather than having been the re-sult of fate, random luck, fortuitous timing, help from exter-nal uncontrolled events, and other such out-of-our-control reasons.
>
> ➤ *Pass/Fail Metric Focus.* It worked or it didn't. There is little to be gained from discussing practices in the Accidental Stage as

they are characterized by their lack of proficiency. Nevertheless, it may occasionally be useful or necessary to explicitly show the accidental nature of what might otherwise be mistaken for a competency. When such is the case, a discussion based on an instance that "passed" is in order; and a facilitator might point out the difference between a simple concern or desire for a fast change, and a studied pursuit of ways to make a change occur faster.

➤ *No competence—Proactively Lucky.* This is not worth belaboring unless it is necessary to show that a success was not the result of a practice, but of uncontrolled circumstances.

➤ *No competence—Reactively Lucky.* Also not worth belaboring unless it is necessary to show that a success was not the result of a practice, but of uncontrolled circumstances.

➤ **Stage 1: Repeatable**

The *Repeatable* stage is typically based on anecdotal "lessons learned" from past change activities. Specialists and talented SWAT teams are recognized for prior successes and abilities to repeat these in acceptable time frames.

➤ *Concepts Knowledge Base.* Awareness develops at this stage. Key concepts are recognized and extracted from examples and lessons learned from both successes and failures, and employed repeatedly in subsequent change activities. The discussion here should identify the key concepts that form the knowledge base.

➤ *Time Metric Focus.* Initially, the principal concern is to have a change occur in time to be useful. A specific example that makes this general point easily is product development. Getting to market while the window is still open is the entry level requirement to play in the game at all. Better yet, get there first—even if you pay more to accelerate the program and compromise some features along the way—such things can be improved later; but only if the product is in play to establish the brand. Conversely, entering a market with little start-up or entry cost (we are not talking production cost here), and with precisely the capability and entry date you predicted is of no value if the market window has closed.

➤ *Creation Competency—Proactively Occasional.* Even a blind hog gets an acorn now and then, and does so because it follows a set procedure that has repeatedly redeemed itself. Blindness and hogs aside, here there should be a statement that supports Creation competency as a general attainment, followed by a specific instance or two that supports the "Occasional" image stemming from the competency. In this case, the word *competency* simply means that there is a known repeatable process that will result in a timely success, though its costs may limit the frequency of application.

➤ *Correction Competency—Reactively Safe.* Pressed to it, a company at this stage that must react knows enough to know that it can accomplish a change when it has to. It may be painful, it may be costly, and it may not get started until the organization is threatened with extinction; but hard work and fear, and the knowledge of a few concepts can get the process through to accomplishment before it's too late.

➤ Stage 2: Defined

The *Defined* stage begins to recognize formal change processes with documented procedures. The base of potentially successful practitioners is broadened as process rather than "natural" talent becomes appreciated. Metrics for the change process are identified, and predictability becomes an elusive desire. Typically, procedures at this stage are rigid and based on studied experience and analysis. Change competency in stages 1 and 2 is required of virtually all companies today in the critical practices unique to their industry sector.

➤ *Knowledge Base of Metrics.* The Defined stage occurs when change processes are sufficiently understood that they have well demarcated start and end points, and a knowledge base of performance metrics develops. How long it took and how much it cost are the metrics that generally get the most visibility and utility for subsequent comparison; but variances from plan and budget (predictability) are usually recorded as well. Here should be a discussion that demonstrates the existence and application of these understandings, keeping in mind that it is not necessary to identify a formal or centralized repository of this knowledge.

➤ *Cost Metric Focus.* At this point, the time to effect a change is acceptable, and the focus turns to cost. Full competency at this level brings the cost of making a change into an acceptable range as well, and the discussion here should make that evident. The acceptability range is often fairly broad, time and cost are frequently traded against each other, and seemingly similar activities have different outcomes.

➤ *Augmentation Competency—Proactively Competitive. Augmentation* is simply another way of saying "improvement." This competency coupled with the earlier stage provides the required capabilities at the heart of today's competitiveness. Here there should be a statement that supports Augmentation competency as a general attainment in the practice being analyzed, followed by a specific instance or two that supports the "Competitive" image stemming from the competency. Discussing the earlier-stage competency can also be useful because together these two provide today's ticket to the game.

➤ *Variation Competency—Reactively Confident.* Variation competency addresses proficient accommodation of real-time changes that are within character but not necessarily predictable: like production expediting, meeting unique customer demands, mass customization, or late supplier deliveries. Like the proactive discussion, the reactive side at this stage completes the minimal requirements for viability in today's business environment: correction (e.g., fixing/replacing broken resources quickly) and variation (e.g., accommodating customer preferences affordably) are entry-level needs for playing today's game. There should be a statement that supports Variation competency as a general attainment in the practice being analyzed, followed by a specific instance or two that supports the "Confident" image stemming from the competency. Discussing the earlier-stage competency can also be useful because together they provide basic viability in today's environment.

➤ Stage 3: Managed

The *Managed* stage is characterized by the appointment of change managers (business engineers), with established responsibilities, though they may neither be called nor recognized as such. An evolving knowledge base of change process fundamentals begins to emerge, appreciation for and participation in the corporate change-process is widespread, rigid procedures are loosened, and predictability is the norm. The more advanced maturity stages (3 and 4) are where preemptive competitive capabilities emerge.

➤ *Responsibilities Knowledge Base.* The Managed Stage occurs when a practice is controlled through the application of a well-formed set of procedures documented sufficiently to function as a manager's rule book. The knowledge base typically consists of the objectives, the rules, and the designation of persons accountable for applying the rules; and should be discussed here.

➤ *Robustness Metric Focus.* At this point, time and cost are within acceptable ranges and the focus turns to predictability, with the goal being "on time, on budget, and on spec." In essence, the focus deals with the quality of the change process, and the discussion should demonstrate that. Again, something should be said about competency *at all lesser metrics,* as well as the competency with the Robustness metric.

➤ *Migration Competency—Proactively Aggressive.* This Migration emphasis anticipates and prepares for inevitable future requirements well enough that when they become present requirements the transitions to accommodate them are smooth. There should be a statement that supports Migration competency as a general attainment, followed by a specific instance or two that supports the "Aggressive" image stemming from the competency. Discussing all earlier-stage competencies is not necessary unless the analysis has a narrow focus.

➤ *Expansion Competency—Reactively Sure.* The change category of Expansion deals with capacity issues, and might address such things as production surge, staff downsizing, or spreading knowledge across a broader base of employees. A statement should support Expansion competency as a general attainment, followed by a specific instance or two that supports the "Sure" image stemming from the competency. Just as for the proactive side, earlier-stage competencies need not be discussed unless the analysis has a narrow focus.

➤ **Stage 4: Mastered**

The *Mastered* stage is characterized by a principle-based deep appreciation of adaptability, an understanding that process alone is not sufficient, and a conscious engineering and manipulation of the structures of business practices and organizational infrastructures. Like a flock of birds swooping and turning as a unit, corporate change loses its event status and takes on constant fluid motion.

➤ *Principles Knowledge Base.* There should be an *articulation of known principles* that govern the subject under analysis. In essence, a principle-based mastery means that practitioners are beyond reading a rule book and following recipes, and into a visceral intuitive understanding of the chemistry that makes the subject work—able to embrace seemingly contradictory situations in this state of understanding—knowing full well that an enumerated discrete (digital) set of principles cannot address all conditions of a naturally continuous (analog) environment. As some sage once said, "The ultimate truth is that we will never know the ultimate truth"; commenting on the belief that our minds build discrete models of a continuous world.

➤ *Scope Metric Focus.* The discussion should demonstrate competency *at all lesser metrics,* as well as the competency with the Scope metric, to give a true sense of the maturing process as opposed to an early preoccupation with the end-game. There will be occasional cases where Scope has been well attended to before some or all of the earlier metrics—these are guidelines not laws. When this is found, it should be noted as an anomaly and not used as a way to elevate the maturity stage—unless it is in an area where the broad norm for the industry or practice must come to grips with Scope before others—in which case it is proper to construct a completely nonstandard Maturity Model and reorder the metric progression.

➤ *Modification Competency—Proactively Formidable.* Modification competency is a high art and addresses proficient addition and subtraction of complete features or capabilities of the subject under analysis. Here there should be a statement that supports Modification competency as a general attainment, followed by a specific instance or two that supports the "Formidable" image stemming from the competency. In broad-based analysis activities where many practices are analyzed, it is not necessary to discuss all earlier-stage competencies here (Migration, Augmentation, Creation); though such an approach is useful and affordable in narrow-focus analysis.

➤ *Reconfiguration Competency—Reactively Automatic.* Reconfiguration competency addresses the ability to take what is already available and proficiently reassemble the different pieces in a new configuration that satisfies new requirements. There should be a statement that supports Reconfiguration competency as a general attainment, followed by a specific instance or two that supports the "Automatic" image stemming from the competency. Just as for the proactive side, discussing all earlier-stage competencies is not necessary unless the analysis has a narrow focus.

■ EXAMPLES

Examples are drawn from the Agile Enterprise Reference Model and Case Study of Remmele Engineering. Here we include 2 of the 24 business practices that were profiled for maturity at Remmele Engineering. In Chapter 2, Remmele's strategic guiding principles were discussed, which form the framework for most of the Remmele business practices and provide the major contribution toward the high maturity scores.

To assess the maturity of a practice, one identifies the knowledge base employed in decision support, the metric focus of active strategies, and the exhibited competencies in both proactive and reactive change—all relative to a previously determined set of change issues. Experience with the Remmele case study found no difficulty in reaching a clear assessment consensus among the three team members for each of the 24 business practices. Though it is generally expected that separate assessments of proactive and reactive competencies in a specific practice will result in two separate maturity levels, this was not the case with Remmele. In all instances, the proactive and reactive competencies for a specific business practice were identical. The team believes that this reflects the content, strength, and pervasiveness of Remmele's specific corporate ideology, which addresses the concept of continuous change at its core without reactive and proactive distinctions.

The first critical business practice example is *Strategic Plan Buy-In* (see Table 9.1). Simply deciding to do something different at the top is a long way from getting a massive company to undertake that process and actually do something different.

For example, in response to a market demand created by Sun's Java and Netscape's browser, Microsoft's rabbit-out-of-a-hat Internet strategy is testament to the ability of a billion-dollar company to turn on a dime. Microsoft accomplished that feat (in the market's eyes) in less than a year. The important difference is in the corporate buy-in process.

For Microsoft and others in their industry, the practice that routinely achieves strategic plan buy-in appears to be a basic competitive requirement for everyone. In other industries, like metal parts machining, the common requirement for competency at this practice may still be in the future. Of course, a machining company with

Table 9.1 Change Issues: Strategic Plan Buy-In

Proactive Change Proficiency Issues

Creation	• Creating a sense of ownership and commitment to the vision
Improvement	• Improving the ability of people to understand and implement the vision and strategy
Migration	• Early understanding and dissemination of the need for major strategy change
Modification	• Encouraging innovative self-directed vision and strategy fulfillment

Reactive Change Proficiency Issues

Correction	• Helping employees that have difficulty with accepting responsibility and commitment
Variation	• Encouraging different Interpretations at different plants to fit different situations
Expansion	• Gaining ownership among new employees quickly
Reconfiguration	• Moving people freely without impediment among different operating modes and incentive programs

unique and decided competency at total and rapid buy-in can differentiate itself from all others quite advantageously.

Exactly what this competency means to Remmele in its industry sector is a relative question that separates practices already commonly recognized in a business sector from ones that are still uncommon. Competency at *future* differentiating advantages generally translates into preemptive advantage today—something borne out by Remmele's uncommon performance.

➤ Strategic Plan Buy-In

This is the process of gaining a sense of ownership for and a commitment to pursue an organization's vision and strategies by the members of the organization. Generally applicable change issues include the depth as well as the breadth of commitment and understanding throughout the organization, the accommodation of substantive changes in the implications of commitment when appropriate, and the ability to bring new membership in the organization to an equal sense of ownership quickly.

Architecture

The foundation of the buy-in process at Remmele is the corporate ideology and its emphasis on accountable empowerment, open communication and trust, and the strong sense of family/team that pervades the organization. Within this framework, the employees, their personal rewards, and the implications of strategic concepts determine local and personal operating modes. Highly mature practices freely reinterpret the relationships between strategic concepts and local and personal implications when appropriate opportunities arise:

Creating a Sense of Ownership and Commitment to the Vision

➤ The employees display a great sense of pride in the company and an expectation to function as accountable contributors, exhibiting a strong family identity and common team spirit. This ideological commitment appears rooted in the corporate Guiding Principles (Chapter 2) and touches everyone with the increasing emphasis on involving all people in the decisions that affect them. Management has not abdicated the responsibility for certain key decisions (e.g., how much will be allocated for capital), but these decisions are only reached *after* formally obtaining a great deal of serious employee input. Periodically, a database of competitive pay scales is developed by looking at other companies and various national sources. Until the late 1980s, a management committee would analyze this data and make general increase recommendations to the president. Now, all employees are given this data along with a form letter to the president that allows them to make a thoughtful and knowledgeable recommendation. Experience shows that the majority of people deliver a well-reasoned number that is considered carefully by the management group. In recent years, the approved increase has been consistently within half a point of the averaged employee recommendation.

➤ One manager offered that psychological ownership is powerful and apparent here, and is the essence of Remmele's success: "People here are so much in charge of what they are doing that they can hardly help but feel ownership. People are employed with the expectation that they will probably be here forever if things work out, and that imposes on Remmele the need to provide tools that will help them be more valuable to the organization. This is the management mind-set."

Improving the Ability of People to Understand and Implement the Vision and Strategy

➤ Exemplifying the involvement-in-decisions-that-affect-you point, as well as showing how the company supports personal knowledge development that enables ownership and deeper understanding: One division manager recently took four machinists on a world search for the best high-velocity machining equipment. They shopped heavily in Germany and France where they spent time talking to customers and users. This involved considerable time for each person away from revenue-generating work and required them to sort through the data and develop a recommendation, which they justified to other employees as well as to management. These people are now the resident experts on high-velocity machining and are responsible for integrating the capability into Remmele, and they own the decision.

Early Understanding and Dissemination of the Need for Major Strategy Change

➤ Remmele maintains an active and ongoing process for uncovering emerging technologies and new market opportunities. This process involves teams of people from both the operations side as well as the sales and marketing sides of the business, with team membership changing frequently to include a representative cross section of the organization. Hands-on technology evaluations and studied market research projects involve the people of the organization in early recognition of both opportunities and drivers that signal pending needs to change business strategies.

Encouraging Innovative Self-Directed Vision and Strategy Fulfillment

➤ Trust-based relationships are actually alive and well at Remmele and quite solid because they are practiced universally in all relationships—not just for the inner circle of management or employees, but also for community, suppliers, and customers. When asked what was unique about working at Remmele, one shop worker offered: "We take pride in our work, look at the T-shirt slogans [*Pride in Quality* displayed on a few chests], and that's what we take to heart. We don't like anything going out the door less than perfect, and we'll talk to the customer about it honestly if he wants us to ship before we have it the way we want it."

Helping Employees That Have Difficulty with Accepting Responsibility and Commitment

➤ Employees take responsibility as peer-to-peer mentors of new employees, helping them assimilate the culture of responsibility and commitment.

Encouraging Different Interpretations at Different Plants to Fit Different Situations

➤ Though the core ideology and corporate strategy establish a foundation, separate divisions are expected to interpret and implement strategic plans in a context that suits achievement best in their markets. The Production Machining Division is organized around "focused-factory" cells dedicated to a single customer's requirement and has evolved a strong cross-functional teamwork mode that accepts responsibility for maintenance, purchasing, recruitment, and other typical support functions among the cell's operators. Whereas station operation in a cell does not require the same capabilities that a machinist employs in another plant, it allows time for active responsibility in a broader set of business support functions. By dispatching these functions within the cell team, support overhead is minimized and employees gain a broader set of skills and an understanding of business operation.

Gaining Ownership among New Employees Quickly

➤ Highly effective information dissemination practices, recruitment screening for self-motivated people, and an active help-your-fellow-employee-learn-the-ropes environment bring new employees up to speed quickly. All employees help the new people learn and practice the company way. Cell teams in the Production Machining Division decide which new team members they will accept. They help each other come up to speed and take pride in saying that nobody has failed to fit in as yet.

**Moving People Freely without Impediment from Different
Operating Modes and Incentive Programs**

➤ Though there are some uncomfortable differences for veteran
employees between the operating modes and skill sets used in
the Automation Division, the Production Machining Division,
and the three other machining plants, enough employees exhibit a willingness to go where the company needs them to satisfy the mobilization flexibility the company sometimes
needs. This is true even at the apprentice level: One of the
stated differences about Remmele apprentices was their willingness to go where the company needed them. On the incentive front, everybody participates in corporate profit sharing,
based on total corporate results, with a floor that guarantees 3
percent of pay minimum will be contributed to the retirement
plan. Anything available above that can be taken as cash or put
into the retirement fund at the employee's discretion. Higher
paid top management has a cap on the amount of profit sharing from this plan. The plan's focus on corporate results facilitates moving people among plants when appropriate.

See Figure 9.6 for a synopsis of the maturity level.

➤ Employee Relationships

This refers to the working interrelationships that exist among all
people engaged by the organization directly as individuals, as well as
the relationship those people have with the organization as a whole
(see Table 9.2). Agility issues generally applicable across industry include creating a sense of ownership and responsibility, delegating
and distributing control and responsibility, reassigning tasks and responsibilities, improving and imparting new skill sets and knowledge, and workforce right-sizing.

Architecture

Employee relationships at Remmele are governed by the Guiding Principles and its emphasis on employee satisfaction through economic
security, trust and open communications, continuous learning, concern for individual needs, involvement in decisions, and a clean, safe
working environment. An employee handbook adds detail to the
meaning of these principles and spells out what should be expected by

Maturity Stage 4 (Mastered) for Both Proactive and Reactive Change Proficiency

Principles Knowledge Base: Remmele's Strategic Policies contribute explicitly: "In the interest of enhancing the psychological ownership of our business by all employees we will continue to (1) involve people in the process of making decisions which affect them, (2) provide for decision making and problem solving at the most appropriate level, (3) encourage risk taking, and (4) empower employees with the freedom and authority to make the decisions necessary for effective job performance."

Scope Metric Focus: Time and cost of securing buy-in for corporate and divisional objectives is not a concern, as the corporate ideology responsible for most of this "practice" is virtually invisible—it just happens. Robustness is a nonissue for the same reason: ideological drivers ensure that responsible ownership is the stable state of the operating environment. Emphasis is now placed on broadening the involvement of employees in the decisions that affect them, and helping them develop the personal skills that they need in order to take on increased responsibility.

Proactive Modification Competency: Innovative contributions to the operating modes that satisfy strategic plans and vision occur as a matter of course, with employees exercising prescreened skills and fulfilling expectations of their relationship to the organization. For instance, the station operators are the process innovators in the mature cells at the Production Machining Division (Plant 30). In another plant it was noted that the suggestion box has been virtually abandoned as a time-delay, if it's good the employees just do it, unless customer approval is needed.	**Reactive Reconfiguration Competency:** The corporate ideology embraces the concept of continuous change at the same time that it relies on a stable set of beliefs and values. The stable foundation of beliefs is what enables the reinterpretation of acceptable strategies. Plant 30, for instance, is under pressure to gain new business, and is considering a wide range of prospects that may require an operating mode different than previous experience. Past examples necessitating such rethinking include both "clean room" and "miniature machining" activities which had no prior precedence, were considerably different than the experience base, and required reinterpretation of strategic concepts into local and personal implications.

Remmele Engineering in 1966. Dove, Hartmen, Benson, *An Agile Enterprise Reference Model with a Case Study of Remmele Engineering*. Agility Forum, 1996.

Figure 9.6 Change Proficiency Maturity: Strategic Plan Buy-In

Table 9.2 Change Issues: Employee Relationships	
Proactive Change Proficiency Issues	
Creation	• Obtaining top-quality people; creating a sense of team, ownership, and responsibility
Improvement	• Improving personnel skills
Migration	• Workforce diversity; top management succession
Modification	• Gaining new skills; guarding against insularity
Reactive Change Proficiency Issues	
Correction	• Correcting mismatches between people and their tasks
Variation	• Filling critical slots when a key employee is absent
Expansion	• Finding more high-quality machinists; handling surge requirements
Reconfiguration	• Reassigning tasks and responsibilities to meet special needs

both the company and the employee. Reconfiguring these relationships generally means changing the people and/or skills assigned to various responsibilities, development programs, teams, and reward systems. Table 9.2 outlines the following change issues:

Obtaining Top-Quality People; Creating a Sense of Team, Ownership, and Responsibility

➤ Common and extensive screening procedures test for like-minded people who expect serious work, a sense of family, and constant learning.

➤ An annual employee satisfaction survey questions peoples' opinions of policies as well as general attitudes. "People are so precious to the business that you have to preserve and protect them. People are told that they will have to work as much as needed when the work is present and in return the company will staff leanly to protect their jobs; reducing the work when business is poor rather than laying off. So the work-week is the variable and everybody expects that. Employee surveys have always had over 90 percent say: 'Yes, keep doing that.' Even the old timers, who for the most part do not ask for full hours in tough times because of seniority."

➤ A Remmele manager comments: "The pyramid chart is alive and well here, and layers of management are not being taken out; but people are involved in the decisions that affect their livelihood, and have always been dealt with from a position of trust."

➤ The machinist's Apprenticeship Program starts with a two-year vocational trades education before they are hired by Remmele and admitted into the program. On admittance, they receive six months of apprentice training credit for the vocational education. They then spend two and a half years rotating through the five Remmele plants at six months each, then a final year of internship in one plant—for a total of four years. In their final six-month rotation at the Repetitive Batch Machining Division, when they are familiar with CNC equipment, apprentices are assigned personal nonsupervisory machinist mentors for each machine they are assigned to operate. Mentors are responsible for providing the day-to-day direction and assistance necessary to assure the completeness of training. Mentors regularly evaluate the apprentice's progress, and apprentices regularly evaluate the mentor's effectiveness as a trainer. These formal two-way performance reviews assure that training is effective and appropriate. Apprentices rank their plant preferences for the final year of training at the completion of the last six-month rotation, and their preferences are instrumental in deciding their assignments.

➤ One employee commenting on the small-plant strategy offered: "People want to know everybody in the plant and have a good relationship as a family." Though there are no formal corporate teaming support structures or standard training classes, people team naturally and effectively. This is likely based on the fact that ego-based individualism is bred/selected out, a sense of family is strong, ownership is pervasive, and the reward system does not favor individualism or create an internal competition. Consultants are brought in on occasion to help train special team skills when necessary, and have been employed at the Automation Division as well as the Production Machining Division, which is organized around focused-factory teams associated with a specific customer. The biannual meetings of Remmele people and sales reps incorporate specific training on development and operation of *selling teams* that will interface with customer's *buying teams*.

Improving Personnel Skills

➤ Though Remmele's observation of cost accounting data shows that approximately 4 percent of payroll is reinvested in formal training of hourly employees, much more is spent on less formal means and not captured specifically as an expense item: There is a strong suspicion that tracking these investments overtly would be counterproductive. There is no training budget; the hourly number is known only because they had to find it for their Baldrige application work.

➤ Remmele will pay for any education that the company can use, regardless of a person's current position. Thus, an accountant's interest in machining courses or a janitor's engineering education are not questioned and are paid for 100 percent up front—not qualified on grade performance. "Here's the money, now what's your excuse. We have to knock down barriers that stand in the way of anybody becoming whatever they want to become."

➤ Knowledge maintenance is valued: With an employee base of 475 people, they send 50 to 60 machine operators to the annual International Manufacturing Technology Show (IMTS) exhibition and conference.

➤ Custom-tailored training is typical. Across the corporation, psychological testing is done down to second-level managers, with skill/leadership development done down to third level. A structured program was put in place for the Production Machining Division's "focused-factory" people that did individual needs assessment and then taught the skills that were needed.

Workforce Diversity; Management Succession

➤ Remmele values the breadth of innovation and approach that comes from diversity in human resources but is having difficulty attaining the breadth it desires from the Minnesota area, which has a dominant ethnic consistency. This is becoming a challenge as the company grows and its annual recruitment volume increases. Rather than compromise its core values on new-recruit qualifications, it has broadened its recruitment activity into surrounding states and beyond.

➤ Senior management at Remmele is approaching retirement age, and succession is once again an issue for consideration. Previous transition practice has basically employed a multiyear gradual phaseover to a designated successor. With growth, the company has recognized the need for a broad-based program of management-skill preparation and has instituted an individualized development program aimed at strengthening the entire management team and growing internal skill sets needed for Remmele's future growth and succession.

Gaining New Skills; Guarding against Insularity

➤ Most of Remmele's senior management team have been recruited from outside rather than promoted from within. This has added to the diversity of thought without polluting the core values and without creating a "dead-end" feeling among long-term employees, who value competency over title in both their own performance and that of their management. Remmele has had to reach outside as it has not had a natural training environment for developing new management, which is now realized and addressed with a new and individualized "leadership development" program specifically aimed at growing internal management skills.

➤ Recruitment efforts target top talent and gifted personnel with a mind of their own; machinist apprentice candidates are screened for breadth of interest and world consciousness, as well as for values and value systems rather than for a specific dogma. Older apprentices are entering the program, bringing with them their experiences in other companies. Occupations other than machinist are not subjected to the same screening template, which adds further to the diversity of thought.

Correcting Mismatches between People and Their Tasks

➤ The specific nature of Remmele's ideology and its consistency among employees has resulted in a self-organizing system of peer-to-peer mentoring. In one division, for instance, the focused-factory cell teams decide who they will team with and then work with each other to develop the necessary complement of skills and responsibility: "Nobody really hasn't fit in, but if all else fails, the pressure is raised on that person and eventually the supervisor will help if they don't move on voluntarily."

Filling Critical Slots When a Key Employee Is Absent

➤ There is a lot of cross-trained job rotation at Remmele on both a formal and informal basis that provides critical backup insurance. In broad terms, apprentices are rotated through each of the five plants for six months at a time, people are moved from job to job within plants as projects come and go, and people are moved from plant to plant as business waxes and wanes in different sectors.

➤ Project Managers have moved successfully between plants, but the Automation Division's project engineers require unique skill sets. Within the plants, there are generally multiple project managers capable of handling each other's responsibilities.

➤ Focused-factory teams in the Production Machining Division are cross-trained on all cell production stations as well as the broader set of support functions like purchasing and maintenance.

Finding More High-Quality Machinists; Handling Surge Requirements

➤ With Remmele growing at 10 to 12 percent per annum and with a base of 475 employees, the current staffing chore is about 50 people per year to cover both growth and attrition. These requirements put a large recruitment load on the plant's human resources people, and machinist apprentices are a particular issue. Though Remmele has always worked closely with the vocational schools, bringing teachers out each year for tours and discussions about changing needs, they are now reaching into the high schools to show that a machinist's life is clean, high paying, and high-technology-oriented.

➤ For surge requirements in the traditional machining businesses, Remmele relies on overtime and borrowing machinists among the plants. Hiring temporary machinists is not an option, as they are simply not available. There is also a strong bias to grow their own as they generally don't even hire journeyperson machinists from elsewhere.

➤ The Production Machining Division does not generally require journeyperson machinists and can utilize outside contractors to fill surge requirements.

Maturity Stage 4 (Mastered) for Both Proactive and Reactive Change Proficiency

Principles Knowledge Base: The corporate Human Resources Department has the principal responsibility for employee relationship management and has an appropriate employee handbook spelling out the details, definitions, and expectations of company employment. This handbook begins with the corporate Guiding Principles statement that in fact establishes the employee relationship framework with its emphasis on employee satisfaction through economic security, trust and open communications, continuous learning, concern for individual needs, involvement in decisions, and a clean, safe working environment. The Guiding Principles are governing, with the remainder of the handbook interpreting their application and providing background and detail for such things as tuition reimbursement and regulatory compliance.

Scope Metric Focus: Though time and cost to find and recruit the qualities and diversity desired in good machinist apprentices are rising, neither are incommensurate with the values attributed to methodical screening and selection. Annual employee surveys and the practices that reflect the ideological core ensure a robust, stable, predictable environment. The company's current emphasis is on broadening its skill development with the new management and leadership training, widening its recruitment pool with its outreach to high schools, and increasing diversity by broadening its recruitment efforts.

Proactive Modification Competency: Remmele has had to reach outside for most of its senior management as it has not had a natural training environment for developing new management. This influx of management trained elsewhere has been successfully added to the corporation without losing or changing the corporate ideology and without creating a "dead-end" feeling among long-term employees. Recruitment efforts for both management and operational people target top talent and gifted personnel with a mind of their own; screening candidates for breadth of interest and world consciousness, as well as for values and value systems—rather than for a specific dogma. That such people can be added to the mix without disruption is a testament to a practice that is well founded and consistent.

Reactive Reconfiguration Competency: Remmele's strong ideological core makes it relatively easy to move people from one part of the company to another, as they share a common and practiced sense of company, working framework, and appreciation for professional competency. This same set of principles values constant learning and continuous change, facilitating quick deployment of resources into areas where they may have little prior experience. The extensive internal networking facilitated by an open communication environment and frequent cross-divisional functional forums provides an ability to identify the right people for urgent needs within the company whenever they arise.

Figure 9.7 Change Proficiency Maturity: Employee Relationship Management

Remmele Engineering in 1966. Dove, Hartmen, Benson, *An Agile Enterprise Reference Model with a Case Study of Remmele Engineering*, Agility Forum, 1996.

➤ The Automation Division (Plant 50) generally needs engineers in times of surge and is able to bring in highly skilled people on contracts.

Reassigning Tasks and Responsibilities to Meet Special Needs

➤ Within plants, the family/team culture provides comprehensive and objective skill visibility. Across plants, the common-function forums convened for purchasing, accounting, technology, and marketing provide similar visibility. When particular needs arise, they can be readily matched with the right people who have the right capabilities.

See Figure 9.7 for a synopsis of the maturity level.

■ HOW AND WHY TO USE MATURITY PROFILING

Maturity is a measure of things like awareness, comprehension, and wisdom, but not necessarily competency. Thus, building a maturity profile will show you how ready you are to do something, but not necessarily show you how well you do it. It is comparative, against an ideal, against another company, against the norms of your industry, or against a normative scale you develop from a role model ideal.

The principal purpose of this chapter is to offer tools and technique for moving this book's information base into your corporate knowledge base, acculturating the concepts of change proficiency. These tools and technique can be used to obtain other immediate objectives as well, and in fact rely on achieving these other objects for their effectiveness at acculturation. Figure 9.8 summarizes objectives and deliverables available from the maturity profiling process. It shows that project team makeup is generally matched to the specific objective, while methodology is fairly universal, and specific results (deliverables) can be chosen from a variety of options for immediate interest and applicability.

Changing the corporate culture requires that we get inside people's heads and change the way they think. To do that, a lot of people are going to have to get engaged, they're going to have to think and look about them to take stock; they're going to have to decide what to take stock of, and then they will need to reach conclusions. This is work. But it can be highly rewarding, both to the company

Objectives(s)	Team	Methodology	Deliverables (any or all)
• Trial Concept Test (Evaluation and Training)	• Facilitators and *Special Teams* People	• Establish Business Practice (BP) Framework	• As-Is Profile (Company State)
• Industry Benchmarks (Reference Base)	• Multiple-Company Team	• Chapter 4 Group Analysis for the Following:	• Supply Profile (Competitors)
• Change Proficiency Acculturation (Cultural Engineering)	• Broad Cross-Company Participants	• BP Definitions	• Demand Profile (Customers)
• Improvement Strategy (Gap Analysis)	• Improvement Team	• BP Framework/ Components	• Best-in-Class Profile (Cross-Industry)
• (Leadership Strategy Opportunity Analysis)	• Strategic Team	• BP Change Domain Issues	• Opportunity Profile (Perceived Advantage)
		• BP Maturity Score	• Possibility Profile (Ideal Optimum)
			• To-Be Profile (Company Objective)

Figure 9.8 Maturity Profiling Projects

A maturity profiling project might be undertaken specifically to develop a foundation for an improvement strategy or a leadership strategy, or perhaps to establish specific benchmarks and an awareness of best-in-class competencies. Very direct objectives with very immediate payoffs. A profiling exercise might also be use as a trial evaluation of general change proficiency concepts, or to train facilitators who will subsequently be deployed across a larger corporate roll-out. In any event, beyond whatever immediate objective is chosen, the exercise will have the longer term effect of acculturating the concepts of change proficiency. It has this effect on the participants by its very nature—and can be employed as a major tool to introduce a broad cross-section of the corporation to these concepts and begin the transformation to response-able enterprise.

with immediate as well as long-term results, and to the individual participants with the development of a new sense and appreciation.

■ DELIVERABLES

The flurry of reengineering activity in the 1990s introduced a broad base of the corporate world to the use of *as-is* and *to-be* process models. Initial thinking recommended that a reengineering project first document the as-is situation, and then design an improved to-be approach. Eventually as the idea of radical change became a clearer necessity, many veterans of the reengineering process questioned the value of time spent recording history when the future needed swift attack.

The usual arguments for ignoring the as-is phase in reengineering exercises assumes that you know what you want to be, or are at least in a position to design what you ought to be, and therefore shouldn't waste any time describing the history you are about to abolish. All fine and well if you really are in a position to begin the to-be design. There are some good reasons, however, for conducting an as-is analysis, principally associated with learning and commitment. Those involved in an as-is exercise come to understand the nature of the problem that a to-be exercise will attack and also develop buy-in. As said in earlier chapters, it is a mistake to assume that everyone (or anyone, for that matter) understands a problem and will buckle down to help find a solution, or even recognize and value a solution when presented with one.

Developing an as-is profile of corporate change proficiency will also define the edge of cultural readiness, which can provide a knowledgeable basis for designing incremental rather than shocking improvement strategies. In the typical corporate environment, change proficiency is not a well understood competency. Developing an as-is profile does a lot more than simply documenting history—it reveals the present in terms never before seen.

Importantly, an as-is profile introduces new notions of competency and measurement without fighting natural defensiveness against new change. It can be a powerful way to start the acculturation of change proficiency values. It can also be a revealing way to evaluate suppliers and their likelihood to be there when you need them the most—though a truly revealing as-is profile here will require the candid participation of a supplier, and will naturally have a defensive undercurrent.

Change proficiency profiles can also be developed for specific industry sectors as well as organizations. These market-wide profiles are best done with cross-organizational participation, though a company may well undertake to privately profile its competitive (supply-side) or customer (demand-side) market with whatever knowledge it possesses or can obtain from industry experts and consultants.

A third type of deliverable (beyond *as-is* and *industry-sector*) builds a hypothetical profile that describes an enterprise which does not exist. Such a profile might be generated to define a desired to-be state in terms of its measurable objectives, and form the basis for guiding the development of an improvement strategy. Another use might be the creation of a theoretically ideal or optimum profile, providing an end-point metric for gap analysis, evaluation of competitors, measurement of progress, or the humbling of the arrogant.

■ OBJECTIVES AND TEAMS

A maturity profiling project may be undertaken specifically as a foundation for an improvement strategy or a leadership strategy, or perhaps to establish specific benchmarks and an awareness of best-in-class competencies. These are direct objectives with immediate payoffs. In addition, a profiling exercise might be used as a trial evaluation of general change proficiency concepts, or to train facilitators who will subsequently be deployed across a larger corporate rollout. Beyond whatever immediate objective is chosen, the exercise will have the longer term effect of acculturating the concepts of change proficiency. It has this effect on the participants by its very nature and can be employed as a major tool to introduce a broad cross-section of the corporation to these concepts and begin the transformation to response-able enterprise.

➤ Trial Concept Test

New management and operational concepts, such as those presented in this book, are rightfully met with healthy skepticism. Suspected merit is weighed against the perceptions of current culture, real people, corporate situations, and political environments. A maturity profiling project can be used to test the long-term potential value of response-able concepts while generating an immediate short-term result. If the principal purpose of the project is either training or evaluation, project team makeup is fairly straightforward, and includes those people who are being trained and/or those who are involved in the evaluation. In either case, participants should be a part of (at least some of) the business practices being profiled so that they participate as contributors as well as profilers.

➤ Industry Benchmarks

Benchmarking for best practices can be an enlightening experience when change proficiency maturity is the focus, especially when cross-industry projects look for best-in-class maturity examples. The focus on maturity looks beyond the practice itself to develop a profile of how an organization understands and perceives the practice in its dynamic realm. Teams are best when they include participants from each company offering a practice for benchmarking, as this deeper involvement amplifies the revelation.

➤ Acculturation of Change Proficiency

This is perhaps the most useful purpose a maturity profiling exercise can serve, but is best when achieved indirectly as a by-product of one of the following strategy development objectives. Changing an embedded culture can be difficult when approached head on: Defenses against change arise, and new values become the focus of academic debate. It is much better to learn and employ a set of tools to gain a more familiar end, like that of developing a meaningful strategy for either improvement or leadership. Long after the strategy objective is met, the new skills and insights remain. To seed a culture effectively, a large cross section of corporate practices should be used, involving participants from as many functional areas as possible and useful. Change proficiency concepts are practice-independent, leaving a residual of common language and common values that cross all functional areas.

➤ Improvement Strategy

Conducting a maturity profiling exercise as an end in itself can provide a learning experience and generate new corporate awareness for some people; but without an actionable objective many people will be left unmotivated or unfulfilled by a seemingly academic exercise. Profiling the as-is situation in any specific business practice can sensitize the participants to the applicable concepts of change proficiency, while presenting them with a set of obvious improvement opportunities. Team participants for this objective are best chosen for their ownership of the practice and the subsequent implementation of an improvement strategy.

➤ Leadership Strategy

The objective here is to find an opportunity to step out in front of the competition—to sense where emerging needs are creating new unfulfilled demands, where the edge of accomplishment and competency exist in a market, and to move one or more steps beyond. Team members are best chosen both for their breadth of understanding and for their vision, and good teams will include outside experts who bring different perspectives and knowledge as well as a blind eye to the internal invisible barriers.

■ METHODOLOGY AND TECHNIQUE

The methodology for developing a maturity profile employs the participative workshop process described in Chapter 4 and summarized in Figure 4.5, especially when the principal objective is to acculturate the organization with change proficiency. An important additional step requires development of a business practice framework, the armature on which the profile hangs.

Participants are of three types: contributors (members of a practice being profiled), profilers (a small group of people who will rationalize the information and make maturity judgments), and facilitators (keepers of the process). Facilitators and profilers can be the same people, should be small in number, and for the sake of consistency should span the entire set of practice analysis workshops if possible. Where workshop participant involvement is not a part of the objectives, a small team of profiles can build a maturity profile by conducting individual and group interviews with appropriate people from the chosen practices, much like the process employed to construct the original Agile Enterprise Reference Model discussed earlier.

Hints on Change Issue/Response Categorization

➤ Often a group is clear on an issue or a response example, but unclear how to categorize it. Four of the change domains are proactive categories and four are reactive. Keeping this in mind helps separate issues and responses more consistently. If a response item occurs spontaneously, it is among the four proactive change domains; if it occurs as a result of external pressure, it is among the reactive group.

➤ The change issues should progress through the proactive and reactive groups with increasing difficulty. It is incorrect to have a reconfiguration issue, for example, describe something simple and commonplace when a variation or expansion issue clearly requires more competency. Since we will be awarding "masters" points to practices that can deal with reconfiguration and modification issues well, these should be appropriately difficult to achieve with rare examples of success. Similar reasoning should be used in the ranking of expansion and migration issues relative to those below them.

➤ Though in reality, change proficiency issues are many, one strong representative and instructive issue per domain is sufficient to create a maturity profile. Sometimes an issue/response example remains elusive or never seems quite right. Don't force it. Leave it blank. This is often the case for issues above the maturity attainment level.

➤ In the development of sequential change domain issues (trying to fill in the table of eight in sequence), it is typical to go back and respin or change some of the proactive issues after starting into the reactive issues—or vice versa depending on which four-tuple you begin with. The issues become interrelated, and together should tell a comprehensive story—they are not disconnected concepts. When finished, the composite of all entries will paint a comprehensive and integrated picture.

➤ To help develop the change domain issues, it is often useful to ask: "Are we focused on the Agility of the practice or the Agility of the enterprise enabled by the practice?" Either or both are valid foci, it is only necessary to establish what the focus will be.

➤ For the advanced student of the change proficiency maturation sequence, migration may seem to be symmetrical with reconfiguration, and modification may seem symmetrical with expansion. People, however, are more inclined to prepare for the next thing (migration) than they are to deal with changing the current thing (modification). Thus, by observation, migration comes before modification. Apparently it is easier to do, at least in the business environment that has molded people's behaviors so far.

Hints on Maturity Categorization

➤ If a workshop approach is employed, a preliminary stab at maturity scoring can be assigned as a 15- to 30-minute silent individual exercise—or as a multiple-small-group exercise—

and subsequently reviewed and discussed by the whole group. All of this would properly precede the official consensus development.

➤ Whether a preliminary group exercise, or a subsequent individual rationalization, the instructions for pegging a maturity level might be: Describe in detail a clear example, and it must be one that is representative of the general situation, for the maturity level that you feel has been attained (in whatever practice is being examined). You should also be able to do this (but don't have to) for every level below the attained level; and you should be able to cite multiple examples at each attained level.

➤ To explicitly justify a contention that a higher maturity level has not yet been attained, identify a change issue of indisputably key importance that is not met. This has the added value of establishing a road map for improvement.

➤ Though you may judge a practice to be fairly mature within its industry, it is important to understand when change proficiency in an industry is still at an early stage of competitive utilization. In early years of industry maturity, it is likely that the change issues in a practice will graduate in difficulty frequently, and having a high maturity score one year may mean nothing the next. In the social structure of high-school teenagers, a 17-year-old senior generally has unchallenged maturity.

➤ There are two dynamic time dimensions to change proficiency maturity: (1) A company progresses through maturity stages in a static industry model, and (2) the model evolves to more sophisticated or difficult issues within each domain as the industry becomes more mature.

■ A SHEEP IN WOLF'S CLOTHING—PUTTING A HARD EDGE ON SOFT SCIENCE

How do we introduce concepts of change proficiency and response ability to an organization and have them embraced rather than suspected as another fad of the day? How do we build momentum and sustain the acculturation rather than lose it in exercises and paperwork? We have explored a methodology for developing a new way of thinking that can't be denied once the inner eye is opened. This chapter provides a technique for creating concept ownership and value understandings among the people in the organization.

Discussion and understanding shape values and beliefs. You are what you think about. This chapter shows how to introduce and embed new thoughts of change proficiency in the culture. The result is like putting on a new pair of glasses that provide X-ray vision — everything looked at thereafter is seen in a different light.

The modeling and profiling processes described in this chapter employ analytical techniques that are neither precise nor unambiguous; nevertheless, they are valuable tools in developing a greater competency. It is suggested that the analytical models speak to the logic of the left brain while helping to create the holistic right-brain patterns of insight, and that a left-brain logical and linear model of change proficiency is generally necessary to gain broad awareness and adoption, yet real insightful competency comes later when the concept of change proficiency transcends the attempts to quantify it.

This chapter showed how to measure your cultural awareness of change proficiency in terms of your organization's deployment maturity, while sensitizing everyone to the need and the concepts. Chapter 10 shows a more advanced technique that takes the budding values and beliefs created here and embeds them deeper by using them to solve pressing problems.

■ NOTES

1. See Dove et al. (1996), *An Agile Enterprise Reference Model with a Case Study of Remmele Engineering.*
2. See Dove (1996), "Business Practices Critical to Early Realization of Agile Enterprise."
3. See Bank (1995), "The Java Saga."

Chapter

10

Becoming and Managing the Response-Able Enterprise

Chapter 9 introduced a method to accomplish something that many corporations do one way or another periodically—assess where they are and decide where to go next. This method has the by-product of residual learning: It develops a working knowledge base of the concepts in this book. However, as it is only an event-based, problem-solving technique, it does little more than introduce RA concepts to those touched by the process. What is needed to build and maintain the RA enterprise is to embed these concepts in the culture of the organization, to make them part of the day-in/day-out operating routine.

In this final chapter, we do not restate the book's contents as a summarized synthesis of its many ideas, but rather introduce another problem-solving technique and a management practice, which together offer a way to embed the contents in the culture, and practice them on a daily basis. Changing the culture means people having to learn something. Using these methods successfully requires the introduction of some new background knowledge as well.

Collaborative learning, communities of practice, organizational learning, and knowledge management are necessary ingredients of the response-able and agile enterprise. They have specific roles to play in the building and managing of the response-able enterprise, and so they are not covered comprehensively, but only as they contribute and pertain to our central focus.

■ A PERSPECTIVE ON KNOWLEDGE MANAGEMENT

That knowledge management is central to the concepts of agile enterprise is an understatement. The only reason we are interested in agile and response-able enterprise is that the business operating environment has become uncertain and unstable; and this has happened because the knowledge that underpins business and business operation is changing faster than business can. Knowledge feeds on knowledge, and we have apparently reached a point where the rate of new knowledge generation outpaces the cycles of organizational response. This thing called knowledge has a mind of its own (see Figure 10.1).

In the agile organization, knowledge management is responsible for having the right knowledge in the right place at the right time. Table 10.1 lists some of the issues encompassed by this responsibility.

Having knowledge at the right time means it is available sufficiently in advance of when it must be utilized to allow for its application. If it is to be applied in an area that is difficult to change, then it must be available early enough to allow for sluggish application. An idea whose time has come generally has many lovers—speed of implementation is at least as important as speed of knowledge acquisition.

Having knowledge at the right place means having it in a specific someone's head, not in the wrong person's head and not in an online repository or a corporate library or a document file. Technology is useful to help people find resources that can help them learn the knowledge they require; but it is neither a substitute nor an alternative for somebody learning something. The knowledge management responsibility includes both a push and a pull side. Knowing who has knowledge is no more important than knowing who needs knowledge, especially in these early times when corporate cultures are not yet naturally collaborative and knowledge seeking.

Having the right knowledge means managing the organizational knowledge portfolio to anticipate emerging needs, satisfy current needs, and weed out the obsolete needs everywhere in the organization. This is *knowledge portfolio management* (Table 10.2) and conveys an important strategic distinction that easily separates knowledge management from the territory staked out by information technology departments and vendors. That the CIO is often confused about owning the CKO responsibility is a measure of how urgently this distinction needs to be made.

Perhaps there will never be a generally accepted definition, structure, and organizational home for knowledge management. With its promise to play a central and deciding role in competitive differentiation, these questions may be best answered differently by

Years Ago

2,500,000	Stone tools—humans live as apes
40,000	Great leap forward (Language-caused? art, houses, weapons, war)
4,000	Horse domesticated, plow invented, wheel invented
500	Water travel begins to homogenize humanity globally
0	Space exploration, nuclear physics, genetic engineering, global communications, networked humanity, . . .

Genetically we last changed around 40,000 B.C.

Knowledge, created and diffused by language, has been driving human evolution ever since.

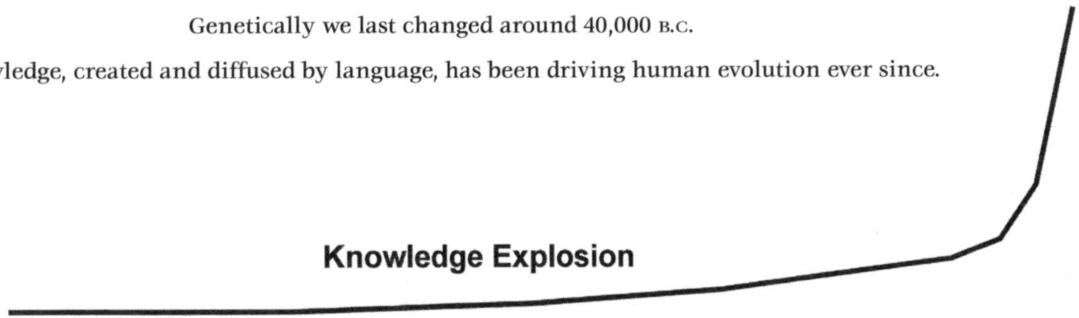

Knowledge Explosion

Figure 10.1 What's Happening

Thanks to Jared Diamond's *The Third Chimpanzee* for general times and characteristics. The statement that we last genetically changed 40,000 years is my interpretation of his writings, however, and should not be held against him if it proves to be wrong. His conjecture was that the voice box was responsible for the *great leap forward* in human development, which provided the uniquely human capability to then incorporate vowels into utterances, which led to a spoken language that could convey complexity and nuance, which led to thought, and to thoughts that could be passed on to others. The emergence of a new form of evolving stuff.

Table 10.1 Key Knowledge Management Issues

What's new and necessary to know changes quickly.

The value of what is already known changes quickly.

Some of what is known is obsolete and toxic.

Applying someone else's knowledge often has no glory.

Knowledge is often not in the heads of the people who need it.

Knowledge is understanding and appreciation, not data and procedure.

Knowledge is learned, and there's no time-out for learning.

Different people learn differently.

Collaborative learning is best, but (usually) culturally unnatural.

Knowledge is not naturally mobile within an organization.

Large organizations are culturally diverse.

Large organizations are geographically dispersed.

Collaboration and knowledge management technology support is in its infancy.

What to know and when to know are vital strategic issues.

Table 10.2 Knowledge Portfolio Management

Knowledge Portfolio Management

The identification, acquisition, diffusion, and renewal of all knowledge that the organization requires.

Portfolio puts strategic emphasis on the dynamics of knowledge value.

Identification recognizes the dynamic nature of knowledge value, and seeks to anticipate new needs in time to acquire knowledge and diffuse it.

Requires is a key word. It assumes a timely evaluation of what knowledge is needed when and by whom to meet operational needs and strategic objectives.

Acquisition recognizes that knowledge may be captured from internal resources, obtained from outside resources, or created by the organization.

Diffusion recognizes that knowledge is understanding, that this occurs in people's heads, and that it involves learning.

Renewal recognizes that knowledge value degrades with time and can become toxically negative.

different firms leveraging their own unique strengths and missions. For example, effective knowledge management in a major consulting organization with its high churn of MBA advisers bears little useful resemblance to what is needed in a manufacturing organization. At some generic level, however, some useful theory and process should emerge.

In the agile organization, knowledge management is first about learning, second about application, third about purpose, and there is no fourth. These are ordered as prerequisites: It is useless to have purpose if it cannot be enacted, and it is useless to be action capable if people cannot understand the purpose and the means. Conversely, prerequisite skills can and do provide benefit even without or before the development of successor skills.

Knowledge management in this light is first and foremost about learning: What should be learned, when should it be learned, and who should be learning it? How these things are done is where the *management* part comes in. You can call it knowledge identification, knowledge acquisition, knowledge diffusion, knowledge renewal or anything else you like—it all boils down to somebody learning something. And that's the rub—partly because learning is generally defined from the controlling perspective of teaching, and partly because squishy human things lack the cold hard edge of black-and-white decision making and technology selection.

■ LEARNING

Carla Hannaford, a neurophysiologist and educator, believes that all people start out as natural-born learning machines. Many, however, get their works gummed up in early-life educational activities mismatched to their individual learning styles and close that part of their minds, often forever. Hannaford explains the neurophysiology of learning: "Evolving [neuronal] patterns become base reference points to understand new information. . . . We continue to elaborate and modify the patterning throughout our lives. The base patterns, 90 percent of which are acquired in the first five years of life, give us the template on which to attach all future learning."[1]

Learning and innovation are closely intertwined. Jacob Bronowski, writing about the creative process, tells us, "A man becomes creative, whether he is an artist or a scientist, when he finds a new unity in the variety of nature. He does so by finding a likeness between things which were not thought alike before, and this gives him a sense both of richness and of understanding. The creative mind is a mind that looks for unexpected likeness."[2]

Bronowski and Hannaford both place heavy weight on the human brain's reliance on metaphor, analogy, and simile as a (if not the) principal learning and creative mechanism. New knowledge is both created and assimilated naturally when it shares some common pattern with old knowledge.

The very knowledge explosion that is creating the need for knowledge management, change proficiency, and response ability is also creating the means to respond. Biology, psychology, and cognitive sciences are generating knowledge about how the human brain learns; and have shown us that we can use this knowledge to intervene effectively in the learning process of virtually all humans.[3] At the same time, technology is bringing us new concepts of distance learning, new access to the world's storehouse of knowledge, and new interpersonal and group communication capabilities.

Educators for some time have understood that traditional teaching techniques do not succeed in creating learned and learning individuals from most who enter traditional educational institutions either in the K through 12 or university systems. It was common in the past to pass this off as the population's bell-shaped intelligence curve, or in many cases, considered a useful fact for early weeding out of students that teachers should not waste time with. Today, most educators are aware that different people learn differently, that there are multiple intelligence types, and that the brain is a natural learning organ whose functional mechanisms we are beginning to understand. Employment of emerging brain-based learning models is beginning to show irrefutable results. Common leverage points are shown in Table 10.3.

Teaching is a push perspective, learning is a pull perspective. Creating and nurturing an environment for self-directed learning takes advantage of the learner who has a driving curiosity or even a deep-felt need to learn specific things.

➤ Communities of Practice

As a youth, I never understood why doctors had a practice but my dad had a job. A little older, in my cynical years, I figured it was because they didn't really know how to do anything well yet, sort of like my sister and her piano lesson homework. With the wisdom of age, however, came the appreciation that the medical profession is up front about how much more there is to learn and that the real learning

---

Table 10.3 Some Brain-Compatible Learning Leverage

Learning

Accelerated when learner sees a solution to a known problem.

Appreciated when learner discovers the solution.

Applied when learner owns the solution.

Collaborative Learning

Different people think differently.

Different people see different things as important.

Different people know different things.

Collectively, people know more than they do individually.

Collective discovery builds comprehensive knowledge.

Collective discovery builds diffused ownership.

Collective discovery can build knowledge at the depth of insight.

Result: Better—Faster—More Mobile Knowledge

---

comes with front line activity and experience—not from books and schooling—and never ends.

"You are what you eat" may say something about your physical makeup, but you are really what you've learned, nothing more, nothing less. Little of what you've learned has come from schools, training classes, and books—most has come from your lifelong social interactions with others: family, friends, enemies, fellow workers, neighbors, your tribe, whoever you meet as you travel through life and whatever you do along the way. That's the way you're wired. Humans have been doing this since long before the invention of institutional education, and long before the invention of a written alphabet.

How we learn is coming under closer scrutiny these days, especially now that lifelong learning and earning have been closely related—a relationship that applies to companies as well as to people, and to top executives as well as hourly employees. Once the eye of science focused, it found that we learn how to do what we do by talking about it with other people who do the same thing. This is why doctors like to hang out with other doctors socializing among their *community of practice.*

But this behavior is not peculiar to doctors, everybody does it: Managers hang out with managers, welders hang out with welders, rock stars and firefighters seek the company of their peers, and so on. We can't help ourselves, that's the way we're wired. We all have other interests and other communities we belong to as well, but the one associated with our income generation has a special place.

People bound by informal relationships who share a common practice,[4] whether it's project management or basket weaving, drag racing or metal forming, is a good definition of a community of practice (CoP). John Seely Brown, head of Xerox's Palo Alto Research Center, underscored this informality in a 1991 white paper for the Institute for Research on Learning: "The communities that we discern are . . . not recognized by the organization. They are more fluid . . . than bounded, often crossing the restrictive boundaries of the organization to incorporate people from outside."[5] A community of practice emerges when people with similar interests seek each other for discourse, experience sharing, and problem-solving assistance. This self-motivated continuous learning has always been present in the workplace—it is not a new concept.

Participation in an active community is not without obligation. "Can you help me" appeals represent a two-way street cultivating a network of people who can provide direct advice. One Bell Labs employee called it "trading in knowledge," and recognized his obligation to possess knowledge of use to others in return for the privilege of seeking another's knowledge. A study[6] at Bell Labs showed that among engineers a higher IQ did not correlate with higher productivity; initiative and networks counted the most—networks composed of people who cultivated respect so they could trade knowledge.

Active communities also learn through indirect conversation and necessarily invest in trust building. Yet in the bottom-line industrial environment, work-hour socializing, war story telling, and water cooler chat is typically discouraged. Many places still restrict access to the Internet—and even the corporate intranet—powerful new expansions to one's community of practice. These policies unwittingly rob the potential for natural learning. Nevertheless, the real work environment has always been based on collaborative learning, even when it is discouraged.

CoPs are becoming fashionable. With the increased awareness and understanding of the value and roles that CoPs play in the workplace, progressive companies are asking how they can get more of them, and how they can make them more effective. Some companies even find the idea novel, and are asking how to build some, not realizing that they already have an active foundation in place. Consultants and information technology vendors never ignore such questions.

Fortunately, science hasn't either. At least one voice of sanity out there has put these fashionable communities of practice in perspective:

"They are not a new solution to existing problems; in fact they are just as likely to have been involved in the development of these problems. In particular, they are not a design fad, a new kind of organizational unit . . . to be implemented. . . . they cannot be legislated into existence or defined by decree. They can be recognized, supported, encouraged, and nurtured, but they are not . . . designable units. Practice itself is not amenable to design."[7]

➤ Collaborative Learning

In the past, I found it easier to collaborate with myself than with others: Committees design camels, meetings waste a lot of time, others don't see things in the same light, and it's hard to help them value what you know if they haven't fought the same demons. My engineering education reinforces these feelings—give me the requirements and the handbooks and creating a solution is a pretty efficient solitary process.

Different engineers do, however, come up with different designs. Maybe some have better handbooks than others, or maybe they have better conversations with themselves—somehow some are more innovative than others. When you consider the innovation factor, engineering isn't so straightforward after all.

This is true for all knowledge work, not just engineering. Any group of professionals has its pecking order. When your ability to solve a problem or explain an effect or respond to a situation is based on the knowledge you have, more knowledge generates more value.

It's been some time since I've practiced engineering. The problems I wrestle with today don't have the handbooks and formulas and clear knowledge that engineering relies on—things like strategies and plans, organizational and human productivity, methods for changing a corporate culture—things that are impacted by the complexity and dynamics of the business environment.

Under these conditions, my feelings about collaboration are very different. I can learn and innovate much better in collaboration with others when the knowledge we collectively explore and create is not so linear and unequivocal. Working toward a common objective with a group of people who think and learn and know differently still has its tear-your-hair-out moments, but that's the price of unparalleled results.

With this realization, I've become curious about the mechanisms and conditions that promote efficient and productive collaborative thought and learning, and about the applications that benefit from collaboration. There are still many projects I'd rather do alone; though now I know many of those would be better with at least some collaboration—even straightforward engineering jobs.

That term *straightforward* is the fallacy. New knowledge is being developed at such a furious pace in virtually every field that complexity and change dynamics are the reality everywhere. The handbook and the past knowledge are necessary but no longer sufficient.

Remember when listening to the voice of the customer became the politically correct thing for product designers? Although this pays big dividends when it is a true collaborative learning activity, collaborative skills and methodologies did not come as part of the package for most. The result was a one-way communication with poor results and occasional outright disaster.

Let's hope that collaboration doesn't become politically correct. Simply deciding to collaborate with others on a certain objective doesn't mean it will be productive. There are times when collaborative learning is more efficient and more innovative, and times when it is not.

Pierre Dillenbourg and Daniel Schneider at the University of Geneva's School of Psychology and Education have investigated the mechanisms at work during collaborative learning. Figure 10.2 shows my simplified adaptation of the eight mechanisms they review:

1. *Disagreement.* Collaboration is a social activity between two or more people, and is governed very much by the participants' common culture and language. When people come together to pursue a common objective, it is likely that they will disagree at some point. Social factors swing into gear and prevent them from ignoring the conflict. This is as true for slight differences in viewpoint as it is for clearly opposing views.

2. *Alternatives.* Bring together different people and you will bring together different viewpoints and conclusions. Most of us tend to define our problems in terms of solutions we can understand. Another viewpoint may not disagree or conflict with ours, but it may offer an alternative interpretation of the same data. Hearing alternatives helps us abandon less reasoned or less sensible conclusions that otherwise go unquestioned. These first two mechanisms are strong arguments for diversity in collaborative group makeup.

3. *Explanation.* When we verbalize or write down a thought sequence or procedure for the first few times, we learn while transforming tacit knowledge into explicit knowledge. We've all experienced teaching something we know to someone else, and learning new

Reaching a common goal while maintainging a mutural understanding.

Individaul	Disagreement	Others will challenge concepts and conclusions individuals take for granted.
	Alternatives	Others will offer alternate concepts and conclusions to individual perceptions.
	Explanation	Externalizing internal thought transforms tacit knowledge into explicit knowledge.
	Internalization	Participative dialogue conveys concepts that integrate with internal knowledge.
	Appropriation	How one's concepts are adopted by others puts the concepts in new perspective.
Collective	Shared load	Multiple levels of thought are explored and integrated simultaneously.
	Regulation	Consistency is monitored and discussed from multiple viewpoints.
	Synchronicity	People tend to help each other achieve a mutual level of understanding.

Figure 10.2 Collaborative Learning Mechanisms

Pierre Dillenbourg and Daniel Schneider at the University of Geneva's School of Psychology and Education have investigated the mechanisms at work during collaborative learning. This synopsis is my simplified adaptation of the eight mechanisms they review in *Collaborative Learning and the Internet*.

things about it in the course of making it understandable to a different mind. Thus, collaborative partners who know more about the subject than others learn and benefit from the interaction as well.

4. *Internalization.* This is the act of integrating new concepts into your internal reasoning that are conveyed during interactive conversation with a more knowledgeable person. Two conditions must be met for this to occur: (a) you must be an active participant in the joint problem solution, and (b) the concepts conveyed by the more knowledgeable person must be close enough to what you already know to integrate readily.

5. *Appropriation.* Similar to internalization but more overt, appropriation is the active reinterpretation of a concept based on how it is incorporated into a larger schema by a more knowledgeable person. This is the primary mechanism at work in apprenticeship learning—where the learner modifies actions based on how the results are appropriated and integrated by the more skilled of the two.

6. *Shared load.* This is not a division of labor by chopping a learning or development task into different parts and then assembling a solution later; but a unique collective ability to monitor different levels of conceptual development simultaneously. Sort of like one person thinking at the tree level, another at the forest level, and a third at the ecological level while all wrestle together with a problem about wood farming. Each takes responsibility for integrating consistency at his or her level of focus. It is difficult for a single individual to operate at multiple metalevels simultaneously, so this division of labor is natural in that it is efficient for the group to work this way.

7. *Regulation.* Members of a collaborative group often have to justify why the thought is proceeding in a certain direction. This activity makes the knowledge explicit and has a mutual regulatory effect that tends to keep the development on solid ground.

8. *Synchronicity.* Collaborators attempt to keep each other synchronized with the same level of understanding. Each person monitors the developing understandings in others, and attempts to correct any misconveyed or misunderstood communication. People are not talking at each other but with each other.

Good collaboration is not compromise and consensus; it is an amplified learning activity. A good collaboration will, however, produce a result that looks comfortably familiar to all participants; it is not one person's design or strategy or discovery with a few other ideas thrown in. The collaboration process helps everyone understand the total concept to the depth of ownership. If some of the ideas don't get published exactly the way a participant would have resolved them, everyone at least understands why they are resolved the way they are. Collaboration does not remove the need for individual judgment. What each of us learns is private and individual.

Collaborative efforts also produce a collective learning that occurs outside any individual, and manifests itself in the way the *group* collectively behaves and deals with the result. This learning emerges from the interactions of all the different individual learnings as they play out the organizational operating dance.

Collaborative learning mechanisms are at work in both organized collaborative projects and in informal communities of practice. People learn faster and better, and are less likely to repeat the mistakes of the past. British Petroleum (BP) nurtures a culture of collaboration and provides infrastructure support for communities of practice; and claims direct dollar values in the tens of millions of dollars from accelerated organizational learning and a reduction in repeated mistakes.[8]

BP began its $12 million pilot program in 1995, and "about a third of the money was spent on behavioral scientists who helped the people in the pilot programs learn how to work effectively in a virtual environment."[9] BP has good bottom line results to show for it: Oil drillers who ran into really expensive problems got on the network and found others who had solved these very same or similar problems before. It's been quite effective for BP and made good times of idle time for the drillers isolated on these drilling platforms—kind of like ham radio with a video link.

That the BP environment consists of engineers on drilling platforms in fairly isolated environments has led some observers to credit boredom and a ham radio alternative to the success of BP's community work. To dismiss BP's benefit as unique to the nature of their business is to misunderstand that they have simply built a collaborative learning environment matched to their situation. Another business with a different situation needs to design the supporting infrastructure appropriately, and not duplicate BP's. Response situation (RS) analysis is well suited to such design, as it focuses on defining the nature of the problem before considering solutions, and then aids the crafting of a response-able solution that both addresses the immediate requirements and evolves as the environment matures and changes.

Information technology plays an important support and enablement role in collaborative learning, both for networked communities of practice and for remote-participation collaborative learning. There is sufficient off-the-shelf support for communities of practice already in various forms such as Lotus Notes, Microsoft's NetMeeting, and Ventana's Group Systems, just to name a few. British Petroleum has perhaps gone the furthest at this writing with an integrated technology and cultural program that makes good use of video and community trust building. Technology alone, however, is insufficient to create communities of practice or collaborative learning—a culture of collaboration and learning is needed first.

■ ORGANIZATIONAL LEARNING

Where does the competency of your organization reside? How about the culture of your organization—where is that located exactly? Does the answer change if your organization is a 150,000-person global company, a 15,000-person division, a 150-person plant, or a 15-person team? How does *your group,* however you want to define it, know what to do and how to behave?

I'm going to suggest an answer that might be uncomfortable at first, but that just might solve an important corporate identity crisis and help us deal with some of the burning decisions of the day. Look at mobs for a moment—not the organized criminal type—but the lynching type, or the Fort Lauderdale spring break type. They're groups, and generally are defined by some specific reactive behavior. We know that mobs behave differently than you would expect from knowing any of the individuals. Nice people for the most part, but there they went and did that unimaginable thing. Maybe from afar you can imagine it, but only because you've seen it so many times and only because it wasn't your boy or your mother involved in the incident. Whatever they reacted to, we know they didn't get their response from a procedures manual.

How about an impromptu jazz ensemble jamming on a magical Saturday. Competent musicians for sure, but something happens when they get together and it isn't in the sheet music—there isn't any.

Ant colonies are collections of many dumb insects that exhibit effective intelligence as a cooperative group. Hive intelligence is a phrase we use to describe seemingly intelligent behavior from a group of bees. At some early stage in life, we all learned that their queens do not tell them what to do, yet some coherent and effective higher-order behavior emerges from this *swarm* interaction.

My point about this emergent behavior in groups is not that nobody is in control, yet coherent things happen anyway; but rather that the "knowledge" driving the group action is not evident anywhere. How do these groups know how to do what they do?

Answering this question might help us understand what *organizational* learning really is. It might help us get a focus on knowledge management. It might unlock the secret of highly effective teams.

Remove all but the worker bees or soldier ants from their insect colonies and watch how ineffective they are. The intelligence of these communities is not manifested in the large numbers, but rather in the interaction and diversity. *In* the interaction and diversity—not *in* the individuals. The knowledge that drives the behavior of these organizations cannot be put in a jar, it cannot be captured, yet it exists.

How can there be *knowledge* if nobody (or no thing) *knows* it? Maybe the human brain can shed some light on this. It is composed of billions of neurons, each interacting with a few or hundreds or thousands of others. Each has its own individual behavior of reaction and stimulus. Each of these behaviors was *learned* from prior interactions, and continues to change and evolve. Though we may say a neuron has memory, we don't honor that stored information as knowledge, nor attribute intelligence to the behavior of that neuron. The intelligence of our human brain emerges at the highest level—and the knowledge that drives our behavior remains illusive in its precise physical location—other than as a large collection of interacting neurons.

Now back to our business organization. Individuals in an organization know things we can describe and categorize—this is evident to us. After all, they are us—and we are egocentric animals. Sort of like one neuron recognizing another but failing to comprehend the larger mind.

Rather than think about your own organization, think of another, in a completely different area of endeavor. What personality and behavior do you expect from a tobacco company, the state motor vehicle department, the U.S. Congress, Microsoft? You know them as organizations that exhibit expected behaviors. But meet one of their employees socially and chances are you will find someone you can relate to, who even agrees with your behavioral assessment but denies any personal responsibility.

When Exxon had its Alaska oil spill problem it wasn't just the doing of the ship's Captain. We all know this down deep inside, so do the Exxon employees; otherwise, we would all be satisfied with the Captain's firing as a sufficient response. We all know that the catastrophe was caused by many interacting events and procedures and behaviors within a complex system, and that no one individual or procedure was solely responsible. And that no Exxon employee wished for this to happen, or was a conscious part of the cause.

If you were an Exxon employee then, no matter in what department, this was a poignant event for you that burned itself into your memory; it probably even altered the way you thought and behaved in your job function thereafter. But not with consistency throughout the organization: Some departments justifiably felt like victims;

some believed they could do something to help preclude such events in the future; while others learned how to deal with these things.

Sort of like the brain again. It has departments in charge of vision and emotion and language and muscles and reasoning and so on, and it is now known that each of these areas in the brain *learns* something from most all events we are subjected to: Input comes through on all channels simultaneously. How you react when Aunt Matilda invites you to her house will depend on your recollections of how it smells, what it looks like, how comfortable the seating arrangements are, what you feel about her emotionally, and of course what you reason your duty to be. And the result is usually not what we call an objective, conscious decision, anymore than IBM's or GM's failures to respond optimally to strategic direction suggestions.

Sometimes by sheer force of will, your reasoning powers can override your true emotional feelings about what you ought to do; but if you don't have the physical skills or, say, the hand-eye coordination, you may not be able to accomplish the task anyway. This is much like the way that stodgy legal and purchasing departments can hamstring a good acquisition or product development strategy. There are also emotional/logical conflicts that might be compared to the marketing/engineering conflicts; and *truth* is not owned exclusively by either.

Learning happens everywhere in the brain and everywhere in the organization (Figure 10.3), and it results in high-level behavior with no one area responsible. Dysfunction occurs when the interaction of these different views and knowledges is too slow, too one sided, or catastrophically nonexistent.

"We have met the enemy and he is us." We know what that means; and we give up trying to do anything about it because it defies localized identification and responsibility. Organizations are hard to change because nobody is really in charge—titles, authorities, and egos notwithstanding. You have to reprogram the neurons before a different behavior emerges.

Auto companies are notoriously paranoid and secretive about what they are doing and how they do things, yet workers and executives switch employers within the auto industry regularly. The really important knowledge doesn't leave because it's not in people's heads; it is in the greater group and how it behaves.

Hitachi has been known to take traveling seminars to their competitors to present and discuss early-stage concepts and technology because they know that they learn more from the interaction and diversity than their close-to-the-chest competitors. Knee-jerk thought about what constitutes intellectual property needs revisited.

It is Distributed—and Defies Localization, Capture, and Defection

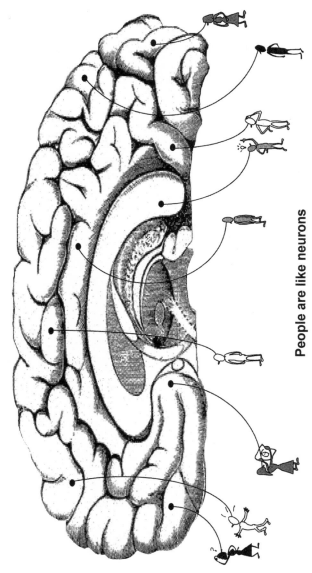

People are like neurons

More people and more interaction and more diversity = More intelligence

A *learning organization* cannot occur without increasing the interaction among the people—more training, more schooling, and more experts don't really do much for the *organization*. And if what everybody must know is determined and regulated and identical, interaction will not matter, there is little diversity of thought. Learning happens everywhere in the brain and everywhere in the organization—and it results in high level behavior with no one area responsible. Dysfunction occurs when the interaction of these different views and knowledge is too slow, too one sided, or catastrophically nonexistent.

Figure 10.3   Group Intelligence Emerges from Interaction and Diversity

So just what is this thing called the *learning organization?* Without increasing the interaction among the people, more training, more schooling, and more experts don't really do much for the *organization.* And if what everybody must know is determined and regulated and identical, interaction doesn't matter much anyway, there's little diversity of thought.

So how can you increase the interaction and diversity of thought within your organization/group/team? Moving your operating culture toward collaboration is an important start, toward collaborative learning even better. Actually, you can't have collaboration without learning; otherwise it's just accommodation.

What about speed of interaction? Are your people plugged in to the greater collaborative environment? Can they tap a *community of practice* for advice and learning? Can you bring together the right minds to advance the organizational knowledge right now? Do they have collaborative access as well as a collaborative skill set and culture . . . or is your company saving money by keeping many of them away from computers and intranet-wasting time?

When knowledge management, organizational learning, teaming, and collaborative strategies recognize the greater group intelligence, a formidable enterprise emerges.

■ ON THE POWER AND NATURE OF INSIGHT

Insights are those nuggets of knowledge that are the shortcuts in our abilities to understand things clearly. They're like X-ray vision: They let us look at something and all the extraneous information just fades away leaving only the essence that explains what we are focused on. Think of insights as *lean knowledge.* The best part is that most insights seem to stem from mental patterns so basic that they have broad applicability—knowledge patterns that are reusable under many seemingly different circumstances.

Nice stuff if you can get it. Geniuses seem to have a lot of it and can make simple sense out of the things that baffle the rest of us. It is obvious we don't get it in school or we'd all have a lot more.

Why is this so important? The knowledge brought to bear on the job, whatever the job, determines how well it is done; and that knowledge, whatever it is, is getting obsolete faster and faster. So the manipulation and renewal of knowledge is a cornerstone of viability today for both your company and for yourself.

The stuff of both personal and corporate core competency is knowledge, the leverageable stuff of knowledge is insight, and people possess insight. So good companies want to know how they can get more insightful people, either those who come with a storehouse of insights or those capable of developing them as needed.

Dan Seligman[10] suggests that intelligence is the attribute to look for, no matter what the job position or responsibility. "In jobs all across the skills spectrum, highest [IQ] test scores are associated with shorter training times, greater productivity, and lower turnover rates." Every job has an ideal IQ range, he says, and companies should attempt to fill those positions with people in the upper, rather than the lower, end of the range. He reminds us that Microsoft hires with this in mind: "promoting worker intelligence as a business strategy."

The Kelley and Caplan[11] study at Bell Labs mentioned earlier disagreed, showing that among engineers a higher IQ didn't help: Initiative and networks counted the most for productivity, and seven other "strategies" played important roles as well. Initiative: Instead of simply identifying a problem, fix it. Networks: Instead of simply asking others for help when stumped, cultivate respect among a group that trades in knowledge.

Interesting concept, this trading in knowledge. A source of indirect insight that allows a person to get beyond the roadblocker problems. It taps into many minds. It isn't teaming in the sense that we employ that term, yet it makes use of a team in the sense that we employ that term: It taps the knowledge of others who are willing to entertain your problem and provide a solution, or at least some ideas that could help enlighten your path to a solution.

After a certain age, we begin to value experience over intelligence and a quick mind. Why? Because experience is a collection of ready-to-use insights indistinguishable from intelligence. Mere intelligence, on the other hand, must create an insight on-the-spot to solve the same problem equally well. Sometimes it can; but if you could find a way to increase your own pool of insightful patterns, you would function at a seemingly "smarter" level. And if you could help others increase their collections of insights, you would have about you a more effective group of people.

The point: It doesn't matter how the insight patterns get there (in your head), it only matters that you have them.

Remember the old plumber's justification for his high price for five masterful minutes of work: "$50 for whacking the pipe, $500 for knowing where to whack it." The plumber's knowledge might fit into one of three categories:

1. Maybe someone showed him where to whack it.
2. Maybe he just "knew" where to whack it.
3. Maybe he understood why to whack it there.

Category 1 is the least leverageable kind of knowledge (it's only information masquerading as knowledge) and the most prevalent form; a set of circumstances repeats itself and you can solve the problem because you've seen it before. This kind is built over many years of exposure to working situations and is the basis of craftsmanship maturation as well as most formal education. "Here are some tools, I'll show you how to use them. Here are some applications, I'll show you how to approach them. Now go out into the world and use this information, and if you run into something different, seek advice from someone wiser."

➤ **Where Do These Wiser People Come From?**

Category 2 is the least predictable but generally the most prevalent form of insightful (rather than rote) knowledge. We exhibit genuine useful insight into the way some things work but we can't explain it, we just apply it. X-ray vision. We all use this form of insight to different degrees every day in the course of just living. Those we call talented often exhibit this unconscious insight in their area of expertise.

Category 3 is the most valuable form of insightful knowledge because it is transferable. It has higher leverage than that which is unconsciously exercised by a single person with a gift. Remember we're talking insight here, we're not talking about an application of formulas and process that cranks out an answer. We're talking about people who come up with an answer in the absence of formula, and then show us how to do it, too. In essence, they have given us a new mental pattern that we use thereafter to filter all the things we see, along with any other such patterns in our mental library.

It's not really that simple. Installing a new insightful pattern needs a receptive mind that is struggling with a problem this new pattern can solve. The mind accepts the new pattern because it recognizes the void that can now be filled. Someone cannot give you one of these patterns when your mind is not in the inquisitive state. Insights cannot be handed out willy-nilly.

Good teachers create this state in our minds before they show us the keys. I had only one such teacher in my entire educational experience. They are all too rare. Guided insight development is unlikely in the classroom: It requires extraordinary teaching insight and a set of thought-provoking problems that feel natural in this artificial environment.

One way to get insight: Tackle a problem for which you have insufficient knowledge to reach a straightforward solution, and no readily available book or expert to consult. One way to accelerate the development of insight: Tackle these problems in the company of others equally in the dark and equally engaged in the discovery process. When are the best insights built? When you are as much in the dark about the problem as you are about the solution. This is why you learn more from benchmarking outside your industry: You have to define the problem first, something we usually take for granted.

According to Kelley and Caplan, engineers at Bell Labs did it. The insight development was actually done by the Bell engineers themselves. They had structured guidance; but they took charge of the initiative defining the problem as well as the solution to higher productivity. They created their own state of inquisitiveness and developed their own insights into high-productivity knowledge work. Powerful stuff, with full ownership. And then these same engineers turned around and organized self-discovery, productivity workshops for all the other engineers. Unlike other forms of productivity training, Bell engineers who went through the six-week training experience continued to improve their productivity over time, rather then showing a short term, quickly decaying, postworkshop effect. They clearly had new leverageable insights, not simply new information.

Importantly, they used workshop exercises to apply the new knowledge they had discovered and found out that fake exercises were not useful, so they brought in the real problems. They researched real problems with real people in real time. I call that *Realsearch,* a process we examine later in this chapter.

➤ Building a Context

"Not invented here" (NIH) is a phrase we all understand from first-hand frustration. An old Calvin and Hobbes cartoon put it straight. Talking to his teacher, Calvin says: "You can present the material, Mrs. Wormwood, but you can't make me care."

Imparting new knowledge to others seems to grow in difficulty in direct proportion to its applicability. Why don't people recognize good information when it stares them in the face? Perhaps it is more fruitful to ask: How can we help people to care?

Eric Drexler puts his finger on it directly in his book, *Engines of Creation.*[12] He suggests that the biological immune system we are all familiar with serves a valuable function when it rejects the cell types that were not present at birth, like bacterial and virus invasions; and that an equally necessary system protects us on the mental plane. "The oldest and simplest mental immune system simply commands 'believe the old, reject the new.' Something like this system generally kept tribes from abandoning old tested ways in favor of wild new notions." He goes on to give some solid grounding for the NIH syndrome, and finally notes: "This simple reject-the-new system once worked well, yet in this era of organ transplantation it can kill. Similarly, in an era when science and technology regularly present facts that are both new and trustworthy, a rigid mental immune system becomes a dangerous handicap."

So it's not just pigheadedness after all. But maybe there's a way to trick this immune system, to insert a new idea disguised as an old, familiar idea. Suggesting that product flow through a factory has a lot in common with traffic flow at commute time helps us understand that high utilization causes accidents, which decreases throughput; and when utilization is really high, the accidents cause accidents, resulting in even lower throughput. The power of the metaphor is mighty.

I remember one postmortem discussion at an auto plant when both union and management representatives decried that their lean production training sessions were not working. People did some things differently after sitting through class but stubbornly refused to change others. They finally asked somebody why: "You guys don't know what you're talking about. If we do what you want, you'll see production go down."

Spoken from the heart; but it wasn't accurate. The class preached a new way to people who had unreceptive mental patterns that could not connect with the new information, patterns that were unable to recognize value in the new suggestions.

We all do it all the time. We understand the problem we have been working on and have found a solution for, so well, that we assume it is obvious to everyone. So we blurt out the solution and provide all its wonderful detail to people who haven't traveled the same road, and aren't prepared to value the same insight.

To transfer knowledge effectively, we must first create a context of understanding. We must build the patterns of understanding and value before we can hope to have new information embraced.

One masterful example: Jack Stack's *Great Game of Business*[13] set out to teach every employee at a discarded International Harvester plant how to read and relate to the monthly corporate financial statements. What an uphill battle that must be—if you try it straight on: "When your shift is finished, we'd like you all to join us for a two-hour session on Balance Sheet reading." What Stack did, instead, was to teach people how to build a personal financial statement, and how to build a financial statement for a family side business like baking muffins and making jams. He captured interest with a personal connection and latched on to existing value patterns before distributing company financial statements. And it works: You have only to read

Open Book Management[14] to see how well this technique has spread throughout all types of companies.

So we use metaphors to connect new information to old trusted knowledge patterns. These are reusable, reconfigurable, scalable knowledge patterns.

■ LOCAL METAPHORS—KNOWLEDGE PACKAGED FOR DIFFUSION

Ever read one of those science fiction books where people have electronic sockets behind their ears (Figure 10.4)? When you want to see a movie, you plug in a chip. When you want to be an expert in something, you plug in a different chip.

Cognitive science tells us that we assimilate new concepts only if they are within a small reach of what we already know—within the zone of proximity, as they say. This is why it takes so long to learn a new subject: We have to do the learning one step at a time, and each step has to sink in before we can build the next one on it.

When robotics were first introduced into the factory environment, retraining electrical service technicians to the level of competency took a long time, and many never made it because the new concepts of soft instructions and programming logic were just too far from past experience. Those that did make it found learning new robot models and new brands of robots successively easier. Like the difference between learning to drive your first car and then moving on to the second and third.

Though the brain can parallel process many input channels, learning appears to be a sequential biological growth process. One way to speed up the learning process is to use multiple channels effectively. *Accelerated learning* [15] is a body of educational techniques that mix verbal storytelling and reading, graphics and visual stimulation, sounds and rhythm, movement and physical experiment, and other forms of input while teaching a student new material and significantly speeds up the learning process in both adults and children.

It isn't just parallel input at work here, but also the concepts of *multiple intelligences*[16] and different *learning styles.*[17] We are not all adept at learning by reading, or by listening to a lecture; nor can all of us follow a global top-down explanation equally as well as a piece-by-piece bottom-up presentation.

In a sense, these accelerated learning techniques employ a shotgun approach, bombarding the student with multiple inputs—at least one is bound to be compatible with the student's learning style.

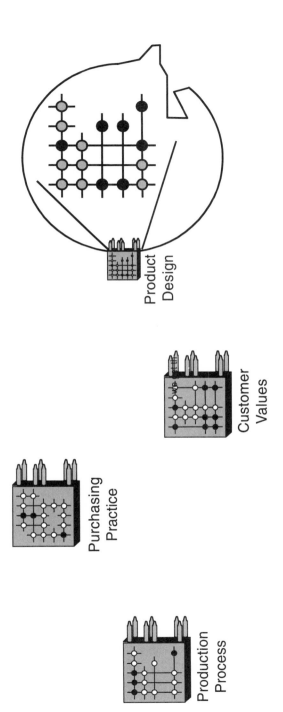

Pretty Fast If It Came in a Plugable Chip!

Plug computability allows us to hook any brand-name speaker up to a Fisher stereo system, put any producer's lightbulb into the living room lamp, and read *almost* any e-mail on our computer regardless of where it came from. These three cases work because they share a common standard for both physical and signal characteristics. Science fiction sometimes paints a future where people have electronic sockets behind their ears. When they want to see a movie, or be an expert at something, they simply plug in an appropriate chip. The science fiction knowledge chip is a fantasy example that goes one step further than the earlier three examples—it is "meaning" compatible as well as physical and signal compatible. The chip transfers instantly usable understanding. How do we get this?

Figure 10.4   How Fast Can You Move Knowledge Around?

In reality, many will be compatible to different degrees, since most of us are a mixture of all learning styles, some more predominant than others. And further, it appears that complex interactions among multiple channels promote and enhance learning to an even greater degree. In a sense, this approach presents information in a form compatible with the way the brain processes information into knowledge.

Plug computability allows us to hook any brand-name speaker up to a Fisher stereo system, put any producer's lightbulb into the living room lamp, and read *almost* any e-mail on our computer regardless of where it came from. These three cases work because they share a common standard for both physical and signal characteristics.

The science fiction knowledge chip mentioned earlier is a fantasy example that goes one step further: It is "meaning" compatible as well as physical and signal compatible. The chip transfers instantly usable understanding. Think of an American product development manager receiving what originated as a Chinese-language e-mail message explaining a product innovation methodology rooted in the Taoist teachings of Lao-Tse; it was translated perfectly, did not convey any thoughts that were culturally unique, and was similar enough to the American's prior knowledge to make total sense.

A respected theory is that cognition is shaped by culture in general and language in particular. Think about it—and you will think in words—and only those words that your sociocultural background gives meaning to. Add to this the proximal-zone concept, that knowledge is assimilated in small steps. Now think about a culturally diverse, or even global, corporation, and its need to speed up the acquisition and mobilization of knowledge.

An organization shouldn't try to solve this problem by eliminating cultural diversity because that would impair the important innovation potential. Language, though, has some possibilities for standardization: Some global companies, the recently merged Daimler-Chrysler for instance, are adopting English as the corporate language. In Daimler-Chrysler's case, however, it will be quite awhile before production workers in Southern California (Hispanic-American culture) can effectively communicate new methods to their counterparts in Detroit (Euro-American culture), let alone Stuttgart (German culture). And that everybody will know almost what they have to learn next (proximal zone) is not likely in a world that throws out surprises fairly regularly.

But what if we could take anyone in the flavor they came in, then mix in an additional common culture, an additional common language, and a new single knowledge pattern so universal that everything else they had to learn was only a small step away? Put like that it sounds as far-fetched as the knowledge-chip fantasy; but bear with me as we move from the slightly exaggerated to the demonstrably possible.

The objective is a way to package a piece of knowledge so that it can be quickly and effectively transferred from one person to another within an organization. The method utilizes concepts of language, culture, and pattern proximity as well as a plug-compatible presentation standard that will require some learning time, but not much, from everyone in the group. And once learned, it streamlines the knowledge transfer process.

This is accomplished by combining various mechanisms we have tested and discussed in this book: a knowledge template called a metaphor model, a cultural context of change proficiency, and a language of change issues and reusable-reconfigurable-scalable principles structured for systems thinking, and communicated simultaneously in textual explanation, bulleted synopsis, graphic depiction, and connected story example (Figures 10.5 and 10.6).

With reference to language, I am not talking about a primary language as rich as the one we all use for thinking and communicating about everything, whether that be English, Chinese, or whatever, but rather the concept of language as vocabulary and communication structure. Think of it as the plug-compatible physical package that allows us to transfer data from one person to another. Like any language it takes some time to master, but not a great deal of time as the concepts we wish to express in this language are very limited.

As to culture, we all have many already. There is the primary societal culture we belong to as well as the usually-secondary work environment culture we belong to; and maybe the subcultures of the soccer team we play with on Saturday, the church group we meet with frequently, and the hunting lodge we visit in the season. One may well be a subset of another, but there are plenty of cases where the same person embraces seemingly contradictory cultures, like the religious physicist or the veterinarian hunter. The point is, we are all capable of embracing another culture under the right circumstances. In this case, we use culture as a set of values and beliefs that give context and perspective. This common culture provides our signal compatibility, giving us a means to transfer information, something beyond transferring mere data.

Finally we come to the transfer of knowledge. Mainly we need a pattern of new knowledge that looks fairly close to old knowledge so that the knowledge receiver has ready-made hooks for attaching new information. Say you want to educate your design engineers on effective ways to gain value from direct customer interaction—

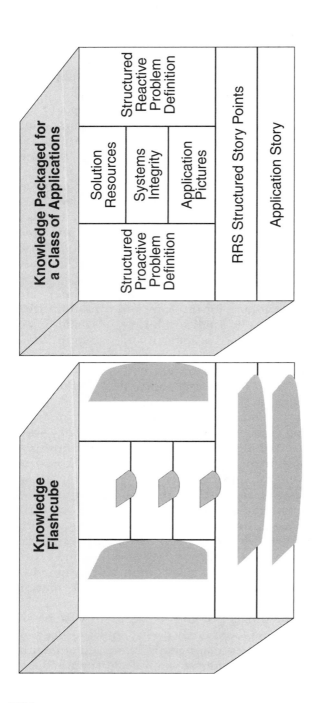

Common Language—Common Architecture
Response-Able Knowledge Packaging

The objective is a way to package a piece of knowledge so that it can be quickly and effectively transferred from one person to another within an organization. The method utilizes concepts of language, culture, and pattern proximity and a plug-compatible presentation standard. It combines a knowledge template called a metaphor model, a cultural context of change proficiency, and a language of change issues and reusable-reconfigurable-scalable principles structured for systems thinking, and communicated simultaneously in textual explanation, bulleted synopsis, graphic depiction, and connected story example.

Figure 10.5 Plug Compatible Knowledge Is Highly Mobile

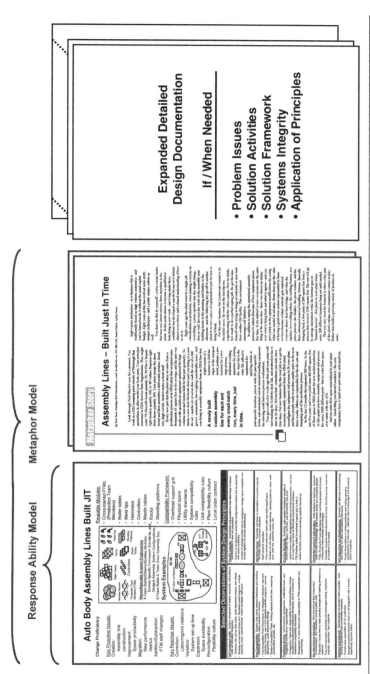

Figure 10.6 Knowledge Packaged as a Metaphor Model

The concept of plug-compatible knowledge packaging was introduced in Chapter 6 with a series of similar graphic presentation patterns called response ability models, which depicted a variety of different processes and practices from very different areas in an enterprise in a common presentation pattern. By adding a textual story to the response ability model that provides contextual detail for the bulleted and graphic synopsis we get what I call a *metaphor model* – a tool which plays an important role in the process called Realsearch.

303

something foreign to them. Help them build a local metaphor model packaged in the knowledge transfer format first, perhaps modeling a departmental new-hire interviewing process that they know and respect. Then introduce the new knowledge packaged in the same manner; assimilation is then much easier because the general concept hooks are all the same. And with the language and culture of change proficiency, one local metaphor model is all that's needed, no matter how many more and different new procedures, processes, and practices will come their way.

Importantly, knowledge is packaged as a solution mechanism, and not simply as a specific solution. Specific examples of solutions are provided as guidance. The knowledge is not packaged as a recipe for solving a single problem, but rather as a process for solving a class of problems in a changing environment.

This concept of plug-compatible knowledge packaging was introduced in Chapter 6 with a series of similar graphic presentation patterns called response ability models, which depicted different process and practices from very different areas in an enterprise in a common presentation pattern. By adding a textual story to the response ability model that provides contextual detail for the bulleted and graphic synopsis, we get what I call a *metaphor model*—a tool that plays an important roll in the process called Realsearch.

■ REALSEARCH—ONE METHOD FOR BUILDING THE RESPONSE-ABLE ENTERPRISE

Insights are the most powerful forms of knowledge, but very difficult to transfer to others. They stem from some internal understanding that is either too complex to convey in language or simply not consciously understood. The specific objective is to help people gain new knowledge about adaptability and adaptable business systems at the depth of insight.

➤ Discovery Workshops

An effective technique for giving people insight is to involve those people in the actual knowledge discovery process. A structured approach in these *discovery workshops* is important, so that the group stays focused and achieves the objectives, both individually as well as collectively.

There is leverage in building new knowledge patterns when a discovery workshop takes place at a "noncompetitive" site where the local examples are not in direct competition with the participants' interests. Unlike benchmarking, where we want to see how a competitor does it, discovery workshops benefit when the shields are down, when the participants don't already think they know the subject cold and have strong filters already in place.

➤ Employing a Local Metaphor

Virtually every business unit within a company has a few practices that exhibit high change proficiency. Typically, these competencies emerge as necessary accommodations to an unforgiving operating environment. Maybe it's the ability to accommodate frequent management changes, each with a new operating philosophy. Or there is a production unit that automatically tracks a chaotically changing priority schedule. Or the logistics department routinely turns late production and carrier problems into on-time deliveries. It might be a purchasing department that never lets a supplier problem impact production schedules. Or an engineering group that custom designs a timely solution for every opportunity or problem. To simply survive today, every company has generally evolved some practices and processes that allow it to accommodate change, no matter how unconscious, brute-forced, or reactionary these processes may appear.

Every business unit has its own brand of tactical chaos it manages to deal with—intuitively, implicitly, routinely, automatically—without explicit process knowledge rooted in change proficiency. Yet at the same time, virtually every business unit today is facing strategic and operating challenges that cry out for this same innate competency.

On the one hand, we can find some processes and practices that exhibit implicit response ability in almost any organization; on the other, there is a real need for more explicit response ability in other processes and practices within these same organizations. Thus, we have the potential to build a metaphor from something that is already response able, and then employ it as a design model when purposely transforming or building something else.

Metaphors can be powerful vehicles for creating and communicating insight, but the trick is to find a meaningful metaphor that can transfer this leverageable knowledge among a specific group of people. One way to accomplish this is to create a metaphor from a business practice that is well known (or at least accessible) and respected within the target group—a *local* metaphor.

Recall the graphic response ability models introduced in Chapter 6; and in the case of the two General Motors examples, how they became metaphor models when a story was added that breathed life into the responsibility model. The Realsearch process builds (or reviews) a *local* metaphor model in each discovery workshop, and then applies the metaphor pattern to the workshop's design objective. In some cases, when introducing the Realsearch technique to an organization, early workshops may build or review two local metaphors; placing more emphasis on the analysis of existing examples to create a knowledge and experience base among the participants.

➤ Framework and Process

Realsearch is an issue-focused, principle-based process summarized in Figure 10.7. In Figure 10.8, the framework/activity diagram (discussed in Chapter 5) shows five framework standards and seven functional activities. The depiction represents the process as a set of core strategic themes and the supporting activities that give life to them. Realsearch is also an adaptable system that can be morphed to suit specific situations, environments, and practitioners, always keeping the strategic themes in mind.

Focus on Change Issues

Realsearch focuses on developing the questions before embracing answers; defining the problem before accepting solutions. The specific activity that achieves this focus is some suitable variant of response situation (RS) analysis, discussed in Chapter 4, which is a methodology for defining problems in terms of their response ability requirements. The key concept here is that the item to be analyzed or designed must first be profiled as a set of change issues to be accommodated.

In a Realsearch workshop, consensus is sought (but never demanded) on the problem definition and not especially on subsequent solution designs. The emphasis on a common problem definition is important so that all solution design activity focuses on an explicit set of requirements.

Base on RRS Principles

The 10 RRS design principles discussed in Part Three are focused on building adaptable systems, which is precisely our objective. In general, however, any specific set of comprehensive design principles would provide the necessary fundamental concepts for a Realsearch process. No two people are likely to employ fundamental knowledge to precisely the same ends. Principle-based design invites collaborative learning as each participant goes away with a deeper but very personal understanding. Principles are tools rather than recipes.

Realsearch Is . . .

a collaborative knowledge development and dissemination
process that employs real people addressing real problems in
real time, typically in mixed workshop groups.

It is an issue-focused, principle-based methodology that first
defines the nature of a problem before considering solutions.

Solutions are then analyzed or designed according to a set
of fundamental design principles.

Insight is fostered with this cause-and-effect understanding
and communicated within an organization through a local metaphor
model—providing a graphic depiction of this cause-and-effect
relationship for a known and respected local business practice.

It Works Because . . .

Comprehension—*You* identify the issues before solutions are entertained, you
root your solutions in fundamental principles, and you cast the results into
repetitive patterns. You understand why and how with the depth and power of
reusable insight.

Commitment—*You* develop the values and priorities, you develop the solution
and strategy, and you design the result to evolve with changing needs. You
own the path and the reasons for walking it.

Completeness—*You* incorporate external knowledge and experience, you
employ a systems-thinking discipline that drives to closure, and you package
the result in communicable form. You ensure that the solution addresses the
problem and that they are both understandable to others.

Realsearch takes place in a structured workshop environment and is not a recipe driven concept by
design because: (1) we need ways to differentiate our businesses, not conformity that eliminates
competition, (2) the nature of the complexity we deal with requires complexity-compatible response,
and (3) though people are generally uncomfortable in the hard work of deep thinking/learning activity, that is what produces insight.

Figure 10.7   Realsearch

The RRS design principles provide enough structure for both the
analysis and the application exercise work to channel the workshop
activity toward its objective; but not enough structure to allow comfortable passive participation. Finding evidence of the principles in a
practice being analyzed and employing them in the design of a new
practice require thought-provoking work. Basing the participant activity on fundamental principles rather than on recipe steps creates
an environment in which people must actively think and struggle
with new concepts.

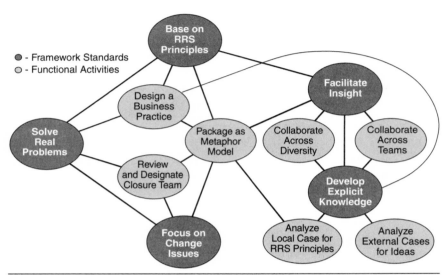

- Framework Standards
- Functional Activities

Realsearch is a general workshop-based process for generating new *response ability* knowledge based on the framework standards depicted here. Some functional activities may be customized to fit the purpose of the effort. When the effort is intended to jump-start a design project that will eventually be implemented, as opposed to simply educate or embed cultural values, the activity called *Review and Designate Closure Team* evaluates the results and passes the initial effort on to a completion team, if warranted. The first action a closure team performs is to complete the design details by using the closure matrix tool discussed in Chapter 7.

Figure 10.8 Realsearch—Framework/Activity Diagram

Package as Metaphor Model

Realsearch employs the concept of metaphor as its principal tool for communicating insightful knowledge. The *response ability model* in Figure 6.5, coupled with its accompanying story in Chapter 6, is in fact one of the *local metaphor models* generated in the Realsearch workshop conducted at General Motors in 1997. In this instance, we wanted to communicate a business practice as responding well to a set of defined change issues precisely because its design is based on RRS principles. It encompasses both a framework/module architecture and the designation of systems integrity persons responsible for maintenance and evolution, enabling the plug-and-play construction and reconfiguration of business systems.

A local metaphor model is not expected to communicate an insight into a specific practice all by itself. It is intended rather as a conceptual map of the knowledge pattern people will learn when studying the business practice, and as a conceptual map to be overlaid on other practices subsequently analyzed or designed.

Analyze External Cases for Ideas

The initial task (Figure 10.9) undertaken in any Realsearch workshop is the review of a few (two to four) relevant cases, generally in the form of written articles. This activity introduces new thoughts relevant to the subsequent analysis and application exercises. Though there may be other ways to accomplish this same end, written articles have some distinct advantages: They can be sent out in advance, they can carry the weight of expert authorship, and people can be assigned to present their salient points and lead a group discussion about them. They can be in a prereading package to all participants; one "experienced" participant is selected to lead a group discussion at the beginning of the workshop. It is generally good practice to send the discussion leaders guidelines on how to conduct an interactive discussion, and how to open it with a personal review of what they discerned as relevant. If three articles are reviewed, three participants get drafted into the leadership rank: Learning is accelerated by teaching.

Analyze Local Case for RRS

Realsearch workshops benefit from tangible exposure to real systems that exhibit response ability. This is best done by selecting a workshop site someplace within the company, or even at another company, where such an example can be studied. The second task activity in the workshop is to analyze such a system. In the absence of a tangible business system, the workshop facilitator must fall back on some commonly exposed response-able system, such as Lego toys or the U.S. Constitution.

For experienced participants, the intent of this warm-up analysis is to sharpen the skills, knowledge base, and insights associated with response-able business systems; for the inexperienced, the effect begins the process of skill and insight development. Candidate analysis subjects may have been consciously designed for adaptability, but have rarely been designed with fundamental principles in mind. Exposing the presence of the principles provides the first tangible understanding for first-time participants, and moves implicit knowledge into the explicit category for those familiar with the practice being analyzed.

At this point, it becomes easier to suggest that these principles can be employed consciously in a purposeful design of another practice—they are not foreign concepts after all. In this light, the analyzed practice becomes a local metaphor that can be pointed to for precedence when suggesting that another practice would benefit from the application of one or more of the RRS principles. This sets the stage for the subsequent design exercise in the Realsearch process.

Day 1	Day 2	Day 3
Review purpose (Objective and benefits) **Review context** (Venue and participants) **Review 2-3 articles** (Majority of morning time)	**Review RA models(s)** (Homework and/or expert) **Examine design problem** General presentation Relevant tour/demo/talk Known/observed issues	**Build FA diagram** Review RA model(s) Identify key RRS elements F/A breakout-team work Group discussion
Build local metaphor Case presentation Breakout-team work Group discussion	**Build RS analysis** RS analysis discussion RS breakout-team work Group discussion	**Build key activities** Closure matrix breakout-team work Group discussion
Group Homework: Construct RA model	**Group Homework:** Skeleton RA model (Lost: Do process reading)	**Consolidate RA model and FA diagram Reflect and adjourn**

Figure 10.9 Pro-Forma Realsearch Workshop Agenda

Intensity is good—evening homework before/during/after a group dinner keeps the minds focused and fosters collaboration. Homework is best done in team groups or team subgroups, as opposed to individual efforts, except the second evening where inexperienced (new) participants may be assigned to read process background material on RA model building—if they haven't done so in advance. Three days appears to be a necessary minimum workshop duration to let the learning develop, sink in, and persist. It is perhaps a necessary maximum duration as well—to keep the thinking innovative rather than detailed. There is value in having inexperienced participants in the group—it sharpens the understandings of the experienced ones. If the inexperienced participants are completely lost (didn't do their preworkshop reading), have them do background process reading the second night rather than the exercise. Keep the pace fast and don't worry about consistency and closure—this process generates innovative ideas to jump-start a studied design effort, creates a sense of ownership of the eventual design by the participants, and establishes conceptual patterns among the participants that typically sink to the insightful level after a few such experiences.

F/A = Framework/Activity, RA = Response-Ability, RRS = Reusable/Reconfigurable/Scalable

Collaborate across Diversity

Good Realsearch results require a conscious attention to team makeup. Composing a genuinely valuable closed corporate Realsearch workshop is difficult at best, and the smartest people in the most successful companies are the worst: They think they're open minded. Bringing outside participants into a corporate workshop adds considerably to the viewpoints and the experience base. Better yet is an open-membership Realsearch team that is involved in a defined-objective, multiworkshop series. Corporate culture and corporate political reality are insidiously strong influences of what is acceptable to consider. Including outsiders as respected participants considerably broadens the knowledge obtained from analysis and applied in design. The more outside, the better; there is real value in finding people with similar interests but from other functional areas and other industries.

All participants must be genuinely interested in the pursuit of the workshop objectives and in a position to employ the knowledge for immediate value: Otherwise, the group suffers from tangential agendas. Participants, whether from inside the company or from outside, should be screened for this interest.

Participant experience with Realsearch should also be mixed when possible. This allows some to take leadership roles, which helps them develop their understanding of the knowledge being explored and sends a message of confidence to first-time participants that the confusion will clear eventually. This mixture of experience levels benefits both new and old hands at the process because it keeps the questions honest, and because questions without answers refuse to go away.

Collaborate across Teams

Breakout groups in workshops are an old concept. The conflict: Keep them small so everyone can and must participate; but don't have too many or there won't be enough time for full-group brief-outs. Balance this conflict by seeking a total participation of 10 to 20 people at any one workshop. In three-day workshops, I have found that breaking the full group in half for breakouts works well; though I often subdivide these two groups when total participation hits the high end of the range.

Duplicate teams means that both breakout groups work on the same objective. This is important in the Realsearch process as we are seeking to develop/refine a specific body of knowledge and apply it. Working with new and incompletely understood concepts typically leads to certain confusion as well as to different interpretations. Both conditions foster a broader exploration and questioning. Having two teams work toward the same objective has never yet in my experience produced duplicate results, and usually produces complementary results. Other important reasons for duplicating the activity: Sometimes one group will get totally lost and make no progress, sometimes one person will dominate a group and take it someplace strange, and sometimes group chemistry follows a different agenda.

Most importantly, the process is trying to develop a familiarity with the knowledge being explored at the depth of insight, in each participant. Insight comes from personal hands-on struggle, not from listening to someone else debrief another group's conclusions. Everyone must explore the same ground.

➤ The Workshop Agenda

Figure 10.9 depicts a pro forma workshop agenda that conforms to many that I have led successfully. Deal with it as a pro forma, a guideline, and think carefully about modifications it might need to fit your situation and facilitation style. This agenda has not always been successful for all workshop groups, especially those with participants who are not fully committed to the endeavor and/or participants who have ignored their prereading assignments.

Organizing a Realsearch discovery workshop is principally a matter of careful participant selection and careful site selection once the subject of interest has been determined.

It is necessary that participants have a vested interest in the subject to be explored: Perhaps they are responsible for solving a similar problem, recommending a strategy for a similar opportunity, designing a similar business practice, evaluating alternatives for a similar issue, or developing the requirements or specification for procuring or developing a solution to a similar problem. Or maybe they are simply going to be on the receiving end of such a design and need to understand it. Participants who do not feel a personal attachment to the workshop subject will impede and distract the effort at best, and can disrupt it badly if they are at odds with the purpose and only there by management command. Also, it is necessary to have complete agreement from all participants that they will follow the workshop structured approach. The techniques employed are at least as important to cultural development as the value of the solutions are to eliminating a problem.

Participants should also be selected with an eye for collaborative diversity. It is important to have different backgrounds and perspectives as well as different specific uses for the general results of the workshop. Ideally, there should be people from different companies and industries, along with people from different functional areas and divisions of your own company. This diversity not only brings a richer pot of ideas and perspectives, but also helps the workshop reach conclusions that are more fundamental and universal fostering a deeper understanding of the problem as well as the solution.

As to site selection, the worst place is the workplace of *principal* participants. Principal participants are those who are part of the principal purpose of the workshop. If the principal purpose is to open the thinking of a sales and marketing organization to new forms of customer service and support, do not conduct the workshop where their daily distractions reign. Take it off site; or better yet, take it to another part of the company geographically remote; or best, take it to another company with a similar interest, as well as something useful to use as a warm-up exercise. Part of this is to ensure unbroken attention and attendance throughout the entire three days, and part is to loosen the ties with old entrenched ideas. With cultural maturity, the necessity for this diminishes.

Participant preparation is important. Prereading assignments should include articles calculated to open the mind to new ideas, such as excerpts from *The Social Life of Information*[18] or *The Cluetrain Manifesto,*[19] and/or provide some fundamental background education, such as Michael Porter's *Harvard Business Review* article "What is Strategy?"[20] These suggestions are merely pro forma. Articles should be chosen for their relationship to the workshop purpose. First-time participants should also receive some background reading material on the workshop process and tools, lest they be totally unprepared for RA principles and RS analysis techniques. It is useful to introduce these tools and techniques to new participants in a preparation meeting the evening or late afternoon before the workshop begins, all the while making sure participants understand the workshop's purpose and have a vested interest. If your company is committed to becoming response-able, it will develop its own prereading and presentation materials from the ideas and concepts in this book tailoring them to fit your environment and the style of your facilitators' style.

First Day

The workshop opens with the necessary why-are-we-here, who-are-we, and what-we-will-do stuff; and quickly moves into the prereading article reviews. The facilitator(s) should not conduct these reviews, but rather different people should have preassigned responsibilities to stand before the group. Each reviewer speaks from a personal viewpoint and bullets the main ideas they encountered, and then leads a discussion soliciting additional or contradictory views.

Working and short lunches should be the norm; there is much to do and little time.

The afternoon is a warm-up exercise, familiarizing and refreshing everyone with the concepts and techniques. To this end, the development of a local metaphor model is preferred, even more so if it is an analysis of a business system indirectly related to the workshop objective. If the workshop objective was the development of new forms of customer service/support for a semiconductor manufacturer, a useful indirect analysis might examine the new guided self-service ideas in the legal and medical fields. In this case the example does not produce a metaphor model *local* to the business at hand, but local in that many people can relate personally to the trends in one or both of these fields.

The analysis case is presented to the group by Someone who can articulate its functional manifestation. This presentation should not replace or eliminate the need for an RS analysis by subsequent breakout teams, as the breakout work breaks the social ice and starts the collaboration process.

Bring the group back together and have each present their results. The facilitator(s) might then help merge the different team results and solicit additional ideas. Generally there is still an opportunity for a final breakout exercise in the evening, which will build a one-page response ability model for presentation the next day. It is useful to have this occur during refreshments preceding dinner, and break the teams into subgroups of no more than four each.

Second Day

A good facilitator might have an exemplary homework surrogate in his or her pocket just in case the prior night's results are dismal. The morning of the second day starts with a quick review of the homework and begins defining the problem to be solved. This can include presentations, tours, demonstrations, anecdotes, whatever; and it should allow for a high degree of interaction and questioning by the group. Their next task will be a response situation analysis, so they should be soliciting the information they will need to accomplish this.

If possible, discuss the RS analysis objectives before lunch and go right into the breakout work during or immediately after lunch. It is good to have a facilitator observing in each breakout session to answer questions related to process, and maybe even to contribute a little if necessary. In the absence of a sufficient number of facilitators, designate someone, preferably the most competently experienced participant, to function in this capacity.

After breakout, each team presents their findings and the facilitator(s) help merge and extend the ideas.

Group homework should again be conducted during the cocktail hour. The principal idea is to develop a skeleton version of a response ability model. Because of the preceding RS breakout exercises, the top part should be fairly straightforward. The real work will be in identifying some key examples of the RRS principles in action. Typically, only a few can be expected at this time, but they are generally the seeds of core solution directions.

If some participants are woefully lost because they do not understand the process, or are at odds with it, the homework hour and private time following dinner will allow them to do some remedial (or perhaps late initial) reading on the concepts and process.

Third Day

The morning of the third day begins with a review and consolidation of the RA model homework, and a group discussion identifies key RRS principles to be employed in the general solution. The morning breakout session is then used to develop a framework/activity diagram identifying major strategic themes and the activities necessary to implement the solution. Group review is inclined to find disparately different opinions at this point, and the facilitator(s) may or may not be able to merge the ideas to the group's satisfaction. No real matter if not, as the afternoon session will have the breakout teams go separate directions anyway.

The afternoon session focuses on only one or two key activities for each breakout team, generally different ones. The closure matrix is used to guide the design of an activity in satisfaction of the original RS analysis solution requirements. The breakout review should describe an activity in general, and then show which of the RS items it satisfies and which of the RRS principles are employed.

At this point, the facilitator(s) lead a consolidation discussion that identifies main conclusions and reflects on the results, and perhaps reflects on the workshop process for subsequent improvement.

Final words: Walk before you run. Don't get carried away with the full depth and breadth of RS analysis and RRS principles the first time out with a cold group. It will baffle them. You can start RS analysis simply by asking for a categorization of proactive and reactive change situations. And you can start the RRS concepts off with a simple reusable, reconfigurable, and scalable focus; introduce the 8 change domains and 10 principles later when participants have had prior exposure to the concepts. Another useful approach is to keep the breakout sessions simply focused, and use the finer grained concepts for the subsequent facilitator-led group reviews and extensions.

➤ Realsearch in Summary

Self-discovery is a powerful way to assimilate and appreciate new knowledge. Working groups from industry that explored the early concepts of change proficiency and response ability at the Agility Forum sent people back to their companies with new visions of possibilities and new ideas on how to realize them. Many of them made something happen in their companies as a result. Not because they heard a seminar. Not because they read a book. And not because they sat around a table and kicked around a few ideas. But because they tried to make sense of something that little was known about, and did it in the company of others with different backgrounds who also wanted a new knowledge and sense of understanding.

As for the development of insight, my observations are that little is evident after a single workshop, the light goes on during the second workshop, and something approaching insight occurs for some in the third and for many in the fourth exposure. At three days per workshop, that's something like 9 to 12 days invested in high-leverage business-related learning with immediate application.

Realsearch is not a recipe-driven concept by design: (1) We need ways to differentiate our businesses, not conformity that eliminates competition; (2) the nature of the complexity we deal with requires complexity-compatible response; (3) though people are generally uncomfortable in the hard work of deep thinking/learning activity, that is what produces insight.

Though the future will continue to evolve the strategic themes of Realsearch and refine the process, common ground revolves around focusing on real and interesting problems, having mixed participants, running parallel teams, building local metaphors, using an issue-focus/principle-base, and making people think and create new insight patterns.

Realsearch is not the only method for building the response-able enterprise, but it does hit all the stepping-stones: It acculturates the theory, concepts, and reality of response ability, change proficiency, and collaborative learning; and it does so while attending to business as usual. Exactly how you employ Realsearch to accomplish these ends is the challenge before you. How you adapt the basic concepts of Realsearch to your political and cultural environment for both initial introduction and eventual evolution will depend on executive vision, executive commitment, introduction strategy, and start-up leadership—people who resonate with the concepts and possess the ability to inspire others.

■ KNOWLEDGE PORTFOLIO MANAGEMENT— ONE METHOD FOR MANAGING THE RESPONSE-ABLE ENTERPRISE

Managing the response-able enterprise requires someone, some group, and/or some mechanism in place to build and maintain response-able systems, and to build and maintain a culture of change proficiency. A culture of change proficiency is codependent on a culture of continuous and collaborative learning. A business practice that I call *knowledge portfolio management* can accomplish all of this.

➤ A Knowledge Portfolio Management Model

Companies have been managing knowledge and people have been collaborating in communities of practice as long as there have been companies and people. This is not new stuff, this is not unnatural stuff. What *is* unnatural is the new abstraction of knowledge management into something artificial that can be dreamed up anew from logic and ideal visions. Something that can be purchased like a box of Cheerios; just add milk to nourish and reinvigorate the corporation.

For a few years in the mid-1990s, the Agility Forum provided a model of *natural* knowledge management facilitated and focused to a specific end. The Forum had two principal objectives: (1) to facilitate the discovery and creation of knowledge about enterprise agility, and (2) to facilitate the adoption and application of that knowledge by industry. It could have taken its meager funds and employed the more-than-competent resources available at Lehigh University to research the field, capture appropriate information, draw reasonable conclusions, and produce books and documents full of valuable information—that would likely go unread for the most part, especially by people with line responsibility who most needed the understanding.

Or it could have pursued one of two paths suggested by various interested factions: (1) the directed approach that convenes a blue ribbon group to determine precisely what knowledge is needed and then engages research to specifically address the agenda, or (2) the grassroots approach that brings together people in the trenches facing real problems and facilitates collaboration among those with similar interests. Approach 1 runs the risk of generating a pile of knowledge that goes unused by real people. Approach 2 runs the risk of solving real problems that have little if any long-term strategic use.

These same choices are faced by corporations every day: the dichotomy between those who would direct a solution from the top down and those who would encourage a solution from the bottom up. Both approaches can demonstrate advantages, and either can work quite well in a corporation with a strong unified culture aligned to the approach. More and more, however, we are finding mixed cultures at corporations as they merge across markets, across industries, and across seas. We're also finding strong control cultures opening the debate on emergent and empowered initiative, and we're finding consensus cultures beginning to see value in directed leadership.

The Agility Forum blended approaches successfully. Not from infinite foreknowledge and wisdom: It simply had no choice, at least for the blending part. As to success, there are plenty of ways to blend and fail; compromise is often one. The Forum needed industry involvement at a committed and intimate level or it would never meet its second objective: the adoption and application of knowledge. The committed level meant that people with strategic responsibilities, and the control of resources, had to get behind the interest in agility. The intimate level meant that people fighting real problems had to work together to find solutions to the problems that kept them up at night.

The Forum convened a group it called the Strategic Analysis Working Group (SAWG), whose purpose was to identify an agenda of critical knowledge development necessary for understanding agility in organizations. Group composition rotated over time and was designed to represent various industries, labor unions, academic groups, government, and related organizations such as the National Center for Manufacturing Sciences. People were sought for their understandings of issues, their real interest/use/need for an agility knowledge base, and their ability to influence the communities they represented.

This strategic group was also responsible for establishing the organizational architecture of the collaborative learning groups that would implement the agenda, and finding and installing the facilitating chairs. Chairs were appointed for one-year terms and chosen for their interest in the subject, their objectivity, and their group facilitation skills. Chairs, with the assistance of a facilitation service group, recruited people from the community at large with interests in the group's general area. The first meeting of each group established individual personal interests and developed an agenda for the year, with specific knowledge deliverables. Groups then met in two-day workshops approximately every six weeks at different locations chosen for their ability to demonstrate or shed light on a group's knowledge quests. These groups were the early development ground for the *Realsearch* process.

Underneath all of this was a facilitation service group that did the logistical and administrative work for both the SAWG and the many individual collaborative groups. The facilitation group administered the formation and logistics of collaborative learning groups, and accepted initiatives for new ones from virtually anywhere. However, they also "packaged" and sold the SAWG agenda, actively seeking people who had problems aligned with the strategic agenda, and then supported them in common pursuit. They also provided the information technology that stored and cataloged the results, and supported the communities of practice that emerged from the collaborative learning groups.

The Forum wasn't active long enough in this industry-involvement mode to really mature the infrastructure it had started to build. Community of practice support, for example, was only in its infancy, as were effective management and search methods for the knowledge repository. Notably, these IT areas were not the lead areas. The Forum led with real people's interest in real problems, both at the strategic level and at the operational level.

For those who find knowledge management too abstract and too distant from the real world, this model brings focus on real problems, and at the same time satisfies both those who need a strategic approach and those who favor a grassroots activity.

I functioned both as the initial chair of the strategic group and as director of the knowledge development groups providing the linkage between strategy and implementation. Though my position was called director of strategic analysis, it is a model for chief knowledge officer. This architecture appears appropriate for a knowledge portfolio management practice in any sizable organization and would potentially have more control over the agenda implementation than we did with volunteers from 250 disparate organizations, each with its own agenda. On the other hand, it is important to value and permit the different agenda perspectives brought to the development groups by individuals with specific and real needs. The SAWG viewed its role as suggestive, not prescriptive—except in certain cases where it actively recruited like-minded group chairs to pursue a critical objective.

A sizable body of knowledge was created in a few short years. Perhaps more importantly, some 1,500 or so participants carried back to their home organizations a new knowledge base that they helped create and that has noticeably influenced many of them. Eventually the Agility Forum chose to abandon the collaborative learning groups and pursue knowledge development in a more traditional research project model. This severed the industry participation mechanism. Shortly thereafter, the Forum downsized considerably and ceased to be a guiding influence for industry.

The collaborative learning groups were the informal networks and communities of practice that outlived the learning projects which originally brought people together. These learning projects helped form the trust and respect bonds across corporate boundaries that nurture effective networks trading in knowledge. In hindsight, it would have been valuable for the staff group to facilitate the formation of CoPs and support them with an infrastructure of Internet tools.

The staff group was small but augmented with industry-loaned executives rotated on an annual or biannual basis. Staff provided support functions for workshop logistics, real-time knowledge capture (workshop work-in-process journals), and Internet-accessible knowledge repository entries. More importantly, staff packaged the SAWG's knowledge agenda into collaborative learning projects and then actively recruited chairs and participants. When a chair was installed for a learning project, staff backed off and provided assistance and support, not direction.

➤ **Using the Model**

Figure 10.10 shows this model adapted to the corporate environment. Independently, this approach offers an interesting model for any corporate university. However, if the collaborative learning projects are modeled after the Realsearch process, the core values of change proficiency and core concepts of response ability become pervasively embedded in the corporate culture, and a response-able enterprise emerges.

Knowledge management is a tool to support an organization's strategic plan. This is its purpose. Many organizations do not sufficiently articulate a strategic plan, particularly one that spans an appropriate time period, to guide the person or group charged with strategic management of the knowledge portfolio—the CKO in Figure 10.10. Corporate vision and mission must also be taken into account when anticipating what knowledge will be needed for the future.

Collaborative learning projects are an effective mechanism for knowledge agenda fulfillment, knowledge diffusion packaging, collaborative culture initiation, and community of practice formation. Communities of practice are an effective mechanism for nurturing a

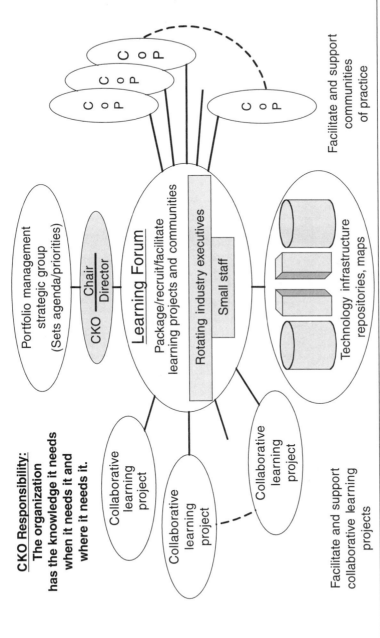

CKO Responsibility:
The organization
has the knowledge it needs
when it needs it and
where it needs it.

Portfolio management
strategic group
(Sets agenda/priorities)

CKO — Chair / Director

Learning Forum

Package/recruit/facilitate
learning projects and communities

Rotating industry executives

Small staff

Technology infrastructure
repositories, maps

Collaborative learning project

Collaborative learning project

Collaborative learning project

Facilitate and support
collaborative learning
projects

Facilitate and support
communities
of practice

C o C o P

C o P

C o C o P

C o P

Figure 10.10 Knowledge Portfolio Management

The Agility Forum employed a successful knowledge portfolio management model that is adapted here to fit the corporate environment. Independently, this approach offers an interesting model for any corporate university. However, if the collaborative learning projects are modeled after the Realsearch process, the core values of change proficiency and core concepts of response ability become pervasively embedded in the corporate culture, and a response-able enterprise emerges.

321

A large-company strategy . . .

☐ Identify one or two strategic pilot areas, e.g., marketing and product design.
☐ Start a collaborative knowledge development project in each.
☐ Facilitate implementation of project results with community of practice support.
☐ Then branch out in both areas with more projects, helping each project spawn a community of practice, developing a culture of collaboration within two focused areas first.
☐ When processes are refined and resources are sufficient, promote general collaborative learning values, and branch into more areas.

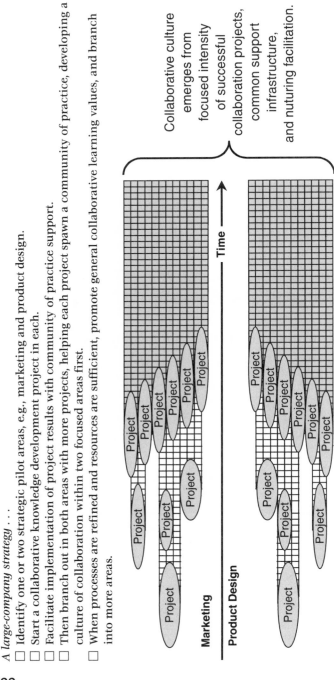

Collaborative culture emerges from focused intensity of successful collaboration projects, common support infrastructure, and nuturing facilitation.

Collaborative learning projects are an effective mechanism for knowledge agenda fulfillment, knowledge diffusion packaging, collaborative culture initiation, and community of practice formation. Communities of practice are an effective mechanism for nurturing a collaborative culture and increasing the velocity and richness of knowledge diffusion. Starting the process of change proficiency acculturation in any company must be fit to the corporate situation. This figure depicts one approach offered as a preliminary plan to a large multicultural auto company.

Figure 10.11 Eating the Elephant One Bite at a Time

collaborative culture and increasing the velocity and richness of knowledge diffusion.

How to start implementing this model or something similar is a question whose answer depends—at a minimum—on the existing corporate culture, the existing political environment, executive vision and commitment, and size, structure, and disbursement of the company. Figure 10.11 shows one approach offered as a preliminary plan to a large multicultural auto company.

■ CONCLUSION

We live in interesting times. In my lifetime, I've talked with a grandfather who grew up with horses and wagons and lived to see man walk on the moon. So far, I've witnessed the introduction of television, nuclear energy, air travel, the computer, robotics, the Internet, personal body-born electronics, and cloning; and expect to live long enough to see human genetic engineering intervene in human life extension and maybe even cold fusion and antigravity become part of everyday life. Genetic engineering and cloning are already used in the production of goods, while material science and atomic level manipulation technology advances rapidly. And there are already two different drugs in clinical trials that significantly affect the human learning process.

The knowledge base is exploding. The duration of value for any given piece of knowledge is shrinking as new knowledge makes old knowledge obsolete faster. This puts pressure on the speed of deployment. If useful knowledge is not deployed quickly enough, it becomes obsolete before it generates a return on investment. This also puts pressure on the speed of knowledge diffusion and a focus on the anticipation of new knowledge needs.

Response ability in all systems of business will determine the ability to deploy knowledge effectively. At the same time, any knowledge management practice spurred into existence to deal with the knowledge explosion must recognize its own needs for being response-able. We will continue to learn about learning and knowledge diffusion mechanisms, and this knowledge must be able to continually influence and mold any knowledge management practice an organization develops.

When an organization needs to learn quicker, it must shorten the time of acquisition and diffusion of knowledge. Collaborative learning supported by a purposeful infrastructure and culture puts more diversity of thought into closer knowledge exchange and development proximity. This creates an architecture from which intelligence at the higher organizational level emerges, much as the anthill and beehive are said to exhibit a collective intelligence separate from individual localization.

Organizational behavior is the collective product of shared common knowledge (see Figure 10.12). Every department in an organization knows things that could be useful to the organization if shared with other departments, but who has time to run around sharing knowledge in the hopes that someone might use it to the greater good? Put that way the answer is no one, but a culture that practices collaboration as a means to solve the front-line problems of the organization as a matter of course has open lines of communication everywhere. And useful knowledge, with a mind of its own, finds its way around the network.

Perhaps more debilitating in today's unforgiving times is the creeping divergence from the strategic and operating plans that occurs in every department caught up with fighting immediate tactical realities

Every department has unshared information and specialized cultures, and slowly discovered deviations from the corporate strategy.

A common language and a collaborative culture increase common knowledge

Organizational behavior is the collective product of shared common knowledge. Every department in an organization knows things that could be useful to the organization if shared with other departments. A culture that practices collaboration as a means to solve the front line problems of the organization as a matter of course has open lines of communication . . . everywhere. And useful knowledge, with a mind of its own, finds its way around the network. Perhaps more debilitating in today's unforgiving times is the creeping divergence from the strategic and operating plans that occur in every department that is caught up with fighting immediate tactical realities, and faced with surprising opportunities. Countless small divergences happen all the time everywhere, and eventually get found and repaired. But in the interim, resources are wasted on activities that no longer require the same intensity or no longer require the effort at all. A good stretch goal for a collaborative culture is zero latency in knowledge diffusion.

Figure 10.12 Organizational Behavior Is the Product of Shared, Common Knowledge

and faced with surprising opportunities. Without conscious purpose, the plan that called for a sales focus to coincide with the development of new production process is sidetracked as an important customer demands more capacity, or threatens to leave. Or the product spec that is driving a next generation design and development activity falls out of touch with the latest understandings of front-line sales-people. Countless small divergences happen all the time everywhere, and eventually get found and repaired. But in the interim, resources are wasted on activities that no longer require the same intensity or no longer require the effort at all. An appropriate (though maybe unattainable) stretch goal for a collaborative culture is zero latency in knowledge diffusion.

An appropriate stretch goal for a response-able enterprise would be zero latency in change accommodation, however you want to define zero latency.

An organization with sufficient competencies in knowledge management and change proficiency, reasonably balanced to complement each other, will be agile enough to live and maybe even lead in these interesting times. Short of a technological mishap-induced return to the dark ages, it is unlikely that knowledge generation will slow down.

In the end, though an organization may well manage knowledge, it will never control it. Viability and leadership will be at least as much determined by organizational *response ability* as it will by knowledge portfolio management.

As promised in the Preface, this book has illustrated what makes a business and any of its systems easy to change, and then has demonstrated how to apply these principles to any system in a company, at any level. It has shown how to analyze opportunities and problems for their operational dynamics, and described ways to use these tools to establish a solution strategy. It has also demonstrated how to measure change proficiency, and how to use this tool to profile a company and establish improvement strategies. Finally, it has focused on the role played by culture, and how to establish and insert these new values and competencies compatibly into an established corporate culture, no matter what it may be.

The next move is yours.

■ NOTES

1. See Hannaford (1995), *Smart Moves—Why Learning Is Not All in Your Head.*

2. See Bronowski (1958), "The Creative Process."
3. See Various Authors (1998), "How The Brain Learns."
4. See Snyder (1997), *Communities of Practice: Combining Organization Learning and Strategy Insights to Create a Bridge to the 21st Century.*
5. See Brown and Duguid (1991), "Organizational Learning and Communities-of-Practice: Toward a Unified View of Working, Learning, and Innovation."
6. See Kelley and Caplan (1993), "How Bell Labs Creates Star Performers."
7. See Wenger (1998), *Communities of Practice—Learning, Meaning, and Identity,* if you really want to know about this thing we all do. Wenger is a senior research scientist with the Institute for Research on Learning in California, and was instrumental in bringing focus to the concept 10 years ago.
8. See Prokesch (1997), "Unleashing the Power of Learning: An Interview with British Petroleum's John Browne."
9. Ibid, p. 153.
10. See Seligman (1997), "Brains in the Office."
11. See Kelley and Caplan (1993), "How Bell Labs Creates Star Performers."
12. See Drexler (1986), *Engines of Creation.*
13. See Stack (1992), *The Great Game of Business.*
14. See Case (1995), *Open Book Management.*
15. See Jensen (1996), *Brain-Based Learning.*
16. See Gardner (1993), *Frames of Mind: The Theory of Multiple Intelligences.*
17. See Jensen (1996), *Brain-Based Learning;* and Hannaford (1995), *Smart Moves.*
18. See Brown and Duguid (2000), *The Social Life of Information.*
19. See Levine et al. (2000), *The Cluetrain Manifesto.*
20. See Porter (1996), "What Is Strategy?"

References

Amidon, D. (1997), *Innovation Strategy for the Knowledge Economy—The Ken Awakening,* Butterworth-Heineman.

Amidon, D. (1998), *Collaborative Innovation and the Knowledge Economy,* Management Accounting Issues Paper No. 17, Society of Management Accountants of Canada.

Asimov, I. (1950), *I Robot,* Doubleday.

Baer, T. (1992), "It All Began with a Handshake," *Managing Automation,* Thomas Publishing, September.

Bank, David (1995), "The Java Saga," *Wired,* December, 166–169, 238–246.

Bennis, W., and Biederman, P. (1997), *Organizing Genius—The Secrets of Creative Collaboration,* Addison-Wesley.

Benson, S., Dove, R., and Kann, J. (1992), "An Agile Systems Framework: A Foundation Tool," *Annual Conference Proceedings,* Agility Forum.

Berger, W. (1999), "Lost in Space," *Wired,* February, 76–81.

Bonabeau, E., and Théraulaz, G. (2000), "Swarm Smarts," *Scientific American,* March, 72–79.

Bronowski, J. (1958), "The Creative Process," *Scientific American,* September.

Brooks, R. (1990), "Elephants Don't Play Chess," *Designing Autonomous Agents,* MIT Press.

Brown, J., and Duguid, P. (1991), "Organizational Learning and Communities-of-Practice: Toward a Unified View of Working, Learning, and Innovation," *Organizational Science,* February.

Brown, J., and Duguid, P. (2000), *The Social Life of Information,* Harvard Business School Press.

Campbel, A. (1993), *Applied Chaos Theory—A Paradigm for Complexity,* Harcourt Brace Jovanovich.

Case, J. (1995), *Open Book Management,* HarperCollins.

Case, J. (1997), "Opening the Books," *Harvard Business Review,* March–April, 118–127.

Collins, J., and Porras, J. (1994), *Built to Last—Successful Habits of Visionary Companies,* Harper Business.

Collis, D., and Montgomery, C. (1995), "Competing on Resources: Strategy in the 1990s," *Harvard Business Review,* July–August.

Cooper, R. (1994), *The Taiyo Group: The Bunsha Philosophy,* Case Study 9-195-080, Harvard Business School.

Cyert, R., and March, J. (1992), *A Behavioral Theory of the Firm,* 2d ed., Blackwell.

D'Aveni, R. (1994), *Hyper-Competition—Managing the Dynamics of Strategic Maneuvering,* Macmillan.

Davenport, T., and Prusak, L. (1998), *Working Knowledge—How organizations Manage What They Know,* Harvard Business School Press.

Davidow, W., and Malone, M. (1992), *The Virtual Corporation,* HarperCollins.

Dewdney, A. (1991), "Insectoids Invade a Field of Robots," *Scientific American,* July.

Diamond, J. (1993), *The Third Chimpanzee,* Harperperennial Library.

Dillenbourg, P., and Schneider, D. (1995), *Collaborative Learning and the Internet,* International Conference on Computer Assisted Instruction, February. (tecfa.unige.ch/tecfa/research/CMC/colla/iccai95_1.html).

Dove, R. (1989), "Complex Automation Systems," *IPC Conference Proceedings,* Engineering Society of Detroit.

Dove, R. (1990), "Systems Engineering and Factory CASE: Critical Enabling Technology," *Proceedings International Conference on Manufacturing Systems and Environment,* Japan Society of Mechanical Engineers.

Dove, R. (1991), "The Competitive Manufacturing Enterprise in 2005—A Vision and Infrastructure," *Proceedings Advanced Manufacturing Research Executive Conference,* Advanced Manufacturing Research, Boston.

Dove, R., et al. (1995), *An Agile Practice Reference Base and Case Study of Remmele Engineering,* Agility Forum.

Dove, R. (1996), "The Voice of Industry Speaks on Agility Priorities," *Automotive Production,* Gardner Publications, March.

Dove, R., Hartman, S., and Benson, S. (1996), *An Agile Enterprise Reference Model with a Case Study of Remmele Engineering,* Agility Forum (available for download from www.parshift.com).

Dove, R., Benson, S., and Hartman, S. (1996), *A Structured Assessment System for Groups Analyzing Agility,* Agility Forum.

Dove, R. (1996), "Business Practices Critical to Early Realization of Agile Enterprise," *Proceedings 1996 Annual Conference,* Agility Forum.

Dove, R. (1996), *Tools for Analyzing and Constructing Agile Capabilities.* Agility Forum. ftp://ftp.parshift.com/PsiDocs/Rkd4Art4.zip

Dove, R. (1998), "Designing Bold, Robust Practices—A Knowledge Management Design Example" (Essays 36–41, December 1997–May 1998, *Automotive Manufacturing & Production,* Gardner Publications), available as a collection at ftp://ftp.parshift.com/PsiDocs/EssBPD.zip

Dove, R. (1998), "Learning: Now More Than Ever," *Automotive Manufacturing and Production,* Gardner Publications, October, 28–30.

Dove, R. (1998), "Realsearch: A Framework for Knowledge Management and Continuing Education," *Proceedings 1998 IEEE Aerospace Conference,* IEEE.

Dove, R. (1999), "Knowledge Management, Response Ability, and the Agile Enterprise," *Journal of Knowledge Management.* MCB University Press, Vol. 3, No. 1, 18–35. ftp://ftp.parshift.com/PsiDocs/Rkd9Art1.zip

Dove, R. (1994–1999), 60 Essay Collection: "Agile and Otherwise," published monthly in *Automotive Manufacturing and Production,* Gardner Publications, November 1994 through December 1999 (collection available at www.parshift.com).

Dove, R. (2000), "Design Principles for Highly Adaptable Business Systems, with Tangible Manufacturing Examples," *Maynard's Industrial Handbook,* McGraw-Hill (revised version available at ftp://ftp.parshift.com/PsiDocs/Rkd8Art3.zip).

Drexler, E. (1986), *Engines of Creation,* Doubleday.

Drucker, P. (1990), "The Emerging Theory of Manufacturing," *Harvard Business Review.* May/June, 94–102.

Fine, C. (1998), *Clockspeed—Winning Industry Control in the Age of Temporary Advantage,* Perseus.

Fitzinger, E., and Lee, H. (1997), "Mass Customization at Hewlett-Packard: The Power of Postponement," *Harvard Business Review,* January–February, 116–121.

Gardner, H. (1993), *Frames of Mind: The Theory of Multiple Intelligences,* Basic Books.

Gleick, J. (1988). *Chaos—Making a New Science,* Penguin.

Goldman, S. (1994), *Agile Competition: The Emergence of a New Industrial Order,* Management Accounting Issues Paper No. 6, Society of Management Accountants of Canada.

Goldman, S., and Graham, C. (Eds.) (1999), *Agility in Health Care: Strategies for Mastering Turbulent Markets,* Jossey-Bass.

Goldman, S., Nagel, R., and Preiss, K. (1995), *Agile Competitors and Virtual Organizations—Strategies for Enriching the Customer,* Van Nostrand Reinhold.

Goldstein, J. (1994), *The Unshackled Organization,* Productivity Press.

Goranson, H. (1999), *The Agile Virtual Enterprise—Cases, Metrics, Tools,* Quorum.

Grove, A. (1996), *Only the Paranoid Survive—How to Exploit the Crises Points that Challenge Every Company and Career,* Doubleday.

Guglielmo, E.J., and Smith, C. (1999), "Enterprise Integration in the Web Era," *Proceedings 13th International Conference on Systems Engineering,* International Council on Systems Engineering, August.

Hamel, G., and Prahalad, C. (1994), *Competing for the Future,* Harvard Business School Press.

Hannaford, C. (1995), *Smart Moves—Why Learning Is Not All in Your Head,* Great Ocean Publishers.

Hock, D. (1997), *The Birth of the Chaordic Century: Out of Control and Into Order,* Chaordic Alliance. www.chaordic.org

Holsapple, C., and Joshi, K. (1998), *In Search of a Descriptive Framework for Knowledge Management,* Kentucky Initiative for Knowledge Management

Research Paper No. 118 (contact cwhols00@ukcc.uky.edu, joshi@cbe.wsu .edu).

Iwata, K., and Onosato, M. (1990), (Osaka University, Japan), "Present Status of Standardization Activity on Factory Automation in Japan," *Proceedings International Conference on Manufacturing Systems and Environment,* Japan Society of Mechanical Engineers.

Jensen, E. (1996), *Brain-Based Learning,* Turning Point Publishing.

Kanter, R. (1983), *The Change Masters,* Routledge.

Kaplan, R., and Norton, D. (1996), "Using the Balanced Scorecard as a Strategic Management System," *Harvard Business Review,* January–February, 75–85.

Kaufman, S. (1995), *At Home in the Universe—The Search for the Laws of Self Organization and Complexity,* Oxford University Press.

Kelley, R., and Caplan, J. (1993), "How Bell Labs Creates Star Performers," *Harvard Business Review,* July–August.

Kelly, K. (1994), *Out of Control,* Addison-Wesley.

Kelly, K. (1997), "Peters Provocations," *Wired,* December, 204–210.

Kidd, P. (1994), *Agile Manufacturing: Forging New Frontiers,* Addison-Wesley.

KMC (1998), Knowledge Management Consortium, www.km.org

Korolkoff, (1990), "Integrated Processing Part 1—Technology in Transition," *Solid State Technology,* August.

Korolkoff, (1990), "Integrated Processing Part 2—Technology in Transition," *Solid State Technology,* October.

Kotter, J., and Heskett, J. (1992), *Corporate Culture and Performance.* Free Press.

Levine, R., Locke, C., Searls, D., and Weinberger, D. (2000), *The Cluetrain Manefesto: The End of Business as Usual,* Perseus (also see www.cluetrain .com).

Lohara, C. (1999), "System Engineering the Enterprise: Experience with Enterprise Frameworks," *Proceedings 13th International Conference on Systems Engineering,* International Council on Systems Engineering, August.

Lohara, C. (1999), "The Living Enterprise," www.parshift.com\Speakers \Speak020.htm, September.

Luehrman, T. (1998), "Strategy as a Portfolio of Real Options," *Harvard Business Review,* September–October.

Magretta, J. (1997), "Growth through Global Sustainability," *Harvard Business Review,* January–February, 79–88.

Maltz, M. (1960), *Psycho-Cybernetics,* Simon & Schuster.

McAlinden, S., and Smith, B. (1998), "World Class Vehicle Launch Timing," *Automotive Manufacturing & Production,* Gardner Publications, February.

McGeehan, J. (Ed.) (1998), *Transformations—Leadership for Brain-Compatible Learning,* Books For Educators.

McGill, I., and Beaty, L. (1992), *Action Learning,* Kogan Page.

Metes, G., Gundry, J., and Bradish, P. (1998), *Agile Networking—Competing through the Internet and Intranets,* Prentice-Hall.

Morgan, G. (1997), *Images of Organization,* Sage.

Nagle, R., and Dove, R. (Principal Investigators), Goldman, S., and Preiss, K. (Eds.), (1991), *Twenty First Century Manufacturing Enterprise Strategy (Volume 1: An Industry-Led View; Volume 2: Infrastructure)*, Iacocca Institute, Lehigh University.

Nakane, J., and Hall, R. (1991), "Holonic Manufacturing: Flexibility—The Competitive Battle in the 1990s," *Production Planning and Control*, 2:1, 2–13.

Newboe, B. (1990), "Cluster Tools: A Process Solution?" *Semiconductor International*, July.

Okimoto, D. (1990), *Between MITI and the Market: Japanese Industrial Policy for High Technology*, Stanford University Press.

Okino, N. (1994), (Faculty of Engineering, Kyoto University, Japan), *Bionic Manufacturing Systems*, CAM-I NGMS Program Workshop, CAM-I, February.

Oleson, J. (1998), *Pathways to Agility*, John Wiley & Sons.

Owen, J. (1999), "Transfer Lines Get Flexible—High-Speed Machining and Modular Design Are Adding Agility," *Manufacturing Engineering*, Society of Manufacturing Engineers, January.

Papert, S. (1980), *Mindstorms—Children, Computers, and Powerful Ideas*, Basic Books.

Peters, T., and Waterman, R. (1982), *In Search of Excellence—Lessons from America's Best Run Companies*, Warner Books.

Pine, J. (1993), *Mass Customization: The New Frontier in Business Competition*, Harvard Business School Press.

Pine, J., Victor, B., and Boynton, A. (1993), "Making Mass Customization Work," *Harvard Business Review*, September–October, 108–119.

Porter, M. (1996), "What Is Strategy?" *Harvard Business Review*, November–December.

Postrel, V. (1998), *Enemies of the Future*, Free Press.

Preiss, K. (1997), "A Systems Perspective of Lean and Agile Manufacturing," *Agility and Global Competition*, John Wiley & Sons, winter, 59–75.

Preiss, K. (1999), "Modeling of Knowledge Flows and Their Impact," *Journal of Knowledge Management*, MCB University Press, 3:1, 36–46.

Preiss, K., and Wadswort, W. (Eds.) (1994), *Agile Customer-Supplier Relations*, Agility Forum.

Preiss, K., Goldman, S., and Nagel, R. (1996), *Cooperate to Compete: Building Agile Business Relationships*, John Wiley & Sons.

Prokesch, S. (1997), "Unleashing the Power of Learning: An Interview with British Petroleum's John Browne," *Harvard Business Review*, September–October.

Ring, J. (1999), "Current Enterprise Models Are *in Conflict* with Mass Customization," www.parshift.com\Speakers\Speak018.htm, July.

Ring, J. (1999), "Toward the Intelligent Enterprise," www.parshift.com\Speakers\Speak019.htm, August.

Ring, J. (1999), "When Enterprise = System," *Proceedings 13th International Conference on Systems Engineering*, International Council on Systems Engineering, August.

Rothschild, M. (1990), *Bionomics—The Inevitability of Capitalism (Economy as Ecosystem)*, Holt.

Sakai, K., and Sekiyama, H., as told to D. Russel (1985), *Bunsha, Improving Your Business through Company Division*, Intercultural Group.

Schneider, W. (1994), *The Reengineering Alternative—A Plan for Making Your Current Culture Work*, McGraw-Hill.

Schneider, W. (1998), "Why Good Management Ideas Fail—Part One: The Neglected Power of Organizational Culture," *Focus on Change Management*. LLP Limited (London). Issue 44, May, 7–13.

Schneider, W. (1998), "Why Good Management Ideas Fail—Part Two: The Importance of Aligning Interventions to Systems and Strategy," *Focus on Change Management*, LLP Limited (London), Issue 45, June, 23–26.

Seligman, D. (1997), "Brains in the Office," *Fortune*, January 13, 38.

SEMI (1989), *Cluster Tool Module Interface and Wafer Transport Standard*, Semiconductor Equipment and Materials International, Document 1796, October.

Senge, P. (1990), *The Fifth Discipline—The Art and Practice of the Learning Organization*, Currency Doubleday.

Simons, R. (1995), "Control in an Age of Empowerment," *Harvard Business Review*, November–December, 80–88.

Slywotzky, A. (1996), *Value Migration—How to Think Several Moves ahead of the Competition*, Harvard Business School Press.

Smith, B. (1998), "World Class Vehicle Launch Timing: General Motors," *Automotive Manufacturing & Production*, Gardner, March.

Smith, B. (1998), "World Class Vehicle Launch Timing: Ford," *Automotive Manufacturing & Production*, Gardner, June.

Smith, B. (1998), "World Class Launch: Chrysler Corporation," *Automotive Manufacturing & Production*, Gardner, July.

Smith, B. (1998), "World Class Launch: Honda and Toyota," *Automotive Manufacturing & Production*, Gardner, October.

Smith, B., and Swiecki, B. (1998), "World Class Launch: The Conclusion," *Automotive Manufacturing & Production*, Gardner, November.

Snyder, W. (1997), *Communities of Practice: Combining Organization Learning and Strategy Insights to Create a Bridge to the 21st Century*, Presented at the Academy of Management, 1997 (contact wsnyder@socialcapital.com).

Stack, J., with Burlingham, B. (1992), *The Great Game of Business*, Currency Doubleday.

Upton, D. (1995), "What Really Makes Factories Flexible?" *Harvard Business Review*, July–August.

Various Authors (1998), "How the Brain Learns," *Educational Leadership*, Association for Supervision and Curriculum Development, November.

Vasilash, G. (1995), "On Cells at Kelsey-Hayes," *Production Magazine*, Gardner, February, 58–61.

Vasilash, G. (1995), "Re-engineering, Re-energizing, Objects, and Other Issues of Interest," *Production Magazine*, Gardner, January, 60–62.

Vasilash, G. (1998), "The Chrysler Operating System," *Automotive Manufacturing & Production,* April, 62–65.

Warnecke, H. (1993), *The Fractal Company—A Revolution in Corporate Culture,* Springer-Verlag.

Wenger, E. (1998), *Communities of Practice—Learning, Meaning, and Identity,* Cambridge University Press.

Womack, J., Jones, D., and Roos, D. (1990), *The Machine That Changed the World,* Macmillan.

Index

Accelerated learning, 298
"Accidental" maturity stage, 12, 241,
    246, 248–249
Activities/issues (in closure matrix),
    202
Agile Competition Model, 20
Agile Enterprise Reference Model,
    47, 240, 242–244
"Agile" response ability state, 12, 69
Agility, 3–29
    autonomous operating concepts, 6
    basic concepts, 3–6
    change proficiency (CP) and, 10
        (see also Change proficiency
        (CP))
    culture and (see Culture(s)/
        cultural)
    degrees of, 22
    enablers, 14
    equals KM (knowledge
        management) plus RA
        (response ability), 9, 10, 14
        (see also Knowledge
        management (KM); Response
        ability (RA))
    evolutionary continuum of
        manufacturing paradigms
        (craft/mass/lean/agile), 6

key concept relationships, 10
knowledge management and, 9,
    10, 14 (see also Knowledge
    management (KM))
vs. management practice, business
    strategy, or manufacturing
    theory, 7
manufacturing metaphor for agile
    resource relationships, 5
organizing for change and
    complexity, 16–20
preferred working definition of,
    14–15
"response ability" and, 9, 10, 14
    (see also Response ability
    (RA))
RRS (reusable/reconfigurable/
    scalable structural
    relationships) (defined), 10
    (see also Reusable/
    reconfigurable/scalable
    (RRS))
size and, 11, 16–17
systemic, 26–27
terminology, 9–13
Agility Forum, Strategic Analysis
    Working Group (SAWG),
    317–320

Allen, Richard, 36
Amazon.com, 68
AMD (Advanced Micro Devices), 23, 26
Apple Macintosh, 20, 86, 165
Applied Materials, Inc. (AMI) (semiconductor-fabrication cluster machines), 32–35, 45, 112–116, 166, 168–169
  change domains, 113
  design issues (product), 45, 112–116
  response ability model, 168–169
Asimov, Isaac, 46, 48, 161
As-is profile, 269–270
AT&T, 68
Autonomous operating concepts, 6

"Battleship" structure, 43
Bell Labs, 189, 192, 283, 294, 296
Best-in-class maturity profile, 240
Brain-based models, 281, 282, 291
Brainstorming for general issues, 123–124
British Petroleum (BP), 288–289
Bronowski, Jacob, 280–281
Brooks, Rodney, 46, 47
Brown, John Seely, 283
Business case justification, 243
Business practice. See Communities of practice (CoPs); Practice(s), business
Business systems analyst (BSA), 232–233

Caplan, Janet, 189, 294, 296
Change, organizing for, 16–20
Change domains, 87, 88, 90, 91, 107, 114, 121, 124, 273
  categorization into (response situation analysis), 124
  correction, 87, 88, 90, 100–102
  creation, 87, 88, 90, 93–95
  developing issues in, 273
  examples (product/process/ practice/people), 91, 113, 114

expansion, 87, 88, 90, 103–105, 209, 273
  improvement, 87, 88, 90, 95–96
  migration, 87, 88, 90, 96–98
  modification, 87, 88, 90, 98–99
  proactive, 12, 69, 87, 88, 92–99
  reactive, 25, 68, 87, 88, 100–107
  reconfiguration, 87, 88, 90, 105–107, 273
  response situation (RS) analysis and, 121
  typical issues (strategic level), 90
  variation, 87, 88, 90, 102–103
Change-enabling structure/culture, 30–63
  adaptable culture, 46–48
  adaptable practices, 40–43
  adaptable processes, 35–40
  adaptable products, 31–35
  adaptable structure, 30–31
  manufacturing enterprise environments (product/ process/practice/people), 30
  perspective on structure/culture, 59–62
  Remmele Engineering (engineered for response ability), 48–59
  RRS structure, 43–46
Change issues, 87–92, 120, 123–124, 191–192, 272–273
  brainstorming for, 123–124
  categorization hints, 272–273
  in closure matrix, 202
  design focused on, 191–192
  establishing, 190–192
  examples (product/process/ practice/people), 91
  examples (strategic level), 90
  proactive/reactive, 123–124, 191–192, 272–273
  RS analysis and, 120, 123–124
Change proficiency (CP), 10, 11, 67–108, 271
  acculturation of, 271
  benefits (viability/leadership), 69

change domains, 87, 88
change issues, typical, 90
comparing among companies, 12
cost (metric dimension), 17–18,
    70, 71, 75–79
defined, 10, 11
dynamic environment, 25
framework, 87–92
language of, 107–108
metrics, 70–87, 107
    balanced scorecard, 72
    four dimensions (time/cost/
        quality/scope), 70, 71–72
    in perspective, 72–73
in perspective, 67–69
proactive, 25, 68, 87, 88, 92–99
product launch, 89
quality (metric dimension),
    71–72, 79–82
    vs. quickness, 70
reactive, 25, 68, 87, 88, 100–107
scope (metric dimension), 70,
    71–72, 82–87, 245
time (metric dimension), 70,
    71–72, 74–75
Change proficiency (CP) maturity,
    12, 72, 239–275
as-is profile (deliverable),
    269–270
best-in-class maturity profile, 240
business practice maturity profile,
    240, 241
categorization hints, 273–274
comparing among companies
    (opportunistic/agile/fragile/
    innovative), 12
competency development, 12
CpMM (change proficiency
    maturity model), 240, 241,
    244–254
CpMP (change proficiency
    maturity profile), 240
definitions, 240
deliverables, 268, 269–270
enterprise maturity profile, 240,
    242, 247

examples, Remmele Engineering,
    254–267
how and why to use, 267–269
hypothetical profile (deliverable),
    270
improvement strategy, 271
industry benchmarks, 271
knowledge acquisition, 12
leadership strategy, 272
maturity reference model, 240,
    242–244
maturity stages, 12, 241, 244, 246,
    248–254
    "accidental," 241, 246, 248–249
    characteristics of, 246
    "defined," 241, 246, 250–251
    "managed," 241, 246, 251–252
    "mastered," 241, 246, 252–254
    "repeatable," 241, 246, 249–250
methodology/technique, 268, 272
metrics, 12, 245
model (CpMM), 12, 240, 241,
    244–254
objectives, 268, 270–272
product innovation, 12
profiling, 239–242, 268
pro forma example (human
    resources skill acquisition),
    241
reactive/proactive, 12
supplier relationships, 12
team, 268, 270–272
trial concept test, 270–271
working knowledge, 12
Chaos theory, 6, 17, 48
Chiat, Jay, 171
Chrysler, 20, 74, 75, 80–81, 85,
    107–108, 159, 300
Client-server structures, 44
Closure matrix, 201, 202, 206, 207,
    213
Coca-Cola, 164
Collaborative analysis team (RS
    analysis), 121–123
Collaborative culture, 98, 99,
    101–102, 103

Collaborative learning, 10, 11,
    151–152, 276, 282, 284–289, 323
  alternatives, 285, 286
  appropriation, 286, 287
  disagreement, 285, 286
  explanation, 285–287
  facilitation (CLF), 10, 11
  information technology and, 288–289
  internalization, 286, 287
  mechanisms of (eight), 285–287
  regulation, 286, 287
  shared load, 286, 287
  synchronicity, 286, 287
Collins and Porras (*Built to Last*),
    47–48, 162
Communities of practice (CoPs),
    276, 281–284, 288, 293
Competency development, 12, 112,
    114, 118–120
Complex adaptive systems, 6–7, 27,
    164
  vs. adaptable systems, 164
  artificial/natural, 152
Complexity, organizing for, 16–20
Components, 17, 139
Control in response-able systems,
    133–135
Correction (change domain), 87, 88,
    90, 100–102
Cost of change, 17–18, 70, 71, 75–79
Creation (change domain), 87, 88,
    90, 93–95
Culture(s)/cultural:
  adaptable, 46–48
  categories of (control/
      competence/collaborative/
      cultivative), 7, 8
  coexistence of core/local, 7
  collaborative, 98, 99, 101–102, 103
  context of change proficiency, 301
  diversity, 300
  as framework, 60, 158–159
  leadership/management focus
      and, 8
  maps, 9
  mismatch, 159
  in perspective, 59–62

Customer, 20, 21, 285
Cyrex, 23, 26

Daimler-Chrysler, 159, 300
Decade of the 1990s, 67–68
Defense contractors, 156, 165
Deferred commitment (principle),
    145–146, 207, 208, 209
"Defined" maturity stage, 12, 241,
    246, 250–251
Dell Computer, 165
Design(s):
  adaptable principles, 164
  integrated, 20
  intuitive, 214–235
  issue-focused, 200–205
  methodology based on issues/
      principles, 191–192
  people system, 118–120
  practice, 117–118, 199
  preparation prior for, 189–190
  principle-based, 205–213,
      306–307
  process system, 116–117
  product system, 112–116
  requirements, four diverse
      examples, 112–120
  RRS principles of (*see* Principles
      of response-able systems)
  strategy, 45
  systematic, 188–213
Digital Equipment Corporation, 68
Dillenbourg, Pierre, 285
Directed systems, 161–162
Distributed control and
    information (principle),
    146–148, 174, 209
Diversity, 150–152, 208, 209,
    263–264, 292, 300, 311
Drexler, Eric (*Engines of Creation*),
    296
Drucker, Peter, 16–17, 43

e-Commerce, and scope, 86
Efficiency programs, 4
Elastic capacity (principle),
    149–150

Emergent behavior/systems, 47,
153–154, 289
Empire Bakery Equipment, 170
Employee relationships, 259–267
Employee turnover, 76–79
cost of, 77
lost productivity costs, 78–79
lost sales costs, 79
new hire costs, 79
recruitment costs, 77–78
training costs, 78
Encapsulation, 141–142, 225–228
Engineering change orders (ECO),
167
Enterprise application integration
(EAI), 217
Enterprise bus, 217
Enterprise maturity profile, 240,
242, 247
Enterprise resource management
(ERM), 214. *See also* Intuitive
design of response-able systems
(Silterra)
Enterprise resource planning (ERP),
97, 214–235
Enterprise systems, response-able,
161–187, 276–326
becoming/managing, 276–326
case stories as models, 180–188
directed and self-organized
dynamics, 161–162
examples of, 163–180
people, 174–180
practice, 171–174, 176–177
process, 167–171, 172–173
product, 164–167, 168–169
insight, 293–298
knowledge portfolio management
model, 317–320, 321
learning, 280–289
local metaphors (knowledge
packaged for diffusion), 180,
298–304
method for building (Realsearch),
304–317
organizational learning, 289–293
Realsearch, 304–317

RRS principles at work, 161
systems integrity management,
162–163
Erector Set (*vs.* Legos), 149
eToys, 86
Evolution, 4
Evolutionary continuum of
manufacturing paradigms
(craft/mass/lean/agile), 6
Evolving standards (framework)
(principle), 158–159, 162–163,
167, 208, 209
Ewasyshyn, Frank, 75, 107
Expansion (change domain), 87, 88,
90, 103–105, 209, 273
Exxon, 290

Facilitated reuse (principle),
155–157, 162. *See also*
Reusability
Factory (battleship *vs.* flotilla
structure), 43
Flat interaction (principle),
143–145, 207, 209
Flexibility *vs.* agility, 6
Flexible capacity, 209
"Flotilla" structure, 43
Ford, 74
Fractal math, 47, 48, 149. *See also*
Chaos theory
"Fragile" response ability state, 12, 69
Framework:
change proficiency, 87–92
culture as, 60, 158–159
defined, 139
evolving standards (principle),
158–159, 162–163, 167, 208,
209

Garrison, Betty, 185
Gates, Bill, 22, 24
Gateway, 165
General Motors, 20, 68, 74, 142,
180–186, 188–213, 305, 308
response ability model (core
competency development),
211–212

General Motors *(Continued)*
  response ability model (JIT
      assembly systems), 182–183
  workshop team, applying RRS
      principles, 188–213
Great Harvest bakeries, 175–180
Group intelligence, 292
Grove, Andy, 23, 24
Guglielmo, Gene, 225

Hanko, Denny, 185
Hannaford, Carla, 280, 281
Hannon, Cy, 215–216, 232
Hewlett-Packard, 145–146, 150
Hitachi, 291
Hive intelligence, 289
Hock, Dee, 162
Honda, 74
Huffy bicycles, 146

IBM, 68, 165
Improvement (change domain), 87,
    88, 90, 95–96
Industry benchmarks, 271
Information technology (IT), 214,
    216, 288–289
Infrastructure architecture, 214, 223,
    234
Innovation:
  creation (change domain), 87, 88,
      93–95
  defined, 14
  indicator of good scope, 84
  management, 243
"Innovative" response ability state,
    12, 69
Insight, 293–298, 304
  context, 296–298
  difficult to transfer, 304
  power/nature of, 293–298
Integrated designs, 20
Integration, 18
Intel, 23–26, 59, 165
Intelligence/IQ, 283, 289, 294, 298
Internal network service, 94, 99, 101,
    106

Internet Service Providers (ISPs),
    149
Intuitive design of response-able
    systems (Silterra), 214–235
  architecture, 224
  assessment, 229–230
  business situation, 228
  change issues, 234
  defining the problem, 218–225
  encapsulation, 225–228
  implementation, 224, 225–228,
      234
  implication, 228–229
  infrastructure architecture, 223
  initial chalk talks with ERM
      vendors, 219
  IT/ERM strategy, 230–231
  IT infrastructure, 234
  objective, 230
  RFI (request for information),
      218–225
  RFQ (request for quotation), 225
  RRS principles, 234
  steps, 224, 226
  strategy, 224, 230–231
  synopsis, 234
  systems integrity management,
      232–233
  trends, 229
  unique competitive advantage,
      228–232
  value-generating sustainable
      differentiation, 231–232
  vendor instructions, 226–228
Issues. *See* Change issues

Java, 22
Joy, Bill, 22

Kelley, Robert, 189, 294, 296
Kelsey-Hayes (adaptable
    manufacturing cell structure),
    35–40, 45, 113, 116–117, 170–173
  design issues (process), 45,
      116–117
  response ability model, 172–173

Knowledge:
  acquisition/capture, 12, 193
  change fueled by, 14–16
  explosion of, 278, 323
  leverageable kinds of,
    294–295
  librarians, 157
  managing/applying (balancing),
    13–14
  metaphor model, 301 (*see also*
    Metaphor)
  packaging:
    common language/architecture,
      302
    for diffusion, 298–304
    as metaphor model, 303
    as solution mechanism, 304
  template, 301
  trading in, 294
  transfer, 301–302
  value (application), 14
  workers, 97–98, 99, 101, 103
  working, 12
Knowledge management (KM), 9,
    10, 11, 15–16, 70, 157, 191, 237,
    243, 276, 277–289, 316
  application, 14, 279
  equals KPM (knowledge portfolio
    management) plus CLF
    (collaborative learning
    facilitation), 10
  formalized, and facilitated
    reusability, 157
  key issues, 279
  learning, 279, 280–289
  mismatched balance, 15–16
  model of natural, 316
  perspective on, 277–280
  process, 191
  purpose, 279
  techniques, 237
Knowledge portfolio management
    (KPM), 10, 11, 277, 279, 325

Launches, 17–19, 75–76
Leadership, 8, 69, 272, 325

Learning, 15, 192, 280–298
  accelerated, 298
  brain-based models, 281, 282
  collaborative, 10, 11, 151–152, 276,
    282, 284–289, 323
  communities of practice (CoPs),
    276, 281–284, 288, 293
  insight, 293–298
  leverage (brain-compatible), 282
  metaphor/analogy/simile, 281
    (*see also* Metaphor)
  organization, 15, 192, 293
  organizational, 289–293
  styles, 298
Legacy, 216–218
Lego, 31, 149–150, 156, 158, 159, 164,
    309
Life metaphor, 4
Local metaphor, 298–304, 305–306
Lohara, Charan, 225
LSI Logic (JIT order fulfillment
    chains), 23, 26, 40–43, 45, 114,
    117–118, 146, 150, 151, 157,
    174
  design issues (business practice),
    45, 117–118
  response ability model, 176–177

"Managed" maturity stage, 12, 241,
    246, 251–252
Mandelbrot set, 47, 48. *See also*
    Chaos theory; Fractal math
Manufacturing. *See also* Process
  evolutionary continuum of
    paradigms (craft/mass/
    lean/agile), 6
  metaphor for agile resource
    relationships, 5
Mass customization, 146
"Mastered" maturity stage, 12, 241,
    246, 252–254, 266
Maturity profiling. *See* Change
    proficiency (CP) maturity
Mauck, Fred, 180
McDonald's, 21
McNealy, Scott, 22–23

Mentor-student relationship,
    rotating, 193, 199–200, 201, 203
Mergers/acquisitions, 159
Metaphor, 4, 180, 186, 298–304,
    305–306
  insight transfer and, 305
  life, 4
  local, 298–304, 305–306
  model, 180, 186, 301, 303, 304
Metrics, 70–87
  balanced scorecard, 72
  of change proficiency, 70–87, 107,
    245
  cost dimension, 17–18, 70, 71,
    75–79
  dimensions (four), 70, 71–72
  focus, 12
  performance, 243
  in perspective, 72–73
  quality dimension, 70, 71–72,
    79–82
  scope dimension, 70, 71, 82–87
  specifying, 125–126
  time dimension, 70, 71–72, 74–75
Microsoft, 22–23, 24–26, 68, 152, 165,
    248, 294
Migration (change domain), 87, 88,
    90, 96–98, 273
Military models, 147
Mobil Oil Company, 151
Mobs, 289
Modification (change domain), 87,
    88, 90, 98–99, 273
Modularity, encapsulated, 141–142,
    225–228
Moore, Tom, 57, 59
Motorola, 41, 68, 146, 174–175
Murray, Mike, 25–26

NASA, Skylab, 17
Netscape, 24, 68, 248
Nintendo, 40
"Not invented here" (NIH), 296, 297

Object-oriented software, 44
On-time delivery issue, 126

Open book management, 148, 298
"Opportunistic" response ability
    state, 12, 69
Oracle, 217, 225, 231
Order entry process, 94–95, 96, 104,
    106–107
Organization, adaptable (RRS,
    response ability), 42
Organizational behavior, 324
Organizational learning, 276,
    289–293
Organizational relationship
    management, 243
Organizational viability, 27

Peer-to-peer communications,
    144
People:
  adaptable, 49–52
  design issues (Remmele
    Engineering's competency
    acquisition), 114, 118–120
  examples, 114
  response-able enterprise system,
    174–180
  typical systems, 164
PeopleSoft, 225, 231
Performance metrics, 243
Peters, Tom, 192
Plug compatibility (principle),
    142–143, 158, 159, 208, 209, 300,
    302, 304
Porter, Michael, 11, 313
Positioning, 11
Practice(s), business:
  adaptable, 40–43
  architecture, 112
  critical (24 listed), 243, 244–245
  design issues (LSI Logic's JIT
    order fulfillment chains), 114,
    117–118
  examples, 114
  maturity profile, 240, 241
  response-able system, 171–174,
    176–177
  typical systems, 164

Principles of response-able systems, 138–159. *See also specific principle*
in closure matrix, 202
deferred commitment, 145–146
distributed control and information, 146–148
elastic capacity, 149–150
evolving standards (framework), 158–159
facilitated reuse, 155–157
flat interaction, 143–145
overview, 140
plug compatibility, 142–143
redundancy and diversity, 150–152
self-contained units (components), 138–142
self-organization, 152–155
Proactive dynamics/change domains, 12, 69, 87, 88, 92–99
creation, 87, 88, 90, 93–95
improvement, 87, 88, 90, 95–96
migration, 87, 88, 90, 96–98
modification, 87, 88, 90, 98–99
Problem perception, 109–111
Process:
adaptable, 35–40
architecture, 112
design issues (manufacturing cells of Kelsey-Hayes), 116–117
examples, 113
models, as-is and to-be, 269–270
response-able system, 167–173
typical systems, 164
Product(s)
adaptable, 31–35
design issues (Applied Materials' cluster machines), 112–116
development, 17–18, 96, 97, 103, 105
examples, 113
innovation, 12
response-able, 164–167
typical systems, 164
Profitability, 3
Proximal-zone concept, 300

Quality of change (metric dimension), 71–72, 79–82

Reactive dynamics/change domains, 12, 69, 87, 88, 100–107
correction, 87, 88, 90, 100–102
expansion, 87, 88, 90, 103–105, 209, 273
reconfiguration, 87, 88, 90, 105–107, 273
variation, 87, 88, 90, 102–103
Real options, 194
Realsearch, 120, 193, 296, 304–317, 319
analyzing external cases for ideas, 309
analyzing local case for RRS, 309
change-issue focus, 306
collaboration across diversity, 311
collaboration across teams, 311–312
description/definition, 307
discovery workshops, 304–305
employing local metaphor, 305–306
framework/activity diagram, 308
framework/process, 306–312
insight development, 316
packaging as metaphor model, 308
participant preparation, 313
principle-based design, 306–307
why it works, 307
workshop agenda, 310, 312–316
workshop site selection, 313
Reconfigurable framework/component concept, 17, 18. *See also* Reusable/reconfigurable/scalable (RRS)
Reconfiguration (change domain), 87, 88, 90, 105–107, 273
Redundancy and diversity (principle), 150–152, 208, 209
Reference model, agile engineering (Remmele Engineering), 47, 240, 242–244

Relationships, key concept, 10
Remmele Engineering, 47–62, 114,
    118–120, 147–148, 150, 180,
    242–244, 254–267
  activity based costing, 147–148
  adaptable people, 49–52
  Agile Enterprise Reference Model,
    47, 240, 242–244
  apprenticeship program, 150
  business practices (reference
    model armature), 243–244
  change proficiency maturity
    profiling examples, 254–267
  competency acquisition, 114
  continuous learning, 60
  correcting mismatches between
    people/tasks, 264
  culture, 60, 61, 62
  customer satisfaction, 54
  design issues for people system
    (competency acquisition),
    118–120
  filling critical slots when key
    employee absent, 265
  gaining new skills, guarding
    against insularity, 264
  guiding principles, 52–54
  handling surge requirements,
    265–267
  improving personnel skills, 263
  management, 56–59
  maturity stage 4 (mastered), 266
  mission statement, 50
  organization, 54–55
  response ability model, 178–179
  workforce diversity, management
    succession, 263–264
"Repeatable" maturity stage, 12, 241,
    246, 249–250
Response ability (RA), 9, 10, 11,
    14–15, 69, 70, 133–160
  agility and, 9, 10, 11, 14–15, 69, 70
  basic definitions, 139
  component, 139
  control in response-able systems,
    133–135

deferred commitment (principle),
    145–146
design requirements, four diverse
    examples, 112–120
distributed control and
    information (principle),
    146–148
elastic capacity (principle), 149–150
enabling, 133–160
enterprise (*see* Enterprise
    systems, response-able)
equals change proficiency (CP)
    plus RRS, 10
evolving standards (framework)
    (principle), 158–159
facilitated reuse (principle),
    155–157
flat interaction (principle),
    143–145
framework, 139
intuitive design of response-able
    systems, 214–235
models (diagrammatic format),
    166
  Applied Materials (product
    system: cluster machine),
    168–169
  General Motors (core
    competency development),
    211–212
  General Motors (JIT assembly
    systems), 182–183
  Kelsey-Hayes (process system:
    matching cell), 172–173
  LSI Logic (practice system: JIT
    order fulfillment chains),
    176–177
  Remmele (people system:
    competency acquisition),
    178–179
plug compatibility (principle),
    142–143
principles of response-able
    systems, 140
redundancy and diversity
    (principle), 150–152

self-contained units (components)
    (principle), 138–142
self-organization (principle),
    152–155
states (opportunistic/agile/
    fragile/innovative), 69
structure, 135–138
system, 139
systematic design of response-able
    systems, 188–213
Response-able enterprise. *See*
    Enterprise systems, response-
    able
Response situation (RS) analysis,
    109–129, 288
change domains, 121, 124
design issues (four diverse
    examples), 112–120
    business practice (LSI Logic's
        JIT order fulfillment
        chains), 117–118
    peopled system—Remmele
        Engineering's competency
        acquisition, 118–120
    process: manufacturing cells of
        Kelsey-Hayes, 116–117
    product (Applied Materials'
        cluster machines), 112–116
language/framework aspect, 121
methodology, 120–128
perspective on "problems," 109–111
problems/opportunities
    definition, 120–128
purpose of, 129
steps in (seven), 121–127
    assembling collaborative
        analysis team, 121–123
    brainstorming for general
        issues, putting them into
        proactive/reactive
        categories, 123–124
    categorizing issues into eight
        domains, 124
    defining boundaries, 123
    identifying errors, 127
    probing questions, 124–125

refining into short list, 125–126
rewording/rationalizing, 127
selecting metric focus, 126
time required for, 128–129
Reusability, 18, 155–157. *See also*
    Reusable/reconfigurable/
    scalable (RRS)
Reusable/reconfigurable/scalable
    (RRS), 10, 11, 31, 33, 43–46, 61,
    72, 140, 162, 164, 301
creating system based on (three
    principal activities), 162
design strategy, 45
explained/defined, 10, 11, 31
framework, 61
natural/artificial systems, 164
principles (*see* Principles of
    response-able systems)
Remmele corporate culture, 61
response ability and, 10, 11, 33, 61
strategy, 45, 72
structure, 10, 43–46
Ring, Jack, 222–225
Robotics, 46–48, 154–155, 161–162,
    298
RRS. *See* Reusable/reconfigurable/
    scalable (RRS)
Ryder Trucking, 20

Scalability, 18, 33. *See also* Reusable/
    reconfigurable/scalable (RRS)
Schneider, Bill, 7
Schneider, Daniel, 285
Scope of change, 70, 71, 72, 82–87,
    245
    e-Commerce and, 86
    examples (product/process/
        practice/people), 83
    indicator of good scope, 84
    lost opportunities (indicator of
        poor scope), 84–85
    metric dimension, 70, 71, 72,
        82–87, 245
Self-contained units (components)
    (principle), 138–142, 174, 208,
    209

Self-organization (principle), 152–155, 161–162, 166, 174, 208, 209
  artificial systems (free market economy), 152
  natural systems, 152
  universal socket wrench, 155
Seligman, Dan, 294
Silterra. *See* Intuitive design of response-able systems (Silterra)
Simmons, Robert, 158
Software technology, object-oriented, 44
Solectron Corporation, 149–150
Sony, 40, 41
Stack, Jack, 197, 297
Stock market, 156
Strategic planning, 243
Structure:
  adaptable, 30–31, 131
  in perspective, 59–62
  response-able, 135–138
  RRS, 43–46
Subcontractor Technical Network (STN), 41–43
Sun Microsystems, 22–23, 248
Supplier relationships, 12
Supply chain management, 96, 97, 102–103, 104–105
Sustainability (value-generating differentiation), 231–232
Swarm interaction, 289
System, 139, 164
Systematic design of response-able systems, 188–213
  accommodating any size group, 205, 209
  accommodating different student types, 204, 208
  allowing flexible student schedules, 205, 209
  analyzing external case for ideas, 198
  analyzing local case for principles, 198–199, 207
  capturing hidden tacit knowledge, 201, 207–208

  closure matrix, 201, 202, 206, 207, 213
  creating student interest/value, 201–203
  designing a business practice, 199
  establishing issues, 190–192
  establishing personal values, 197–198
  excising poor value knowledge, 204, 209
  facilitating insight, 196
  finding/fixing incorrect knowledge, 204, 209
  focus on change issues, 194–195
  framework standards, 194–196
  functional activities, 196–200
  improving knowledge accuracy/effectiveness, 203, 208
  injecting fresh outside knowledge, 204
  issue-focused design, 200–205
  metaphor model, 199
  migrating knowledge focus, 203–204
  packaging knowledge as response ability models, 199
  preliminary framework/component architecture, 192–213
  preparation prior to design work, 189–190
  principle-based design, 205–213
  quality review/selection, 200
  reinterpreting rules for new applications, 205, 209–213
  relating to fundamental principles, 195–196
  rotating student/mentor roles, 199–200, 201, 203
  sequence of (seven steps), 210
  solving real problems, 196
  students renewing knowledge, 196
  systems integrity management in action, 197
System control, two styles of, 59–60
Systemic agility, 26–27

Systems integrity management, 162–163, 170–171, 232–233
 component evolution management, 163
 component inventory management, 163
 customer account manager, 171
 evolving standards and, 162–163
 framework evolution management, 163
 general manager, 170
 operations manager, 170
 personnel, 170–171
 responsibilities (four), 163
 Silterra, 232–233
 system configuration management, 163

Teams, 121–123, 147, 188–213, 268, 270–272, 311–312
Texas Instruments, 156–157
Time of change (metric dimension), 70, 71–72, 74–75
Time-to-market, 74
Toy industry, 39, 86

Toys "R" Us, 86
Training, and employee turnover, 193
Transformation programs, 4
Transition period, cost of, 17–18
Trial concept test, 270–271

Unit redundancy, 207
Upton, David, 60, 189

Variation (change domain), 87, 88, 90, 102–103
Viability, 3, 27, 69, 325
Visa Corporation, 153, 156

Weick, Karl, 17
Workshop process, participative, 122, 188, 272, 273

Xerox PARC, 16

Y2K, 97, 152

Zero latency (in change accommodation), 325